Database Pr

and Design

This book is to be returned on or before the last date stamped below.

Database Principles and Design

Third Edition

Colin Ritchie

COURSE TECHNOLOGY
CENGAGE Learning

Australia • Brazil • Japan • Korea • Mexico • Singapore • Spain • United Kingdom • United States

COURSE TECHNOLOGY
CENGAGE Learning

Database Principles and Design
3rd Edition
Colin Ritchie

Publishing Director: John Yates

Publisher: Gaynor Redvers-Mutton

Editorial Assistant: Matthew Lane

Content Project Editor: Alison Walters
Leonora Dawson-Bowling

Production Controller: Maeve Healy

Manufacturing Manager: Helen Mason

Marketing Manager: Jason Bennett

Typesetter: Newgen, India

Cover design: Nick Welch

Text design: Design Deluxe, Bath, UK

© 2008, Cengage Learning EMEA

For product information and technology assistance, contact
emea.info@cengage.com

For permission to use material from this text or product, and for permission queries, email
clsuk.permissions@cengage.com

Products and services that are referred to in this book may be either trademarks and/or registered trademarks of their respective owners. The publishers and author/s make no claim to these trademarks.

British Library Cataloguing-in-Publication Data
A catalogue record for this book is available from the British Library

ISBN: 978–1–84480–540–2

Cengage Learning EMEA
High Holborn House, 50-51 Bedford Row
London WC1R 4LR

Cengage Learning products are represented in Canada by Nelson Education Ltd.

For your lifelong learning solutions, visit
www.cengage.co.uk
Purchase e-books or e-chapters at:
http://estore.bized.co.uk

Printed by C & C Offset Printing Co Ltd, China
1 2 3 4 5 6 7 8 9 10 – 10 09 08

Brief contents

Contents

3   Conceptual database design 61

8   Network and distributed systems 215

Hands-On Section B: Microsoft Access B1–B56

9 Post relational databases 231

11   XML and databases **335**

Preface

Overview

This text provides an introductory treatment of the principles and practice of relational databases, and is intended for students in HND and degree courses in computing or information technology in which the students are expected to develop competence in designing practical database systems.

No previous knowledge of databases is assumed but some knowledge of general principles of computers and a little programming experience would be helpful. The text is not a guide to any particular database system, although both Oracle, Microsoft Access and the (SQL) syntax of MySQL are used as exemplar systems.

Database design properly forms part of the broader process of systems analysis and design. However, data modelling and the consequent construction of a database are sufficiently distinct tasks to be worthy of treatment in a separate textbook. In addition to aspects of database design, this book also deals with other aspects of databases such as integrity and concurrency.

SQL is one of the most important elements of modern database technology. It is used very extensively by virtually all database systems and is a major vehicle in facilitating inter-database communication. Accordingly, it is important that students studying database principles obtain a good grounding in the language. To this end, this text contains a tutorial on Oracle SQL as well as guidance in using SQL in Access and MySQL. Other laboratory exercises on SQL are available from the text's support website www.cengage.co.uk/ritchie

Microsoft Access is used to demonstrate some of the aspects of database design. While Access is intended only for small scale database applications, it does provide a wide range of features such as forms and report generators that are found in larger systems and it is simple and very convenient to use – in short, it is ideal for student use.

Objectives

The objectives of the text are to provide the following:

- an introduction to the principles underlying relational databases
- instruction in the techniques used to design and develop practical database systems
- an introduction to some of the practical considerations with database systems, such as security and integrity, distributed systems, etc.

- instruction in the use of SQL

- an introduction to other database technologies that are currently significant, such as object, object-relational and XML databases.

Summary of chapters

The text consists of thirteen chapters. The two Hands-On sections are somewhat distinct from the others: one is a tutorial on SQL, while the other is a simple introduction to Microsoft Access. The contents of the chapters are indicated below:

1 **Introduction and background**

   This chapter provides a non-technical intuitive introduction to the subject.

2 **The relational data model**

   The underlying principles of relational databases are introduced.

3 **Conceptual database design**

   This chapter describes the process of developing a conceptual design for a proposed database application. Because of the size of this topic, the chapter has been divided into three sections, as follows:

   Part 1: Entity-Relationship (ER) model

   Part 2: Converting an ER model into a relational database model

   Part 3: Normalisation of the relational model

4 **Physical database design**

   Aspects of building a practical system based on the conceptual models discussed earlier.

   Hands-On Section A: Learning SQL

   A practical guide to learning SQL.

5 **Interfacing with the database**

   How the database can be accessed using a range of programming tools.

6 **Transactions**

   This chapter describes the basic concepts of the transaction mechanism which is fundamental in maintaining system integrity.

7 **Integrity and security**

   Considers techniques that are utilised in maintaining the integrity and security of database systems.

8 **Network and distributed systems**

Many if not most database systems now operate in a networked environment. We explore the implications of this for database systems.

Hands-On Section B: Microsoft Access

A practical guide to learning Access.

9 **Post relational databases**

This chapter describes database variants, object and object-relational systems, that provide object-oriented features.

10 **Web databases**

This chapter examines techniques used to provide database facilities within the context of a website.

11 **XML and databases**

XML is an increasingly significant factor in modern computing and this chapter indicates current developments regarding the storage of XML documents in conventional and purpose-built databases.

Appendix Answers to review questions.

Treatment

In order to make the text as readable as possible, each chapter, with the exception of the two Hands-On chapters, has the following structure:

- The chapter starts with a set of learning objectives that indicate what the student should learn from the chapter.

- After the main body of the chapter, a summary section recaps on the most significant points covered in that chapter.

- The summary is followed by a set of review questions. These are questions requiring a short answer and are intended simply to test the student's recall of the material covered. The review questions are answered in the appendix at the end of the book.

- A set of exercises is also provided. These are either appropriate practical exercises, and/or questions that might appear in an examination paper. Answers to exercises are provided on the text's support website.

The Hands-On chapters are intended to support the students' laboratory work:

1 Hands-On Section A: Learning SQL is a fairly extensive tutorial on SQL intended to be used in the laboratory to instruct the student in SQL. A set of exercises

based on the same database is available from the text's support website. These exercises can be attempted by the student after working through the corresponding part of the tutorial.

2   Hands-On Section B: Microsoft Access is a simple introduction to using Microsoft Access to create tables, queries, forms and reports. This might form the basis for project work in Access, in which a full application is generated consisting of tables, transaction forms and business reports.

Supporting material

Additional resources are available on the website, **www.cengage.co.uk/ritchie**. These include:

- Answers to the chapter exercises.

- Sets of presentation slides for lecture use.

- Sample databases corresponding to the case studies introduced in Chapter 1, implemented in Microsoft Access. SQL scripts are also provided to enable the tables for these databases to be constructed in Oracle and MySQL.

- Sample examination-type questions for some topics.

- Sample specifications for project assignments.

1

Introduction and background

LEARNING OBJECTIVES

The main purpose of this chapter is to cover some of the groundwork, some of the basic principles that we need to support the rest of the text.

After studying this chapter, you should be able to do the following:

- Describe in outline the main methods of modern systems analysis and design.

- Identify the role of database design within the overall systems design.

- Describe the historical background to record-based storage systems.

- Provide a basic definition of a database.

- Describe the nature of data models and their characteristics and list the main data models in use.

- Outline the essential principles of hierarchical, network and relational database models.

- Provide an intuitive description of how a relational database is composed of a set of tables.

Introduction

Most computer applications require a means of holding *persistent data*; i.e. data that preserves its value between successive invocations of the software that produces it and, indeed, between successive 'switch-ons' of the computer itself. For some systems, including commercial applications such as order processing and human resources, the storage of data is a major part of their function, while for others it is perhaps more subsidiary to their purpose.

While our main concern in this text is the design and implementation of database systems, it is important to see database design within the context of overall systems development, of which database design is just a part. Accordingly, we start out in this chapter by providing a brief overview of the systems development process to see the role of the database within this. Note that we are primarily discussing systems employed in commercial enterprises; not all databases are used in such environments – many are technically-based or used for purposes such as air traffic control. Also, commercial enterprises are of greatly varying size, and this factor has a significant effect on the processes one might employ in the development of an information system. However, the essential disciplines presented by modern analysis and design methodologies are generally worthwhile in most development situations and hence are worthy of study.

Information systems analysis and design

This term is used to refer to the technical and organisational processes involved in developing an information system, from initial ideas to full implementation. Put simply, an information system is a grouping of people and computers; its design will include the activities of people – 'users' – and computerised processes. The main purpose of the majority of information systems is the processing of transactions and consequent management of data derived from them. A transaction in this context is some human/computer interaction that provides a service to the human agent. Simple examples of transactions are:

- Buying goods from a department store
- Renting a DVD from a rental shop
- Booking a holiday in a travel agency
- Ordering a book on the internet
- Ordering parts from another company

In these transactions, from the point of view of both the customer and the company providing the service, it is very important that the transaction is handled accurately. Errors in recording the information related to the transaction cannot be tolerated. Customers do not want the wrong goods delivered from the department store or to find that they are not booked on their holiday. Hence the various processes involved must be thoroughly planned and implemented, and a major objective of information development procedures is to provide techniques and disciplines that, as far as is possible, ensure that errors will not occur.

To this end, various development 'methodologies' have been introduced that provide a formal framework for the activity. Within the constraints of this text, we will only provide a brief description of the overall scope of these methodologies; for more detailed descriptions, refer to *Hoffer et al 2002*. The various methodologies that have been proposed and designed are in a sense competing systems, although they should achieve the same objectives; different development teams and individual developers have their own preferences which they feel are most likely to provide the best results for them. In addition to achieving the desired accuracy and integrity in their delivered system, another major factor for the developer is the effect of a methodology on the time and resources it takes to implement the system. Some methodologies emphasise this factor, although, of course the same expectation of accuracy and integrity still holds.

Current methodologies

The reader is warned at this point that the terminology and description in this topic area is somewhat unsettled. There seems to be little standardisation and agreement about what a methodology should be called and what it should contain; in short, it does not have the precise formalisation of other techniques in the computer field, such as the ER model for instance. Thus you may find that the notes below do not accord fully with other descriptions of the same subject. However, such differences are generally not too significant and the central principles are usually quite clear.

Methodologies are generally defined within the framework of a 'life cycle'; this expresses a sequence of phases from project initiation through analysis and design to implementation. A series of discrete stages are defined, each of which contains a number of activities and objectives.

A popular version is the so-called classic or 'waterfall' model, which is summarised here. Figure 1.1 illustrates this model.

The diagram is intended to indicate that the project proceeds in a series of steps, shown going from top to bottom, with each step being completed before the start of the next. This diagram assumes that the project described has previously been identified and initiated. For example, a system may be required to manage the processing of a new company, or it may be a replacement for a current, aging system.

The nature and purpose of these phases are summarised below:

Systems analysis

The requirements of the system in terms of the enterprise's expectations are determined.

Logical design

The logical design expresses the system design in terms not tied to any specific hardware or software so that, in principle, it can be implemented on a number of different hardware and software platforms. It is perhaps concerned more with the underlying requirements and objectives of the system and hence is often thought of as the 'business design' phase. This stage is significant in terms of our specific interest in databases, since it is here that the design of database structures takes place. This topic is addressed in some depth in Chapter 3.

Physical design

The logical design is rendered in a more detailed version within the context of selected hardware and software products. Our attention is now focussed on the technical aspects of the system. For instance, we need to decide at this point which database system we will use and, possibly, which web technology to employ. This text covers many aspects of the physical design of databases in Chapter 4 and later chapters.

Implementation

The physical design is implemented. This phase includes the production, testing and installation of software code, databases and web systems and is therefore of considerable importance in the overall scheme. At this stage, a number of techniques are available that aim to ensure the smooth and failure-free introduction of the new system. Possible methods include

1 Pilot running. A part of the full system is initially introduced to verify, with minimal risk, that the design is correct and workable. The scope of the pilot could be restricted to a limited group of customers or a specific geographical area. If all is well, full implementation can then begin.

2 Parallel running. The new system is introduced but the old system continues to run. The results from the two versions can be compared for consistency.

3 Phased introduction. The system is introduced piecemeal; i.e. only part of the full functionality is initially available and new features are added when previous sub-systems are proven.

4 Direct introduction. The full new system is introduced and the old system is terminated at the same time. Some contingency planning for reversion to the old system is desirable in case of serious failure.

The relative merits of these alternatives are dependent on a number of factors such as:

■ The criticality of the system – how important it is that it succeeds and how serious the consequences of failure.

■ The feasibility of using pilot, phased introduction or parallel running.

■ The size of the system.

Maintenance

After delivery and installation, it is usually necessary to address problems arising from the use of the system. Maintenance may be necessary as a result of problems which come to light after 'going live'. The word 'problems' clearly can cover a multitude of possibilities, from total failure of the system shortly after going live to relatively minor inconveniences not

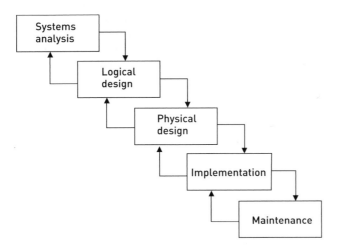

FIGURE 1.1 Waterfall model

critical to the system operation. Maintenance also arises as a consequence of natural changes to the environment of the system, such as increased transaction rates, statutory changes, etc.

As illustrated in Figure 1.1, the life cycle consists of a number of separate phases and in general progresses from the 'top' to the 'bottom'. In the strict interpretation of this scheme, there is the implication that each stage is fully completed before progressing to the next level. In practice, this is often found to be impractical; it can be very difficult to be so definitive regarding the exactness and completeness of each stage. In adapted versions of the waterfall model, some movement up the waterfall is possible, as implied by Figure 1.1; this would occur when developments later down the waterfall expose problems not anticipated earlier on and a reassessment is necessary. For instance, during the physical design some potential performance bottlenecks may be identified, necessitating a change to the logical design. One of the activities of the implementation phase is testing which is specifically intended to reveal necessary amendments to the physical design. However, even allowing for this adaptation, the classical waterfall model is often considered too limiting and realistic; hence, a number of alternative methodologies are also employed, a few of which are briefly described below.

Alternative life-cycle techniques

Prototyping

Prototyping proceeds on the basis of developing the full system in a series of investigation, design and implementation cycles, where each cycle provides a partial implementation that tries to prove the design and demonstrates the system to the users. Successive cycles refine and expand the system until an end product is reached. Within each cycle, some form of classical life cycle model would probably be used.

Prototypes will often utilise software tools that can rapidly simulate a required functionality. While these simulations are not suitable for final implementation, they can prove the concepts involved and transfer to a more robust final system is straightforward. For instance, a user interface and database design could be implemented on a small scale using Microsoft Access. Development in Access can be achieved rapidly and can be used to prove the database schema design and demonstrate representative forms and reports to users. For implementation in a large multi-user system, the designs established can be transferred to a larger scale database such as Microsoft SQL server.

Spiral model

This model utilises aspects of prototyping and waterfall models but also introduces a new aspect – risk assessment. It proceeds from an initial tentative design that is implemented and presented to users for approval. Based on this assessment, a revised, enhanced version is produced which is again assessed. After the phase objectives are established and, before each implementation phase, a risk assessment takes place which is intended to identify potential problems in alternative implementation strategies.

Data storage in computers

The need for persistent storage has traditionally been met by the use of magnetic storage devices such as tape and disk, with magnetic 'hard disks' being the predominant form at the current stage of technology. Quite possibly other forms of storage may become prevalent, with optical systems being the current most likely contender. However, the principles discussed in this book are likely to remain valid regardless of the storage technology used. For convenience, we will refer to 'disk' storage in this book, although this should be taken to mean any current or new form of mass storage.

The storage space on disks is generally controlled by 'file management' software, which can be part of the operating system, a layer of software above the operating system, or both. The basic tool provided is the 'file' abstraction. A file is a group of binary digits of arbitrary length, recorded on the disk surface, which the operating system treats as a unit of storage. To support the use of files as a storage medium, the system also provides a naming and categorisation mechanism (in the form of a hierarchical file and directory system), and reading, writing and positioning facilities. The file can have an arbitrarily complex internal structure, but this is generally only recognised by the application software and is not visible to the operating system. For instance, the file may consist of purely text characters, it may be a binary image of a graphical picture. The operating system, however, views it purely as a series of bits and is not aware of the interpretation placed on these bits by the application software.

The file system provides the user with the means to store programs and associated data (text and binary data such as graphics, sound, etc.) and as such is an indispensable part of the computer. End-user applications such as word processing, graphic design and spreadsheets extensively utilise the file system for storage of documents, designs, etc.; in doing so, such applications use their own specialised formatting of data, though many de facto standard formats, such as TIFF, BMP and RTF, are also used.

Our main concern in this text is systems – databases – that provide generalised facilities for the storage and retrieval of data of arbitrary conceptual structure and format, but predominantly textual and numerical. Databases are used extensively, but not exclusively, in commercial applications. In the earlier days of such systems, application programs normally used the file system directly to provide persistent storage, with each program using its own file formats. Of particular note in this respect is the COBOL language; this was the earliest commonly-used language to provide the programmer with extensive file handling facilities including, notably, the ability to store data in the form of **records**. A record is a compound data item consisting of a number of component **fields**, each of which is an elementary data item such as a text item or a numerical amount. This is a convenient format to use to represent 'real-world' entities such as orders, invoices, bank accounts and customers.

For instance, if we design a file to hold data on cinema films, a possible record format, together with sample data, might be as detailed below.

Title	30 characters
Director	20 characters
Year	4 numeric digits
MainStar	20 characters
SupportStar	20 characters

The 'fields' of this file are 'Title', 'Director', etc. and a typical record of this file might hold the values

Titanic	James Cameron	1997	Leonardo DiCaprio	Kate Winslett

If we were to write COBOL programs to create, read and update such a file, *each such program* would contain a description of the file format, which, in COBOL notation, would look something like this:

01 Film-Record.

02	Title	PICTURE	X(30).
02	Director	PICTURE	X(20).
02	Year	PICTURE	9999.
02	MainStar	PICTURE	X(20).
02	SupportStar	PICTURE	X(20).

This record definition effectively allocates main memory spaces, of the sizes indicated by the **PICTURE** clauses (e.g. **X(30)** specifies a field of thirty characters, **9999** specifies four numeric digits) in one contiguous sequence of bytes. This record space can then be populated with valid data values and transferred to disk using a **WRITE** instruction.

Subsequently, the record could be retrieved using a **READ** instruction. It is important to realise that the record specifications provided in COBOL programs were the only definition of the data structures being used; on disk, the data was held in a basic file system. Clearly, with many programmers working on one system, it was critical to maintain consistency in the design of the records. If it became necessary to modify a record design, all programs using that record type would need to be amended and recompiled. In addition, all programmers working on the system would need to be kept informed of such changes.

COBOL records can be arbitrarily complex; each record can have any required number of fields (within system limits) and, with some constraints, can have variable length fields and a variable number (i.e. an array) of fields. If we wanted to include a list of stars rather than just the two as used above, an alternative format might be:

01 Film-Record.

02	Title	PICTURE	X(30).
02	Director	PICTURE	X(20).
02	Year	PICTURE	9999.
02	Star	PICTURE	X(20) OCCURS 6 TIMES.

Different record formats within the one file are also possible, provided some 'record type' field is employed to enable the application programs to distinguish between the various formats. Additionally, COBOL provided very effective file organisation and access facilities including random, relative and indexed files. The merits of these facilities at that point in computing history account for COBOL's long-lived dominance of the commercial computing market.

However, technology marches on, and problems and limitations were soon encountered in file-based systems. The development of the concept of a 'database' arose at this time to meet these difficulties and, later again, the *relational* database ultimately provided more effective solutions. In the rest of this chapter, we provide an overview of the database concept and, in particular, its implementation using the relational model. The treatment in this chapter is essentially intuitive; later chapters provide more detailed and formal descriptions of relational techniques.

The database concept

The problems with file systems that became apparent were:

- The structure of the records is defined *in the application program*. This produced two unfortunate consequences:

  1 In order to change a file format, every program using the file had to be modified.
  2 At the same time, the file had to be rebuilt in the new format using 'one-off' conversion programs.

- The files were designed to suit the application currently being developed. When attempts were made to integrate different applications, the files were often found to be incompatible.

- Because files were created to meet the requirements of each separate application, the same data, such as customers' names and addresses, were often duplicated. In addition to the waste of space implied by this, amendment of such data was made more complex and the possibility existed of the various versions of the data being different.

- The ability to create files of arbitrary complexity made it difficult to provide generalised querying and maintenance facilities. For instance, the conversion process mentioned above could not be readily automated.

The database concept arose as an attempt to solve these problems. The conceptual leap made was to consider the *data*, instead of the application *programs*, to be of prime importance in the design of systems. Typically file-based systems concentrated on the functionality of the programs, with files being constructed to serve the persistent storage needs of these programs. The alternative approach – the database approach – is to look first at the design of the application's data and then write programs to process it. This is illustrated in Figure 1.2.

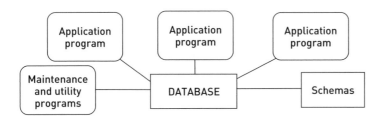

FIGURE 1.2 Database concept

Figure 1.2 shows that the data is the centre of interest and is maintained *independently of the application programs* that access and update it. Note also that we can employ general maintenance and utility programs (the nature of these will be described later) which are concerned only with the database and are not associated with any particular application. To facilitate this, the database must contain, not just the data, but also descriptions of the data within the database. This takes the form of **schemas** that define the structure of records held in the database. A schema is roughly equivalent to the COBOL record definition, but is stored separately from the application programs that use it.

In effect, we want the database to represent the application's data; i.e. the database *models* the application. The concept of modelling introduced here is very important in computing and recurs elsewhere in this text.

NOTE

It is too much to expect this process of modelling to be complete, i.e. fully representative of the system being modelled. Real systems are sufficiently complex that an exhaustive model is rarely possible. Attempts to capture every inter-relationship, exception and dependency of the real system are likely to fail and are probably unnecessary. What we need to model is not the real system *per se* but the computer application that interacts with the real system.

Realisation of the features described above requires a software system that manages the data and the schema information and provides an interface to the user. This software is called a **Database Management System** (usually abbreviated to **DBMS**). The term 'database package' is often used; this is used to refer to a DBMS implementation offered by a particular vendor, such as Microsoft Access, Borland Paradox or Oracle.

Definition of 'database'

We can perhaps at this stage attempt a definition of 'database'; unfortunately, like many terms used in computer technology, there is considerable variation in interpretations placed on the word 'database'. These range from the least prescriptive: 'a collection of data' to the over-specific: 'a large centralised shared data repository', which seems to exclude a database on a personal computer.

Rather than trying to capture the full import of the database concept in a single compact sentence, it is perhaps more productive to outline the essential features of a database and use this as a defining description. To be worthy of being called a database, a system must have two essential properties:

- it holds data as an integrated system of records
- it contains self-describing information.

These properties are explained in more detail below:

Integrated organisation

We imply by this term that all the data pertaining to the application or applications being served by the database is held under the control of one software management system, so that any data relevant to an application transaction is directly available. Any inter-relationships between the data can be exploited by application programs. For instance, an order processing system might contain a set of customer records and a set of order records; integration implies that the order records that belong to each of the customers can be readily determined.

Self-describing

The database must contain 'meta-data', i.e. descriptions of the data held in the database. These are referred to as **schemas.** In principle, a schema corresponds to a record description held in a COBOL program: it defines the position, size and type of each component field of each database record type. Practical database systems vary in the techniques used to define schemas; some of these will be explored later in this text. The significance of the schema concept is that it enables the database to exist independently of any program. Programs can discover the format of the data from the schema and hence process the data appropriately. For instance, if the previous cinema film file example was transferred to a database, the schema would show that the first 30 bytes of the stored records were the name of the film, the next 20 were the Director's name etc. The software can therefore 'unpack' the data according to the pattern supplied by the schema.

In order to implement these features in an application system, we require the assistance of appropriate software in the form of a DBMS. Application programs are not expected to probe unassisted into the schemas and the database data store; they must operate through the intermediary of the DBMS software. The DBMS presents a user interface to the users and to users' application programs and provides access facilities to the database data. We can now re-express the diagram of Figure 1.2 more precisely as in Figure 1.3.

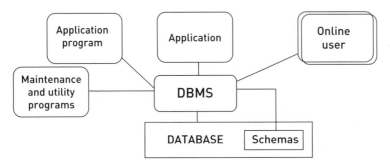

FIGURE 1.3 Conceptual view of database system

Figure 1.3 is intended to illustrate the following important points:

- Access to the database application data and to the schemas or 'meta-data' (i.e. the stored specification data that describes application data formats) is vested entirely in the DBMS. Direct access to the stored data, even in 'read-only' mode, is not possible.

- The schemas are stored within the database itself, so the database effectively contains its own description.

- Different modes of access to the DBMS are possible:

    1 we can write a program in a high-level language that 'talks' to the DBMS to provide the required services, or
    2 we can use interactive facilities provided by the user interface of the DBMS.

- Additional services can be provided by specially written maintenance and utility programs. These might include report generators, system documenters, etc.

The nature and facilities of DBMS packages is covered in more detail in Chapter 4.

Data modelling

In general usage, a model of some 'real' system is another representation that shares certain relevant features with the real system. A model can be a set of equations, an actual physical scale model, a computer program, etc. Models are useful in that the characteristics of the real system can be analysed by studying the nature and behaviour of the model. The rationale for this approach will depend on the system being modelled; for instance, in order to examine the behaviour of a new ship design, a scale model is economically more feasible than building an actual ship. Equally a computer model of a queuing system in a post office is more useful when investigating different queuing disciplines and numbers of service points than actually experimenting with a real post office.

In the study of databases, our interest is in **data modelling**. The role of data modelling is to provide techniques that allow us to represent, by graphical and other formal methods, the nature of data in real-world computer applications. The principal justification for the use of data modelling is to provide a clearer understanding of the underlying nature of 'information' and the processing of information in this area. It provides analysts and designers with a means of characterising and describing the structure, relationships and transformations of information. It is expected that the use of data models will provide a better understanding of the application area being studied and hence will enable the design of better database systems.

There are a number of data models, some of which are covered to varying degrees in this text over a number of chapters. The data models that are of interest to us are:

- the Hierarchical Model
- the Network Model
- the Relational Model
- the Object-Oriented Model
- the Entity–Relationship (ER) model.

Note that the ER model is somewhat different from the others above in that it is a technique used solely in the design of a relational system and does not directly influence how data is organised within data storage.

The **Hierarchical Model** formed the basis of the earliest databases and, as the name implies, organised data in a hierarchical structure. An outline description of this model can be found later in this chapter.

The **Network Model** followed the hierarchical model and solved some of the problems of that model. It is also described later in this chapter.

The **Relational Model** (RM) was first introduced by Codd in 1970 and forms the basis of most current database management systems. Its essential simplicity has been effective in fuelling its rapid rise in popularity; this has been tempered only by the fact that practical relational database systems can require considerable computer processing power.

The **Object-Oriented (OO) model** has become more prominent in recent years, particularly in the field of programming and systems development. Of interest to us in this text is its application to data management, in the form of the object-oriented database. The latter provides a competitor to the relational database and appears to have some advantages for certain applications.

The **Entity–Relationship (ER) model** was devised by Chen in 1976. It is a diagrammatic technique that provides a generalised approach to the representation of data and which is particularly suitable and helpful in the design of relational database systems. The main idea here is that the ER model provides a simpler approach to the understanding of the data content and relationships within a specified application and yields a diagrammatic definition of these. This model can then readily be converted to an equivalent in the Relational Model; i.e. in terms of constituent database tables and relationships. The principles and practice of the ER model are covered in some depth in Chapter 3.

General properties of data models

In addition to these specific models, there are a number of general terms in common use pertaining to the representation and interpretation of data that require explanation in the context of these models. In this and the next two chapters we cover the topics of the relational model and the entity relationship model. The object-oriented model is described in Chapter 5 in the context of newer database implementations.

- The first point to be made here is that the term 'data model' is something of a misnomer. Such models are not concerned with 'just' the data, but also the processing of the data, and hence all models provide not only a conceptual view of the representation of data and data structures, but also define allowable operations on these. For instance, the relational model represents data as a set of two-dimensional tables but also defines operations such as *restrict, project* and *join* on those tables.

- The real-world system being modelled is usually referred to as an 'enterprise'. Elements within the enterprise, such as human workers, goods, transactions, etc., are modelled by concepts such as *entities* or *objects*.

- One difficulty in data modelling is the difference between the 'human' view of an information system and the way it has to be implemented within a computer system. To resolve the difficulties caused by this difference, we can view the architecture of a database system as a series of 'levels' that provide varying degrees of abstraction of the system.

- To address the problem mentioned above, a standard architecture called the **ANSI/SPARC** architecture has been widely adopted. The ANSI/SPARC architecture is divided into three levels, known as the *internal, conceptual* and *external* levels, as follows:

    1 *External level*. This refers to the users' logical view of the enterprise; i.e. it refers to how the user perceives the data. A user view will consist of information received from the system in the form of queries, reports, screens, etc. In general, there can be several end-user views for the same whole system.

2   *Conceptual level*. The conceptual level provides a formal representation of the real data and procedures. It is essentially a 'mapping' between the internal and external views and describes the semantics of entities, relationships, constraints, etc.

3   *Internal level*. Refers to the implementation of the system in terms of tables, columns, indexes, etc.

On this basis, the relational model can be seen as a conceptual model. It expresses the data of the 'real' application in terms of a set of tables that define entities and relationships. However, it does not define how the tables are to be stored on disk or how specific data is to be accessed. Earlier data models tended to smudge the distinction between these levels; for instance, the hierarchical model required explicit record pointers embedded in the data records to specify connections such as Order – OrderItem links. Thus the logical notion of data linking was implemented by actual physical links. In effect, the conceptual and internal layers were intertwined. Such an arrangement is deemed to be undesirable, since it ties the levels together too intimately, making modification and evolution of the system at any of the levels more difficult. This conflicts with the critical notion of **data independence**, i.e. it is deemed important to be able to effect changes at some level without being concerned with the ramifications of the changes at some other level. For instance, in a relational system, we can alter the table structure (e.g. add a new column, change the size of a data item, etc.) without having to attend directly to the physical reorganisation of the table.

Modelling concepts

Before we can proceed to work with a data model, we have to develop a set of semantic concepts to help us to describe 'the real world' and its relationship with the database. One must be warned that this area of study is fraught with difficulties, dealing as it does with philosophical notions that do not have precise definitions. For this reason, it is important to appreciate the limitations of the modelling process. We are not trying to produce a comprehensive representation of the real world; this would be too problematic and is not in any case necessary. In practice we must be content to model those aspects of the application domain that are relevant to the database design.

A number of these modelling concepts are described below.

Application domain

The **application domain** of an information system is the real-world environment in which the information system is to be applied. Common examples are university student management, company stock control, hotel room reservation, etc. An alternative term for this is 'universe of discourse'.

Entities

When we perceive the world, we see that it contains a number of recognisably separate 'things', such as people, vehicles, products, offices, etc. We can also appreciate the existence of less tangible notions, such as sales orders or hotel booking. In data modelling, we refer to these as **entities**. A database application system will be concerned with a number of such entities, within the [...] representation of each relev[...] also be represented in some [...]

A problem presented by the e[...] entity and what would be bett[...] is no single 'correct' interpretati[...] possible. Generally though, one [...] convenient that the others.

We really ought to distinguish betw[...] a generic classification while the fo[...] university, for example, students coul[...] on the BSc course for Chemistry is ar[...] terms are not strictly applied and entit[...] referred to as 'entities'.

Attributes

An **attribute** of an entity is some property or characteristic that is relevant to the application. An entity is essentially defined by a set of attributes. For instance, an employee has attributes *name*, *address*, *salary*, *department*, etc.

Attribute domain and type

The **domain** of an attribute is the range of possible values that the attribute can have. Some domains are very large (e.g. the set of all employee's names) while others can be more precisely delineated (e.g. the range of possible salary values in a company). Data '**type**' refers to the classification of the data used for the attribute; common types are *text*, *number* and *date*. The terms 'domain' and 'type' are clearly related; in general, the datatype determines the maximum possible extent of the domain. The actual domain will be equal to or smaller than that extent. For example, in practice, an employee's salary would be represented as a number datatype with potential value of negative millions to positive millions, whereas the real domain of values might only be 15 000 to 100 000.

Relationship

A **relationship** is an association or interaction between two or more entities. For instance, the relationship 'employs' exists between entities 'company' and 'employee', the relationship 'teaches' exists between 'teacher' and 'pupil'.

Earlier forms of database

Hierarchical model database

The earliest databases were designed to meet the data processing demands of large organisations. In particular, large assembly type industries often needed to manage data which had an inherently hierarchical structure. The classic example of this is in Bill of

Materials applications where the company's products are constructed from a number of component assemblies, each consisting of a number sub-assemblies, which in turn contained further sub-assemblies and so on, eventually to the individual component parts. For instance, a car consists of 'top-level' assemblies such as the body, engine, wheels, etc.; the engine can be further broken down into the engine block, carburettor, air filter, etc. This process of subdivision continues until we reach the level of basic 'atomic' components such as nuts and bolts. If the structure of a car is represented in a database that can reflect this hierarchy, it can be used to yield useful information; one of its main tasks, for instance, is to generate a complete parts listing from which, given the individual costs of parts, the overall cost of the product can be produced. The costs of the various intermediate sub-assemblies are also generated during this process.

The first type of database, therefore, was based on a hierarchical structure, the so-called **Hierarchical Model Database (HMDB)**, which could directly represent the structure of the data used in these applications. In fact, the data of many applications has an inherent hierarchical structure; for instance, a sales order consists of 'root' information such as the customer involved, the date of the order, etc., but associated with this would be a set of data items representing the individual items of the order. We can visualise this as shown in Figure 1.4.

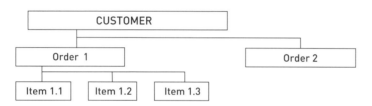

FIGURE 1.4 Hierarchical view of sales orders

This technique meets the 'integrated' database criterion; it enables data pertaining to different entities (e.g. customers, orders, etc.) in the application domain to be united such that associations among these entities are reflected in the structure of the database: given a customer, it is possible to find data about that customer's orders.

It is perhaps less obvious how this type of database meets the 'self-describing' criterion. In fact, the hierarchical database uses a two-level architecture; the **physical schema** defines the physical structure of the full database, while the **logical schema** specifies different views of the data for the purposes of each application.

The physical database is implemented using a system of pointers; using the structure illustrated in Figure 1.4, the details for one customer would include a pointer that linked to the data related to the first order and then from there to the first of the order item records. This brings us to the bottom of the tree and the next action would be to follow other links from the order record to subsequent order items, and so on. In effect, the data items in that tree would be traversed in the sequence known as a *pre-order traversal* of the hierarchy:

Customer → Order1 → Order Item 1.1 → Order Item 1.2 → Order 2 → Order Item 2.1, etc.

This is referred to as '**navigational access**' because programmed access to the information involves navigating through a series of items by means of the embedded pointers.

The main problems of the hierarchical model are:

- The hierarchical structure only permits the use of one-to-many relationships; an application whereby one engineer works on one or more projects and each project employs one or more engineers cannot be directly represented. To circumvent this serious limitation, practical systems introduced the idea of '**logical relationships**' which superimposed another set of connections between data items separate from the 'physical' tree structure. However, this introduces yet more complexity to the art of design and programming of these databases.

- The embedded pointers produce a lack of data independence, since implementation mechanisms are intermixed with actual data. Modifications such as addition of a new data item to a record are difficult.

- Accessing the database involves navigational traversal through the data, although indexed access to 'starting points' – for example, a selected customer – is possible. The hierarchical traversal means that the performance of the system is dependent on the placement of data within the hierarchy. However, it also has to be said that navigational access can often be much faster than indexed access.

- The production of ad hoc queries is not possible. Queries must be implemented by programs specially written for the purpose.

- The design and maintenance of the system requires highly skilled staff.

In spite of these problems, the HMDB was a substantial improvement over the basic file-based systems that preceded it. Its main benefit, in common with all database technologies, is the centralisation of the data definition so that applications can refer to an accurate, managed representation of the stored data.

The first implementation of a hierarchical database was called Information Management System (IMS) and was developed by the companies IBM, Rockwell and Caterpillar in the late 1960s to meet the challenge of managing the bill of materials for the Apollo space program. IBM has continued to develop and market the product and it still constitutes a major factor in its sales. Hence the hierarchical model does yield the means of facilitating a practical large-scale database system. Its decline can be attributed to the relative benefits provided by the relational database.

Network model database

The Network Model Database was designed by the Database Task Group (DBTG) of the Programming Language Committee (later called the COBOL committee) of the Conference of Data Systems (CODASYL), the group responsible for the definition and standardisation of the COBOL language. It was intended first of all to address some of the shortcomings of the hierarchical model. It was also hoped that this standard database model might be adopted universally, thereby making applications and programmers' skills in the database area more portable. A major contribution of the

DBTG was a final report that contained the specifications for three essential database components:

- A **Network Schema**, which was the conceptual design of the entire database and was managed by the database administrators. This defined the structure of the database and the format of the records and fields within each record type.

- A **Network Subschema**, which in effect provided virtual views of portions of the database that were visible to application programmers. This enabled individual programs to deal only with the records and fields of interest for the application.

- A **Data Management Language (DML)** that enables definition of, and access to, the schema and subschema. It consisted of a data definition language to construct the schemas and a data manipulation language to develop programs.

The main enhancement is that the one-to-many limitation was removed. The model still views data in a hierarchical one-to-many structure, but now a record can have more than one parent. The hierarchical model can therefore be seen as a subset of the network.

However, this system was also found to be cumbersome and difficult to work with as applications became increasingly large and complex. The main problems were the complexity of structural changes, which required significant time and processing, and the lack of facilities for ad hoc reports, which required specific programming effort.

The relational database

The invention of the relational database is largely attributed to Edward Codd, whose seminal paper on the subject is referenced at the end of the chapter. The relational database has an underlying mathematical basis which has been important in its development and acceptance. In this chapter we will not deal with this mathematical aspect, which will be described briefly later; for our current purposes, we will content ourselves with an intuitive description of the technique.

The simplest (but far from complete) view of relational databases is that they represent the application data as 'two-dimensional' tables. Using file processing terminology, the columns of the table represent component fields of the record, and each row details an instance of a record. An example is shown in Table 1.1.

Film Title	Director	Year	Main Star	Support Star
Gone with the Wind	Victor Fleming	1939	Clark Gable	Vivien Leigh
Forbidden Planet	Fred Wilcox	1956	Leslie Neilson	Walter Pidgeon
Shane	George Stevens	1953	Alan Ladd	Van Heflin
Casablanca	Michael Curtiz	1942	Humphrey Bogart	Ingrid Bergman
Titanic	James Cameron	1997	Leonardo DiCaprio	Kate Winslett
Schindler's List	Steven Spielberg	1993	Liam Neeson	Ralph Fiennes

TABLE 1.1 Film table

1

Note that as conventionally drawn, each column of the table has a heading such as *Film Title* that specifies the content of the column. The heading is part of the schema, the stored description of the data, and not part of the data itself. In physical terms, the headings and the data would be stored separately.

> **NOTE**
>
> The sample data of film titles shown above uses some classic films of recent times and older. As well as celebrating some of the great films, use of classic names prevents the data in this textbook from ageing quite so much!

Rather than the 'files', 'records' and 'fields' of file processing, relational database parlance introduces its own new terminology – in fact we have a choice! The most common terms in use are **table**, **rows** and **columns**, which are intuitively meaningful. More formal terms used, which are derived from their mathematical basis, are **relation**, **tuples** and **attributes**. These terms will be explained in Chapter 2.

The conceptually simple tabular arrangement can be readily understood by most people and this simplicity is an important factor in the popularity of relational databases. In particular, its ease of understanding for simple tasks has made the relational database amenable for use by 'end-users' in addition to professional system developers.

However, the apparent simplicity is perhaps misleading; the precise requirements for the construction of tables, the techniques employed in representing all the elements of a complex application, and the practical problems of designing and using relational databases, provide many interesting problems. Additionally, we need a supporting software environment to provide the necessary storage and access facilities and, importantly, to provide the aforementioned characteristics of 'integration' and 'self-description'. Study of techniques that support these characteristics constitute a major proportion of this text.

Case studies

In this section we present a set of case studies which will be used to assist in the delivery of the rest of the text. At this point, we have provided only an overview of the case studies, sufficient to meet the immediate requirements of the next few chapters. The scenarios described are deliberately simple to avoid complexities that would obscure the messages that they are intended to convey. A version of each of these case studies implemented in Microsoft Access is available on the website for this text. Scripts for creating the tables used in these case studies are available for Oracle and MySQL on the website.

CASE STUDY 1 – EMPLOYEES

This basic scenario is used as the subject for SQL tutorials in Hands-On Section A: Learning SQL. Its simplicity helps in explaining the querying process, although it is sufficiently rich in content to provide a wide range of query possibilities. The information maintained includes:

Employee identification number

Name

Job position

Hire date

Salary

BranchCode indicating company branch in which employee works

Department code indicating department (within their branch) in which employee works

Name of branch

City where branch is located

Manager of branch (the employee identification of the manager)

Supervisor code (the employee identification of the employee's supervisor in the company)

CASE STUDY 2 – DVD HIRE SHOP

A DVD rental shop requires a database system to assist in managing the hire and return of DVDs. The application is chosen because the requirements and working of such systems are easy to understand and familiar to many people.

The database maintains details of customers, films, DVD copies of films and rental transactions. The system must record transactions (i.e. when a DVD is rented and when it is returned), calculate how much a rental costs and determine which rentals are overdue. Additionally it must record the arrival in stock of new DVDs and the disposal of obsolete and faulty DVDs. DVDs are grouped into rental price categories; the category of a DVD will normally change during its lifetime in the shop – it will become cheaper as it 'ages'. The cost of rental is based on the rental price times the number of days it has been rented. The standard period of rental is two days; additional days are charged at a reduced rate. A DVD is considered 'overdue' if it is not returned within one week.

Reports are required showing rental histories for selected clients, usage reports for selected DVDs and popularity ranking for current films available for rent.

Case study extension: Add data pertaining to the stars and directors of the films.

1

CASE STUDY 3 – TRAINING COURSES COMPANY

A training company holds courses on a range of topics, within a number of subject areas such as bookkeeping, accounting, IT, management, etc. Courses have a duration of one to five days and are held on company premises. The company has a number of tutors that present the courses, one tutor per presentation. One tutor may present different courses at various times. Each course is scheduled at a number of dates in the future; for instance, a bookkeeping course may be scheduled to run on 20th December, 7th January and 1st February. For each presentation of the course, a maximum number of places available is specified. For instance, the 20th December presentation may be limited to 20 enrolments.

When customers make a booking for a course, the booking is recorded in the name of one person making the booking but the booking may reserve one or more places on the course.

A database system is required to manage the company's customers, course and presentation information and course bookings and produce reports on income from courses and course occupancy.

CASE STUDY 4 – JOB AGENCY

A job agency offers to find jobs for clients looking for employment. A database system is used to record the clients' personal and resumé details. Personal details include name, address, date of birth, sex and phone number. The resumé detail includes a history of employment and a set of qualifications. Each client is assigned to one job consultant within the agency, who negotiates with the client and endeavours to locate suitable employment for them.

CASE STUDY 5 – CORRESPONDENCE COLLEGE

This case study provides a more elaborate example to study but is still of manageable proportions as a source of instruction. It is based on a correspondence college that offers courses in a range of topics. The full system to support this application is divided into four sub-systems.

1. **Students management**. Initial enrolment of students; attachment to specific study programmes and modules; maintenance of student information, e.g. names and addresses.

2. **Payments**. Students may opt to pay for their courses by subscription; this consists of an initial one-off payment followed by a set number of monthly subscriptions. Provision is made to dispatch letters to students who default in their payments.

3 **Assignments**. For each course module, students complete a series of assignments which are sent to the college office; the assignments are marked by external tutors and the results recorded in the students' records. Completion of a programme of study will result in the award of a diploma or certificate.

4 **Tutors**. The written assignments received from students are gathered into batches, which are then dispatched by post to tutors for marking (i.e. complete batches of up to ten assignments are sent to tutors). Assume that there can be an indefinite number of tutors. The tutors mark the assignments, then return them, retaining them within the same batches. The subsystem enables 'tracking' of the assignments, so that the college knows what assignments have been received, sent to tutors or marked. The system also keeps a running total of the total number of assignments that have been marked by each tutor, to enable them to be paid.

Tables in practice

Let's look in more detail at the way we construct a relational table. As we saw earlier, a table can be used to store data on some application topic, such as films. However, in a more complex application environment, there may be more than one subject about which we need to hold data. For instance, consider the application described by Case Study 2 earlier – the DVD hire shop; in this application, we would store data about films recorded on DVD and also data on the shop's customers who hire the DVDs. In this context we refer to subjects such as 'films' and 'customers' as entity types and the application environment (the DVD shop in this example) as the application domain.

NOTE

The term **entity type** refers to the *category* of subject, e.g. **customer**. We would refer to an actual instance of this entity class, such as Mr John Smith, as an **entity**. In common with much terminology in computing, these terms are often used rather loosely; in particular, 'entity' is often used for both meanings described above, confusing the general with the specific. In most cases, this should not cause a problem in understanding what is intended; this note is provided to reassure those readers who may have already noticed the need for this distinction.

In general, each entity class is represented in a relational database by a separate table. In our DVD shop example above we would need two tables, the Film table (as shown in Table 1.1) and a Customer table (shown in Table 1.2).

Customer Number	Name	Address	Balance Owing
5567	Jones	Cross Road	2.50
2913	Anderson	River Lane	0.00
4890	Murray	West Street	1.50
1622	Richards	Mill Lane	3.00

TABLE 1.2 Customer table

For each table there is a certain column (or possibly more than one column) that has a unique value and serves as an identifier for the row. This is called the **primary key** of the table. For instance, the primary key of the Customer table above is the Customer Number.

Notice, however, that the data in these two tables does not provide any information about which customer has hired which film: from the point of view of the DVD shop, it is clearly necessary that this information is represented somewhere. We say that there is a **relationship** between these two tables, which we could call **Hired By**. This is the sort of inter-data information that was represented in the network and hierarchical databases as physical pointers in the data, but such techniques are not used in relational databases. One tentative (and not very satisfactory) solution might be to add a column to the Customer table to indicate which film (if any) the customer currently has on hire. This is illustrated in Table 1.3.

Customer Number	Name	Address	Balance Owing	Film Title
5567	Jones	Cross Road	2.50	Forbidden Planet
2913	Anderson	River Lane	0.00	Titanic
4890	Murray	West Street	1.50	Casablanca
1622	Richards	Mill Lane	3.00	Schindler's List

TABLE 1.3 Customer table version 2

What is wrong with this arrangement? Well, since there is only one column to indicate the hired film, the tables as they stand can only record one hired film per customer; it is unlikely that either the DVD shop or the customer would be happy with that restriction!

An obvious solution to this difficulty, and one which might be adopted in a file processing system, would be simply to add more Film Title columns, say, allowing up to three films:

Customer Number	Name	Address	Balance Owing	Film Title 1	Film Title 2	Film Title 3
5567	Jones	Cross Road	2.50	Forbidden Planet	–	–
2913	Anderson	River Lane	0.00	Titanic	Shane	Casablanca
4890	Murray	West Street	1.50	Casablanca	Titanic	–
1622	Richards	Mill Lane	3.00	Schindler's List	–	–

TABLE 1.4 Customer table version 3

In principle, the number of titles could be extended indefinitely in this way. In effect, in programming terms, these columns constitute an array of titles.

While this appears to be an acceptable method of dealing with the situation, the use of an array of items like this is *specifically disallowed* in relational database tables. Certainly, there is nothing to prevent you from specifying a table as shown above with three title columns, but they would be treated as three distinct columns and not as a true array of values. Use of multiple columns in this way is not in the spirit of relational systems and would cause some difficulties and awkwardness when defining queries and in other operations. Note in particular that the relational system only permits a fixed number of columns in any one table.

So how do we specify the films on loan to each customer? In effect, what we are trying to specify is a *relationship* between entities – customer and film. In relational systems, relationships are most often represented by another table; for instance, in our current example, we could use a **Hired By** table shown in Table 1.5.

Customer Number	Film Title	Date Hired
5567	Forbidden Planet	12-Sep-07
2913	Titanic	14-Sep-07
2913	Shane	10-Oct-07
2913	Casablanca	16-Oct-07
4890	Casablanca	25-Oct-07
4890	Titanic	20-Nov-07
1622	Shindler's List	29-Nov-07

TABLE 1.5 Hired by table

> **NOTE**
>
> The description in this chapter is deliberately informal; the expression of relationships between tables is rather more involved than that implied by the above example. The later chapters of this book will, of course, deal with this topic in much more detail.

The DVD shop, therefore, can be represented by a set of three tables, one of which links the other two tables together. Note that the link values refer to columns of the tables (Customer Number and Film Title) which identifies the appropriate rows. We can illustrate this diagrammatically as shown in Figure 1.5, which, for clarity, shows only one customer and one film.

Customer Table

Customer Number	Name	Address	Balance Owing
5567	Jones	Cross Road	2.50

Hired By table

Customer Number	Film Title	Date Hired
5567	Forbidden Planet	12/9/07

Film Table

Film Title	Director	Year	Main Star	Support Star
Forbidden Planet	Fred Wilcox	1956	Leslie Neilson	Walter Pidgeon

FIGURE 1.5 DVD shop table system

Note that the database tables do not actually hold any representation of the links shown in Figure 1.5; linkage is achieved by having equal values in the linked fields of each table pair. If this point is not clear, look back at the three Customer tables shown earlier and Figure 1.5, and note how the **Hired By** table shows that Mr Murray (Customer Number 4890) has two films on hire given by the two rows.

4890	Casablanca	25-Oct-07
4890	Titanic	20-Nov-07

These correspondences are used by database software to extract required information from the respective tables. If, for example, we wanted to print out the titles and stars of all films currently on loan to Mr. Murray, the database software would need to access all three tables.

We indicated earlier that one required feature of a database is 'integration'; the example above shows how a set of separate tables are inter-related to provide a model of the application domain. This is one important aspect of data integration.

The other required database feature is 'self-description'; in terms of the above example, if we wanted to use the database software to access information from the DVD shop tables, the software would obtain the format of these tables from the table schemas stored (on disk) along with the tables.

What do we mean by 'specification of a table'? As we have seen, a table consists of a fixed number of columns, each of which represents some property or attribute of the entity being described and which is given a descriptive symbolic name, such as *Film Title*. Each column must hold values of one type only; i.e. each value in any one column must be all text, all numeric or all dates, etc. Specification of the table therefore consists of detailing the names and types of each of the columns of the table.

The actual method of doing this varies from system to system, although a standard database language exists called **Standard Query Language** (or **SQL**) which provides a system-independent way of specifying the schema information. SQL is described in some detail in Hands-On Section A. In most database packages, the schema information is supplied to the system using a form or table-based input routine.

In addition to the basic name and type information, database packages will also allow the specification of additional features such as validation criteria and formatting controls; these topics will be covered in Chapter 7.

A further example

As a further illustration of how relational tables can be applied, we will develop here an intuitive design of another application. We will use the fourth subsystem of Case Study 5 – the Tutor Management subsystem of the Correspondence College. It may be worthwhile to re-read the definition of this Case Study and to give it some initial thought. Assume the existence of student and course information; these will be referred to simply by appropriate codes.

First we make a list of all of the data items that the system appears to require:

Tutor Code

Batch Number

Student Code

Course Code

Assignment Number

Total Assignments marked (per tutor)

Date Batch sent to Tutor

Date Batch returned from tutor

However, this list does not reflect the relative numbers of these items; for instance, one batch contains several assignments. We can illustrate the structure of the data using a diagrammatic approach; Figure 1.6 is intended to show the data representing one batch.

FIGURE 1.6 Table design – first attempt

It shows *one* batch. Note that, for each batch, there is a single value for the first five items in Figure 1.6 but that there can be several occurrences of the fields Student Code, Course Code and Assignment Number. One possible way of storing this data is shown in Figure 1.7.

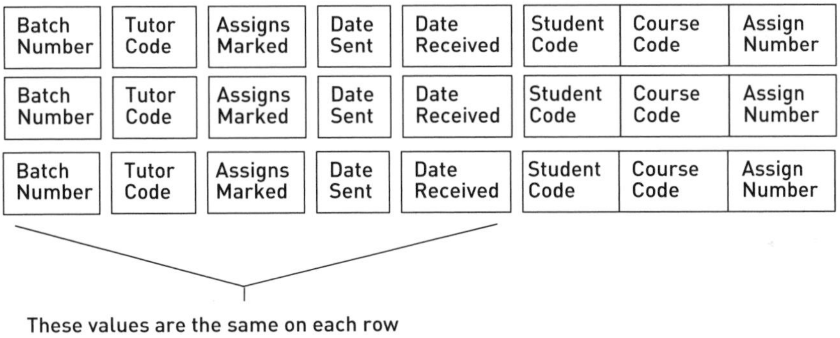

| Batch Number | Tutor Code | Assigns Marked | Date Sent | Date Received | Student Code | Course Code | Assign Number |

| Batch Number | Tutor Code | Assigns Marked | Date Sent | Date Received | Student Code | Course Code | Assign Number |

| Batch Number | Tutor Code | Assigns Marked | Date Sent | Date Received | Student Code | Course Code | Assign Number |

These values are the same on each row

FIGURE 1.7 Possible data design

At this stage it is possibly easier to visualise if we look at sample data in a tabular format in Table 1.6.

Batch Number	Tutor Code	Assigns Marked	Date Sent	Date Returned	Student Code	Course Code	Assign Number
23	JS	87	26-Apr-07	07-May-07	981230	PR007	3
23	JS	87	26-Apr-07	07-May-07	978001	AB003	1
23	JS	87	26-Apr-07	07-May-07	980239	PR009	7

TABLE 1.6 Possible table design – sample data table

This is clearly wasteful, since the first five fields are repeated in all the rows; there is considerable redundancy in this representation of the data. A better solution would be to separate the data into two tables; the batch information is stored in one row of the 'Batch' table (Table 1.7) and the individual assignment data is stored in a separate 'Assignment' table (Table 1.8).

Batch Number	Tutor Code	Assigns Marked	Date Sent	Date Returned
23	JS	87	26-Apr-07	07-May-07

TABLE 1.7 Batch table – first attempt

Student Code	Course Code	Assign Number
981230	PR007	3
978001	AB003	1
980239	PR009	7

TABLE 1.8 Assignment table – first attempt

There is a problem here though! There is now no indication in the Assignment table as to which batch each row belongs. To resolve this problem, we need an extra field in the Assignment table to specify the relevant batch number (see Table 1.9).

Batch Number	Student Code	Course Code	Assign Number
23	981230	PR007	3
23	978001	AB003	1
23	980239	PR009	7

TABLE 1.9 Assignment table

The data now looks quite efficient, with minimal duplication; the Batch Number has to be repeated in each of the Assignment rows pertaining to that batch, but otherwise no duplication occurs.

However, the limited scope of the above example data does not reveal another problem: if we were to show more of the Batch table data (more of the separate batches) the problem becomes more apparent (see Table 1.10).

Batch Number	Tutor Code	Assigns Marked	Date Sent	Date Returned
23	JS	87	26-Apr-07	07-May-07
24	GH	91	28-Apr-07	06-May-07
25	GH	91	1-May-07	06-May-07
26	CR	129	4-May-07	9-May-07
27	JS	87	5-May-07	10-May-07

TABLE 1.10 Batch table with more data

The point to note is that every row pertaining to a particular tutor repeats the Assignments Marked value for that tutor. For instance, every time **GH** appears in the **Tutor Code** column, **91** will always appear in the **Assigns Marked** column, because the **Assigns Marked** value only depends on the Tutor. We can eliminate this duplication by, once more, factoring the table into two separate tables and removing the duplicate rows. For clarity, we show below the final version of all three tables; note that the Assignment table only shows one batch.

Batch Number	Tutor Code	Date Sent	Date Returned
23	JS	26-Apr-07	07-May-07
24	GH	28-Apr-07	06-May-07
25	GH	1-May-07	06-May-07
26	CR	4-May-07	9-May-07
27	JS	5-May-07	10-May-07

Tutor Code	Assigns Marked
JS	87
GH	91
CR	129

TABLE 1.11 Batch table (left) and Tutor table (right)

Batch Number	Student Code	Course Code	Assign Number
23	981230	PR007	3
23	978001	AB003	1
23	980239	PR009	7

TABLE 1.12 Assignment table – revised

This process of factoring the data into a number of storage efficient tables can be specified in a more formal procedure called **normalisation**, described in Chapter 3. It will also be shown that, in addition to reducing data duplication, normalised data also avoids certain difficulties or **anomalies** which can arise with un-normalised data.

Elements of a practical database system

The foregoing sections have shown how relational database tables can be used to represent the data in an application domain. We saw that the data in the **Film**, **Customer** and **Hired By** tables represents or models aspects of the DVD shop and its customers. Figure 1.5, for instance, represents the fact that customer Jones has the film Forbidden Planet on hire. When such information has been captured for a company's activities, it directly facilitates the development of systems to drive the transactions of the company.

In order to enable the setting up, maintaining and accessing of a database, a DBMS would provide a range of features serving the needs of the application system developers and the end-users. A practical database package would typically provide facilities for:

- The design and maintenance of database tables. This involves the schema specification previously described.

- The formulation of **queries**, i.e. requests for information from the database. This is a fundamental mechanism in database technology: having stored the data, it is important that retrieving it is made as convenient and efficient as possible. Hence much of the study of databases is concerned with aspects of querying. A number of techniques are used for this, including languages such as SQL and table-based methods such as that used in Microsoft Access and other systems.

- The design of **forms**: a form is a full screen display of data from a database table, normally showing a single row of the table at a time. This is a more convenient method for users to view, amend and enter data.

- The design of **reports**: a report is a printed presentation of data extracted from the database (typically using a query) in a format convenient to the user.

- The construction of **macros** and programs. A macro is a method of automating a sequence of steps involved in implementing some database operation. Programs are used to implement the functionality of applications.

The current database software market

In order to be able to use a database in an application, you will require a software implementation that provides the required facilities. Although some current systems still exist that use a network or hierarchical database, these are primarily 'legacy' systems.

The relational database has been so dramatically successful that it forms the heart of virtually all new development work in commercial information processing.

However, databases based on non-relational data are available; these include object-oriented databases (e.g. db4o, Versant and Objectivity), extended relational and object-relational (e.g. Oracle object features introduced in Version 8, InterSystems Cache and Matisse). The object-oriented databases have achieved some success in specialised applications; typically, they perform best for applications with large volumes of relatively static data which require fast access. These newer forms of database are described in Chapter 9.

The current market can be roughly divided into 'large-scale' and 'small-scale' database systems; the former are designed to cater for more complex applications involving large numbers of users, tables and table rows. The principal vendors in this market are Oracle, Microsoft (SQL Server), IBM (DB2) and MySQL. These database systems are intended primarily for systems development by professional system developers for use in commercial applications and are not used extensively by end-users.

'End-user' in this context refers to office staff, managers, and accountants who require access to the data held in the corporate database, and also to personal users who design and build a database for their own applications. It is assumed that such users have a very good knowledge of their own field of work and, in particular, the application area of the intended database system, but they possibly lack the level of knowledge expected of a professional software engineer. The challenge in the design of database packages suitable for end-users is to provide a system that makes it as easy as possible to develop a system while providing a reasonable level of assurance that it will perform as intended.

Small-scale database packages are those running on personal computers. While many of these are now high-powered systems suitable for the development of substantial multi-user applications, they have also been designed with the end-user in mind. The particular features of such systems are:

- The use of graphical user interfaces, which facilitates the design of tables, forms and reports.

- An extensive interactive capability, which minimises the need for programming.

There are a large number of personal computer database packages currently available, but the most common are Microsoft Access, Fire (public domain) and Borland's Interbase. Examples used in this text are drawn from Microsoft Access.

Summary

The purpose of this chapter has been to provide some of the background to the world of databases and a gentle intuitive introduction to the central concepts of relational databases. We have seen that database design and development normally takes place within the wider context of overall systems design, and that there are a number of alternative data models on which we can base a practical database system. Our main focus will be on the relational database model, although post-relational databases will also be considered in a some detail. We have also introduced a set of case studies that will be used to illustrate many of the topics to be covered.

The most significant points introduced in this chapter are:

1 A database is an *integrated* and *self-describing* system of data storage. The schema of the database holds the database description.

2 A number of data models are described: hierarchical, network, relational and object oriented. These are used as the underlying conceptual bases for database organisation. Also described was the entity relational model; this is not used as a basis for database organisation but is a valuable aid for the design of specific relational databases.

3 The predominant form of database today is the relational database. Earlier database models are the hierarchical and network models. Post-relational databases, based on the object model, are also important in today's market.

4 Database design and development is a integral process within the broader subject of information systems development.

5 The relational database uses two-dimensional tables to represent application entities such customers, orders, parts, etc. and also to represent relationships (associations) between entities.

6 The columns of a relational table represent properties or attributes of the entity class described by the table. For instance, in a Customer table, likely columns would be Name, Address, Credit Limit, etc.

7 The rows of a relational table represent *instances* of the entity class; in a Customer table, each row represents one customer.

Review questions

1 How do older file systems and the database approach differ in terms of the relationship between the data and the application programs?

2 What are the two most significant properties of a database?

3 List the data models that provide the bases for database organisation.

4 What are the principal disadvantages of hierarchical and network databases?

5 List the stages of the waterfall development model.

6 List the possible methods of introducing a new system.

7 Outline the basic structure of a relational database table.

8 Explain the meaning of the rows and columns of a relational database table.

9 Explain how separate tables in a relational database are linked together.

10 What is meant by the term 'schema'?

References

Textbooks

Bowman, K. (2003): *Systems Analysis: A Beginner's Guide*, Palgrave Macmillan.

Chen, P.P.-S. (1976): 'The Entity Relationship Model – Towards a United View of Data', *ACM Transactions on Database Systems*, Vol 1, No. 1, March 1976.

Codd, E.F. (1970): 'A relational model of data for large shared data banks'. *Communications of the ACM*, 13(6):377–387. Obtainable from the ACM at http://www.acm.org/ classics/nov95 /toc.html

Hoffer S.A., George J.F., Valacich J.S. (2002): *Modern Systems Analysis and Design* (third edition), Englewood Cliffs, NJ Prentice-Hall.

Oppel, A. (2004): *Databases Demystified*, McGraw-Hill Education.

Shelly, GB., Cashman T.J. and Rosenblatt, H.J. (2005): *Systems Analysis and Design* (sixth edition), Course Technology.

Skidmore, S. and Eva, M. (2003): *Introducing Systems Development*, Palgrave Macmillan.

2

The relational data model

LEARNING OBJECTIVES

In the first chapter we outlined some of the basic principles of data modelling, and the basic notion of a relational database, based on the relational model, was introduced via informal examples. With these elementary ideas in place, the more formal principles underlying the relational model can now be readily examined. We begin our description of the relational model by starting at its roots in the mathematical theory of sets. This leads us into the details of the principles and properties of relations and the techniques used to construct a database from a set of relations.

After studying this chapter, you should be able to do the following:

- Explain, in simple terms, the concepts of sets and relations and how these relate to the Relational Data model.

- Explain the terms relation, attribute, tuple, row, primary key, foreign key and candidate key.

- List the properties of a relation.

- Explain the concept of functional dependency and determine dependencies from examples.

- Explain the concepts of entity integrity and referential integrity.

- Explain the concepts of Relational Algebra.

- List the common Relational Algebra operations: RESTRICT, PROJECT, JOIN, UNION, PRODUCT, DIFFERENCE (also known as MINUS or COMPLEMENT), INTERSECTION.

- Solve examples using these operations.

- Explain the relationship between Relational Algebra and SQL.

- Explain the concept of a relational view and identify the benefits of using views.

The relational model

Sets and relations

Basic set principles

The concepts introduced in this section are perhaps not essential to an understanding of the relational model, but it is helpful to be able to appreciate that the model has a strong theoretical underpinning. The relational model is based on the mathematical theory of *sets*. A set can be viewed as a collection of zero or more items of similar type. For instance, a set of numbers could be {32, 5, 99, 1 066}; another set of numbers could be {1}. A set of people could be {Thomas, Frank, Anne, Joe}. An empty set is valid and shown as {}. The theory is not concerned with the nature of the contained items, only about the common properties of such sets and the ways in which sets can be processed mathematically. For instance, we can define operations on sets such as 'union' that combines two sets into one: the union of the sets {32, 5, 99, 1 066} and {1} is the set {32, 5, 99 1 066, 1}.

The three most important characteristics of sets for our purposes are:

- All members of the set are of the same type.

- Only one instance of any item is held in a set. For instance, a set {999, 111, 999} is not a proper set and would be expressed correctly as {999, 111}.

- The sequence of items in the set is not significant. Therefore, the sets {999, 111} and {111, 999} are the same set.

These simple set principles can be used to develop the concept of a relation, as described in the next section.

Relations

Given two sets X and Y, we can take any element from x from X and y from Y to form an ordered pair (x, y). The set of all ordered pairs is called the **product set** and is denoted by X.Y.

e.g. X = {1, 2}   Y = {A, B , C}
then X.Y = {1A, 1B, 1C, 2A, 2B, 2C}

A subset of X.Y is called a **relation** and can be denoted R(X, Y). A relation can be considered as a mapping from one set to another and given a functional name.

e.g. X = {Jones, Smith, Brown}
     Y = {Accounts, Sales, Despatch, Personnel}

and the relation R(X, Y) is to be interpreted as 'works in', so that the ordered pair (Jones, Sales) represents the fact 'Jones works in Sales'.

The set X could be mapped into a number of other sets, in addition to Y; for instance,

Y1 = {Clerk, Accountant, Manager, Salesman}
Y2 = {5, 10, 15, 20, 25}

to give ordered pairs like (Jones, Salesman) and (Jones, 15)

These can be combined into a single expression such as:

(Jones, Sales, Salesman, 15).

Such an expression is called an **n-tuple** (where **n** is the number of sets involved; e.g. the above example is a 4-tuple) or just **tuple**. Each of the elements of the tuple is called an **attribute**. Each attribute has a name identifying its 'meaning' in the application area of the data. For the example above, we might use the attribute names:

Employee Name, Department, Occupation, Years of Service

A relation can now be viewed as a set of tuples (shown in Table 2.1).

Employee Name	Department	Occupation	Years of Service
Jones	Sales	Salesman	15
Smith	Accounts	Clerk	5
Brown	Accounts	Accountant	10

TABLE 2.1 A set of tuples

Hence the data of an application can be modelled as a two-dimensional table; in effect, each relation defines and/or describes some area of the application and provides a mapping from an identifying value (in our example, the Employee Name) to other descriptive or qualifying attributes (Department etc.). The identifying value is sometimes called the **ruling part** while the rest of the attributes are collectively referred to as the **dependent part**.

If we were to store data in this form, it is convenient to use the following correspondences between the relation concept and more conventional file processing notions:

Relation is synonymous with *table* or *file*

Tuple is synonymous with *row* or *record*

Attribute is synonymous with *column* or *field*

Ruling part is synonymous with *primary key* (described in next section).

For example, while most file processing uses a record as a 'unit' of input/output, a relational system reads and writes one *row* at a time. Each row of a relation describes one 'entity' within the application area. Unfortunately, *all* of the above terminology is found in current usage and not always within consistent groupings. In general, the terms 'relation' and 'table' tend to be used interchangeably. The term 'attribute' is used in preference to 'column' when talking about a property of an entity, while 'column' is used when referring to a specific column of a table. The term 'row' is definitely preferable to the alternatives.

Notice that each of the columns of a table is drawn from a set of similar values such as

Y1 = {Clerk, Accountant, Manager, Salesman}
Y2 = {5, 10, 15, 20, 25}

so that all items in any one column are all of the same datatype (i.e. numeric, text, date, etc.). The range of available datatypes is dictated by the particular database software used.

You will recall that in Chapter 1, the concept of a domain was introduced. We can repeat the definition in terms of our current example: the *domain* of an attribute is the set of *all possible values* of that attribute. In the above example, the domains of Y1, Y2, etc. were assumed to be the enumerated list of values shown. In general, the domain of a column is prescribed by the column's datatype; a column defined as an integer type is limited to values in the range (for a 16-bit representation) of −32 768 to +32 767. However, in a practical system, the actual domain of the data will often be more restricted. For instance, an attribute such as Years of Service might be represented by an integer value having the aforementioned domain, whereas a more realistic range of values would be, say, zero to 50 years. In current database packages it is not possible to 'fine-tune' a column's domain by defining a new datatype, such as Age; i.e. user-defined types are not available. (Note that this is a technique used in 'extended relational' systems which are now appearing in the market. This topic is covered in more detail in Chapter 9).

However, most database packages allow the simulation of a narrower domain by means of column constraints which can be specified within a table definition. In effect, when a table structure is defined, the user can specify the range of admissible values that can be entered in the table for each column. For instance, a Years of Service column might be given a constraint of 'between 0 and 50'. The purpose of such constraints is to prevent invalid data being entered into the table; this topic is covered in much more detail in Chapter 7, which deals with integrity and security.

Properties of a relation

Based on the foregoing principles, a relation can be seen to have the following properties:

1 Columns in the relation are all single values; i.e. arrays of values or other compound structures are not allowed.

2 Entries in any column are all of the same datatype; e.g. integer, real number, character, data, etc.

3 No two rows of the relation are identical.

4 The order of the rows in the table is immaterial.

5 The order of the columns in the table is immaterial.

6 Each table contains an identifying column or columns (the ruling part or primary key).

Some comments on the above items are worth making.

NOTES

Property 3:   This property is effectively saying it is meaningless to have two identical rows – both rows identify the same real entity. Some query operations in SQL or relational algebra (both described later in this chapter) will naturally yield duplicate rows; for example, if you execute a query asking only for the names in a personnel relation, then duplicate rows are quite likely. However, the same philosophy still applies – if multiple 'Smith' rows are generated, these can be reduced to one such row with no loss in meaning.

Property 4:   It is likely, in a particular application, that you might want to 'see' the data in a certain sequence; for instance, you might want to list a customer table in order of surname. However, such ordering of the data is *not* achieved by reorganising the table rows into the required sequence. Instead, the data is extracted from the (unsorted) table in that sequence. Normally, the data in a database table is simply held in the order of physical writing to the table.

Another point is that since the row order is not meaningful, it cannot be used for any purpose. For instance, in a relation describing people (say, in a sports club application) you cannot use consecutive rows to indicate that the people described by the rows are married.

Property 5:   Application programs access the table columns *by name* independently of the position or sequence of the columns. In a similar sense to Property 4 dealing with rows, the juxtaposition of columns cannot be used to indicate any association between the columns.

Property 6:   The primary key concept is covered in more detail shortly.

Practical database systems based on relational principles, by and large, conform to these criteria. In addition to these essential properties, there are a number of other issues contributing to relational theory which need our attention. Some of these are described in the remainder of this chapter, while the rest are covered in Chapter 3.

Other relational concepts and terminology

Primary key

In an earlier section we introduced the idea of the **ruling part** and the **dependent part** of a table row. The ruling part, usually called the **primary key**, plays a very important role in relational database theory and practice.

The **primary key** of a table is a column (or a combination of two or more columns) that serves to *identify* the individual rows of the table. For instance, in the customer table described in Chapter 1, the primary key is the Customer Number; since this number has a unique value for each customer, it can be used within the database to reference a specific customer. We can see from this definition that the non-key columns are dependent on the primary key. This leads to an important concept called **functional dependency** which is described in more detail later in this chapter.

Customer Number	Name	Address	Balance Owing
5567	Jones	Cross Road	2.50
2913	Anderson	River Lane	0.00
4890	Murray	West Street	1.50
1622	Richards	Mill Lane	3.00

primary key   dependent part

TABLE 2.2 Customer table, primary key and dependent part

The adoption of a set of unique codes such as the Customer Number in Table 2.2 is often used to simplify the definition of a primary key. Such codes are of course well established in general use, independent of their application in relational databases, and for much the same reason – to guarantee proper identification of customers, products, orders, etc. Where there is no natural or existing code available for a relation, it is common practice simply to assign a sequential number to successive rows to serve as the key. Databases often provide a facility to generate these numbers automatically – for instance, the Autonumber datatype in Microsoft Access.

Composite primary key

Note that the primary key may consist of more than one column; the key value may effectively be a concatenation of two or more columns. The reasons for this will be more evident later, but a simple example may clarify the nature of this usage. Suppose we have a table holding data on which engineers have been assigned to which projects and the date of the assignment. An extract of this table may appear as shown in Table 2.3.

Project Number	Engineer Name	Assignment Date
A2367	Connelly	31–Nov–07
G0814	Chapman	22–Dec–07
G0814	McDonald	12–Jun–07
P9890	Connelly	01–Feb–07
V0122	McDonald	23–Apr–07
V0122	Stewart	15–Apr–07

TABLE 2.3 Assignment table

This table represents assignment 'events'; each row records one instance of such events and hence has a unique identity. Neither Project Number nor Engineer Surname can suffice as a primary key value on its own because the values in each column are not unique. For example, Project V0122 occurs twice and engineer Connelly occurs twice. The combination of Project Number and Engineer Surname *does* produce a unique value which is suitable as a primary key.

It may be necessary to use more than two columns; to extend the previous example, let's assume that the name is not sufficient to identify the engineer, due to the possibility of duplicate names. We could of course adopt an 'engineer code', but if we wanted to persist with the name then some other distinguishing attribute must be found, such as a first name. If we assume that there are two 'McDonalds', namely Angus and Hamish, then our table would now appear as shown in Table 2.4.

Project Number	Engineer Surname	Engineer Firstname	Assignment Date
A2367	Connelly	James	31-Nov-07
G0814	Chapman	David	22-Dec-07
G0814	McDonald	Angus	12-Jun-07
P9890	Connelly	James	01-Feb-07
V0122	McDonald	Hamish	23-Apr-07
V0122	Stewart	Alan	15-Apr-07

TABLE 2.4 Assignment table

We now have a three-column primary key. This example is somewhat contrived, but multiple column primary keys can occur quite naturally in practice. Examples of this will be encountered later in this text.

Functional dependency

The concept of **functional dependence** was mentioned briefly above in the description of primary keys. We can define functional dependence formally as follows:

If we say that one column B of a table is **functionally dependent** on another column A (or group of columns), it means that every value of A uniquely determines the value of B. This is often written using the notation $A \rightarrow B$.

This concept is important in relational data theory and it is worth some thought to ensure that it is understood. If $A \rightarrow B$, then it means that every time a particular value appears in the **A** column, then another particular value will appear in the **B** column.

If in one row the **A** column value is 999 and the **B** column value is POLICE, then if another row has **A** = 999, column **B** must be POLICE.

Let's consider another example: a car hire company. A representative sample of data from their rental charges table is shown in Table 2.5. The charges are based on a daily rate assigned to each model and an additional mileage rate.

Make	Model	Engine Size	Daily Rental £	Mileage Charge p.
Ford	Escort	1 400	15	10
Ford	Mondeo	1 600	20	15
Nissan	Almera	1 400	16	10
Renault	Megane	1 400	16	10
Vauxhall	Vectra	1 600	22	15
Vauxhall	Vectra	2 000	25	15

TABLE 2.5 Car hire company

Note that for any value of engine size, say 1 400, the mileage charge is always the same (in this case 10p). Hence, the mileage charge is functionally dependent on the engine size. We would write this as:

Engine Size   →   Mileage Charge

Functional dependency must be determined from knowledge of the application domain; it is important to understand that it is a feature of the *real world domain* of the database application and is not an observation of chance coincidence of column values. It follows from this that you cannot determine whether a dependency exists simply by inspection of the table data – which is why we said in the above example that the table was a *representative* sample of data. In practice, such dependencies are often derived from 'business rules' of the application domain; in the car rental example, the company has decided that such a rule will apply.

Foreign keys

The primary key is used to refer to a specific row in a table. Primary key values can be included in a column of another table which is related in some way to the first table. Columns containing such values are called **foreign keys**. An example will clarify this concept.

In Chapter 1 we presented an example of a table system which included the pair of Batch and Tutor tables shown in Table 2.6.

Batch Table

Batch Number	Tutor Code	Date Sent	Date Returned
23	JS	26-Apr-07	07-May-07
24	GH	28-Apr-07	06-May-07
25	GH	1-May-07	06-May-07
26	CR	4-May-07	9-May-07
27	JS	5-May-07	10-May-07

Tutor Table

Tutor Code	Assigns Marked
JS	87
GH	91
CR	129

TABLE 2.6 Batch Table (left) and Tutor Table (right) (reproduced from Chapter 1)

Note that the primary key of each table is the first column. The Tutor Code column of the Batch Table contains values that refer to the Tutor Table primary key values, and hence is a *foreign key* within the Batch Table.

To put this definition more succinctly, *a foreign key is a column in one table that refers to the primary key of another table.* This is the basic 'linking' mechanism that allows a set of tables to form an integrated database.

Note that relational databases do not use any form of stored 'pointers' between foreign and primary keys; the linking is done purely on a match of values.

Candidate keys

In some tables it is possible to find that more than one column, or combination of columns, could serve as a primary key. Such alternative primary keys are called **candidate keys**. One of the possible candidate keys is chosen to be the primary key. In most cases this choice is obvious; for example, a code (such as a customer number) is often specifically created to identify the instances within the table. Such codes will be guaranteed to be unique, will generally be compact, and may be convenient for use externally to the database system; for example, a product sales catalogue would typically display the same codes as used within the database.

Within the basic data, however, it is often possible to identify other potential candidate keys. For example we may have a lecturer table (from a university database) with the structure shown in Table 2.7.

Lecturer Id	Name	Department	Room No	Subject Leader
123	Harrison	Finance	A029	Taxation
145	Cooper	Mathematics	M074	Algebra

TABLE 2.7 Lecturer table

The 'obvious' primary key is the Lecturer Id, the role of which is solely to act as a unique identifier for lecturing staff. However, depending on the particular conditions prevailing in the university, several other candidate keys are theoretically possible:

- The **name** is a possibility if we are sure that no duplicate names will occur.

- It may be that there is only one lecturer per room; in this case, the **room number** will be unique in the table.

- The Subject Leader is (presumably) unique, at least per department (if not in the whole university) so **Department–Subject Leader** is a candidate key.

On grounds of effectiveness and economy, none of these options is very appealing and would not be used in practice. The candidate key concept is not very significant in practical systems, but is a factor in the process of normalisation which is described in Chapter 3, Part 3.

Nulls

It often happens when inserting data into a database table that some of the attribute values cannot be entered for a variety of reasons. Possible reasons are:

- The data is not available; e.g. a new employee has failed to provide their date of birth. The rest of the employee information has to be added to enable the payroll program to proceed.

- The data is not applicable to this entity; e.g. the attribute is salesman's rate of commission but this salesman doesn't earn commission.

To provide a standard means of filling in columns of a table that would otherwise be empty, the null concept was devised. Although sometimes referred to as a 'null value', a null is *not a value*, but is an indicator held in the column to specify that the attribute does not have a value. One merit of the null concept is that, since it is not a value, a null is type-less, hence it can be used for a date, a text value, a number or any other datatype.

The use of nulls in relational systems is very controversial; there is a strong school of thought that believes that their use is, at best, confusing and awkward, and at worst definitely dangerous in terms of accuracy in queries. While the idea may appear fairly innocent, it has far-reaching consequences that affect many aspects of the use of relational databases. Particularly in the area of database queries, one has frequently to take special account of the likely effect of null attributes within the query parameters.

What is the alternative to null? A technique used by some designers is to adopt a system of default values; within an attribute column, say a salesman's commission rate, values not within the normal domain of values for the column are adopted to represent 'missing' and 'inapplicable'. One problem here is that the default values must conform to the datatype of the column, so that a 'missing' date would be some artificial date, while a 'missing' numerical amount must be a numeric value.

There are pros and cons for both the null and anti-null approaches, but the inescapable fact is that for current database systems the null mechanism is well entrenched and cannot be completely avoided. It figures significantly, for example, in the SQL query language: see the section dealing with joins in Hands-On Section A.

Entity integrity

It is a defining principle of relational tables that each row of a table uniquely represents a one entity in the application domain. One row in a customer table represents one customer. It is also necessary that no two rows of the table are the same; if this were allowed it would mean that the same application domain entity was represented by two rows of the table. Preservation of this principle is referred to as **entity integrity**. In general, the use of unique primary key values guarantees that this principle is complied with. Note however that the use of any nulls within the primary key value would invalidate the principle; a null expresses some uncertainty about a value and hence is inappropriate for a key that serves as a unique defining label. Consequently, the definition of entity integrity is usually expressed as:

"Entity integrity is the principle that no part of a primary key can be null".

As an aside, it is interesting to note that the principle of 'one row – one entity' is routinely broken in relational database applications! The philosophical notion that real world entities require one-to-one representation within a database breaks down when the individual entities being dealt with are sufficiently trivial. So, for example, if we had a database representing the stock within a hardware store, it is unlikely that we would record each nut and bolt individually. Instead, we would have one row per nut and bolt type and an associated 'quantity in stock' value. Thus the row represents an entity type rather than the individual entities. This technique would be employed until the entities became worthy of separate identification on the grounds of value or other reason.

It is also perhaps worth noting that the uniqueness of rows in a relation applies specifically to 'base relations', i.e. the relations that constitute the designed database, and not to relations created as intermediate answers within a query, which can often contain duplicate values.

Referential integrity

Referential integrity is concerned with the linkages between tables defined by the foreign and primary key fields. As we indicated above, a foreign key is an attribute in one table that refers to the primary key in another table. For a set of database tables, all foreign key values in all tables *must* be matched by a row in another table. A database table for which this is true is said to conform to referential integrity; otherwise, it does not.

A typical situation is shown in Table 2.8. The primary key of each table is the first column.

Courses

CourseCode	CourseTitle	CourseDept
A123	Maths	Mathematics
B654	Economics	Business
C299	Computing	Comp Science

Students

MatricNum	StudentName	CourseCode
990134	Jones	B654
992011	Smith	D333
992888	Brown	A123

TABLE 2.8 Course and student tables

The Course table defines courses offered by a college; the Student table holds information on each student. In the Student table, the column CourseCode is a foreign key referring to the primary key of the Course table.

In the first row of the Student table, the CourseCode value B654 is valid because it refers to an existing row in the table (economics course). However, the CourseCode in the second row (D333) row breaks referential integrity because there is no corresponding row in the table. In application terms, it implies that the student Smith is on a non-existent course.

We indicated above that referential integrity deals only with non-null foreign keys. If student Smith in the above table was not enrolled on any course, this could be specified by means of a null value in the CourseCode column. This does not conflict with referential integrity since no reference is being made to a non-existent course.

Note that the C299 CourseCode in the Student table is not matched with any value in the Student table; this is OK, however, since CourseCode is not a foreign key in the Course table. It simply implies that the Computing course has currently no enrolled students.

A database that does not exhibit referential integrity is in an anomalous and impractical condition and will likely produce serious run-time failures. Hence, it is important that referential integrity be maintained throughout the database and most database systems now provide facilities to assist in complying with this. For instance, the current SQL standard provides clauses that define referential relationships, enabling the database software to check for consistency. In current interactive environments such as Microsoft Access, referential integrity can be enforced by defining to the system the relationships that exist between member tables of a database using a graphical interface. The screen shot shown in Figure 2.1 illustrates the link between the two tables.

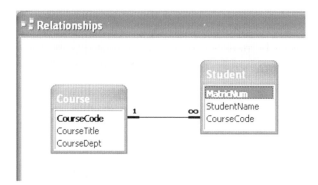

FIGURE 2.1 Referential integrity screen

The example shows the referential link between the two tables using the CourseCode. The effect of establishing this link is that the database software will not permit any modification to the database that breaches this referential integrity requirement. For instance, we cannot delete a row of the Course table if some row or rows of the Student table refer to it. This corresponds to the application domain restriction that you cannot cancel a course while there are still students on it. However, most systems (including Microsoft Access) allow deletion of rows from the primary table by use of a technique called *cascaded delete*. This has the effect of deleting all dependent rows when a primary table record is deleted. For instance, if the Course table record referring to, say, course B654 is deleted, reference to all students on this course in the Students table will also be deleted, thereby preserving referential integrity. The admissibility of this technique will of course depend on the design of the particular application. It is likely that the correct approach in most applications would be to delete the dependent rows individually before deleting the parent.

Additionally, there is a related technique called *cascaded amendment*; this compensates for changes to a primary key value by amending all foreign key values that refer to it. For example, if it was decided to renumber CourseCode B654 as B654X, then all foreign keys on the Student table referring to B654 would be altered to B654X. Since modification of primary key values in this way is generally not advisable, this technique is much less used.

Relational algebra

Relational databases are based on the mathematical notion of a relation; i.e. a set of mappings from independent values (keys) to dependent values. The mathematical theory defines a number of algebraic operations on relations that produce new relations from one or more originals. The fact that the algebra operates on a relation or relations to produce a new relation (i.e. the operations exhibit *closure*) is important, because it means that a succession of operations can be applied to 'output' relations in order to implement a compound operation.

The operations defined are as follows:

RESTRICT	Form new relation from selected *rows* of input relation.
PROJECT	Form new relation from selected *columns* of input relation.
JOIN	Form new relation by 'joining' rows of two or more input relations.
UNION	Form new relation by combining rows from two input tables.
PRODUCT	Form new relation by joining every row in one table with every row of a second; i.e. the *Cartesian product* of the relation members.
DIFFERENCE	Form the difference of two relations, a third relation containing rows that occur in the first relation but not in the second. Also known as MINUS or COMPLEMENT.
INTERSECTION	Form the intersection of two relations, a third relation containing rows that appear in both the first and second relations.

NOTE

The RESTRICT operator is often (and probably better) known as SELECT; however, 'SELECT' is used extensively as a command in the SQL query language, but with a much broader meaning than that used in relational algebra. To avoid confusion, the operator will be called 'RESTRICT'.

For UNION, DIFFERENCE and INTERSECTION the relations must have the same structure; i.e. they must have the same number of attributes drawn from the same domains.

Of the above, the RESTRICT, PROJECT and JOIN operations are the most significant from the point of view of practical database working, and are described first. Table 2.9 illustrates the principles. Note that the expressions used in the examples are *not in any recognised standard format* – they are descriptive only.

Orders

OrderNo	CustNo	OrdDate	Carrier
AJ123	5567	12-Dec-06	DHL
GK300	3488	13-Dec-06	TNT
NN125	5567	10-Dec-06	SEC

OrderItems

OrderNo	ItemCode	Quantity	Size
AJ123	A/23	100	L
AJ123	F/12	250	M
AJ123	M/66	30	M
GK300	B/10	500	S
GK300	F/12	300	L
NN125	M/66	50	M

TABLE 2.9 Orders and OrderItems

Principal operators

RESTRICT

RESTRICT Orders WHERE CustNo = '5567' would give the relation:

OrderNo	CustNo	OrdDate	Carrier
AJ123	5567	12-Dec-06	DHL
NN125	5567	10-Dec-06	SEC

PROJECT

>PROJECT Columns OrderNo, OrdDate FROM Orders

would give the relation:

OrderNo	OrdDate
AJ123	12-Dec-06
GK300	13-Dec-06
NN125	10-Dec-06

JOIN

>JOIN Tables Orders, OrderItems

>Matching Columns Orders.OrderNo With OrderItems.OrderNo

would give:

OrderNo	CustNo	OrdDate	Carrier	ItemCode	Quantity	Size
AJ123	5567	12-Dec-06	DHL	A/23	100	L
AJ123	5567	12-Dec-06	DHL	F/12	250	M
AJ123	5567	12-Dec-06	DHL	M/66	30	M
GK300	3488	13-Dec-06	TNT	B/10	500	S
GK300	3488	13-Dec-06	TNT	F/12	300	L
NN125	5567	10-Dec-06	SEC	M/66	50	M

NOTE

This is technically known as a **natural join**. There are other forms of join; in particular, there is an **equi-join**, which is the same as the natural join but with the 'matching' columns left in. In the above example, this would give a relation with two OrderNo columns.

The join can be considered as a combination of a product (i.e. referring to Table 2.9, a 'perm' of all rows in the Orders table with all rows in OrderItems table) with a restriction (extracting rows with equal values in the 'join' columns) and, for a natural join, a projection eliminating the duplicate matching column. Joining of tables in this way is a fundamental part of relational database working; in effect, it is a 'drawing together' of data held in a number of separate entity and relationship tables. There are other variations on the theme of joining, which will be described in Hands-On Section A, that deal with SQL.

All these operations yield another relation so that, for example, a restriction could be applied to the result of the join. Notionally, this involves using compound statements containing two or more of the above operations.

Other relational operators

From a practical point of view, the restrict, project and join operations are by far the most significant. In this section we examine the other operators, namely, UNION, DIFFERENCE, INTERSECTION and PRODUCT which are used less frequently.

The operators UNION, DIFFERENCE and INTERSECTION can only be applied to relations of identical structure. For the purposes of describing these, let us suppose that two departments within a university keep their own separate database table of students called STUDENT1 and STUDENT2, (with, fortunately, identical structures) as shown in Table 2.10.

STUDENT1

MatricNo	Name	Address
951234	Smith	Glasgow
952356	Jones	Aberdeen
953388	Brown	Dundee
954001	Adams	Edinburgh

STUDENT2

MatricNo	Name	Address
952991	Gray	Paisley
953777	White	Glasgow
953388	Brown	Dundee

TABLE 2.10 Student1 and Student2 records for two university departments

Note that Mr Brown has managed to get himself onto both tables.

UNION

A union forms a new relation by combining rows from both input relations, removing any duplicate rows. Hence, STUDENT1 UNION STUDENT2 would yield

MatricNo	Name	Address
951234	Smith	Glasgow
952356	Jones	Aberdeen
953388	Brown	Dundee
954001	Adams	Edinburgh
952991	Gray	Paisley
953777	White	Glasgow

Note that the duplicate row is dropped. Such an operation might be useful if the two departments were merged and a single table formed from the two originals. The most common application of a union is in combining two or more relations of intermediate results (with the same structure) obtained from other queries. Examples of this are encountered later when we deal with SQL programming in Hands-On Section A.

DIFFERENCE

The difference of two relations A and B (sometimes written A − B) is the set of all rows in A that *do not* appear in B. Note that A − B is different from B − A. Another way of looking at this is that A − B is what is left of A after rows common to A and B are removed. The difference STUDENT1 − STUDENT2 is shown below:

MatricNo	Name	Address
951234	Smith	Glasgow
952356	Jones	Aberdeen
954001	Adams	Edinburgh

The above relation shows STUDENT1 − STUDENT2; note that it consists of all the rows of A (i.e. STUDENT1) except for:

953388	Brown	Dundee

which is common to both tables and hence not part of STUDENT1 − STUDENT2.

INTERSECTION

The intersection of two relations contains the rows that are in both relations. Again, it is essential that the two input relations have the same structure.

MatricNo	Name	Address
953388	Brown	Dundee

In terms of our two student tables, this operation would immediately reveal which students were in both tables.

PRODUCT

The product, also known as the *Cartesian product*, is the result of combining each row of one relation with every row of a second relation; in other words, it is a condition-less join of the two relations. It would normally be applied to relations of different structure. Note that a join is defined as a subset of a product, as explained earlier in this chapter. The product has limited practical application. However, we can offer the following (almost practical!) example. In a sports club system, club members can book tennis courts for specific time slots, say, each hour from 8.00 to 20.00. Suppose we have a table of available courts, Courts, and a table of possible time slots, Times (Table 2.11). Then we could generate a relation of all bookable court/time slots by the product of Courts and Times (Table 2.12).

Court No.	Court Description	Time Slot
1	Lawn Court 1	8.00 – 9.00
2	Lawn Court 2	9.00 – 10.00
3	Indoor Court 1	10.00 – 11.00
4	Indoor Court 2	11.00 – 12.00
5	etc.	etc.

TABLE 2.11 Table of Courts and table of Times

Court No.	Court Description	Time Slot
1	Lawn Court 1	8.00 – 9.00
1	Lawn Court 1	9.00 – 10.00
1	Lawn Court 1	10.00 – 11.00
etc.		etc.
2	Lawn Court 2	8.00 – 9.00
2	Lawn Court 2	9.00 – 10.00
2	Lawn Court 2	10.00 – 11.00
etc.		etc.

TABLE 2.12 Table of Courts × Times

Relational algebra and SQL

Relational algebra provides a useful mathematical basis for relational databases, demonstrating that complex processing can be performed on such databases with a relatively small number of basic set operations. It could, in principle, be implemented as a 'language' which could be used to manipulate relational database tables. However, in practice, the operations provided by this algebra are implemented in a more user-friendly form by declarative query languages such as SQL. SQL is by far the most significant query language in current use, and knowledge of SQL is an essential requirement for anyone working in the area of relational databases. SQL originated in 1974 and was initially called SEQUEL; 'SQL' is still pronounced 'see-quel' by many people, although ANSI (the American National Standards Institute) who are responsible for standardisation of the language, has defined the offical pronunciation as 'ess-q-ell'. In 1979, the company now known as Oracle announced the first commercial SQL-type product. Other products appeared in the early 1980s from INGRES and IBM. Standardisation of the language began in 1982 by ANSI and was joined in these efforts by ISO in 1983. The first ISO standard appeared in 1987. For a considerable time, a later version known SQL2 or SQL-92 became the established standard, and most database systems during the 1990s conformed to that standard. During that time another standard was developed, originally called SQL3; this eventually appeared around 1999 and was called SQL:99. This version introduced object-oriented features, some of which are described in Chapter 9. The primary innovation of later (and, at the time of writing, current) versions SQL:2003 and SQL:2006 was integration of XML features which are described in Chapter 11.

SQL is described in some detail in Hands-On Section A, but we show here how the main SQL command, SELECT, implements the basic relational algebra operations.

SELECT is the most common SQL command and is used to implement most of the relational algebra operations described earlier. We can illustrate these operations using the Orders and OrderItems tables used in Table 2.9 and its principal operator results, reproduced here as Table 2.13 for convenience.

Orders

OrderNo	CustNo	OrdDate	Carrier
AJ123	5567	12-Dec-06	DHL
GK300	3488	13-Dec-06	TNT
NN125	5567	10-Dec-06	SEC

OrderItems

OrderNo	ItemCode	Quantity	Size
AJ123	A/23	100	L
AJ123	F/12	250	M
AJ123	M/66	30	M
GK300	B/10	500	S
GK300	F/12	300	L
NN125	M/66	50	M

TABLE 2.13 Orders and OrderItems Tables

The format of the basic SQL query is:

SELECT *list of values* FROM *list of source tables* WHERE *condition(s)*

The effect of such a SELECT query is to generate a new relation by performing restrict, project and join operations on the source relations (tables or other query output). This should be seen as three 'clauses' – the SELECT, FROM and WHERE clauses – each of which performs a separate function. Consider the following example:

SELECT OrderNo, OrdDate FROM Orders WHERE OrdDate > '10-Dec-06'

would give the result:

OrderNo	OrdDate
AJ123	12-Dec-06
GK300	13-Dec-06

The SELECT list specifies the columns to be output, and hence is performing a PROJECT operation.

The WHERE clause specifies which rows are to be output, and hence is performing a RESTRICT operation.

The FROM clause indicates the source table; since only one is specified, no JOIN operation takes place. We can introduce a JOIN by accessing both tables:

SELECT OrderNo, OrdDate, ItemCode, Quantity FROM Orders, OrderItems

WHERE OrdDate > '10-Dec-06'

AND Orders.OrderNo = OrderItems.OrderNo

This query includes columns which are in the OrderItems tables and hence the two tables must be joined. This is accomplished by listing the other table in the FROM clause and providing an additional condition that specifies how the tables are to be joined – i.e. the foreign key to primary key link. The result is:

OrderNo	OrdDate	ItemCode	Quantity
AJ123	12-Dec-06	A/23	100
AJ123	12-Dec-06	F/12	250
AJ123	12-Dec-06	M/66	30
GK300	13-Dec-06	B/10	500
GK300	13-Dec-06	F/12	300

In summary, this SQL query uses PROJECT, RESTRICT and JOIN operations on the source tables.

The other relational algebra operations can also be performed using SQL, but are less frequently used. UNION is achieved simply by using two SELECT statements connected by the word UNION. Referring back to the example in Table 2.10:

SELECT MatricNo, Name FROM STUDENT1

UNION

SELECT MatricNo, Name FROM STUDENT2

Note that the SELECT list must be the same for each component query. This would give the result:

MatricNo	Name
951234	Smith
952356	Jones
953388	Brown
954001	Adams
952991	Gray
953777	White

However, this result could be achieved more directly avoiding use of the UNION operation.

Generation of the PRODUCT is simple: just avoid specifying the JOIN condition!

2

SELECT OrderNo, OrdDate, ItemCode, Quantity FROM Orders, OrderItems

WHERE OrdDate > '10-Dec-06'

This is same as the JOIN query above, but with the crucial join condition omitted. This would combine each selected rows of the Orders table (rows 1 and 2) with every row of the OrderItems table, giving $2 \times 6 = 12$ rows in the output.

OrderNo	OrdDate	ItemCode	Quantity
AJ123	12-Dec-06	A/23	100
AJ123	12-Dec-06	F/12	250
AJ123	12-Dec-06	M/66	30
AJ123	12-Dec-06	B/10	500
AJ123	12-Dec-06	F/12	300
AJ123	12-Dec-06	M/66	50
GK300	13-Dec-06	A/23	100
GK300	13-Dec-06	F/12	250
GK300	13-Dec-06	M/66	30
GK300	13-Dec-06	B/10	500
GK300	13-Dec-06	F/12	300
GK300	13-Dec-06	M/66	50

This result is simply not meaningful within the application; it combines OrderNo values with ItemCode values, which belong to another order. Hence, use of this device is rare; however, it can be a good indication in practice that you have forgotten to specify a join correctly: look out for an unexpectedly high number of rows in the output!

Relational views

A **view** is a virtual relation; i.e. it appears to the user (end-user or programmer) as a named table, but it does not in fact exist as an actual stored table. It is, in effect, a relation created by a query on actual tables; the 'result' table of this processing is managed by the DBMS software to provide the illusion of a real table. The system will store the definition of the view (as a query specification) and can hence be used as if it was a real table.

Reasons for using a view are that it:

- provides a mechanism for hiding sensitive parts of actual tables from specific users

- simplifies certain processing, such as the production of reports, by providing a predefined virtual table as the source of the report

- enables the same data to be 'seen' in different ways by different classes of users, suited to their individual needs, without any effort on their part.

To provide a transparent view service, the DBMS has to ensure that any changes to the underlying base relations of a view are reflected consistently in the view. Since a view is based on execution of a query, changes in the base tables will necessitate re-evaluation of the query. While this has potential time/processing implications, it is essentially easy to comply with. The converse, namely, to propagate *changes to a view* through to the base tables, is much more problematic and is not, in fact, always possible.

Views are considered again later when we study SQL in detail in Hands-On Section A. Note that the term 'view' is not used by Microsoft in this sense. The functionality of a view is achieved simply by a named, stored query. See Hands-On Section B for details of how stored queries are used in Access.

Summary

1 In this chapter we have covered a number of very important concepts which we meet again in later work.

2 A data model is a representation of data within some application domain. In this chapter we have looked at the relational model.

3 An application domain is a real-world environment within which an information system and/or a database is being employed.

4 The relational model is based on the theory of sets. A relation represents a mapping of one set onto one or more other sets.

5 Null is a presentation used in relational databases to indicate that an attribute value is missing.

6 The primary key of a relation is a column or columns of a relation that uniquely defines the rows of the table.

7 Functional dependency expresses the concept that one attribute may depend for its value on the value of another attribute.

8 A candidate key is a column (or columns) of a relation that could potentially be used as a primary key.

9 Relations are associated with one another by means of a foreign key in one relation that holds the value of a primary key in another relation.

10 Referential integrity is the principle that within a database a (non-null) foreign key in one table must be matched with an existing primary key in the referenced table.

11 Entity integrity is the principle that no part of a primary key can be null.

12 Relational algebra is a system of algebraic operators that operate on relations. These operations define the ways in which data in relations can be retrieved and transformed. In practice, relational algebra is implemented using the SQL language.

13 The common relational operators are RESTRICT, PROJECT and JOIN. Others are UNION, INTERSECTION, DIFFERENCE and PRODUCT.

14 A view is a virtual table; the DBMS can treat it (in many respects) like a real table, but it is generated from the execution of a query.

Review questions

1 Distinguish between the application domain and the domain of an attribute.

2 List the properties of a relation.

3 The properties of a relation indicate that the sequence of the rows and of the columns is immaterial. How can a particular row and column be located?

4 Distinguish between the terms primary key, candidate key and foreign key.

5 What does it mean to say that one attribute of a table is 'functionally dependent' on another?

6 Explain the purpose of nulls in database tables and indicate why it is not quite correct to talk of a 'null value'.

7 How are separate tables in a relational database notionally connected together?

8 Explain the concept of referential integrity and its importance in relational database practice.

9 Define the term 'view'.

10 What is the essential nature of relational algebra?

Exercises

1 Using Table 2.14, evaluate the relational algebra operations listed below.

Table A

Order Number	Company	City
A1002	Rentokil	London
A3333	Eurotunnel	Paris
B0987	Kwikfit	Glasgow
C7521	BT	Edinburgh
E0102	Halifax plc	Halifax

Table B

Order Number	Company	City
E0102	Halifax plc	Halifax
D2489	Hanson	London
B0987	Kwikfit	Manchester

TABLE 2.14 Chapter 2 Exercise 1

Union of A and B

Difference A – B

Difference B – A

Intersection of A and B

2 The following **Tutor** and **Student** tables show tutors who are assigned to students. The student's tutor is identified by the Tutor column of the Student table. The primary keys are Tutor Id and Student Id respectively. Do these tables conform with (a) entity and (b) referential integrity? If they do, state why you think so. If not, identify where the integrity is lacking.

Tutor

Tutor Id	Tutor Name
21	Newman
34	Martin
56	Wright
78	Adams

Student

Student Id	Student Name	Tutor
990199	Young	56
990278	Fletcher	56
990445	Chung	45
null	Cohen	21
990721	Kennedy	78

TABLE 2.15 Chapter 2 Exercise 2

3 Using the sample of data shown in Table 2.16, explain the concept of *functional dependency* and say whether the following functional dependencies are verified by the data or not.

a) Employee No → Position

b) Position → Salary

c) Salary → Position

d) Position → Branch

e) Branch, Position → Salary

Employee No	Position	Salary	Branch	Branch Name
101	Programmer	32000	02	Glasgow
102	Salesman	27500	01	London
103	Salesman	38000	02	Glasgow
104	Accountant	27500	03	Manchester
105	Manager	41000	01	London
106	Accountant	27500	03	Manchester

TABLE 2.16 Chapter 2 Exercise 3

References

The seminal work in the relational model is the paper by Codd:

Codd, E.F. (1970): 'A relational model of data for large shared data banks'. *Communications of the ACM*, 13(6): 377–387. Obtainable from the ACM at http://www.acm.org/classics/nov95/toc.html

Textbooks

The following books provide more formal treatment of the topics in this chapter:

Date, C.J. (2005): *Database in Depth: The Relational Model for Practitioners*, O'Reilly
Elmasri, R. and Navathe, S.B. (2007): *Fundamentals of Database Systems*, Pearson International

Website

Wikipedia: http://en.wikipedia.org/wiki/Relational_model

3

Conceptual database design

LEARNING OBJECTIVES

After studying this chapter, you should be able to do the following:

- Show how the concepts of 'entity' and 'relationship' are represented in Entity-Relationship (ER) modelling.

- Show how an ER diagram is drawn.

- Explain the term 'cardinality' and itemise the possible cardinality values.

- Explain the term 'optionality' and 'partial participation'.

- Explain the concepts of weak and strong entities.

- Draw ER diagrams based on a given scenario.

- Convert an ER diagram to an equivalent relational model.

- Explain the concept of normalisation as it applies to the relational model.

- Explain the meaning of the 1st, 2nd and 3rd normal forms.

- Describe the anomalies (update, insert, delete) that can occur as a result of using un-normalised data.

- Apply the rules of normalisation to specific examples.

Introduction

Database design can be considered as having three phases: conceptual design, logical design and physical design.

In conceptual design, a data model is developed that reflects the nature of the application data but does not specify any implementation details such as a database platform or programming languages; the end-product of this is a set of entity-relationship (ER) diagrams and attribute specifications.

In logical design, the ER design is used to develop a specific data model such as the relational model. In relational terms we now have a set of relational tables that represent the application data. The final phase, physical design, is concerned with the actual implementation of the logical design on a specific hardware and software platform. This chapter is concerned with the conceptual and logical phases of this development process; the physical design phase is the subject of the Chapter 4.

For convenience in presenting the subject in manageable chunks, the chapter has been divided into three parts, each of which ends with a review and a set of exercises. The parts are:

Part 1:   The Entity-Relationship (ER) model.

Part 2:   Converting an ER model into a relational database model.

Part 3:   Normalisation of the relational model.

Part 1 describes how we can use the entity-relationship modelling technique to generate a graphical representation of our application data. In Part 2, we describe how to convert this ER model into an equivalent relational model – i.e. the schema design of a set of relational tables. Normalisation, described in Part 3, is an alternative design technique that complements ER design and provides additional confirmation of the correctness of the design.

Part 1: Entity-Relationship (ER) model

Introduction

The nature of entities and relationships was described in the previous chapter. To recap, an entity is a term used to denote any real thing or abstract notion that we wish to recognise as a separate concern within the domain of a database application. A relationship is some association that exists between these entities.

Entity-Relationship (ER) modelling is a diagrammatic technique used by analysts and designers as a top-down method for analysing an application system, its objective being to help in understanding the nature and relationships that exist within the data of the system. The ER diagrams thus produced provide a graphical design which can then be used to derive a set of relational tables that model the data of the application system. The ER system was devised by Peter Chen and presented in a seminal conference paper (Chen 1976). The relational model which we described in the previous chapter predates Chen's work, so relational databases were designed before then; however, the introduction of ER diagrams gave designers a significant new technique in their work.

The first requirement before any attempt is made to design an ER diagram is a proper understanding of the problem domain. No design methodology can compensate for a lack of knowledge and/or understanding of the problem that is being tackled. We described the process of analysis and design in Chapter 1, and ER modelling fits into the logical design stage of that process.

While general and intuitive rules can contribute to the ER design, many of the factors to be taken into account in this respect can be called 'business rules'; i.e. stipulations and/or restrictions on how things will be done within an enterprise. For example, the management of a company may decide that 'each client will only be dealt with by one salesperson', or 'every project will have at least two engineers but each engineer will work on only one project'.

In Part 1 of this chapter, we describe the nature of ER diagrams, and show how they are produced and how they are used in designing. In the next part we will explain how ER diagrams are used in the design of relational database tables.

Entities and relationships

Introduction

Entity types and relationships are expressed diagrammatically in ER diagrams, with a rectangle representing an entity and some form of connecting line for a relationship. There are, unfortunately, several different conventions used in drawing ER diagrams. Three main conventions in use are Chen's original system, the so-called crowsfoot system and UML-type diagrams. Even within the crowsfoot system, there are variations in conventions. UML has certain advantages: it is being widely adopted as the standard modelling language, it is a much richer object-based system, and it covers the whole development process of business analysis, design, programming and documentation. For ER modelling, only one component of UML, class diagrams, is used.

However, for the purposes of learning ER design, we have adopted the crowsfoot notation, since it is arguably easier to read and provides all the features required within the limited scope of ER modelling. Where UML is used for ER design only very limited features of the UML system are used; for instance, a class diagram is inherently object-based, but object features such as method descriptions are not required for ER work. An outline of UML diagramming (as used for ER design) and how it corresponds to the crowsfoot system is provided later.

ER diagrams

ER diagrams are intended to show the entities involved in a database application and the relationships between the entities. The basic configuration is shown in Figure 3.1.1.

FIGURE 3.1.1 Simple ER diagram

The entities Student and College are shown as rectangles; the relationship **attends** is shown as a labelled connecting line between the entities. We can 'read' this diagram as 'Student attends College' and in its inverse sense, 'College is attended by Student'.

It is important to realise that, in general, ER diagrams express relationships between entity types (such as Student); another way of looking at it is that each entity box in an ER diagram refers to a *set* of entities (e.g. a set of Students) of the given type and that every member of that set is potentially involved in the specified relationships.

Figure 3.1.2 shows a more elaborate system (School/Head/Teacher/Child).

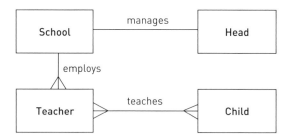

FIGURE 3.1.2 School ER example

You will note that the ends of the connecting lines terminate in a splayed fashion, commonly referred to as a 'crowsfoot'. This device is used to specify the **cardinality** of the relationship; the cardinality specifies, for one member of the first entity set, the possible number of members it can be related to in a second entity set. There are three flavours of cardinality:

1:1	One-to-one	- e.g. Head manages school
1:n	One-to-many	- e.g. School employs teacher
m:n	Many-to-many	- e.g. Teacher teaches child

The crowsfoot is used to indicate the 'many' end of the relationship. Instead of using just 'many', it is also possible to specify the cardinality with explicit numbers such as 2 or 10 if the system design specifies such definite limits. This is a feature of UML. Each of the relationships can be 'read' in two directions and each interpretation depends on the type of line ending, one or many. The sense of the relationship name has to be suitably reversed to suit the direction of reading; for instance, 'teaches' becomes 'is taught by'. Thus, a complete interpretation of Figure 3.1.2 is:

- One head manages only one school and each school has only one head.
- One school employs many teachers but each teacher is only employed by one school.
- One teacher teaches many children and each child is taught by many teachers.

3

NOTE

We interpret each relationship from the point of view of *one* instance of the entity; for example, even for the many-many relationship, we refer to '*one* teacher teaches many children'. To emphasise this point, the entity names are always expressed in the singular: 'teacher', not 'teachers'.

To interpret a relationship within a diagram, for instance *school employs teacher*, we start at one end and move towards the other end, interpreting the relationship and the terminal crowsfoot, if any:

- Starting at the school end we say – **one** school employs (crowsfoot=) **many** teachers.
- Starting at the teacher end we say – **one** teacher is employed by (no crowsfoot=) **one** school.

We emphasise again that we always read the relationship by starting with '**one** teacher teaches . . . ' and we ignore the crowsfoot, if any, at the starting end. You should not read it as '**many** teachers teach . . . ' An alternative is to use 'each' instead of 'one' in the above expressions.

Optionality and participation

Consider the relationship between School and Teacher originally defined in Figure 3.1.2 and shown again in Figure 3.1.3.

FIGURE 3.1.3 School – Teacher relationship

As already described, this expresses the rules:

'one School employs one or more Teachers'

'one Teacher is employed by one School'

However, it may be that some teachers are not employed by any school. This might be the case where a specialist teacher is employed by the central education authority and visits many schools. Thus the second rule given above is incomplete – it should really indicate the 'zero school' possibility. For instance, the rule could be expressed as:

'one Teacher is employed by one School *or by no School*'

We need some additional convention for use in ER diagrams to allow us to express this kind of condition. Regrettably, this topic has produced a variety of different terminology and diagramming conventions in the database literature. In an area that is already potentially quite confusing, it is unfortunate that database literature is so inconsistent in its handling of the topic. In our explanation below we try to cover the more common terminology and conventions in current use.

Optionality

The School-Teacher rule given above could be viewed as expressing the fact that the relationship, from the point of view of the Teacher, is optional; i.e. a Teacher may or may not be employed by a School. This can be indicated on an ER diagram as shown in Figure 3.1.4. The circle is intended to suggest 'zero' or 'optionally'.

FIGURE 3.1.4 Example of optionality

We read Figure 3.1.4 as:

'One Teacher is employed by one School or (circle) zero Schools'

This convention permits convenient reading of the diagram, but has the unfortunate aspect that the zero indicator (the circle) is at the opposite end of the relationship line from the entity concerned in the optionality.

In reality, optionality is a way of expressing minimum cardinality; a common notation, used in UML diagrams, is to qualify a relationship with a notation such as 0..1, where the zero indicates a minimum cardinality of zero (in other words optional) and a maximum of 1. See the description later of the UML notation for this method. It is also not uncommon to see cardinality range used with crowsfoot notation.

Participation

An alternative approach to the optionality concept is to highlight the fact that some instances of the Teacher entity set do not participate in the relationship; there are Teachers that are unconnected (through the Employs relationship) with any School. This is expressed by saying that the Teacher entity class has **partial participation** in the relationship: the alternative is **total participation**.

Note on variant conventions

An alternative convention in the crowsfoot system makes the optionality indicator explicit; if an entity is not optional, a vertical bar is used instead of the circle. Figure 3.1.4

above would then be changed to that shown in Figure 3.1.5(a); this means that a school *must* have at least one teacher. Other authors take this further by using the vertical bar to indicate the 'one' end of a relationship (the crowsfoot being the 'many' end). This would produce Figure 3.1.5(b).

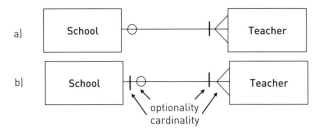

FIGURE 3.1.5 Alternative conventions

Visualisation of relationships

Relationships represent a mapping from one entity set to another. For instance, a one-to-many relationship is one in which an entity in one set 'maps to' one or more entities in the other set. Mapping diagrams can help in visualising the notions of cardinality and optionality. These illustrate the mapping by means of explicit connecting lines between entities in example sets. Figures 3.1.6 and 3.1.7 show a few examples using the School model above.

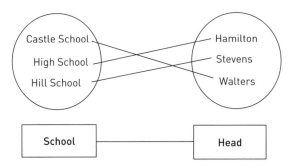

FIGURE 3.1.6 One-to-one, mandatory

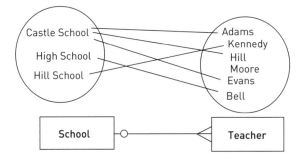

FIGURE 3.1.7 One-to-many, part optional with an unattached Teacher entity

Notice that in the fully mandatory case (Figure 3.1.6) no entity is left 'unattached'. In Figure 3.1.7, the Teacher entity set has partial participation in the relationship; this is illustrated by teacher Moore, who is not connected to any school. In Figure 3.1.8 the School entity set is partially involved; in particular, we can see that the High School does not participate in the relationship.

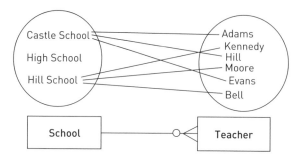

FIGURE 3.1.8 One-to-many, part optional with an unattached School entity

Attributes

First-level ER diagrams only show the general structure of the system; the next step is to identify **attributes** or **properties** of the entities. In the school example, possible attributes are name, address, type of school and name and number of teacher. These can be represented in the ER diagram as ellipses, as shown in Figure 3.1.9.

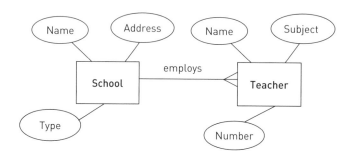

FIGURE 3.1.9 Entity attributes

For most practical systems, displaying the attributes in this fashion would make the diagrams too complicated. At the risk of confusing the reader with yet another notation, it is worth noting that attributes can be represented more neatly using the box convention shown in Figure 3.1.10. The entity name is shown at the top with the attributes listed in the section below. It is important to identify attributes at this stage, as it helps to clarify what we mean by each entity and often reveals alternative formulations of the model. It is also helpful in highlighting certain particular cases, namely, *multi-valued attributes* and *time-varying attributes*. Discussion of these is included in Part 2 of this chapter.

FIGURE 3.1.10 Attribute display

Another difficulty that often arises at this stage in ER design is that in some situations there is uncertainty about whether something should be treated as an entity or an attribute. In most cases the attributes of an entity can be readily identified: a person's name and age, the colour of a car, the cost of a refrigerator, are all fairly clear. However, consider the case of a film catalogue, which could be represented as in Figure 3.1.11; we make the assumption that a Film has only one Director.

FIGURE 3.1.11 Film catalogue

The Director certainly seems to be a valid entity in this scenario, but in practice the only attribute of this that we would probably record would be the director's name, a single value. In this case it could be absorbed into the Film entity with no serious effect on the model. Conversely, we may initially have decided that Director was to be modelled by a simple attribute, but later decided that we wanted to store other information about directors, such as age and nationality. In this case, it would make sense to form a new Director entity for the model.

Example

We can illustrate the principles we have covered so far by referring back to the example introduced in Chapter 1. The description of the database application is repeated below for convenience.

A small correspondence college offers courses in a range of topics. For each course, students complete a series of assignments which are sent to the college office; the assignments are gathered into batches, which are then dispatched by post to tutors for marking (i.e. complete batches of up to 10 assignments are sent to tutors). Assume that there can be an indefinite number of tutors. The tutors mark the assignments, then return them, retaining them within the same batches. A system is required that enables 'tracking' of the assignments, so that the college knows what assignments have been received, sent to tutors or marked. Also, the system should keep a running total of the total number of assignments that have been marked by each tutor.

In designing an ER diagram, we try to identify the distinct 'entities' in the application. In the above scenario, we appear to have entities STUDENT, TUTOR, ASSIGNMENT, BATCH. We then establish the relationships between these entities, including their cardinality and optionality.

Relationships are:

STUDENT sends ASSIGNMENT (one-to-many)

TUTOR processes BATCH (one-to-many)

ASSIGNMENT contained in BATCH (one-to-many).

NOTE

A commonly asked question at this point is: the college is mentioned in the scenario description; why does it not appear in the ER diagram? In effect, the diagram models the 'whole college' so it is not appropriate for it to appear *in* the diagram. This is a general rule: the environment being modelled should not appear in the ER diagram; it is represented by the whole diagram.

From this information, the basic diagram can be derived; see Figure 3.1.12.

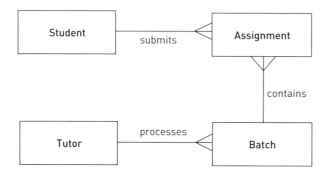

FIGURE 3.1.12 Correspondence college example

You should satisfy yourself at this point about the cardinalities indicated in Figure 3.1.12. Read each relationship both ways and express it in English. You should get the following relationships:

One STUDENT submits many ASSIGNMENTS and one ASSIGNMENT is submitted by one STUDENT.

One ASSIGNMENT is contained in one BATCH and one BATCH contains many ASSIGNMENTS.

One TUTOR marks many BATCHES and one BATCH is marked by one TUTOR.

The question of which relationships to include often arises; for instance, do we need a relationship between TUTOR and ASSIGNMENT called 'marks'? From our understanding of the situation, we can see that the relationship between TUTOR and ASSIGNMENT is implied through the TUTOR – BATCH – ASSIGNMENT relationships; it tells us that the tutor marks all the assignments in a batch. An additional 'marks' relationship would not define anything new.

In our example, we also have to establish optionality. Examine each relationship and determine whether either (or both) entities is optional or mandatory in the relationship. As in all aspects of the ER modelling process, this can only be determined from a knowledge of the application domain. Take each relationship in turn:

STUDENT submits ASSIGNMENT: an Assignment *must be* submitted by a Student, so Assignment participation is total. A Student *may* send no Assignments, so Student participation is partial.

BATCH contains ASSIGNMENT: an Assignment is always part of a Batch and a Batch must have at least one Assignment, so both entities are mandatory.

TUTOR processes BATCH: a Tutor *may* have no Batches to process, so Tutor involvement is partial. A Batch *must* have an associated Tutor so participation is total.

We can now draw the ER diagram incorporating the optionalities; see Figure 3.1.13.

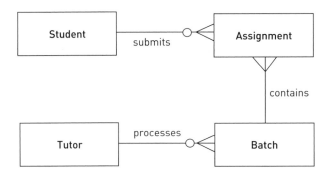

FIGURE 3.1.13 College model with optionalities

Many-to-many relationships

Some relationships appear at first analysis to be many-to-many. When we study the process of conversion of an ER diagram into relational tables in the next section of this chapter, we will find many-to-many relationships present us with a problem – in short, we can't do it! However, it is always possible to eliminate a many-to-many relationship by expressing it as two one-to-many relationships. This process is shown in Figure 3.1.14.

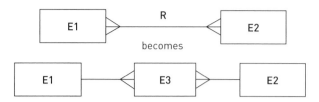

FIGURE 3.1.14 Redefining many-to-many relationships

In effect, the original relationship **R** has become an entity. In many situations, this new entity corresponds to some valid concept in the application domain, albeit abstract. If we take the case of engineers and projects within an engineering company, it may be the rule that each engineer works on many projects at once and each project employs several engineers, giving us the ER diagram shown in Figure 3.1.15(a).

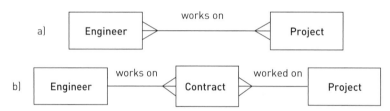

FIGURE 3.1.15 Example of many-to-many conversion

The relationship here can be interpreted as a noun 'Contract' which could be modelled by an entity. Two new relationships now arise, which could be interpreted as 'Engineer Works on many Contracts' and 'Project Worked on by many Contracts'. See Figure 3.1.15(b).

We can see that this is probably an entity that should have been adopted in the first place, since it can have its own attributes; for instance, 'hours worked' – the number of hours worked by one engineer on one project is an attribute of the contract, not of the engineer or the project.

In summary, it is worthwhile to see if many-to-many relationships can be converted to one-to-many, since there may be another entity hidden there. As previously mentioned, elimination of many-to-many relationships simplifies the conversion of ER diagrams to relational tables.

Weak entities

A **weak entity** is one which cannot exist without the existence of some other entity. In a DVD hire shop, for instance, we would have entities FILM, representing actual films such as 'Braveheart', and FILM COPY, which represents physical DVD copies of that film. Clearly, each FILM COPY instance must correspond to an instance of a FILM entity; it makes no sense to have a DVD which has no associated film. In ER diagrams, a weak entity is represented by a double box, as shown in Figure 3.1.16.

FIGURE 3.1.16 Weak entity

A little thought will show that weak entities arise in *mandatory many-to-one* relationships; the FILM entity in the above diagram is the 'one' end and must exist for any corresponding FILM COPY instance. A normal or 'non-weak' entity is sometimes called a **strong entity**.

Weak entities have a strong bearing on the integrity of a database. Within a database, we must maintain consistency between entities related in this way; for instance, if a FILM is to be deleted from the DVD shop database, all related FILM COPYs must also be deleted or the database will contain weak entities with no related 'owning' entity. This is the concept known as **referential integrity** which was described in Chapter 2. Note that it also illustrates an example of the use of the **cascaded delete** process described in Chapter 2.

An alternative terminology for expressing this concept is to say that the weak entity is **existence dependent** on the other entity.

More unusual relationships

The ER models described so far are all based on straightforward binary relationships. In practice this is not sufficient for some situations.

Unary relationships

We should recall that an ER model represents relationships between entity *sets*; i.e. it expresses relationships between each member of one set with one or more members of another set. However, we may wish to show a relationship between two members of the same set. Typical examples are shown in Figure 3.1.17.

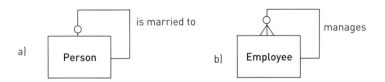

FIGURE 3.1.17 Recursive relationships

Figure 3.1.17(a) says that each Person is (optionally) married to one other Person. Figure 3.1.17(b) says that each employee manages zero or more other employees and that each employee is managed by one other employee. These are sometimes referred to as **recursive** relationships.

Ternary relationships

Some situations call for a ternary relationship, i.e. *three* entities are involved in the one relationship. Figure 3.1.18 shown below illustrates one possibility.

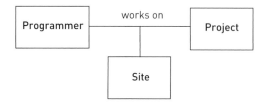

FIGURE 3.1.18 Ternary relationship

The situation represented here is a set of programmers who are working on a number of projects at specific work sites. We are trying to express the fact that specific members of all three entity sets are simultaneously related; for instance, that a specific programmer Fred works on Project P at Site S. Note that it is not possible unambiguously to specify the appropriate cardinalities in such diagrams, since the line terminating at an entity, say Site, connects to two other entities, Programmer and Project.

If we split this relationship into two binary relationships, we might produce the diagrams shown in Figure 3.1.19, adopting an ad hoc set of cardinalities.

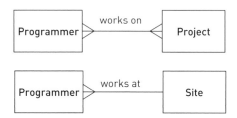

FIGURE 3.1.19 Ternary conversion

Figure 3.1.19 certainly show that Fred works on Project P and that he works at Site S, but they fail to indicate which project at which site. Project P may be worked on at a number of sites, while each site might host several projects.

It is desirable to transform a ternary relationship into something more manageable; the recommended technique is to change the relationship itself into an entity, with relationships with the other entities. This is illustrated in Figure 3.1.20.

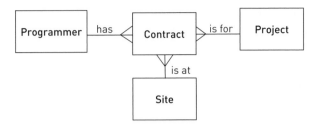

FIGURE 3.1.20 Ternary relationship re-expressed

More than one relationship between entities

Although not explicitly stated earlier, there is nothing in the 'rules' of ER diagrams that prevent entity types being related by more than relationship. This is of course necessary to reflect real life situations. A typical example is shown in Figure 3.1.21.

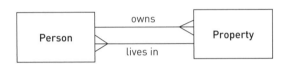

FIGURE 3.1.21 Multi-relationship

This diagram indicates that one person can own zero or more properties and one person lives in one property. Also, one property can be occupied by one or more people and is owned by one person. It is worth noting at this point that the diagrams are expressing general relationships between members of the specified **sets** of entities, which should be treated independently. For instance, the 'owns' and 'lives in' relationships are independent and do not imply, for instance, that a person necessarily lives in one of the properties that they own.

Case studies

Like most disciplines, ER is best learned by seeing worked examples, and we provide a number of examples based on the case studies introduced in Chapter 1. The case studies elaborated here are numbers 2 and 4. The text of these is repeated below for convenient reference.

These case studies are implemented as a Microsoft Access database available on this text's support website. Examination of a working version is a persuasive way of verifying the model.

Developing the ER diagram

The first thing to be aware of when tackling an ER design is that it is not a mechanistic process: there is no fixed set of steps to proceed through that will automatically yield the 'correct' solution. It may be found that initial decisions have to be abandoned and reassessed. In other words, it is an iterative process that requires successive passes through the design. The elements of this iterative process can be defined as shown below:

1 Obtain a thorough understanding of the system, including the customer's requirements and expectations, business rules that govern the working of the required application and limits and quantities involved.

2 Identify from the above a set of entities and relationships.

3 Construct an initial ER diagram, adopting suitable primary and foreign keys.

4 Review the ER design, look for potential problems and simplifications.

5 Seek approval of the design from the future users of the system. One benefit of the ER method is that the design can be understood by non-computing staff.

6 Revise the ER design in the light of the reviews.

CASE STUDY 2 – DVD HIRE SHOP

A DVD rental shop requires a database system to assist in managing the hire and return of DVDs. The application is chosen because the requirements and working of such systems are easy to understand and familiar to many people.

The database maintains details of customers, films, DVD copies of films and rental transactions. The system must record transactions (i.e. when a DVD is rented and when it is returned), calculate how much a rental costs and determine which rentals are overdue. Additionally it must record the arrival in stock of new DVDs and the disposal of obsolete and faulty DVDs. DVDs are grouped into rental price categories; the category of a DVD will normally change during its lifetime in the shop – it will become cheaper as it 'ages'. The cost of rental is based on the rental price times the number of days it has been rented. The standard period of rental is two days; additional days are charged at a reduced rate. A DVD is considered 'overdue' if it is not returned within one week.

Reports are required showing rental histories for selected clients, usage reports for selected DVDs and popularity ranking for current films available for rent.

Case study extension: Add data to the tables pertaining to the stars of the films.

Discussion for case study 2

The case study definition indicates reports required from the system; while the ER model does not reference report construction directly, it is necessary within the design to include any attributes that are required to implement the requested reports. This is of relevance in the following discussion.

An early design decision to be made in this scenario relates to representation of the multiple DVD copies of each film. This is a situation that occurs in many applications where the existence of a collection of identical objects is to be recorded. The question is: do we uniquely identify each such object, or do we 'lump' them altogether and simply record the number in stock? If we were dealing with a stock of bricks in a DIY store, then it is clear that a quantity in stock value would suffice. In the current case study, however, it is not so clear-cut. Do we want to individually track each DVD, or can we deal simply with a number in stock (for each film)? Both of these schemes are probably workable; however, the former method would enable monitoring of the usage of each DVD, which is specified as a requirement for a report in the case study definition. Hence, in this example, we have opted for this scheme.

We can initially identify in the main scenario (ignoring the extension for the moment) the following entities: Customer, Film, DVD copy. We can also see that there must be a relationship between Customer and – what? A little thought should show that it is the DVD that is being rented, not the 'film' as such. So we have a tentative relationship of Customer to DVD.

We now have to assess the cardinality of this relationship. We test this by trial statements such as 'one Customer rents . . . ' and should get the answers:

One Customer rents zero or many DVDs

One DVD is rented by zero or many Customers

The second assertion is possibly a little contentious; surely one DVD is rented by only one customer? This is a situation that occurs frequently in ER design. In effect, we need the model to represent the database situation over a period of time, and taking this into account it is clear that one DVD can be rented out to many customers over different time periods. Hence we must allow for a many-to-many relationship in this situation. We mentioned earlier that many-to-many relationships are best resolved at this stage into two one-to-many relationships, although this can be deferred to the next stage. Figure 3.1.22 shows the current model. 'Rental' can be described as a relationship entity. The Rental entity could also be called a 'transaction entity' since each instance represents one transaction, i.e. one rental of a DVD. Note that at this stage the model only allows for one DVD per transaction; typically, of course, we would want to be able to rent several DVDs at one time – with this model this would imply a series of separate transactions. We will extend the model in this respect shortly. Figure 3.1.22 also includes indications of optionalities; examining the figure, we can see that we allow for Customers who have not rented any DVDs and DVDs which have not been rented, both contingencies that could naturally occur. For instance, the figure shows that one Customer can have zero or many Rentals.

FIGURE 3.1.22 DVD Rental version 1

How does the Film entity fit into this scheme? Clearly, it has a relationship with the DVD entity, which can be expressed as: 'one Film is recorded on many DVDs'. We can complete the entity configuration as shown in Figure 3.1.23.

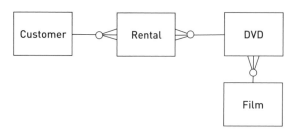

FIGURE 3.1.23 DVD Rental version 2

The DVD–Film optionality indicates that we can have a film with no related DVDs; this would enable the storing of Film information prior to having available any recordings of it.

It is necessary now to establish the attributes of the model. Most of the attributes should be fairly evident, but we must take account of the required functionality and output of the planned database. Another factor that must be taken into account eventually is the choice of primary keys and the foreign key connections between the entities. At the ER diagram stage it is not essential fully to resolve this matter, as it is best considered when we generate relational tables from the ER design in Part 2 of this chapter. In the attribute lists below no specific reference is made to key values; you should bear in mind at this stage that each entity will have a primary key and each relationship requires a foreign key. Figure 3.1.24 shows a possible set of attributes.

FIGURE 3.1.24 DVD Rental attributes – Customer, Rental, DVD, Film

The purpose of most of these should be fairly obvious but a few points of clarification may be in order. In each entity we have included an identifying value (such as ReferenceNo in Rental) and these are destined to be primary keys in the final relational database. In Rental, the ReturnDate and AmountPaid will be irrelevant until the DVD is returned; in practice, they would normally be filled with nulls until available. In DVD, the Status code is intended to specify certain states such as 'in stock', 'on hire', 'faulty', etc.

The StockDate allows the age of the DVD to be determined. The PriceCode indicates the rental price for a DVD. The Usage figure is a count of the times the DVD has been on hire for purposes of balancing its use against other DVDs of the same film. The Film-Code identifies the film that is recorded on the DVD.

Model extension 1

It would be more natural to allow for multiple DVDs in one rental transaction. This implies that the Rental entity would need to hold multiple values for many of its attributes which, as we saw in Chapter 2, is not admissible in the relational model. Hence we have to associate the Rental entity with another, say, Rental Item entity in a one-to-many relationship. A revised model would look like Figure 3.1.25.

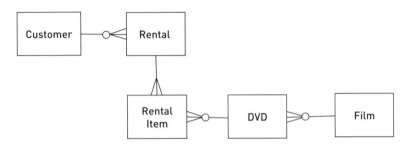

FIGURE 3.1.25 DVD Rental extended

The Customer is still related to a Rental transaction, but the latter now consists of a number of Rental Items, each corresponding to one DVD. The new Rental entities are now as shown in Figure 3.1.26. The Rental – Rental Item relationship is mandatory in both directions for the following reasons: Rental Item is a weak entity and hence must have an owning Rental entity instance; secondly, there is no point in a Rental of zero items.

Rental	Rental Item
ReferenceNo	ReferenceNo
IssueDate	ReturnDate
AmountPaid	DVDCode
CustomerNo	

FIGURE 3.1.26 DVD Rental attributes – Rental, Rental Item

You should make sure that you understand the implications of Figure 3.1.26. Note the following points:

- The IssueDate is still in the Rental entity, as we assume that all DVDs are issued at the same time.

- Conversely, the ReturnDate is in the Rental Item, since the individual DVDs could be returned separately.

- The Rental entity refers to the customer but the Rental Item refers to the DVD.

The primary key of Rental Item instances will be discussed in Part 2 of the chapter.

Model extension 2

We want to add information on the stars that appear in each film. This would be useful, for example, for producing a report grouping DVDs in stock by each star name. Stars are clearly related to Films, but what is the cardinality? One may feature many stars, and each star may be in many films, so the relationship is many-to-many, as shown in Figure 3.1.27.

FIGURE 3.1.27 Film – Star relationship

This should be resolved as two one-to-many relationships, but we will leave this as an exercise for the next part when the relational tables are developed.

Do you agree with the optionality indications? It says 'one film has zero or more stars' and 'one star is in zero or more films'. The former assertion is probably necessary, since we could have films such as documentaries or cartoons with no stars as such. The latter assertion would be necessary only to allow recording of star information prior to having any films of that star. This is perhaps not so important; in implementation terms, it would be easy to add a new star prior to adding a new film in which they starred.

CASE STUDY 4 – JOB AGENCY

A job agency offers to find jobs for clients looking for employment. A database system is used to record the clients' personal and resumé details. Personal details include name, address, date of birth, sex and phone number. The resumé details includes a history of employment and a set of qualifications. The employment history will include current position (if any) and a record of job positions, employer name and final salary. The qualifications refer to an award (e.g. MSc), an awarding body (e.g. University of Oxford) and a graduation year. Each client is assigned to one job consultant within the agency, who negotiates with the client and endeavours to locate suitable employment for them. The consultant typically will deal with a number of clients.

3

Where do we start?! We have itemised a series of observations and decisions which may help in this analysis.

1 The best approach is to identify potential entities in the text without worrying too much about their validity at this stage. This might yield the following list:

   Client, Client details, History of employment, Employer, Qualifications, Award, Awarding Body, Consultant.

2 There are a number of other items which are mentioned, such as award year, but it is probably easy to see that this is simply an attribute. It is best at this early stage to identify the most obvious and least contentious entities and to try to relate other potential entities to these.

3 In this respect, Client appears to be pre-eminent; the purpose of the projected database, after all, is to manage the agency's clients. Note that one relationship which we must *not* entertain is 'Client to Agency'; as we indicated earlier, the subject of the ER model must not itself appear in the model. The model as a whole *represents* the Agency, so it makes no sense to include it *in* the model.

4 The Client details, such as name, address, date of birth, etc. are all single values and can be managed simply as attributes of Client.

5 Client's employment history also suggests Client attributes, but in this case is it potentially multi-valued. As we saw in the previous chapter, the relational model does not permit multi-valued attributes within one relation. It appears therefore that a one-to-many relationship exists: one client has many job history records. It is possible also that a client may have no previous job history, so a more accurate relationship is 'one client has zero or more job records'. The reverse relationship is 'one job history refers to one client'; job history is a weak entity and hence it makes no sense to consider 'one job history refers to no client'. We will attend to the component attributes of job history in due course.

6 A similar argument applies to qualifications: 'one client has zero or many qualifications' and 'one qualification applies to one client'. Now you may argue that many clients may have the same qualification; for instance, two or more clients may have an MSc from Oxford in 1995. However, we should view each qualification instance as referring to a single client and each will embody all the relevant details specifically for that client.

7 The agency consultants each deal with many clients, but each client is assigned to one consultant. What about optionality is this relationship? The possibilities are that a client is not assigned to any consultant and that a consultant is not assigned to any client. These are potentially temporary conditions that may occur at some stage in the database's lifetime; for instance, a new consultant may be hired and until given a client will be 'client-less'. If we failed to make the relationship optional in this case, we could not add the consultant to the database unless we simultaneously added their first client. To avoid such anomalies it is best to use optional relationships, so we have: 'one client has zero or one consultant and one consultant

has zero or many clients'. The effect this has on the design of the database tables will become clear in the next part of this chapter.

We are now in a position to draw our initial diagram, Figure 3.1.28.

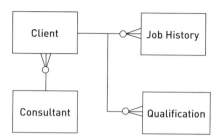

FIGURE 3.1.28 Job agency model

We can turn our attention now to the attributes; the client and consultant attributes are fairly clear and non-contentious, but the other entities are more interesting. Taking Qualifications first, we can identify the following attributes, with examples in brackets:

Award (MSc), grade (second class), awarding body (Oxford University), year of graduation

A decision we need to make here is whether any of these need to or should be modelled as separate entities. The awarding body is the prime candidate for this. Clearly, bodies such as universities appear to merit being viewed as distinct entities, but on the other hand all that is required in terms of our application is to record the body name, which would suggest a simple attribute. However, it may be important to ensure that occurrences of the same awarding body are represented by the same name – University of Oxford and Oxford University would appear to a query as different bodies – and one way to ensure this is to use a separate awarding body entity. This is perhaps more of an implementation matter, since there are other techniques available to guarantee such consistency in naming; for our purposes at this stage we will adopt simple attributes in such cases.

While a similar argument might seem to apply to the employer details in the job history, in fact this instance is more complex: the employment information would probably also include the address and phone information to facilitate contact with previous employers. Hence, being more than a single value, a separate employer entity is necessary. This would be related to the job history as shown in Figure 3.1.29. The relationship is not optional in any direction. For instance, a Job History would need to refer to an Employer.

FIGURE 3.1.29 Job history – Employer relationship

We can now show (Figure 3.1.30) a possible set of attributes based on foregoing analysis.

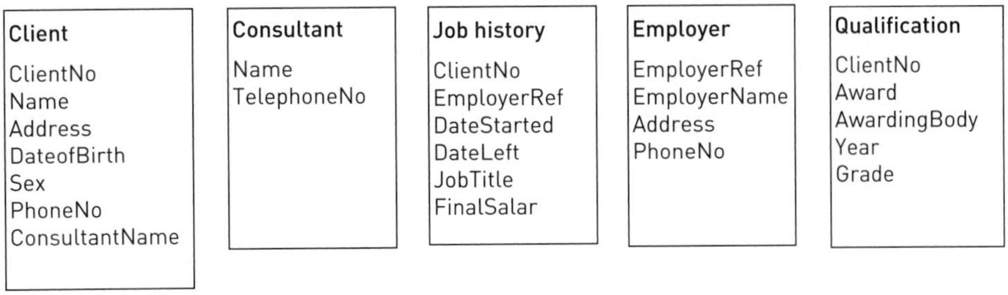

Client	Consultant	Job history	Employer	Qualification
ClientNo Name Address DateofBirth Sex PhoneNo ConsultantName	Name TelephoneNo	ClientNo EmployerRef DateStarted DateLeft JobTitle FinalSalar	EmployerRef EmployerName Address PhoneNo	ClientNo Award AwardingBody Year Grade

3

FIGURE 3.1.30 Job agency attributes

Case studies 1, 3 and 5

These are left as exercises for the student. They should be tackled at this stage as reference is made to them at later stages of the book. In particular, Case study 1, Employees, is used as the model for the SQL tutorials in Hands-On Section A. Solutions can be found on the book's website along with Microsoft Access, Oracle and MySQL implementations.

UML system for ER modelling

While the crowsfoot system is used in this text for the purposes of learning the concepts of ER modelling, it is important to be familiar with the UML class diagram system, since it is often used in professional design and development environments. Accordingly, we provide a brief summary of UML diagramming for ER design based on class diagrams. Note that the UML system is very extensive and what we indicate here is a very small part of the whole sufficient to represent ER models.

As in ER diagrams, UML uses rectangles to represent entities (strictly, they represent classes) and connecting lines to indicate relationships (associations). At both ends of the relationship line a notation, of the form $m..n$, is used to express the **multiplicity** of the relationship in each 'direction'. The term 'multiplicity' used in this context is a combination of cardinality and participation (optionality) as previously described for ER diagrams. In effect, in the $m..n$ notation, the m indicates the participation and the n, the cardinality. To put it another way, the multiplicity expresses the range of possible occurrences of one entity type that is related to a single occurrence of an associated entity type. The table below indicates the interpretation of a range of possible multiplicity values relative to one related entity:

Multiplicity constraint	Interpretation
0..1	Zero or one. Note: zero indicates optional participation
1..1 (can be just 1)	Exactly one
0..* (can be just *)	Zero-to-many
1..*	One-to-many
3..6	Minimum of two and a maximum of six

Note that the final notation, 3..6, defines very specific constraints on the relationship which might for example be indicated by a business rule. This would not impact on the structure of the ER model; the constraint would need to be enforced within the physical implementation of the database – refer to Chapter 7 for techniques in this respect.

The diagram in Figure 3.1.31 expresses the following relationships:

One project employs one or more engineers.

One engineer works on zero or one project.

Hence a project must have at least one engineer (mandatory participation) and each engineer is assigned to one project or to none (optional participation).

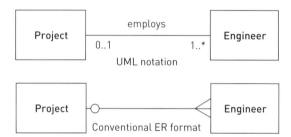

FIGURE 3.1.31 UML versus crowsfoot

The example in Figure 3.1.32, based on an Employee database illustrates the abbreviated notation for a one-to-many relationship:

One employee must work in exactly one branch.

One branch employs zero or more employees.

FIGURE 3.1.32 Employee example

Note carefully that the 'many' notation, the lone asterisk, includes the zero possibility; i.e. a branch may have no employees.

Entity attributes

As in some variants of the crowsfoot system, the UML diagram would normally include a list of the attributes of the entity. In the full realisation of a class diagram, it would also include the methods of the class; i.e. the allowable procedures and functions that can be applied to class objects.

Summary

1 Entity Relationship (ER) diagrams are used to model the nature of data within the domain of a database application.

2 Entities are identifiable things or concepts that are relevant to the application. These are modelled in the ER diagrams by boxes. The entity box represents a *set* of entities of one type.

3 Relationships express associations between entities. They are drawn as lines connecting the related entity boxes.

4 Relationships can be one-to-one, one-to-many or many-to-many. This is referred to as the cardinality of the relationship.

5 Entities have associated attributes (properties).

6 Relationships can be mandatory or optional (also called full and partial participation).

7 Many-to-many relationships can be re-expressed as two one-to-many relationships.

8 A weak (or dependent) entity is one that cannot exist without being related to another entity.

9 Most relationships are binary but some can be unary or ternary. Ternary relationships are better re-expressed as three binary ones.

10 UML class diagrams can be used (in a restricted form) to represent ER diagrams.

Review questions

1 Distinguish between an *entity* and an *entity set*. Which one is represented in an ER diagram?

2 List the possible variants of cardinality.

3 How is the 'many' end of a relationship denoted in ER diagrams?

4 Explain what is meant by saying that a relationship is 'optional'.

5 Explain what is meant by saying that an entity set may have 'partial participation' in a relationship.

6 What is meant by the term 'weak entity'?

7 Explain what is meant by a unary and a ternary relationship.

8 Why is it not possible to represent a many-to-many relationship with two tables?

Exercises

1 Draw an ER diagram, in both crowsfoot and UML format, to model the following set of conditions pertaining to Students, Lectures and Courses:

Each student is on only one course.

Each course must have one or more students.

Each course is taught by one or more lecturers.

Each lecturer reaches on one or more courses.

2 Express the diagrams, Figure 3.1.33(a) and (b), in sentences. For Figure 3.1.33(b), replace the many-to-many relationship with two equivalent one-to-many relationships.

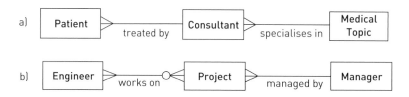

a)

b)

FIGURE 3.1.33 Chapter 3 Part 1 Exercise 2

3 Is the diagram in Figure 3.1.34 a valid possibility? If so, what is its practical interpretation?

FIGURE 3.1.34 Chapter 3 Part 1 Exercise 3

4 Using the mapping diagram shown in Figure 3.1.35, determine the cardinalities of the relationships involved; i.e. complete the following assertions:

a) One Engineer works on . . . . Projects.

b) One Project is worked on by . . . . Engineers.

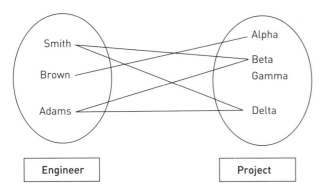

FIGURE 3.1.35 Entity mapping question

More challenging questions

Construct ER diagrams to represent the scenarios in questions 5–7:

5 Order processing system

A company processes orders each of which consists of a number of order items. Each order refers to a particular customer and an order date. Required customer information is a name and address and phone number. Each order item specifies a product and a quantity. Products are specified by a product code and have a description and a unit cost. Each product may have one or more possible substitutes; i.e. such substitute products may be shipped when the requested product is out of stock. Products may be delivered in one or more separate shipments and orders may be paid for in one or more separate submissions.

6 Diet system

A hospital prepares special diets for patients for which the nutrient value must be known. Each diet consists of a number of ingredients (meat, potatoes, carrots, etc.) in specified quantities per week, each of which have a number of nutrient values (calorific value, protein, vitamins, fibre, etc.) per unit weight. Each patient has a recommended daily amount (RDA) of each nutrient value. Design a database that can hold this information and hence enable the formulation of suitable diets.

7 Soccer league

A database is required to manage the fixtures and results of a soccer league. Assume there are twenty teams and that in the full playing season each team plays every other team twice – once at home and once away. After each game, the game results (goals per side) are recorded in the system in addition to details of players 'booked' and sent off. Note that a player booked twice is automatically sent off; thus the possible status values of a player in this respect is 'not-booked', 'booked' or 'sent-off'. For a win, a team is awarded three league points and, for a draw, one point, otherwise no points.

The system must be capable of producing, during the playing season, a league table showing the current team standings, including games played, total home goals scored, total away goals scored and points won.

Part 2: Converting an ER model into a relational database model

Part 2 Overview

In Part 1 of this chapter we looked at how ER diagrams can be designed to model the data of an application system. In this part, we investigate the important topic of deriving a relational model of our application from the ER design. The end result of this process should be the design of a set of interconnected relational database tables which can then be physically implemented on a chosen database product. Aspects of the latter phase – the physical implementation of the database – is the subject of Chapter 4.

Deriving a table design from an ER diagram

We can use an ER diagram, together with details of the entity attributes, to produce a set of relational tables that model the data requirements of the application. We begin, in the next section, with an overall summary of the procedure, then in the subsequent sections we examine each step in more detail.

For the purposes of illustration, we will use the simple example shown in Figure 3.2.1, based on a scenario in which Engineers are assigned to work on Projects.

FIGURE 3.2.1 Example ER diagram

In Figure 3.2.1 we have not indicated any cardinality or optionality at this stage, as various alternatives for these are examined as part of the process explanation.

Summary of design process

The following stages define the conversion process:

1 **Entity tables**. Create a table to represent each entity in the ER model.

2 **Relationships**. Represent relationships according to their cardinality and optionality. Some relationships will generate another table, while others can be represented within the entity tables.

3 **Primary and foreign keys**. Linkages between the tables must be established by the selection of suitable primary and foreign keys. This process actually occurs in parallel with the other two.

Detailed process

1. Entity tables

This process is relatively straightforward. The attributes of the entity set determined at the ER design stage simply become the column attributes of the table. It is necessary to adopt one (or more) of the columns as a primary key. Frequently this choice is obvious: there is often some identification code, such as a Product Code, Order Number, Matriculation Number, etc. already in use in the application domain that will serve this purpose. Where no such code is available, it is necessary to choose from one of the candidate keys of the relation or to invent a new identity code. A common practice is to use an automatic number generator to assign a unique number to each row. Such a facility is provided by most DBMSs: Microsoft Access provides a datatype called Autonumber that adopts a new value for each row created. Oracle does not provide an actual attribute datatype, but offers a CREATE SEQUENCE command that defines a variable that increments by 1 each time it is referenced.

The essential requirement, of course, is that the primary key must have a unique value for each row of the table.

For our Engineer-Project model our tables would look as shown in Table 3.2.1.

Engineer

EngId	Name
12	Kelly
34	Ross
56	Smith

Project

ProjectCode	Title
S03	Mercury
X99	Venus
Z22	Apollo

TABLE 3.2.1 Engineer and Project model tables

The primary keys are EngId and ProjectCode.

2. Relationships

Incorporating the ER relationships into the tables can be somewhat more complex. In the notes below, we consider separately the different cases of cardinality, namely, one-to-one, one-to-many and many-to-many.

Case 1: One-to-one relationship

a) Using a single table

In principle the two tables can be combined into one. Using our sample model and arbitrary assignments, this might produce the table shown in Table 3.2.2.

EngId	Name	ProjectCode	Title
12	Kelly	X99	Venus
34	Ross	S03	Mercury
56	Smith	Z22	Apollo

TABLE 3.2.2 Engineer-Project table

Note that we have two candidate keys (EngId and ProjectCode) and one would have to be adopted as primary key. If the relationship is mandatory in both directions then either candidate key can be used; the choice would made purely on grounds of convenience.

However, if the relationship is optional in one direction, then a free choice is not available and the primary key depends on the optionality. If it is possible to have an Engineer not assigned to any Project, then the situation shown in Table 3.2.3 could arise.

EngId	Name	ProjectCode	Title
12	Kelly	X99	Venus
34	Ross	S03	Mercury
45	Jones	*Null*	*null*
56	Smith	Z22	Apollo

TABLE 3.2.3 Engineer-Project table version 2

The ProjectCode column can be null and hence cannot be used as a primary key; the only choice therefore is EngId. Conversely, if it is possible for there to be a project with no assigned engineers, then EngId is not valid as primary key and the ProjectCode must be used (Table 3.2.4):

EngId	Name	ProjectCode	Title
12	Kelly	X99	Mercury
34	Ross	S03	Venus
null	*null*	T15	Zeus
56	Smith	Z22	Apollo

TABLE 3.2.4 Engineer-Project table version 3

b) Using two tables

In many if not most examples, it is advisable to use a separate table for each entity. This clarifies the entity-table representation and is more amenable to amendment. The two tables have to be 'linked' and a foreign key must be inserted in one of the tables. In the Engineer-Project model, we can put ProjectCode in the Engineer table (Table 3.2.5).

Engineer

EngId	Name	ProjectCode
12	Kelly	X99
34	Ross	S03
56	Smith	Z22

Project

ProjectCode	Title
X99	Venus
Z22	Apollo
S03	Mercury

TABLE 3.2.5 Engineer-Project table version 4

or EngId in the Project table, Table 3.2.6:

Engineer

EngId	Name
12	Kelly
34	Ross
56	Smith

Project

ProjectCode	Title	EngId
X99	Venus	12
Z22	Apollo	56
S03	Mercury	34

TABLE 3.2.6 Engineer-Project table version 5

The foreign keys in the above tables are ProjectCode in Engineer table (Table 3.2.5) and EngId in the Project table (3.2.6).

Case 2: One-to-many relationship

One-to-many relationships can be represented by two or three tables. The design decisions are described below. We will assume for this section that the relationship is one Project to many Engineers.

a) Using two tables

Since any one Engineer is only associated with one project, it is possible to adopt a foreign key of ProjectCode for the Engineer table, Table 3.2.7.

Engineer

EngId	Name	ProjectCode
12	Kelly	X99
29	Brown	S03
34	Ross	S03
56	Smith	Z22
62	Adams	Z22

Project

ProjectCode	Title
X99	Venus
Z22	Apollo
S03	Mercury

TABLE 3.2.7 Engineer-Project table version 6

Note that Brown and Ross both work on S03 (Mercury) and Smith and Adams both work on Z22 (Apollo).

A helpful fact is to notice that for any tables linked by a one-to-many relationship, the foreign key (FK) will be in the table at the 'many' end, and the referenced primary key (PK) at the 'one' end. The diagram in Figure 3.2.2 may help you to remember this.

FIGURE 3.2.2 Foreign key rule

In a complex ER diagram, this enables the validity of the PK/FK pairings to be quickly checked.

b) Using three tables

The most general way of dealing with one-to-many relationships is to form a third table, a 'relationship' or 'association' table, that specifies the assignment of engineers to projects. The three tables would look like this:

Engineer

EngId	Name
12	Kelly
29	Brown
34	Ross
56	Smith
62	Adams

Project

ProjectCode	Title
X99	Venus
Z22	Apollo
S03	Mercury

Assignment

EngId	ProjectCode
12	X99
29	S03
34	S03
56	Z22
62	Z22

TABLE 3.2.8 Engineer-Project-Assignment table

The primary key of the Assignment table can be formed by concatenating EngId and ProjectCode. EngId and ProjectCode columns in the Assignments table are each foreign keys linking with the primary keys in the other two tables.

Note that the table designs would be the same regardless of whether the relationship was one engineer to many projects or one project to many engineers.

Case 3: Many-to-many relationship

In a many-to-many relationship, we have no choice: we must form a third table to represent the relationship.

Engineer

EngId	Name
12	Kelly
29	Brown
34	Ross
56	Smith
62	Adams

Project

ProjectCode	Title
X99	Venus
Z22	Apollo
S03	Mercury

Assignment

EngId	ProjectCode
12	X99
29	S03
34	S03
34	X99
56	Z22
62	Z22
62	S03

TABLE 3.2.9 Engineer-Project-Assignment table version 2

We can see from Table 3.2.9 that engineer 34 (Ross) is working on two projects (S03 and X99) and engineer 62 (Adams) is working on two projects (Z22 and S03). An attempt to condense this information into two tables will fail; these multiple project assignments cannot be expressed within the Engineer table because it would require multiple values in the ProjectCode (foreign key) column, as Table 3.2.10 shows.

Engineer

EngId	Name	ProjectCode
12	Kelly	X99
29	Brown	S03
null	*null*	X09
56	Smith	X99
62	Adams	Z22
		S03

TABLE 3.2.10 Engineer table errors

These multiple values in the ProjectCode column are not allowed; hence three tables must be used.

It is possible that the Assignment table as shown in Table 3.2.9 could itself be viewed as an 'entity' table; i.e. the allocation of engineers to projects could be considered a distinct concept within the application domain which merits its own table. Recall that we have encountered this idea before in the context of ER diagrams: many-to-many relationships can be interpreted as two one-to-many relationships. This is especially true where additional information pertaining to the *assignment* (as opposed to either the engineer or the project separately) can be represented; e.g. we might want to record hours worked per engineer per project:

Assignment

EngId	ProjectCode	HoursWorked
12	X99	210
29	S03	35
34	S03	90
34	X99	200
56	Z22	65
62	Z22	15
62	S03	47

TABLE 3.2.11 Assignment table with additional data

This shows, for example, that a total of 290 hours were worked by engineer 34, 90 on project S03 and 200 on X99. We could not represent the hours worked figure without using a separate table for assignments.

3. Primary and foreign keys

We have noted in the sections above that we have to insert foreign key columns into certain tables to implement a link to another table. In general, a foreign key value must be the same as a primary key value in the linked table. This is the principle of referential integrity that has been mentioned before. However, a foreign key value is allowed to be null if the relationship is optional. While it is possible to be very prescriptive about the combinations of cardinality and optionality that would allow a null to be used, it is easier to manage if the basic principle is understood: *if a relationship is not mandatory, the foreign key value can be null.*

The Engineer – Project example given earlier in this chapter illustrates this point. If the relationship 'works on' between Engineer and Project is mandatory, then the Project-Code column of the Engineer table *cannot* be null: every engineer must connect to some project (Table 3.2.12 and Figure 3.2.3).

FIGURE 3.2.3 'Engineer works on one project'

Engineer

EngId	Name	ProjectCode
12	Kelly	X99
34	Ross	S03
56	Smith	Z22

Project

ProjectCode	Title
X99	Venus
Z22	Apollo
S03	Mercury

TABLE 3.2.12 Engineer and Project tables – mandatory relationships

If however the relationship is optional (Engineer has only partial participation, Figure 3.2.4) then the ProjectCode column of the Engineer table can be null. Table 3.2.13 shows that Smith is not currently assigned to a project and hence has a null ProjectCode.

FIGURE 3.2.4 'Engineer works on zero or one project'

Engineer

EngId	Name	ProjectCode
12	Kelly	X99
34	Ross	S03
56	Smith	*null*

Project

ProjectCode	Title
X99	Venus
Z22	Apollo
S03	Mercury

TABLE 3.2.13 Engineer and Project tables – optional relationship

Database systems typically allow you to specify whether or not a foreign key attribute can be null; SQL, for instance, provides a NOT NULL clause in the CREATE TABLE command for this purpose. The NOT NULL clause would always be used in respect of the primary key and it should also be specified for foreign keys within a mandatory relationship.

Example

We will describe an example to illustrate the conversion process.

Problem

A software company employs a number of programmers who are assigned to work on specific projects. Each project is controlled by one manager. Each programmer works on only one project but contributes to the writing of several programs. Each program may be written by one or more programmers. Construct an ER diagram to represent this scenario and hence construct suitable relational tables. Assume that the entities shown have (at least) the following attributes:

Manager: Employee number, name

Project: Project code, start date, planned finish date

Programmer: Employee number, name, programming language,
                    Years experience in language

Program: Program number, title, language

Solution

The ER Diagram is shown in Figure 3.2.5.

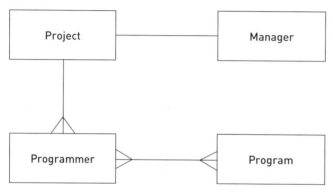

FIGURE 3.2.5 Software company ER model

Table design

The first step is to create a table for each of the entities shown and to identify their attributes. This yields Manager, Project, Programmer, Program (Table 3.2.14).

Manager

Employee Number	Name

Project

Project Code	Project Name	Start Date	Finish Date

Programmer

Employee Number	Name	Language	Years Exper

Program

Program Number	Title	Language

TABLE 3.2.14 Manager, Project, Programmer, Program example table

We now have to examine the relationships to determine the requirements for additional tables and the placement of foreign keys.

Manager–Project relationship

This is a one-to-one relationship where we have chosen to keep the entity information in separate tables. The only requirement is to establish a foreign key to link the tables. The most natural representation is probably to put the manager's employee number in the Project table. This is based on the principle that a project is unlikely to have more than one manager. It is more likely that the system could be modified to allow one manager to have more than one project; in this event, no modification to these tables would be necessary. So the Project table gets an additional column to hold the manager's employee number as a foreign key, given by column Manager Number in Table 3.2.15.

Project

Project Code	Project Name	Start Date	Finish Date	Manager Number

TABLE 3.2.15 Project table with foreign key

Project–Programmer relationship

This is a one-to-many relationship and will require a foreign key column in the table at the 'many' end of the relationship, i.e. the Programmer table (Table 3.2.16). This table now becomes:

Programmer

Employee Number	Name	Language	Years Exper	Project Code

TABLE 3.2.16 Programmer table with foreign key

It is important to appreciate why the foreign key must go in the Programmer table and not the Project table: there are potentially several Project → Programmer links, so they cannot all be specified by one foreign key in the Project table.

Programmer–Program relationship

This is a many-to-many relationship as it currently stands. As we noted earlier, we must convert this to two one-to-many relationships. We will introduce a new relationship entity called Assignment that shows the assignment of programmers to programs. The relevant part of the ER diagram now looks like Figure 3.2.6.

FIGURE 3.2.6 Resolving a many-to-many relationship

Since the new Assignment table is at the 'many' end of both of the new relationships, it will contain both the foreign keys. The Assignment table will have the following structure, (Table 3.2.17).

Assignment

Programmer Emp Number	Program Number

TABLE 3.2.17 Example additional requirements and FK placement – assignment table

Each of the columns are *individually* foreign keys linking to the other tables. The two columns *combined* form the primary key of the table.

This completes the design of the tables; it is worthwhile at this point to try to build the tables using sample test data (either invented or, better still, drawn from the real application environment) to verify that the structure is correct. Below we have composed a set of tables using sample data (Table 3.2.18).

Manager

Employee Number	Name
432	Morrison
512	Kennedy

Project

Project Code	Project Name	Start Date	Finish Date	Manager Number
P001	Website	12/02/06	30/09/06	512
P002	Sales	5/04/07	20/11/08	432

Programmer

Employee Number	Name	Language	Years Experience	Project Code
127	Jones	Oracle	4	P001
258	Green	Oracle	8	P001
361	Allen	Java	2	P002
677	Orr	Java	10	P001
780	Grant	Oracle	4	P002

TABLE 3.2.18 Example tables with data (continued over page)

Program

Program Number	Title	Language
A001	Home pages	HTML
A002	Forms input	Java
A003	Database interface	Java
S101	Enter New Sales	Oracle
S102	Invoicing	Oracle
S103	Sales Enquiry	Oracle

Assignment

Programmer Emp Number	Program Number
127	S102
258	S101
361	A002
677	A003
780	S103

TABLE 3.2.18 Example tables with data (continued)

The reader should examine these tables to confirm that the data is consistent with the ER model and that it inherently 'makes sense' from a general understanding of the application.

Additional techniques

In this section we examine some additional techniques that can usefully be employed when building relational tables. These include:

- An alternative approach to primary keys
- Multi-valued attributes (already mentioned in the previous section)
- Time-varying attributes
- Generalisation

Primary keys – an alternative approach

In our treatment of relational database tables so far, we have adopted the usual practice of using what could be called 'natural' primary key values, such as codes and identifiers that would be used in the application domain. Sometimes it is necessary to invent new attributes for the purposes of identification in a database table where no suitable value exists in the current domain. A common technique is to use a sequential counter, such as the Microsoft Access Autonumber datatype, to generate unique key values.

An approach which is adopted by some database designers is to use a sequential number for the primary key of *every* table. Sometimes this key value will be adopted as a conventional key within the application, but frequently it can be superfluous to the application and only exists to provide a unique key value. To show how this would affect the structure of tables, we have redefined the tables of the example given in the previous section to add a Row Id value (Table 3.2.19).

Manager

Row Id	Employee Number	Name
1	432	Morrison
2	512	Kennedy

Project

Row Id	Project Code	Project Name	Start Date	Finish Date	Manager Id
1	P001	Website	12/02/99	30/09/99	2
2	P002	Sales	5/04/99	20/11/99	1

Programmer

Row Id	Employee Number	Name	Language	Years Experience	Project Id
1	127	Jones	Oracle	4	1
2	258	Green	Oracle	8	1
3	361	Allen	Java	2	2
4	677	Orr	Java	10	1
5	780	Grant	Oracle	4	2

Program

Row Id	Program Number	Title	Language
1	A001	Home pages	HTML
2	A002	Forms input	Java
3	A003	Database interface	Java
4	S101	Enter New Sales	Oracle
5	S102	Invoicing	Oracle
6	S103	Sales Enquiry	Oracle

TABLE 3.2.19 Example tables with data – alternative approach (continued over page)

Assignment

Row Id	Programmer Id	Program Id
1	1	5
2	2	4
3	3	2
4	4	3
5	5	6

TABLE 3.2.19 Example tables with data – alternative approach (continued)

This is an extreme example that assumes that none of the generated key values (Row Id) are used in the application domain and are used purely to interconnect the tables. The following points can be made about this method of working:

1 For a given table, a generated key value is never reused, even a value used in a row that is deleted. This guarantees lifetime (of the table) uniqueness of the key values.

2 The technique is similar to the use of 'identity' codes in object-oriented systems where the system generates a unique identifier for every object created. We will return to this point when object systems are covered in Chapter 9.

3 A consequence of the technique is that no table will ever have a composite key.

4 More indexes will generally be required; in addition to the index on the generated primary key, indexes will usually be necessary for the other candidate keys previously used as the primary keys, such as Program Number, Project Code, etc. in the above example. If for no other reason, these additional indexes would be desirable to ensure uniqueness of these values in new rows of the table.

5 All foreign key columns will contain numerical values matching the generated primary key values. In the case of Microsoft Access, the generated keys are long integer (32 bit) values and hence the foreign key columns must use a long integer datatype.

Multi-valued attributes

The Programmer table of this example has one column representing the Language attribute. If the programmer was conversant in more than one Language, it would notionally require a set of values (per row) in the Language column; this is not possible with conventional relational database tables, as it conflicts with the relational model requirement that all values must be 'atomic'. In terms of ER diagrams, the Programmer – Language situation might be drawn as shown in Figure 3.2.7, using only a sample number of attributes.

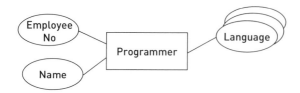

FIGURE 3.2.7 Multi-valued attributes – multi-language programmers

To represent multiple values within one column, one might be tempted to hold several values concatenated together into one string; e.g. 'Java, HTML, C++'. In some circumstances, this could be acceptable, but the main limitation of this technique is that it complicates searching (using say, SQL) for values embedded in the middle of the string. An index created for the language column, for instance, would only see the whole string value (Java, HTML, C++) and not the individual components.

Another alternative would be to have several language columns; this again might be OK for a limited situation with a predictable small number of values. The main problems here are:

1   A fixed upper limit has to be set on the number of such columns; we could allow for, say, three languages to be recorded. If a fourth was required – too bad!

2   It complicates querying on the language values, because every language column would need to be tested for a particular value.

3   Essentially, it is not in the spirit of relational databases.

The recommended procedure for multi-valued attributes is to create a new table to hold the values. The need for this table may not be obvious at the ER design stage, as the table is somewhat abstract: it does not seem to correspond to any real-world entity. The ER diagram would then be as shown in Figure 3.2.8.

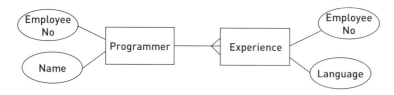

FIGURE 3.2.8 Multi-valued attributes – recommended procedure

The new table would have a primary key composed of the primary key of the original table (programmer's employee number) together with a qualifying value (since there will typically be more than one row per programmer), often simply the attribute value itself.

For the programmer-language example, we would modify the Programmer table and create a new Experience table as shown in Table 3.2.20.

Programmer

Employee Number	Name	Years Experience	Project Number
127	Jones	4	P001
258	Green	8	P001
361	Allen	2	P002
677	Orr	10	P001
780	Grant	4	P002

Experience

Employee Number	Language
127	Oracle
258	Oracle
258	Access
361	C++
361	HTML
361	Java
677	HTML
677	Java
780	Oracle

TABLE 3.2.20 Example modified Programmer table and new Experience table

It is also possible that an entity class could have a *group* of repeating attributes. This would be handled in exactly the same way, namely, by using a new entity class with several attributes. For example, a company Employee entity could require attributes Child Name, Child Sex and Child DOB (date of birth). In table terms, this would be represented by a new table 'Dependent' with the format shown in Table 3.2.21.

Dependent

Employee Number	Child Name	Child Sex	Child DOB

TABLE 3.2.21 Example dependent table

The primary key is Employee Number (the primary key of the Employee table) and Child Name.

This topic is handled in a different manner by the process of normalisation, which is the subject of the next part of this chapter.

Time-varying attributes

In virtually all applications, the value of database contents will naturally vary over time. In a stock control application, for instance, the cost of an item in stock can change and the quantity-in-stock will generally change even more frequently. In many applications, it is sufficient simply to know the current values of such variables: the previous history of changes is of no consequence. In a stock control system, for example, if the quantity-in-stock changes from 120 to 100, it probably not necessary to record that it was previously 120.

However, in some applications it is necessary to record a history of value changes. An investment management system, for instance, would typically monitor the prices of stock market shares which vary from day to day, with a view to predicting future price movement. Hence, for one table attribute, say share price, we need to record a series of prices and date values. As we have already seen, we must handle this in relational database terms by forming a new table to hold the multiple values: see Figure 3.2.9.

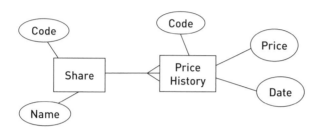

FIGURE 3.2.9 Time-varying attributes

Typical data from this model might look like Table 3.2.22.

Share

Code	Name
BT	British Telecom
MS	Marks & Spencer
SP	Scottish Power

Price History

Code	Price	Date
BT	3.34	12/10/06
BT	3.36	17/10/06
BT	3.41	24/10/06
. . . etc.		
MS	5.12	12/10/06
MS	5.22	17/10/06
MS	5.37	24/10/06

TABLE 3.2.22   Share–Price History table

Even in applications where no specific requirements for historical data exist, it may still be necessary to allow for changes in values over a period of time. For instance, if we work to a rule that says 'one Engineer will only work on one Project' and design the tables accordingly, the tables can only show the Engineer–Project assignment at one point in time. When an engineer moves a new project, the tables cannot represent a temporary situation in which the engineer is working on both projects. It is often advisable to make such relationships one-to-many to provide more flexibility in this respect.

Generalisation

Generalisation (the opposite of *specialisation*) is the process of grouping similar entities under more general or 'higher order' types to indicate commonality in certain properties. A type hierarchy can then be formed, as shown in Figure 3.2.10.

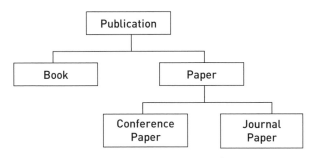

FIGURE 3.2.10 Generalisation example

In Figure 3.2.10, the most general type is Publication; this can 'sub-typed' or specialised into Book and Paper and so on. All entities share certain common properties, defined by publication while each sub-type has its own special properties. This situation is illustrated in Table 3.2.23.

Type	Properties
Publication	*Publ_code, Title, Authors, Keywords*
Book	As for publication plus: *Publisher, ISBN, Year, Edition*
Paper	As for publication plus one of the following:
Conference Paper	*Name of Conference, Date, Proceedings Publisher*
Journal Paper	*Journal, Date, Vol, Number*

TABLE 3.2.23 Publication sub types

This concept is an essential part of the object model where it is implemented as an *inheritance structure*; e.g. the Book class inherits the characteristics of the parent class Publication. We can also say that the structure represents 'IS-A' relationships; i.e. a Book 'is-a' Publication.

In the relational model, the representation of this situation is cumbersome; if we put all data pertaining to any publication in one table (e.g. Publication_Table), then it would need to have columns for all the data items given above. However, for a particular reference, say a book, the columns not relevant to a book (such as *Journal Name*) would have to be null. Alternatively, we would require three separate tables, which would make general queries over all the data rather awkward. This topic is discussed in more detail in Chapter 9, where the limitations of the relational model are discussed.

Case studies

We can now revisit the case studies for which we developed ER models in Part 1 of this chapter and convert the models to relational tables. In fact, the ER models take us well down the necessary road and most of this table development process is quite straight-forward. A significant factor is whether or not we have converted many-to-many into one-to-many relationships; if not, then this has to be done at this stage. As an illustration of this process, in the DVD Rental ER model, we left unresolved a many-to-many relationship between Films and Film Stars.

CASE STUDY 2 – DVD RENTAL

The first stage is to convert each entity from our ER model into a table. In fact, the attribute lists from the ER model are sufficiently developed that they can be adopted at this stage. To reduce the complexity of depicting table descriptions in future, we will adopt a commonly used compact notation, illustrated below for the DVD Rental case study, omitting for the time being the Stars entity. Each line represents one table and the table name precedes a list of the attribute names. The primary keys, where decided, are shown in italics. Similarly, the foreign keys are shown bold.

CUSTOMER (*CustomerNo*, Name, Address, PostCode, PhoneNo)

RENTAL (*ReferenceNo*, IssueDate, AmountPaid, **CustomerNo**)

RENTAL ITEM (**ReferenceNo**, **DVDCode**, ReturnDate)

DVD (*DVDCode*, StockDate, Status, PriceCode, Usage, **FilmCode**)

FILM (*FilmCode*, Title, Director, Year)

The next stage is to set up the appropriate relationships between the entities. There are no issues with many-to-many relationships here, so relationships are established based on suitable primary and foreign key selection or creation.

The primary keys are straightforward apart from the Rental Item table. As discussed earlier in this part of the chapter, we have a number of choices in forming a primary key in situations like this where the entity is contrived and does not have a 'natural' primary key. What are the candidate keys in this entity? Let's consider the possibilities:

1 Clearly, the ReferenceNo on its own is not sufficient, since one rental transaction (identified by one ReferenceNo) could be associated with many Rental Items.

2 How about ReferenceNo combined with ReturnDate? Two or more items corresponding to one ReferenceNo could be returned on the same day, so that is no use.

3 How about ReferenceNo combined with DVDCode? This is better. The DVDCode refers to one physical DVD so, within one transaction, it must be unique. Hence

the combination of ReferenceNo and DVDCode would give a workable primary key value.

So the revised entity would be:

RENTAL ITEM (***ReferenceNo***, ***DVDCode***, ReturnDate)

As discussed earlier, another option is to employ a surrogate key, which means adding an additional artificial key, for example called ItemId:

RENTAL ITEM (*ItemId*, **ReferenceNo**, **DVDCode**, ReturnDate)

Almost certainly you would adopt an automatic sequence number for this key, to avoid having to contrive unique values by some other means. This could be done in Microsoft Access by use of the Autonumber datatype and in other systems by means of an SQL CREATE SEQUENCE command.

Another factor worth examining at this point is the effect of relationship optionality on the table design. The difference optionality makes is that if a relationship is optional, the foreign key may legitimately be null. To put it another way, if the foreign key attribute can potentially (and legitimately) have no related *entity instance* to refer to, then it can be set to null. In our current example, no such optionality exists; for instance, CustomerNo in Rental and FilmCode in DVD are both mandatory and hence non-null. Schema design facilities in database management systems allow the designation of foreign keys as 'non-null'; this is necessary to manage referential integrity in the database.

Addition of Stars information

The previous part, we derived an ER diagram with a many-to-many relationship, reproduced in Figure 3.2.11.

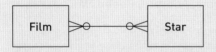

FIGURE 3.2.11 Film star relationship

This enables us to illustrate the process of dealing with a many-to-many relationship at this stage in the process. The situation demands that we form an intermediate entity connected to the others by one-to-one relationships. With a contrived relation such as this you may be stuck for a name, and awkward combinations such as FilmStar are often suggested (and used!). However, a little thought often produces an alternative which is quite apt in the circumstances. If you examine Figure 3.2.12 you can see that we have adopted the name 'Role' for this entity. As in many such cases, you may find a good application for the entity – we could add another attribute that provides the name of the part the star played in that film. For instance, this might yield an association such as Goldfinger – James Bond – Sean Connery.

FIGURE 3.2.12 Film star relationship using role

The additional entities are therefore:

STAR (*StarName*, Nationality, DateofBirth)

ROLE (**FilmCode**, **StarName**, RoleName)

For the Star relation we have chosen the star name as the primary key. Being simply a person's name, this is perhaps slightly contentious, but since stars usually take some care to have unique names we will assume that this is acceptable. The natural primary key of such intermediate entities is the concatenation of the primary keys of the other entities, as shown. Primary keys are in italics, foreign keys are bold.

CASE STUDY 3 – JOB AGENCY

The design of this case study is derived from the ER model shown below, with an incomplete specification of primary and foreign keys:

CLIENT (*ClientNo*, Name, Address, Date of Birth, Sex, PhoneNo)

CONSULTANT (*Name*, Telephone No)

JOB HISTORY (**ClientNo, EmployerRef**, Date Started, Date Left, Job Title, Final Salary)

EMPLOYER (*EmployerRef*, EmployerName, Address, Phone No)

QUALIFICATION (**ClientNo**, Award, Awarding Body, Year, Grade)

The main decisions to be made are with regard to the primary keys of the multi-valued derivatives of Client, namely, Job History and Qualifications. ClientNo is not a sufficient key for either, so we will look initially for some natural attribute combinations that will work.

Taking Job History first, consider the combination ClientNo and EmployerRef. This looks promising *but* there is the possibility that a client may have had more than one period of employment with the same company, so we need a further qualification to guarantee unique key values. If we further add Date Started this should suffice – it would appear unlikely that one would start twice with the same company on the same date! So our chosen primary key is the composite ClientNo/EmployerRef/Date Started.

The Qualification entity is just as awkward; ClientNo plus Award looks promising, but it is not uncommon for people to have two BSc or MSc degrees. Even if we qualify this with the awarding body, we are still not guaranteed uniqueness, so it looks as if we also need to include the year. This gives a composite primary key ClientNo/Award/Awarding Body/Year.

Of course the option is open, as always, of simply using automatic surrogate keys, and in this example it seems an eminently sensible approach. Adopting this design decision, using surrogate keys of HistoryID and QualID, the revised table design is:

CLIENT (*ClientNo*, Name, Address, Date of Birth, Sex, PhoneNo)

CONSULTANT (*Name*, Telephone No)

JOB HISTORY (*HistoryID*, **ClientNo**, **EmployerRef**, Date Started, Date Left, Job Title, Final Salary)

EMPLOYER (*EmployerRef*, EmployerName, Address, Phone No)

QUALIFICATION (*QualID*, **ClientNo**, Award, Awarding Body, Year, Grade)

3

Summary

1 Entity-Relationship (ER) diagrams are used to assist in the design of relational database tables.

2 An ER diagram representing a database application can be converted to a set of tables that can be employed in the application.

3 In general, an ER diagram entity converts to a relational table.

4 Relationships between entities can be represented either by foreign key additions to entity tables or by additional tables, depending on the cardinality and optionality.

5 Foreign key values must match a primary key value in the related table *or* be null if the relationship is optional.

6 Multi-valued attributes and time-varying attributes can be represented by an additional table related to the base table in a one-to-many relationship.

Review questions

1 List the stages of the conversion process from ER diagrams to relational tables.

2 How do you represent a many-to-many relationship with relational tables?

3 When is it permissible for a foreign key value to be null?

4 How do you represent multi-valued attributes in relational tables?

5 How do you represent time-varying attributes in relational tables?

Exercises

1 Describe in detail the procedure for conversion of ER diagrams to relational tables.

2 **a)** The ER diagram shown in Figure 3.2.13 describes the situation in a college in which each student is enrolled on one course, each of which is managed by one department. Each course consists of a set of modules and one module can be included in one or more courses. Making any necessary changes to it, convert this ER diagram into a set of relational tables.

   b) Suppose that each course can have a number of optional modules that each student can select. It is therefore necessary to record the module choice for each student. Extend the ER diagram to accommodate this change.

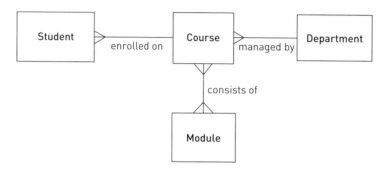

FIGURE 3.2.13 Exercise 2 Chapter 3 Part 2

3 A university computer laboratory requires a booking system to enable students to book a specific lab computer at a specific time. The students must be enrolled on certain authorised courses. Some of the computers have special facilities and/or additional equipment such as large memory, scanner, speech input, etc.

Design an ER diagram to model this application and then derive a set of relational tables from the ER diagram, using appropriate choices for the table attributes. Indicate the foreign keys used and for each specify whether a null entry would be allowable.

Part 3: Normalisation

Part 3 Overview

One of the principal objectives of relational databases is to ensure that each item of data is only held *once* within the database. For instance, if we hold customers' addresses, then the address of any one customer is only represented once throughout all the tables of the application.

The reasons for this are, first, simply, to minimise the amount of space required to hold the database, but also and more importantly to simplify maintenance of the data. If the same information is held in two or more places, then each time the data changes, each occurrence of the data must be located and amended. Also, having two 'copies' of the same data gives rise to the possibility of their being different.

In many cases, it is relatively easy to arrange the tables to meet this objective. There is, however, a more formal procedure called **normalisation** that can be followed to organise data into a standard format which avoids many processing difficulties. The process of normalisation is described in this chapter.

Overview of the normalisation process

In order to understand the process of normalisation, it is necessary to refer back to the concepts, mentioned earlier, of the *ruling part* and *dependent part* of the rows. The ruling part, also known as the **key** value of the table, is the column or columns that specify or identify the entity instance being described by the row. For instance, the key of the Batch table is the Batch number since this value uniquely specifies the batch being described by the other columns of the row, the dependent columns.

The purpose of normalisation is to:

- Put data into a form that conforms to relational principles; e.g. single-valued columns; each relation represents one 'real world' entity

- Avoid redundancy by storing each 'fact' within the database only once

- Put the data into a form that is more able to accommodate change

- Avoid certain difficulties in updating (so-called 'anomalies', described later)

- Facilitate the enforcement of constraints on the data.

Normalisation involves checking that the tables conform to specific rules, and, if not, re-organising the data. This will mean creating new tables containing data drawn from the original tables. Normalisation is a multi-stage process, the result of each of the stages being called a **normal form**; successive stages produce a greater and greater degree of normalisation. There are a total of seven normal forms, called, in increasing degree and grouped for the convenience of description:

- **First**, **Second** and **Third Normal Forms** (abbreviated to 1NF, 2NF and 3NF)

- **Boyce-Codd** (BCNF)

- **Fourth Normal Form** (4NF)

- **Fifth Normal Form** (5NF) and **Domain-Key Normal Form** (DK/NF).

The normal forms 1NF, 2NF and 3NF are the most important and all practical database applications would be expected to conform to these. The likelihood of a set of tables requiring modification to comply with these is quite high.

The Boyce-Codd normal form is a more stringent form of 3NF and again should be applied to a practical system. There is less chance of this normal form affecting the structure of the tables.

The Fourth and Fifth Normal Forms are unlikely to be significant in a practical system that has been designed, say, using the ER approach.

The highest normal form, the Domain-Key, was devised by Fagin in 1981. Fagin proved that this normal form was the 'last'; no higher form is possible or necessary, since a relation in DK/NF can have no modification anomalies. However, this is mostly of theoretical interest, since there is no known procedure for converting to this form.

The first three normal forms are the most significant and are usually sufficient for most applications. These will be described in some detail in the following section; the other normal forms will be covered in the subsequent sections in somewhat less detail.

Normal forms 1NF, 2NF and 3NF

The normalisation process assumes that you start with some informal description of all the data attributes that the database application appears to require; this is often called 'un-normalised data'. This set of attributes is then tested using criteria defined by each of the normalisation stages. If the data fails the criteria, there is a prescribed procedure for correcting the structure of the data; this inevitably involves the creation of additional tables.

The overall process of normalisation for the first three stages is summarised in Figure 3.3.1.

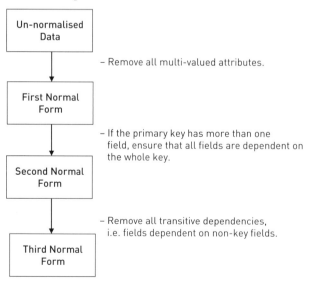

FIGURE 3.3.1 The normalisation process and normal forms

To understand what these steps imply, we can refer to one of the case studies (Case Study 5) initially introduced in Chapter 1 concerning a correspondence college, and in particular the subsystem dealing with the management of tutors and assignments. For convenience, the specification of this example is reproduced again below.

CASE STUDY 5 – CORRESPONDENCE COLLEGE

Tutors: The written assignments received from students are gathered into batches, which are then dispatched by post to tutors for marking (i.e. complete batches of up to ten assignments are sent to tutors). Assume that there can be an indefinite number of tutors. The tutors mark the assignments, then return them, retaining them within the same batches. The subsystem enables 'tracking' of the assignments, so that the college knows what assignments have been received, sent to tutors or marked. Also, the system keeps a running total of the total number of assignments that have been marked by each tutor, to enable them to be paid.

As we did in Chapter 1, we can represent the data diagrammatically as shown in Figure 3.3.2. We view this data design as a first attempt at forming a relational table to represent the application data. Naturally, we would prefer as few tables as possible, so we have combined all the data into one tentative table design. The attribute Batch Number will be used as a provisional primary key.

FIGURE 3.3.2 Correspondence college example

First normal form

In Figure 3.3.2 we are not pretending that we have anything resembling a proper relational table at this stage: it is simply a trial combination of all relevant data items. Note however that the cardinality of the attributes is shown correctly: there is a group of attributes that have several values for each value of the others. If we were to attempt to organise this data into a table, it might look something like Table 3.3.1.

Batch Number	Tutor Code	Assigns Marked	Date Sent	Date Returned	Student Code	Course Code	Assign Number
23	JS	87	12/4/07	07/5/07	20071230	PR007	3
					20078001	AB003	1
					20070239	PR009	7
24	GH	91	21/09/07	15/10/07	20078001	AB003	4
					20079851	GM201	3

TABLE 3.3.1 Trial combination of relevant datatypes

As we have already noted, we cannot have multiple attribute values in one 'cell' (i.e. row/column intersection) of a relational table. In other words, there is no way to create a relational table with this format. The objective of 1NF is to produce a table with no such multiple attributes. In other words, 1NF is the first most primitive form of the data that can in fact be used to construct a table in a practical relational database system such as Oracle or Access.

Before we look at the process a producing a 'true' 1NF representation, we could explore other attempts at dealing with the repeated data groups. Note that the issues discussed here have already been considered in Chapter 3 Part 2 (page 101) but are re-examined here in the context of normalisation. One possibility would be to repeat the columns horizontally to give, in outline, something like Table 3.3.2.

Batch Number	Student Code	Course Code	Assign Number	Student Code	Course Code	Assign Number	Student Code	Course Code	Assign Number

TABLE 3.3.2 Alternative attempt repeated data groups – columns repeated horizontally

However, a relational table must have a fixed number of columns, and hence you would have to set a fixed upper limit on the number of repetitions. In many rows, several of the repeated columns would be empty, thereby wasting space. Also, this format complicates querying of the table; if we wanted to search for a particular Student Code, then we would need to search multiple columns of the table.

Another possibility would be to use a character string containing a list of items for each repeated data value. For example, the list of Student Codes for batch 23 could be held as the character string value '20071230, 20078001, 20070239'. This would appear to conform to the 'single value' criterion of 1NF, but this is an illusion, since it hides the presence of multiple values. One problem arising from this format is the fact that a maximum string length would need to be specified, which would place an arbitrary limit on the number of items in the list. A more serious problem again relates to the difficulty in querying such data; a search for a particular Student Code would require a 'sub-string' scan along the list of values, which would be grossly inefficient. In any case, this is not supported by standard SQL queries.

The formats described above in an attempt to cope with multiple attribute values are not usable and we require a more productive approach to the problem. This approach is described in the next section.

1NF procedure

There are two methods we can use to produce a valid 1NF representation of our data. For clarity, we can refer to these as the 'one-table' and 'two-table' solutions respectively.

In the one-table solution, we extend the table rows by replicating the non-repeated columns for each repeated item value. This yields the table shown in Table 3.3.3.

Batch Number	Tutor Code	Assigns Marked	Date Sent	Date Returned	Student Code	Course Code	Assign Number
23	JS	87	12/4/07	07/5/07	20071230	PR007	3
23	JS	87	12/4/07	07/5/07	20078001	AB003	1
23	JS	87	12/4/07	07/5/07	20070239	PR009	7
24	GH	91	21/09/07	15/10/07	20078001	AB003	4
24	GH	91	21/09/07	15/10/07	20079851	GM201	3

TABLE 3.3.3 Batch table – one-table solution

This table is now in 1NF since each table cell has a single value. There is of course very evident redundancy in this table; for instance, the data pertaining to batch number 23 requires three rows of the table. Since elimination of redundancy is one of the objectives of normalisation, this does not appear too clever; however, this redundancy is removed in the next normalisation stage.

In the two-table method, we immediately separate the repeating and non-repeating data into separate tables. An appropriate primary key value has to be adopted for the repeating data table and a foreign key inserted to refer back to the other table.

Since a two-table procedure is generally more intuitive and simplifies the second normal form process, it is used as the basis of the rest of the coverage of normalisation. To start with, we describe the two-table 1NF procedure in more detail.

We require to remove the repeating items (i.e. Student Code, Course Code, Assign Number) and to form a new table called Batch Items; this is the action needed to arrive at the First Normal Form (or 1NF). The steps involved in this are detailed below:

- Remove the repeating items from the original table and form them into a new table (Table 3.3.4).

Batch Items

Student Code	Course Code	Assign Number
20071230	PR007	3
20078001	AB003	1
20070239	PR009	7
20078001	AB003	4
20079851	GM201	3

TABLE 3.3.4 Table with repetitions removed

The original table is reduced to that shown below, with a primary key of Batch Number (Table 3.3.5).

Batch

Batch Number	Tutor Code	Assigns Marked	Date Sent	Date Returned
23	JS	87	12/4/07	07/5/07
24	GH	91	21/09/07	15/10/07

TABLE 3.3.5 Batch table with the primary key Batch Number

- Create a new column in the new table which is the key value of the original table, i.e. Batch Number. This is the foreign key column that enables the two tables to be joined (Table 3.3.6).

Batch Items

Batch Number	Student Code	Course Code	Assign Number
23	20071230	PR007	3
23	20078001	AB003	1
23	20070239	PR009	7
24	20078001	AB003	4
24	20079851	GM201	3

TABLE 3.3.6 Batch Items table – version 1

- Devise a primary key for the new table. In this example, we could form a primary key by some combination of the available attributes; for instance, Batch Number – Student Code, as illustrated above. Remembering that we require a unique value for the primary key, this choice would be dependent on there being only one assignment per student in each batch. If this is not the case, the primary key may also need to include the Course Code; this assumes that, if a batch contains more than one assignment from one student, then the assignments are from different courses. If this is not the case then the Assign Number would also need to be included in the key.

Another possibility is to use the technique described in Part 2 of this chapter whereby the table primary key value is an automatically generated numerical value. This value would number from 1 upwards as new records are created. This is illustrated in Table 3.3.7.

Batch Items

Sequence Number	Batch Number	Student Code	Course Code	Assign Number
1	23	20071230	PR007	3
2	23	20078001	AB003	1
3	23	20070239	PR009	7
4	24	20078001	AB003	4
5	24	20079851	GM201	3

TABLE 3.3.7 Batch Items table – version 2

Note that the Batch Number attribute still acts as a foreign key to link the Batch Items table to the original Batch table.

For the purposes of further discussion, we shall use the Batch Items table version 1 shown in Table 3.3.6, with the primary key of Batch Number – Student Code.

Second normal form

This form requires that *all non-key attributes are dependent on the whole primary key* and not on a part of it. The definition indicates that it is only applicable to relations that have primary keys consisting of two or more columns. In our example we see that Batch Items (using version 1 above) has a compound key consisting of Batch Number and Student Code. Do any of the other dependent attributes depend on just one of the component key fields? This question is not immediately answerable; it depends on the Student–Course relationship. *If* each student is on one and only one course at any time, then the Course Code depends solely on the Student Code (i.e. knowing the student, we can determine the course). In this case, we should separate the Student–Course information into a separate table, Table 3.3.8.

Batch Items

Batch Number	Student Code	Assign Number
23	20071230	3
23	20078001	1
23	20070239	7
24	20078001	4
24	20079851	3

Student

Student Code	Course Code
20071230	PR007
20078001	AB003
20070239	PR009
20078001	AB003
20079851	GM201

TABLE 3.3.8 Using two tables with the second normal form

Note that the new table consists of a primary key (the partial key component from the original table, namely, Student Code) and the dependent column(s), in this case, Course Code. The dependent columns are removed from the original table.

However, if it is possible to be dealing with a student working on two different courses, then the simple correspondence between student and course implied by the Student table above would not apply. Hence, in order to specify to which course the Assign Number refers in a particular batch, we need the Course Code, as in the original version.

Third normal form

This form, 3NF, requires us to ensure that *no attributes are dependent on other non-key attributes*. We noted earlier that the Assigns Marked attribute was a characteristic solely of the tutor and is unrelated (directly) to the Batch table key value. To comply with the 3NF requirements, we must separate the tutor information into a separate relation, as shown in Table 3.3.9.

Batch

Batch Number	Tutor Code	Date Sent	Date Returned
23	JS	12/4/07	07/5/07
24	GH	21/09/07	15/10/07

Tutor

Tutor Code	Assigns Marked
JS	87
GH	91

TABLE 3.3.9 Using batch and tutor tables with the third normal form

Non-key dependency is also referred to as **transitive dependency**, because a transitive link exists between the key and the other attributes involved, as shown in Figure 3.3.3.

FIGURE 3.3.3 Transitive dependency

To summarise this example, the original data has been factored into four normalised tables, namely, Batch, Batch Items, Student and Tutor. Thus we arrive at the design dictated by the normalisation process corresponds to our intuitive design which was developed on page 26. The normalisation discipline helps us to understand more formally and clearly why we build the application relations in a particular way. The need to define the precise nature of the data in the application domain (e.g. can a student be on more than one course?) makes us study the situation more closely; in developing a practical application, we must be careful to specify definitely what features of the data and its processing our design is intended to manage.

Anomalies

If we try to use tables in an application that do not conform to 1NF, 2NF or 3NF, we will encounter certain processing 'anomalies'; i.e. inconvenient or error-prone situations arising when we process the tables. They can classified as **update**, **delete** and **insertion** anomalies. Table 3.3.10 is used as an example.

Enrolment

Student Number	Course Number	Student Name	Address	Course
S21	9201	Jones	Edinburgh	Accounts
S21	9267	Jones	Edinburgh	Maths
S24	9267	Smith	Glasgow	Maths
S30	9201	Richards	Manchester	Accounts
S30	9322	Richards	Manchester	Computing
S41	9267	Ferguson	London	Maths

TABLE 3.3.10 Anomalies example

This table is in 1NF but not 2NF. The key of the relation is shown the composite Student Number – Course Number; we can see that Student Name is dependent on one part of this key, namely, Student Number. That is, given a particular value of Student Number, say S24, the value of Student Name is predetermined, namely Smith. Similarly, Course is dependent on Course Number. Observe that every time the number 9267 appears in the Course Number column, the course name Maths appears in the Course column. In general, there will be one row of this table for each student–course combination, hence these dependent items will be repeated with each occurrence of each value of either Student Number or Course Number. (It is important to note that this example assumes that a student can be on more than one course.)

This data is subject to three types of anomaly: update, deletion and insertion anomalies.

Update anomaly

Information about the address of students is repeated, once for each course they are on. If Jones moves to Aberdeen, every row in the table that refers to Jones would have to be amended. Failure to update all instances of Jones' address would result in two different versions of the address.

Delete anomaly

If the last student registered for a course withdraws from it, the details about the course are lost as well. The table only retains information on existing student–course combinations, not on courses independently. If student S30 leaves course 9322, no record remains of this course.

Insertion anomaly

This is the converse of the delete anomaly: we cannot record the existence of a new course without at least one student being assigned to it. If we introduce a new course on Physics, we cannot record any information about it until we enrol the first student. Note that we cannot use empty (null) columns; for instance, a row of the table such as that illustrated in Table 3.3.11 is not allowed.

Student No	Course No	Student Name	Address	Course
Null	9300	*Null*	*Null*	Physics

TABLE 3.3.11 Insertion anomaly – not allowed

The use of nulls in the primary key of a relational table conflicts with the concept of entity integrity described in Chapter 2.

These anomalies can be avoided if the data is normalised to 2NF. For this example, the data would then also conform to 3NF. To comply with 2NF we must factor the table into additional tables where dependency on a partial key exists; this applies to Student Name and Address, dependent on Student Number, and Course, dependent on Course Number. This gives us a new table for Students and for Courses. These, and the residue of the original table, are shown below.

Student

Student Number	Student Name	Address
S21	Jones	Edinburgh
S24	Smith	Glasgow
S30	Richards	Manchester
S41	Ferguson	London

TABLE 3.3.12 Student table

Course

Course Number	Course
9201	Accounts
9267	Maths
9322	Computing

Enrolment

Student Number	Course No
S21	9201
S21	9267
S24	9267
S30	9201
S30	9322
S41	9267

TABLE 3.3.13 Course and Enrolment tables

The example illustrates the effect of anomalies arising from a design that does not conform to 2NF, but anomalies can also arise from failure to comply with 3NF. Consider Table 3.3.14. Assuming the usual interpretation of such data, we can see that the dependency

Salesman Number → Salesman Name exists; this conflicts with 3NF and is subject to update anomalies. If the Salesman's name is changed, multiple rows would need updating.

Order Number	Order Date	Cust Number	Salesman Number	Salesman Name

TABLE 3.3.14 3NF anomalies with non-key attributes

Boyce-Codd normal form

This normal form was developed because of observed limitations of the third normal form that allowed redundancy and anomalies to arise under certain circumstances. It is sometimes referred to as 'strong' 3NF. Note also that some authors adopt the Boyce-Codd version as *the* third normal form. In practice, conditions necessitating Boyce-Codd normalisation are relatively rare.

The definition of BCNF is very compact:

A relation is in BCNF if every determinant in the relation is a candidate key.

NOTE

A *determinant* is the 'left-hand' attribute in a functional dependency: for instance, if we have the dependency **OrderNumber** → **OrderDate**, meaning OrderNumber determines OrderDate, then OrderNumber is the determinant. A *candidate key* is an attribute or combination of attributes that could serve as a primary key because its value will be unique for all rows of the relation. One candidate key is chosen to be the actual primary key.

To understand the implications of BCNF, consider the sample relation in Table 3.3.15.

Student

Student Number	Subject	Subject Lecturer
10001	Accounting	Williams
10001	Maths	O'Connell
10022	Maths	Davis
10333	Economics	Edmonds
10333	Management	Fisher
14444	Accounting	Williams

TABLE 3.3.15 Implications of BCNF

The Student relation describes Students, Subjects that the student are studying and the Subject Lecturers. The following rules apply to this application; the bracketed items indicate an example of each rule:

1 Each student can take one or more subjects (10001 takes Accounting and Maths).

2 Each lecturer teaches only one subject (Williams only teaches Accounting).

3 Each subject can be taught by one or more lecturers (Maths is taught by O'Connell and Davis).

Let us first look for candidate keys in this relation. The Student Number cannot be a primary key since it is not unique. However, Student Number and Subject combined would provide a unique value, as would Student Number and Subject Lecturer. Each of these candidate keys produce a functional dependency; in addition there is, by definition (rule 2 above), a functional dependency between Subject Lecturer and Subject. Hence, we have three functional dependencies, as follows:

1 Student Number, Subject → Lecturer

2 Student Number, Lecturer → Subject

3 Lecturer → Subject

Note that the relation is in 3NF: regardless of whether we choose Student Number, Subject or Student Number, Lecturer above as the primary key, all non-key attributes are dependent on the whole key. For instance, if we choose a key of Student Number, Subject then we have the dependency:

Student Number, Subject → Subject Lecturer

However, referring back to our definition of BCNF, we can see that functional dependency 3 conflicts with the requirements: Lecturer is a determinant but not a candidate key. Hence this relation is not in BCNF.

Non-BCNF relations can produce anomalies under certain circumstances; in the Student relation above, if we delete the row for Student 10022, we lose the fact that Davis teaches Maths – this is a delete anomaly. If we want to introduce the fact that Peters teaches Management we must also find a student to enrol in the course – this is an insertion anomaly.

As always in normalisation, the solution is to divide the relation into new relations that comply with BCNF. The example relation above becomes the case shown in Table 3.3.16.

Student

Student Number	Subject Lecturer
10001	Williams
10001	O'Connell
10022	Davis
10333	Edmonds
10333	Fisher
14444	Williams

Lecturer

Subject Lecturer	Subject
Williams	Accounting
O'Connell	Maths
Davis	Maths
Edmonds	Economics
Fisher	Management

TABLE 3.3.16 BCNF compliance by dividing the tables

These relations each have only one candidate key and hence must be in BCNF. Anomalies arise in non-BCNF relations when:

- There is more than one candidate key
- The candidate keys are composite
- The attributes of the candidate keys overlap; i.e. they have an attribute in common.

Note that the BCNF definition does not mention lower normal forms; it is evaluated purely on the basis of the definition given above. This means that in principle you could 'jump' directly to the BCNF stage without needing to examine for 2NF or 3NF; if the relation complies with BCNF, it must also comply with 2NF and 3NF. In practice, derivation of 2NF and 3NF is intuitively easier to understand and hence these forms are more commonly used.

Fourth normal form (4NF)

The fourth normal form is concerned with a concept called a **multivalued dependency** (MVD). The presence of MVDs in a relation leads to anomalies in the data. The un-normalised data shown in Table 3.3.17 refers to personnel information about employees in respect of their dependents and their leisure activities. In general, each of these (dependents and activities) will be multi-valued.

Employee	Children	Activities
Andy Evans	Ann	Golf
	Martin	Tennis
		Gardening
Gillian Walker	Eileen	Swimming
	Mark	Badminton
	Karen	

TABLE 3.3.17 Un-normalised data and multivalued dependency

One possible way of organising this data is shown in Table 3.3.18.

Employee	Children	Activities
Andy Evans	Ann	Golf
Andy Evans	Martin	Tennis
Andy Evans	*null*	Gardening
Gillian Walker	Eileen	Swimming
Gillian Walker	Mark	Badminton
Gillian Walker	Karen	*null*

TABLE 3.3.18 Organised data – version 1

An obvious feature of the data is that the two multi-valued attributes are independent. Accordingly, to organise the data as shown in Table 3.3.18 is inappropriate, since it seems to suggest some relationship between children and activities. In order to avoid this interpretation we need to replicate each occurrence of a child value with every value of the activity producing the relation as shown in Table 3.3.19.

Employee	Children	Activities
Andy Evans	Ann	Golf
Andy Evans	Ann	Tennis
Andy Evans	Ann	Gardening
Andy Evans	Martin	Golf
Andy Evans	Martin	Tennis
Andy Evans	Martin	Gardening
Gillian Walker	Eileen	Swimming
Gillian Walker	Mark	Swimming
Gillian Walker	Karen	Swimming
Gillian Walker	Eileen	Badminton
Gillian Walker	Mark	Badminton
Gillian Walker	Karen	Badminton

TABLE 3.3.19 Organised data with replicated data values – version 2

This form of table exhibits multi-valued dependency. Since the primary key of this relation would need to be all three attributes, it must be in BCNF, but there is still manifestly considerable redundancy in the data. The obvious solution to this is to decompose the relation into two separate relations, as shown in Table 3.3.20.

Employee	Children
Andy Evans	Ann
Andy Evans	Martin
Gillian Walker	Eileen
Gillian Walker	Mark
Gillian Walker	Karen

Employee	Activities
Andy Evans	Tennis
Andy Evans	Gardening
Andy Evans	Golf
Gillian Walker	Swimming
Gillian Walker	Badminton

TABLE 3.3.20 Organised data reducing duplication – version 3

The key of each of these relations consists of both attributes. As well as being in BCNF, these relations are also now in 4NF because the MVDs have been eliminated. The formal definition of 4NF is:

> A relation is in fourth normal form if it is in BCNF and all dependencies are functional dependencies.

The solution arrived at in Table 3.3.20, of course, is that which would have been developed if using ER modelling or even an intuitive approach. However, there are more formal aspects to MVDs that we will not address in this text. Readers interested in further study of this topic should consult Elmasri and Navathe (2007).

3

Higher forms: Fifth normal form (5NF) and DK/NF

The fifth normal form is concerned with the concept of **join dependency**. This is an assertion that, if a relation is subdivided into a number of projections, then the original relation can be reconstituted without loss of information by joins.

The Domain-Key Normal Form was defined by Fagin in 1981. The formal definition of DK/NF is:

> A relation is in DK/NF if every constraint on the relation is a logical consequence of the definitions of keys and domains.

Fagin proved that this is the ultimate normal form: no other normal form is necessary or possible. Unfortunately, there is no known standard procedure for converting a relation to DK/NF.

Neither of these normal forms is used to any extent in normal practical database design and will not be pursued further in this text. For further details on these, consult the texts by David Kroenke and CJ Date given at the end of the chapter.

Summary of normalisation

Normalisation is a formal procedure that can contribute to the design of relational tables and, using the notion of functional dependency, can allow you to verify that the designed tables do not contain any anomalies. It should be noted that the table designs emerging from normalisation show the natural usage of tables; i.e. each entity class in the application domain and (most) relationships between the entities are each represented by a separate table.

ER diagrams and normalisation

ER modelling and the techniques of normalisation are both used in the design of relational database systems. In this respect, the ER technique works in a 'top-down' fashion; i.e. we proceed by identifying the 'large scale' objects in the application domain (such as Programmers, Projects, Customers) and their relationships with one another, before analysing their component attributes in depth. This contrasts with the 'bottom-up' normalisation approach where the entity descriptions 'emerge' from an analysis of the component data attributes.

However, it must not be thought that the two methods are 'in competition' or even alternatives. In general, both will be used in the design process for a new system. The ER approach is probably best in deriving the overall design, producing a set of relations; normalisation can then be applied to these tables to ensure that they conform to normalisation rules. Note that a design produced in this fashion is unlikely to need attention beyond the 3NF stage of normalisation.

CASE STUDY

We will use Case Study 4, Job Agency, to illustrate the normalisation process. For convenience, the specification of this Case Study is given below.

A job agency offers to find jobs for clients looking for employment. A database system is used to record the clients' personal and resumé details. Personal details include name, address, date of birth, sex and phone number. The resumé details includes a history of employment and a set of qualifications. Each client is assigned to one job consultant within the agency, who negotiates with the client and endeavours to locate suitable employment for them.

We start by forming a list of all the data items that the application requires. To assist this activity it is helpful to focus on the various elements, such as Client and Consultant, that are mentioned in the case study specification.

Client Details:

Registration No, Name, Address, Date of Birth, Sex, Telephone

Agency Consultant:

Consultant Id, Name, Extension

Qualifications:

Award, Awarding Body, Level, Year

Previous Employment:

Employer Name, Address, Telephone, Job Title, Reason for leaving, Date Started, Date Left, Final Pay.

The table below shows the transformation of the un-normalised data through the successive normal forms. The keys of the tables are shown in italics. The numbers in parentheses refer to notes that are supplied below the table. The → symbol indicates that the referenced table is unchanged by that stage.

3

Un-Normalised	First Normal Form	Second Normal Form	Third Normal Form
Client Data	**Client Table**	→	**Client Table**
RegNo	*RegNo*		*RegNo*
Name	Name		Name
Address	Address		Address
DOB	DOB		DOB
Sex	Sex		Sex
Phone	Phone		Phone
Consultant	Consultant Id		Consultant Id (FK)
Consultant Id	Name		**Consultant Table** (4)
Name	Extension		*Consultant Id*
Extension			Name
Qualifications			Extension
Award			
Awarding Body	**Qualifications Table**	→	→
Level	*RegNo* (1)		
Year	*Award*		
Prev Employment	Awarding Body		
Employer Name	Level		
Address	Year		
Telephone			
Job Title	**Employment Table**	**Employment Table**	→
Reason for leaving	*RegNo* (1,2)	*RegNo*	
Date Started	*Employer Name*	*Employer Name*	
Date Left	*Date Started*	*Job Title*	
Final Pay	Job Title	*Date Started*	
	Address	Reason for leaving	
	Telephone	Date Left	
	Reason for leaving	Final Pay	
	Date Left		
	Final Pay	**Employer Table**	→
		Employer Name (3)	
		Address	
		Telephone	

TABLE 3.3.21 Normalisation of Job Agency Model

Notes on this example

1 The qualification and the previous employment data occurs several times for each client and hence must be factored into separate tables as shown. The RegNo must form part of the key of the new tables to form a foreign key link to the Client table. It is assumed that the Award entry is sufficient to make the combined key unique.

2 The requirements for the primary key of the Employment table are somewhat complex. RegNo is required as already mentioned. The addition of Employer Name is probably not sufficient, since one could be employed by a company on more than one occasion. If the key is qualified by appending the Date of Starting, this would presumably give a unique key value.

3 The 2NF conversion required arises because, in the initial Employment table design, the employer address and telephone are dependent on only part of the key (Employer Name).

4 The 3NF conversion arises because of the functional dependency:

Consultant Id → Name, Extension where Consultant Id is not a key.

Summary

1 Normalisation is a set of procedures that aid in analysing the design of a database.

2 Normalisation removes unnecessary redundancy from a database.

3 Normalisation can identify potential anomalies in the structure of the database tables.

4 An anomaly is a difficulty or inconvenience in the processing of the tables.

5 Normalisation is a multi-stage process where the product of each stage is referred as a 'normal form'.

6 Normal forms 1NF, 2NF, 3NF and Boyce-Codd are the most significant from the point of view of practical design.

7 Other normal forms are 4NF, 5NF and DK/NF.

8 Normalisation is used as part of the database table design process and complements ER diagram design techniques.

Review questions

1 Define the term 'normalisation'.

2 What are the benefits of normalisation?

3 Outline the process of converting from un-normalised through the first, second and third normal forms.

3

4 List the types of anomaly that can arise if database tables do not conform to 2NF and/or 3NF.

5 Define the Boyce-Codd normal form.

6 List the conditions that give rise to anomalies in non-BCNF relations.

7 What is the significance of the Domain-Key normal form?

Exercises

1 Normalise the data shown in Table 3.3.22, showing the development of your design through the forms 1NF, 2NF and 3NF.

OrdNo	Date	CustNo	Name	Address	ProdNo	Desc	Price	Qty
1	05-01-96	22	Smith	London	A95	Jacket	55	4
					G17	Coat	120	8
					K10	Suit	90	5
2	19-01-96	47	Jones	Paris	G17	Coat	120	9
					D77	Shirt	35	20
3	27-03-96	25	West	Glasgow	E30	Tie	5	25
					D77	Shirt	35	4

TABLE 3.3.22 Exercise 1 Chapter 3 Part 3 Un-normalised data

2 For Table 3.3.6 Batch Items table version 2 shown earlier and reproduced below, suppose that the same student number could appear more than once in one Batch. Suggest and justify an alternative key attribute combination.

Batch Items

Student Number	Student Name	Address	Course Code	Course Name	Course Start Date	Exam Result
9300111	Smith	Glasgow	BS002	Accounting	05/10/92	Pass
9300123	Anderson	Edinburgh	BS004	Maths	12/10/92	Pass
9300123	Anderson	Edinburgh	BS016	Economics	12/10/92	Fail
9300789	Jones	Dundee	BS002	Accounting	05/10/92	Pass

3 (a) Outline the kinds of anomalies that can arise in a relational database system by using un-normalised tables, using table as a means of illustration.

(b) Show how the above data could be re-organised into separate tables to avoid these anomalies.

4 Anomalies arise in non-BCNF relations under certain conditions which are explained earlier in the chapter. Show how the Student relation table used in this explanation (reproduced below as Table 3.3.23) satisfies these conditions.

Student Number	Subject	Subject Lecturer
10001	Accounting	Williams
10001	Maths	O'Connell
10022	Maths	Davis
10333	Economics	Edmonds
10333	Management	Fisher
14444	Accounting	Williams

TABLE 3.3.23 Student relation table

5 (a) A financial consultancy company provides consultants to work on clients' projects. Each consultant works on only one project at a time, but a project may employ more than one consultant. Table 3.3.24 (un-normalised), provides an extract of data pertaining to the current assignments.

Consultant Id	Project No	Hours	Project Name	Consultant Name	Project Location	Fee Rate
21	A92	450	Apollo	Gray	Glasgow	100.00
25	Z50	90	Zeus	Brown	Edinburgh	90.00
33	Z50	20	Zeus	White	Edinburgh	95.00
37	M75	135	Mercury	Green	Aberdeen	150.00

TABLE 3.3.24 Exercise 5 Chapter 3 Part 3

(b) The Hours value is the total hours worked on the project so far, per consultant. The Fee Rate value depends on the combination of the consultant involved and the project.

i) Design a set of normalised tables derived from this data. The primary keys must be identified.

ii) Explain what changes would be required in the tables' design if the consultants were allowed to work on more than one project at a time.

6 (a) Explain how, in a relational database application, anomalies can arise from the use of un-normalised data, using Table 3.3.25 as a means of illustration.

Project Number	Project Name	Employee Number	Employee Name	Department Spent	Hours
1	Apollo	1001	Smith	Engineering	127
1	Apollo	1003	Jones	Accounts	45
2	Mercury	1002	Stewart	Marketing	70
3	Venus	1001	Smith	Engineering	21
3	Venus	1006	Brown	Engineering	124

TABLE 3.3.25 Exercise 6 Chapter 3 Part 3

3

(b) Design a set of relational tables that would avoid the anomalies arising from the above table design, identifying the primary key in each table.

7 Table 3.3.26 has been designed by an unskilled database user to hold data on student exam results. Convert the table to a more efficient format.

Student Number	Subject	Student Name	Lecturer	Lecturer Dept	Assess-ment 1	Assess-ment 1	Assess-ment 1
991010	Maths	Stewart	Mackay	MAT	45	23	69
991010	Stats	Stewart	Mackay	MAT	31	66	57
992001	Accounts	Ridley	Robinson	FIN	77	58	80
992001	Economics	Ridley	Ford	BUS	41	30	43
. . .							

TABLE 3.3.26 Exercise 7 Chapter 3 Part 3

8 Examine Table 3.3.27, which describes the working experience of a group of programmers in languages and database systems. What normal form is the table in? Convert the tables to 4NF.

Programmer Name	Language	Database
David	COBOL	Oracle
David	COBOL	Access
David	C++	Oracle
David	C++	Access
William	Smalltalk	Informix
William	Smalltalk	Oracle

TABLE 3.3.27 Exercise 8 Chapter 3 Part 3

References

The following texts provide more in-depth treatment of the subjects of this chapter:

Date, C. J. (2005): *Database in Depth: The Relational Model for Practitioners*, O'Reilly
Elmasri, R. and Navathe, S.B. (2007): *Fundamentals of Database Systems*, Pearson International
Kroenue, D. and Auer, D. (2006): *Database Concepts* (third edition), Prentice Hall
Rob, P. and Coronel, C. (2007): *Database Systems: Design, Implementation and Management*, Thomson Course Technology

4

Physical database design

LEARNING OBJECTIVES

The previous chapters have described how a conceptual design of a database application can be developed using tools such as ER modelling and normalisation. The next stage in the process is to convert this conceptual design into an actual working system using a chosen database product. This is known as 'physical database design'. In effect, much of the remainder of this text deals with various aspects of this task. The current chapter deals with a number of initial significant topics in this area.

After studying this chapter, you should be able to do the following:

- Explain how the physical design phase of database development relates to the earlier phases.

- Describe the features of a typical database management system.

- Explain the factors to be considered when choosing a database product for an application.

- Understand the nature of datatypes commonly available for attribute design.

- Explain how different datatypes are employed in table design.

- Explain the advantages of introducing controlled redundancy into the design of database tables.

- Describe different techniques of controlled redundancy.

- Describe the benefits of indexing and how indexes can be employed.

- Explain different aspects of indexing, including multi-field indexes, indexing overheads, etc.

Introduction

We have described the activities involved in developing a conceptual model of the database that is required to support the target application. The conceptual design should include ER diagrams and the structure of each of the tables derived from the component relations and relationships. The nature of the conceptual design is such that it should be independent of an actual database product; i.e. it should be possible to take the design and implement it using a range of different products. It is quite likely in practice that you have a particular database in mind or that you have no choice; for instance, you may work for a company committed, by virtue of previously implemented systems, to a particular database product. Nevertheless, it is desirable that the design should progress through an implementation-independent phase so that the requirements of the application system are not confused with the limitations of the database product.

Once we have clear conceptual design for our database, it is then necessary to chose a database product and to start to construct the target database system. A good deal of the rest of the book is concerned with the process of doing just that. In the current chapter, we deal with a number of topics that are of initial significance within the sphere of physical design. The specific topics covered are:

- Features of a typical DBMS

- Choosing a database product

- Introduction to example DBMS systems

- Table design

- Controlled data redundancy in tables

- Indexing

Database management systems

Features of a DBMS

A database management system, usually abbreviated to DBMS, is the software system that provides the facilities necessary to design and support a database application. A DBMS typically has many components; the most significant of these are listed and briefly described below.

The DBMS components described are:

- Database engine

- Query processor

- Schema manager

- Forms manager

- Report generator
- Data dictionary

Database engine

The database engine is the part of the DBMS that does the actual work of storing and accessing application oriented data (i.e. tables, rows, etc.) from physical storage. As implied by the name, the engine is the operational heart of the database system.

The database itself may be stored in a number of separate files or it may contained entirely in one physical file. The role of the engine is to maintain this data and to enable it to be accessed for the purposes of the application. For instance, we may wish to examine the contents of a Personnel table; the engine needs to have information available on the structure of this table (from the database schema) and how it can be retrieved from the database file(s). In effect, the engine provides the user with an abstraction layer that deals with tables and rows and columns, while the engine converts these concepts into physical disk locations and blocks.

The engine has other responsibilities in addition to those indicated above; the list below summarises all its roles. For completeness all its roles are documented at this point, but note that many of the topics mentioned are the subject of later chapters, and hence the description here is brief.

- Physical data management and accessing, including:

  (i) Index Management. Indexes are special tables created and maintained by the engine which speed up retrieval of data from the database. Indexes are described later in this chapter.

  (ii) View Management. A view is essentially a 'virtual table' generated from a query on normal tables. The view query can be stored in the system as if it was a conventional table. The principles of views were described in Chapter 2.

- Accessing the data dictionary.

- Transaction control. Most commercial databases are accessed by multiple online users; this requires special handling to avoid corruption of data and/or loss of updates.

- Security: access rights.

- Integrity: validation, referential integrity, transactions, recovery.

Query processor

The query processor executes query requests, typically specified in a query language such as SQL. Some systems such as Access and Paradox provide a graphical tableau for the expression of queries, referred to as 'query by example' (QBE). The term 'QBE' does not refer to a standardised system but to a generic type of table-based, language-free, querying technique that is available in various forms in several database packages. The term QBE is not actually used by these products which, rather unfortunately, leaves the method with no actual label by which to refer to it.

The original QBE was developed as a research project on IBM mainframe systems. The first PC implementation of a QBE interface appeared in the Paradox package, originally marketed by Borland and later by Corel. Access provides both an SQL and QBE facility which are largely interchangeable.

SQL is described in some detail in Hands-On Section A and Access' version of QBE is demonstrated extensively in Hands-On Section B.

Schema manager

The schema management facility is responsible for the maintenance of the database's self-describing information. An essential part of this is the definition of the table designs. In some systems a separate interface is available to manage this function, but often it is handled by means of system-specific SQL commands.

Forms manager

A form manager provides a user-friendly interface to the database, enabling the display of query results and the management of input transactions. A forms manager would provide forms design facilities and also manage the execution of forms. The forms manager can be an integral part of the DBMS (as in Access) or be provided by a free-standing program. Forms are described in more detail later in this chapter and also in Hands-On Section B, where we describe Microsoft Access.

Report generator

The report generator produces formatted results from the database, usually destined for printed output. It can be an integral part of the DBMS (as in Access) or be provided by a free-standing program such as Crystal Reports. Reports are described in more detail later in this chapter and also in Hands-On Section B.

Data dictionary

A data dictionary is a centralised repository used to record all information about a database including the names of all tables, the schemas for each table, the location of tables, view definitions, details about indexes, access rights, etc. In other words, it is a database about a database. In most systems, the data dictionary system tables that hold the user definitions are also accessible to database users (such as system developers); access to this data would normally be in read-only mode to avoid any risk of corruption.

We can distinguish between *active* and *passive* dictionaries; in a passive system, the information held is purely documentary, to be referenced by database developers and administrators. In an active dictionary the data is used by the database software as a repository of name references to database objects such as tables, attributes, forms, etc.

In Microsoft Access everything associated with a database, including the data dictionary and the data itself, is held in one physical file with an .MDB extension. A more typical arrangement, used in Oracle, is that the data dictionary itself consists of a large number (more than 200) of relational tables held along with the application tables. In addition to the 'real' tables there is also a large number of synonyms, i.e. alternative names for some of the tables. Each user has access rights to their own tables plus a number of the dictionary tables. The database administrator will have access rights to all the tables. As an indication of the general nature of Oracle dictionary tables, a select few are described below:

ALL_TABLES ALL_INDEXES ALL_VIEWS	Tables with the ALL_ prefix hold information about database objects accessible to the user.
DBA_USERS DBA_VIEWS	Tables with the DBA_ prefix hold information accessible only to the Database Administrator.
USER_TABLES	Tables with the USER_ prefix hold information created by or directly applicable to the user. USER_TABLES holds a list of all the tables created by the user.
USER_TAB_COLUMNS	USER_TAB_COLUMNS contains a list of all the columns of all the tables created by the user.
TABS	The system holds a number of synonyms, i.e. alternative names for system objects. TABS is a synonym for USER_TABLES.
COLS	COLS is a synonym for USER_TAB_COLUMNS

It is worth noting the fact that these data dictionary tables are themselves relational tables within the same database; for instance, we can view the tables simply by using suitable SQL commands:

```
SELECT * FROM TABS         would list all tables created by the user.
SELECT * FROM USER_INDEXES would list all the user's indexes.
```

Choice of database

In many cases we have no choice in the selection of a database product, but where a 'green-field' situation exists there a number of factors to be considered. In assessing the wide range of database products that are currently available, it is helpful to identify some major distinguishing features to simplify the process of selection. A number of such features are given below.

Scale

This term refers to the maximum number of users and the maximum disk space supported by the database. These parameters can also be limited by the host computer system; the system overall must be able to cope with the expected loading.

Performance

The number of transactions per hour that can be handled. This of course is also heavily dependent on the computer system used, but it is important that the database and the computer are matched in power.

Support for datatypes

For example, you may require support for storing multimedia data. For specialised applications you may require to hold high precision floating point values or 'long' integer values.

Connectivity

This term refers to support for accessing other database or file systems. There may be a need, for instance, to access some legacy system that uses an older database package. Also, your database may need to communicate with another system in another office. This is an area of considerable activity in the database market at present fuelled by the current interest in promoting commerce via national and international networks.

Processing complexity

Many modern database products, particularly those addressing the PC market, provide extensive interactive facilities that can be used by end-users (as opposed to professional systems developers). Some, indeed, *only* provide for such usage. If the interactive facilities cannot cope with your proposed application, then you need to look for products that have some degree of additional programmability. It may be that your application requires some computation that is best handled by a conventional programming language. In this event, database access via a programmable interface may be required. Chapter 5 describes a range of such interfaces.

Sample DBMS systems

This text uses a number of database products to illustrate the principles being expounded, the chief of these being Microsoft Access, Oracle and MySQL. Access constitutes the major exemplar, not because it is deemed superior in general to others, but because of its pedagogical value: it presents a wide range of features and facilities in a convenient and accessible fashion. Oracle is used primarily as a vehicle for teaching SQL and for programming features such as its procedure and post-relational languages. MySQL is described as it is an important player in the current database field and is used extensively by teaching environments.

Microsoft Access

Microsoft Access Version 1.0 was first introduced in 1992. It was directed at small businesses and advanced end-users such as engineers, managers and accountants rather than the systems development community. At this time other PC-based database products such as dBase III and Borland Paradox had already generated a market for such tools. Access grew rapidly in popularity and soon became the market leader, a position it has maintained ever since through many improved versions. Recent versions have been 'bundled' within the Microsoft Office suite.

The fact that Access was targeted at end-users and small business systems has lead at times to a lack of appreciation of the product's capabilities. It fact it has many important and significant features, making it a powerful system for many applications within the limits of its scalability. It has a fully-featured powerful database engine supporting multi-user working with record locking, transactions and constraints, including referential integrity. The main user interface provides a graphical 'point and click' style environment for table, form, report and macro design. To enhance the system's potential, an underlying programming environment based on VBA (Visual Basic for Applications) modules is available. Each form and report design owns a set of VBA modules that provides event-driven response to user interactions (such as button clicks, data entry, etc.) and processing events. Many of the event-handling routines such as buttons to perform record save or delete operations are generated automatically by 'wizards'.

Access also supports macros; these can be used to provide a degree of programmability and may be preferred by non-expert users who do not have knowledge of VBA coding. Macros mostly automate operations such as menu option selection which would otherwise have to be done manually.

The forms design facility allows the creation of forms using a range of controls such as text boxes, labels, command buttons, list and combo boxes, radio and check buttons, images, sub-forms, etc. Queries can be specified either in a QBE tableau or by SQL. Queries can be saved (the SQL version is stored) and subsequently used in other queries or as the source of a form or report.

The principal limitation of Access is its scalability; although it has multi-user capability, the number of simultaneous users is relatively small due to the limitations of the database engine.

Access has been chosen for use in this text because it displays a wide range of capabilities and concepts within a relatively compact environment, making it very suitable for the explanation of many important database principles. Hands-On Section B provides a practical introduction to the features of Access.

Oracle

Oracle is a major player in the large multi-user enterprise computing arena. Originally developed by a company called Relational Software Inc., founded by Larry Ellison in 1979, it has evolved through many versions, each adding to the facilities offered and the system performance. Significant milestones were the introduction of PL/SQL in version 6 (1988), object-oriented features in version 8 (1999) and the ability to read and write XML (2001). At the time of writing, the current version is Oracle 10g (version 10.2.0.1).

MySQL

MySQL is a powerful, multi-user DBMS marketed by the Swedish company MySQL AB, which was founded by David Axmark, Allan Larsson and Michael Widenius. The first formal release of the product was in 1996. MySQL is available as an Open Source product and versions are available free of charge. It is commonly associated with other Open Source products such as the Linux operating system, Apache web server, the web language PHP and other languages such as Perl and Python. Combinations of these products potentially provide cheaper implementations of database and web systems than would be possible with conventional proprietary products. At the time of writing, MySQL offers production version 5.0.37.

Design of tables

The major decisions regarding the design of tables are generally tackled during the conceptual design of the system; the subdivision of the data in respective tables and the design of relationship tables should have been worked out. However, there remain a few factors worthy of your attention, dealt with in the subsections below. Some of the points covered overlap with topics studied elsewhere, but are provided here for completeness.

Attribute design

Choosing the datatype

The conceptual data design should establish the domains of the data items to be represented in the database tables. Factors like the maximum admissible length of text attributes such as names and addresses and maximum values and required precision for numerical items need to be determined. From this knowledge, appropriate datatypes can be chosen for the table columns. Note that the datatype determines the storage mode, the behaviour of the data item on input and output and the permissible processing operations on the data. A summary of the main categories of datatypes generally provided by database systems is given in Table 4.1.

DataType	Explanation
Text	Character data; letters, numerical digits, special symbols, etc. based on standard character sets such as ASCII or Unicode.
Numeric	Numerical values, either integer or real (floating point) numbers, with varying size and precision.
Counter	System-generated serial sequence of numbers, often used to create primary key values.
Date/Time	Date and time values.
Boolean	Logical values which can be interpreted as any pair of values, e.g. true/false, 1/0, Yes/No.
Binary	Set of binary data, held as an unstructured item. Often used to store multimedia data.
Object	Binary data in standard object-based format such as OLE or COM.

TABLE 4.1 Datatype categories

The following sections provide some additional information about some of these datatypes.

Text

In general the defined size of a text column is governed by the users' expectations of the data to be encountered in the application. Choosing an appropriate length in this respect involves a trade-off between accommodating the data and the disk space required to hold the data; an extra 10 bytes per row in a table of 10 000 rows adds 100 000 bytes to the size of the table. Most systems support variable-length text fields, which do not store trailing spaces and hence optimise storage requirements. An example of this is the VARCHAR2 type in Oracle. Many systems now provide a facility for storing large volumes of text; examples are the 'memo' type in Microsoft Access which can hold text of up to 64 Kbytes and the Oracle 'LONG' which has a theoretical storage limit of 2 gigabytes. Also available in Oracle is the CLOB type, which stands for 'character large object'; these objects can hold up to 4 Gigabytes, although they will generally be accessed by special functions.

Such fields are limited in functionality. Typical restrictions are that CLOB data objects:

- Cannot be used in SQL Select lists

- Cannot be indexed

- Can only exist one per table.

- Are used simply for the recording of textual information that cannot be conveniently accommodated in conventional text fields.

Numbers

For numerical items there is a major split between integer, fixed point and floating point values. If the data is purely a whole number (e.g. a quantity in stock value), some integer representation is best; again, knowledge of the application domain should indicate the maximum value of the item. Most systems provide for more than one integer type; the SQL standard specifies INTEGER and SMALLINT. The actual size of these (in bits) is implementation-dependent, subject to the former being larger than the latter, but possible values are 16 bits for SMALLINT and 32 for INTEGER. Microsoft Access provides Byte (8 bit), Integer (16 bit) and Long (32 bit).

A fixed point representation provides a fixed number of total digits, which includes a fixed number of decimal places. Standard SQL has a datatype NUMERIC(n, p) where the total number of digits is $n+p$ and p is the number of decimal places. A fixed point format would be used for currency amounts in the absence of a specific currency type (e.g. Microsoft Access). A floating point value is represented in standard SQL using the FLOAT datatype.

An example of numeric datatype provision, is shown in the table below, which summarises the types available in Microsoft Access.

Datatype name	Range of values	Storage
Byte	0 to 255, integer	One byte
Integer	−32,768 to +32,767, integer	Two bytes
Long Integer	± 2 billion, approx, integer	Four bytes
Single	$\pm 3.4 \times 10^{\pm 38}$, approx, floating point, six digit precision	Four bytes
Double	$+ 1.8 \times 10^{+ 308}$, approx, floating point, ten digits precision	Eight bytes

It is important to distinguish carefully between integer and floating point representations: integers are inherently exact but ultimately limited in maximum value; floating point values are never 'exact', but can represent very large or very small values with a defined precision.

A point to note when deciding on a datatype is that numerical types should only be used for actual numeric values. Some data items consist entirely of numerical digits although they are not numerical quantities; identification codes such as product numbers fall into this category. In general, such items should be defined as text fields. As well as defining how the data item is stored, the datatype defines the behaviour of the data on input and output. For instance, if a field is defined as text rather than numeric, it will be left-justified in printed output and report generators will not try to generate automatic totals of the field.

Date/Time

Handling of date and time information in databases is quite complex. Each system will have its own internal representation of dates which is not relevant to the users of the system. The real complication is the wide range of possible formats in which the date and the time can be input and displayed. An additional complication is the different conventions used for numerical dates in the USA (MM-DD-YY) and Europe (DD-MM-YY). The SQL standard date/time formats are YYYY-MM-DD and HH:MM:SS, but most systems permit considerable variation. Possible date formats are:

- 18-01-07 and 18/01/07 (Europe),
- 01-18-07 and 01/18/07 (US)
- 18-Jan-07 (unambiguous)
- 06-06-07 (ambiguous). Interpretation of such dates will depend on the international settings of your system.

Most systems are remarkably adept at sorting out all these variations; Access, for instance, allows you to specify a specific date format for a field, but will accept a date in any of the other valid formats. Oracle allows you to 'build your own' format so that, for example, you can display a date in the format '18th January 2007'.

Attribute domains

The datatype cannot generally fix the data values within the precise domain dictated by the application. For instance, a numeric attribute may have a range of value of 1 to 500, but the nearest representation available is, say, a 16-bit integer with potential range of $-32\,768$ to $+32\,767$. Ideally, it would be desirable to set the domain of an attribute to the exact values that exist in the application; this facility is not widely available, but some current developments are moving in this direction. For instance, in the SQL standard, a CREATE DOMAIN command is defined (albeit with limited functionality) and several products now offer 'extended relational' facilities that include user-defined attribute types.

In the absence of datatypes that precisely define the attribute domain, suitable validation must be applied to prevent erroneous data from being entered into the database. The general principle is that no data that is outside the domains of the table attributes should be allowed into the database. If this principle is to be imposed by validation, it places the onus for its implementation on the database developer.

Data redundancy

Earlier in this text, the benefits of normalisation were described, namely, the removal of redundancies and avoidance of anomalies. It may come as a surprise then that it may be acceptable to tolerate data redundancy in the interests of convenience and/or performance. A common example is very widespread – the use of a postcode within an address. If we have an address consisting of a street, town and district, then inclusion of a postcode is actually redundant and breaks third normal form, because the address is functionally dependent on the postcode; given a postcode, the city and street name is predetermined. The alternative here it not too attractive; it theoretically requires a separate table mapping the postcode to the city and street address. Normally one would not implement this, since the problems created by the redundancy are far outweighed by the convenience.

Another example is also very common and relates to applications having a one-to-many relationship, such as order to order items. The main order information is held in an Order table (customer, date etc.), with details of each item ordered (product code, quantity, etc.) stored in an Order Detail table. This is illustrated in Figure 4.1. Additionally, it is likely that the item price may be held in a third table, say Products.

FIGURE 4.1 Derived attribute example

The total order value can be computed by querying the Order Items and Products tables and totalling the individual amounts. However, if a large number of items is involved, this causes a fair amount of accessing. Although it is clearly redundant, it would be possible to hold the total order value in the Order table, thereby having this value readily accessible without further querying. A table attribute that can be calculated from other database data is often called a **derived attribute**. It is clearly essential that the correspondence between the redundant total and the component Order Item values is maintained continuously; any change to the Order Item or Product tables must be reflected immediately in the Order table. This can be reliably achieved by the using a **transaction** to update the Order and Order Item tables together, guaranteeing that the two tables will always be 'in line'. Transactions are a database mechanism that allows database operations to be 'bracketed' together to ensure that all the operations therein are carried out as a unit. Transactions are covered in Chapter 6.

The examples described above could be viewed as relatively trivial, and deciding to use them should not require any serious heart-searching. In circumstances where the database system and/or host computer are under considerable performance pressures, it may be necessary to denormalise in more substantial measure. What this implies is that we deliberately design relations that are not in 1NF, 2NF or 3NF. The next sections discuss briefly the prospects and implications inherent in denormalising at the various NF stages.

First normal form

Strictly speaking, it is not possible to represent data not in first normal form within a relational database, because it implies the storage of more than one value in one table 'cell'. However, we can create an implicit non-1NF format by repeating a column definition. For instance, if we look again at an example shown in an earlier chapter, the difficulty here can be identified as shown in Table 4.2.

Customer Table

Customer Number	Name	Address	Balance Owing	Film Title 1	Film Title 2	Film Title 3
5567	Jones	Cross Road	2.50	Forbidden Planet	—	—
2913	Anderson	River Lane	0.00	Titanic	Shane	Casablanca
4890	Murray	West Street	1.50	Casablanca	Titanic	—
1622	Richards	Mill Lane	3.00	Schindler's List	—	—

TABLE 4.2 Customer table first normal form

In this example, representing a video hire application, the videos currently on hire to a customer are held in a set of three identically defined columns called Film Title 1, Film Title 2 and Film Title 3. Unused film title 'slots' are filled with null.

The problems introduced by non-1NF relations are:

- Rows must be of a fixed number of columns, so there can only be a fixed number of repeated attributes.

- Typically, many of the attribute columns will be unfilled, representing wasted space.

- There is added complexity in querying: since values of the same attribute are held in one row, querying these values involves multiple references to the attribute.

Using Table 4.2, if we wanted to issue a query to find the occurrence of a particular film name in the Film Title columns, it would require an SQL query like:

```
SELECT CustomerNo, Name FROM Customer WHERE   FilmTitle1 = 'Titanic'
                                     OR       FilmTitle2 = 'Titanic'
                                     OR       FilmTitle3 = 'Titanic'
```

This would be very inconvenient for more than a few columns.

It is perhaps worth noting that 1NF differs in nature from 2NF and 3NF in the context of redundancy. If we have a relation not in 1NF, it does not introduce any redundancy or anomalies. Indeed, it could actually economise in storage space. Failure to conform to 2NF or 3NF does introduce redundancy and anomalies, the implications of which must be clearly identified and managed within the system design.

Second and third normal forms

If we choose to relax the 2NF or 3NF rules, the consequences are relatively obvious; we are introducing redundancy and the potential for anomalies for the possible advantage of increased performance. In effect, we are hoping to improve querying times by avoiding a join to another table. As an example, consider the example of postcodes mentioned above. The conventional format for a name and address application is shown in Table 4.3.

CustomerNo	CustomerName	Address	City	PostCode
B1717	Smith	30 Moon Street	Sunville	SV12 9TR
C2346	Jones	20 Moon Street	Sunville	SV12 9TR

TABLE 4.3 Customer table with redundant PostCode

In fact, given the postcode, the street name and the City can be determined as indicated in the example. Customers Smith and Jones are near neighbours and hence have the same postcode. This format conflicts with 3NF, since the Address and City columns are functionally dependent on the non-key column PostCode. The 'ideal' representation of this data would be as shown in Table 4.4.

CustomerNo	CustomerName	Street Number		PostCode	Address	City
B1717	Smith	30		SV12 9TR	Moon Street	Sunville
C2346	Jones	20				

TABLE 4.4 Customer table normalised version

In most application involving addresses it is unlikely that the properly normalised design would be used; the normalised version is not likely to save much space, and other than adherence to the principles of normalisation, has little advantage. Having said that, it is worth noting that in the UK, for example, commercially available databases can provide the translation between postcode and address.

The circumstances that might indicate potential benefits in terms of using non-2NF or non-3NF tables are:

- Large tables that would take some time to join.

- Relatively limited duplication of data inherent in the de-normalisation.

- Relatively static data such as the postcode – address relationship.

It is generally possible to avoid anomalies by employing a transaction to guarantee that the duplicate updating is done correctly. So, for example, if an item of data is stored in several different rows of a table, a transaction would be used to amend all occurrences at the same time, ensuring that they all maintain the same value. Provided the above conditions are satisfied, the duplication of data is probably more of an inconvenience in the development and maintenance of the system.

Indexing

Principles

Indexes are used to speed up the retrieval of data from databases. They are an implementation requirement of practical systems rather than a theoretical feature. Somewhat surprisingly, it is the availability of very efficient indexing systems that primarily accounts for the success of relational databases. In the immediate period after the invention of the relational database idea, it was thought by many that it would not be feasible as a practical system because of the processing and accessing overheads implied. The databases current at that time were so-called 'navigational' systems, i.e. the records of the database were linked by explicit pointers in the data, although various indexing systems were also used. This reduced the need to search for data based on key values, as is the case for the relational database. The development of the B-tree indexing system dramatically improved the management of large indexes and made key-based accessing feasible. In addition, the B-tree index facilitates browsing forwards and backwards in key sequence and searching with partial key values (i.e. 'starting with' type searches).

In effect, an index holds all the values of a specified column or columns of a table, together with the corresponding disk addresses of records with those values. To illustrate this, we will use a simple tabular structure, but note that a practical (e.g. B-tree) index is not organised in this way. For the purposes of this explanation, refer to the 'fragment' of a table as shown in Table 4.5.

Customer Table

Record No	Customer No	Customer Name	Town
1	CD1234	Jones	Glasgow
2	AB3344	Smith	London
3	ZZ8811	Anderson	Belfast
4	RT0189	Campbell	London
5	FN2178	Harper	London
6	BC0012	Collins	Belfast

TABLE 4.5 Customer table using indexing

(The 'Record No' shown above indicates where the row is stored in the database; this value is *not* part of the row data.)

It is possible to build indexes for one or more fields of the file; this enables fast access to the data based on a known value of the chosen field. Fields used as indexes are often referred to as **index keys**. For example, a Customer No key would *conceptually* look as shown in Table 4.6.

Customer No	Record Number
AB3344	2
CD1234	1
BC0012	6
FN2178	5
RT0189	4
ZZ8811	3

TABLE 4.6 Customer Number Index

An index based on the Customer Name would look like Table 4.7.

Customer Name	Record Number
Anderson	3
Campbell	4
Collins	6
Harper	5
Jones	1
Smith	2

TABLE 4.7 Customer Name Index

Note: Indexes are *not* held in relational tables and have an internal structure that is hidden from the database users.

It is possible for the index keys to have duplicate values; an index based on the Town attribute shows the effect in Table 4.8.

Town	Record Number
Belfast	3, 6
Glasgow	1
London	2, 4, 5

TABLE 4.8 Town Index showing duplicate values

It is possible to specify whether duplicate key values are allowed; primary key indexes, of course, must be unique, but other indexes often need to allow duplicate values.

The rationale for using indexes is that the index table would typically be much smaller than the data table, could be held substantially in main memory, and hence can be searched more quickly. In the absence of an index, a search for a particular column value would necessitate a serial read of the entire table. In fact, in practice, the index is structured in such a way as to reduce further the time to find a particular value. From the above description, you may see that there are two separate ways in which an index helps:

- Searching rapidly for a single value
- Presenting the table in a specified order

To follow the second point, if for example we used the Customer Name index, and viewed the table using a database facility, the table records would appear to be in

Customer Name sequence. Typically, the data is actually held unordered, and the indexes are used to present the data in the required sequence. The nature of B-tree indexes make this operation particularly easy; for an explanation of the internal working of a B-tree, refer to the references given at the end of the chapter.

Note that the user would never 'see' the index data, nor are they required to do anything to service the indexes other than to specify which columns require indexing. The database engine automatically maintains and uses the indexes and they are entirely transparent to the user.

An index may consist of one or more columns; this enables us to use any arbitrary sorting sequence of the data. For instance, we could sort the above data tables into Town–Customer Name sequence. This would order the data firstly into Town sequence; since there will typically be more than one customer in each town, the records pertaining to each town will then be sorted in Customer Name sequence. Note that there is no point in joining index fields in this way if the first field has unique values. For instance, consider Table 4.5, shown earlier in this section, and reproduced as Table 4.9.

Record No.	Customer No	Customer Name	Town
1	CD1234	Jones	Glasgow
2	AB3344	Smith	London
3	ZZ8811	Anderson	Belfast
4	RT0189	Campbell	London
5	FN2178	Harper	London
6	BC0012	Collins	Belfast

TABLE 4.9 Customer table using indexing

An index key of Customer Number–Town makes no sense since the first field (Customer Number, presumably unique values) determines the sequence; the Town value would not affect the overall data sequence.

Choosing indexes

In general, the primary key of a table would be indexed; other fields might be indexed if a fast search on that field value was desirable. The database engine would use an index if one were available; otherwise a serial search of all rows would take place. To help to clarify this point, consider a query on a Customer table that is required to list all customers with the name 'Smith'. In SQL this query would be expressed as:

```
SELECT Name, CustomerNo FROM Customer
WHERE Name = 'Smith'
```

In the absence of an index on the Name attribute, this query would be evaluated by reading every row of the table; there is no alternative, since any row could have Name equal to 'Smith'. If an index existed for the Name attribute, then the index would effectively provide the SQL interpreter with a list of the rows that contain 'Smith'. The benefit of this increases as the number of rows increases.

Query interpreters, in working out how best to resolve a query, will take account of what indexes are available and use these if it will speed up the query execution. Systems will generally construct an index for the primary key column of each table; it is up to the application developer to create additional indexes for columns that feature in frequent and/or 'heavy' queries. Specifically, an index should normally be created for:

- the primary key
- foreign keys used in joins
- columns used in GROUP BY and/or ORDER BY clauses
- columns referred to in selection criteria of commonly used queries.

Conversely, creation of indexes is not indicated in the following cases:

- Very small relations: the time taken to search the whole relation will be quite small and probably less than the overheads of indexing.
- Where the index is only used in an infrequently used query. Again, the overheads associated with the indexing would outweigh the benefits.

Indexing overheads

Note however that indexes have to be kept constantly up to date, so that amendments to the data may require modification of the indexes. For instance, the addition of a new row to the table will necessitate the update of every index for that table. This can constitute a considerable overhead during updating. A balance has to be found between the necessary speed of access and the updating overheads. In some situations, for example in periodic reports or updates run, say, once a month, it is better to 'drop' the index during normal operations then rebuild the index specially for the monthly job. For an example, refer back to the Order – Order Item tables illustrated in Figure 4.1. The Salesman attribute identifies the salesperson responsible for the sale. If we assume that a report is required summarising the total sales per salesperson for the month, then an index based on the Salesman attribute would be desirable. However, this index would need constant updating during the month as new rows were added and amended. A better procedure might be to drop the index after one month's report and rebuild it again before the next report is produced. SQL commands for creating and dropping indexes are described in Hands-On Section A.

Indexes also require disk storage space, which can be substantial. For every index defined, the index will contain the index key value and a disk address, plus some additional space required by the B-tree structure. If an index key is a substantial part of the row, then that index could be larger than the data storage space. In most cases, the index space will not be a cause for concern, but it is factor that ought to be considered during the database's physical design.

It is worth noting that most of the work involved in indexes is transparent to the user. For instance, updating and searching of indexes are carried out automatically by the database engine. When issuing an SQL query, the SQL interpreter decides which indexes to use.

Multi-field indexes

An index can be based on two or columns combined together. Typically, this can be done without regard for the column types; e.g. an index can be formed from a concatenation of a text value and a date. Multi-field indexes are necessary for compound primary key values and to speed up queries using GROUP BY and/or ORDER BY operations on multiple columns. Examples of these cases are given below.

Compound primary key

In many applications, compound primary keys arise in tables representing a 'relationship' between two other tables, e.g.:

Orders Table:	*OrderNo*	CustomerNo	Date	
Products Table:	*ProductNo*	Description	Cost	BinNo
Order Detail Table:	*OrderNo*	*ProductNo*	Quantity	

Primary keys are shown in italics.

SQL Order By clause

In the above tables, we may want to list all Order table data in customer number order and, for each customer, in date order. Using SQL, this would look like:

```
SELECT OrderNo, CustomerNo, Date
FROM Orders ORDER BY CustomerNo, Date
```

ORDER BY and GROUP BY operations can sometimes extend to more than two columns. For instance, in Chapter 3 we described an example based on a staff employ-ment agency. To generate a unique primary key for the previous employment table, a combination of the attributes RegNo, Employer Name, Job Title and Date Started was required. This combination would need to be specified in the ORDER BY clause to dis-play the data in this sequence.

Note that an index for compounded columns can also serve as an index for 'left-hand' subsets of these columns. In general, a compound index consisting of columns $c1$, $c2$, $c3$ ... can also serve as an index for $c1$ and $c1$-$c2$ and $c1$-$c2$-$c3$ etc. This effect arises from the nature of the ordering process itself and the fact that index systems can search using only a left-hand portion of the search value. In the case of the SELECT example above, if an index was built on the CustomerNo-Date combination, this index is accept-able as a CustomerNo index alone, since it is in the appropriate sequence. The following list shows customer data sorted by date within CustomerNo. Note that the customer numbers are in sequence; hence this index could be used, for example, to display the data in customer number sequence:

CustomerNo	Date
10	12 Jan 98
10	27 Feb 98
10	4 Apr 98
20	15 Dec 98
30	10 Nov 98
30	6 May 99
. . .	

The same is *not* true of the 'right-hand' subsets, since these are in separate sequences grouped within the major key. For instance, the aforementioned CustomerNo-Date index cannot serve as a Date index and a, separate index would need to be built if required.

The practical consequence of the 'left-hand' subset effect is that if you have an index for say columns c1-c2, then you do not need to build an index explicitly for c1 alone.

Note that there is no point in forming an index based on compound fields if the first field has unique values. For instance, the index key of CustomerNo-Town makes no sense, since the first field (CustomerNo, presumably unique values) determines the sequence; the Town value would not affect the overall data sequence.

Summary

This chapter has described some important aspects of the physical design of the database. First we looked at the common features of a database management system or DBMS, the software that underpins the hardware of the database. The DBMS consists of several components: database engine, query processor, schema manager, and possibly a data dictionary and form and report managers.

We next examined the factors, such as scale and performance, that would be considered in choosing a database for a particular application. The DBMS systems that are used in this text as the main exemplars and teaching vehicles (Access, Oracle and MySQL) were briefly described.

Next, we considered the significant factors in the design of database tables. This involved a study of common datatypes provided by DBMSs, such as text, numeric, etc. The potential benefits of disregarding conventional advice about normalisation and redundancy was introduced as a possible way of improving performance at the (minimal) risk of incurring processing anomalies. The nature and benefits of indexing was explained, showing that, although it is not a theoretical feature of a relational database, it is nevertheless indispensable from a performance viewpoint.

Review questions

1 Outline the role of the database engine.

2 Distinguish between an active and a passive data dictionary.

3 Identify the benefits of using indexes.

4 Identify the main factors to be considered when choosing a database product for a proposed new application.

5 What datatype would be the best choice for:

   a) an amount of money?

   b) quantity of televisions in stock?

   c) the dimensions of molecules?

6 Can you suggest conditions within which a limited denormalisation might be acceptable?

7 It was stated earlier that to end-users the set of forms supporting a database application 'is' the database. Explain what is meant by this statement.

8 Why is it advantageous that each form within an application system has a consistent appearance and uses similar functionality?

9 What is meant by saying that indexes are an 'implementation feature' and not a theoretical feature of relational databases?

Exercises

1 Explain what is meant by a database management system (DBMS) and outline the main functions that a DBMS performs.

2 Describe the facilities you would expect to find in a DBMS for the production of forms, reports and indexes.

3 In what respects is the use of validation less satisfactory than datatypes as a means of preventing the input of invalid data?

4 Using the example datatype descriptions given in the chapter, we can see that a long integer datatype and the single precision floating point datatype both use four bytes. Compare the range of values and contrast the applications of the two types.

5 a) In a sales order processing system, information on orders received is entered into a database using principally two tables, namely, an Order table and an Order Item table. There is one row per order in the Order table and the Order Item table has several rows per order, i.e. one row per product within the order. Within the Order Item rows, the Product Description and Product Price

(obtained from the Product table) is stored in each row. This facilitates the production of invoices without reference to the Product table. The format of these tables is shown below:

Order Table

Order No	Customer No	Order Date	Total Order Value

Order Item Table

Order No	Product No	Product Description	Product Price	Quantity

b) Within this scenario, indicate where and how the tables do not conform to rules of normalisation. For each such case, discuss the merits of the case in terms of potential benefits compared with the disadvantages.

6　Using the table shown in Table 4.10, show the order of the rows of the table indicated by the following indexes:

a) Product Code, Branch

b) Branch, Product Code

c) Branch, Sales Value

Product Code	Branch	Total Sales
B342	North	350
C100	South	100
C100	North	250
E501	North	400
B342	South	300
E501	South	150

TABLE 4.10 Exercise 6 Chapter 4

d) Why would it be inefficient to create two indexes, Product Code and Product Code, Branch, for this table?

References

Textbooks

There are vast numbers of books on the featured database systems. Those identified here are larger, more complete references.

Oracle

Loney, K. (2004) *Oracle Database 10g: The Complete Reference*, Osborne Oracle Press.

Microsoft Access

Prague CN, Irwin MR and Reardon J, (2003) *Access 2003 Bible*, Hungry Minds.

Dubios P, (2006) *MySQL Cookbook* (second edition), O'Reilly.

Kofler M, (2005) *The Definitive Guide to MySQL 5*, Berkeley: Apress.

B-tree index

This text gives a good explanation of the theory and internals of B-tree indexes.

O'Neil P. and O'Neil E. (2004) *Database Principles, Programming and Performance* San Francisco: Morgan Kaufmann.

4

Websites

Again, a vast amount of information is available on the Internet, but it is sometimes difficult here to separate the good from the bad. The main sites for the respective database vendors are often the best.

Oracle

http://www.oracle.com/database/index.html

Microsoft Access

http://office.microsoft.com/en-us/access/default.aspx

MySQL

http://www.mysql.com/

HANDS-ON SECTION A: LEARNING SQL

Introduction

In Chapter 2 we described the concept of database querying and introduced Structured Query Language (SQL) as the most significant query language. SQL is by far the most important standard within the modern-day relational database market. It provides a measure of standardisation in an area crowded with competing and divergent technologies. A significant application of SQL in modern database usage, for example, is its role as a communication language that enables systems using different database technologies to operate successfully together. In particular, it facilitates use of client-server techniques for database access.

SQL is mostly employed within some other language system, such as C++, Visual Basic or 4GL languages (e.g. Oracle PL/SQL, Informix 4GL), or as a communication language in a client-server environment. For the purposes of learning the syntax, however, a command interpreter is ideal, and these notes will be most beneficial if the student has access to such a facility. See the section below, Implementations, for information about running SQL exercises.

This chapter provides an introductory description of the principal features of the SQL language through a series of tutorials. Accompanying the book is a set of practical exercises, available from the book's website, which are intended to provide the student with the practice essential in developing competence in the language. Both this chapter and the tutorials consist of a series of related 'sessions' to provide a convenient subdivision of the work involved in studying the language and in doing laboratory exercises. In addition, each tutorial session contains a brief resume of the SQL commands and techniques used in that section.

It should be noted that we are providing here a general introduction to the most common features and facilities of SQL, conforming as far as possible to the current SQL standard. Practical systems, such as IBM DB2 or Oracle, will typically provide a much richer set of SQL commands that are designed to manage and optimise that particular system. There are variations in the interpretation of SQL commands by the various proprietary systems; these notes have been prepared using Oracle's SQL*Plus interpreter, but reference is also made to MySQL and Microsoft Access versions of the SQL commands.

SQL is a declarative command language that enables you to perform a range of operations on relational tables. These operations are traditionally divided into three categories, as indicated below.

Data Definition Language (DDL): commands that:

- create a table
- amend a table
- specify integrity checks
- delete a table
- build an index for a table
- define a virtual table (view).

Data Manipulation Language (DML): commands that:

- query the database to show selected records
- insert, delete and update rows of the table
- control transactions when updating a database.

Data Control Language (DCL): commands that:

- control access rights to parts of the database.

We will cover most of these operations in this chapter, starting with DML, since this contains the most frequently used commands and presents the most complex problems for the student. A very simple database application is employed in order to provide a basis for the SQL tutorials. This application is described in the next section.

Scenario

The narrative in this section and the tutorials are based on the simple set of tables described below. They describe personnel within a company that has a number of separate branches. Employee information is held in the table Employee; a separate related table, Branch, contains information on company branches. Interpretation of the tables is quite straightforward and requires only a few points of clarification:

1 The two tables are related by means of the foreign key BranchCode column in the Employee table referencing the primary key of the Branch table.

2 The 'departments' exist within the branches; i.e. the sales department for Branch 01 is different from the sales department of Branch 02.

3 The Supervisor column refers to the employee id (EmpId) of the person's supervisor. In other words, the Supervisor column is a foreign key value that references the same table.

4 The Salary column holds an annual salary figure.

5 The Budget column of the Branch table is expressed in thousands of pounds.

6 The Manager column in the Branch table refers to an EmpId value in the Employee table.

The format and content of the two tables is shown below. In some instances, the headings have been edited to clarify the text.

Employee table

Name	Null?	Type
EmpId	NOT NULL	VARCHAR2(4)
Name		VARCHAR2(10)
Position		VARCHAR2(12)
HireDate		DATE
Salary		NUMBER(7,2)
BR	NOT NULL	VARCHAR2(2)
Department		VARCHAR2(10)
Supervisor		VARCHAR2(4)

EMPID	NAME	POSITION	HIREDATE	SALARY	BR	DEPARTMENT	SUPERVISOR
1001	Kennedy	Director	16-JAN-94	50 000	01		
1045	Smith	Salesman	12-MAY-05	18 000	04	Sales	3 691
1271	Stewart	Clerk	30-APR-91	16 000	03	Accounts	3 255
1534	Bell	Supervisor	28-NOV-95	20 000	01	Admin	3 876
1653	Walker	Secretary	03-AUG-97	15 500	04	Admin	3 876
2244	Chung	Programmer	09-APR-06	21 500	01	Technical	7 663
2906	Stein	Supervisor	04-FEB-89	15 500	03	Sales	
3198	Roxburgh	Salesman	21-SEP-89	20 000	01	Sales	3 255
3255	Young	Chief Accnt	19-MAR-92	30 000	01	Accounts	1 001
3691	Adams	Supervisor	01-OCT-96	23 000	04	Sales	4 206
3876	Hill	Administrator	27-JAN-00	27 000	04	Admin	
4102	Monaghan	Clerk	13-JUN-99	17 000	02	Admin	4 206
4206	Gomatam	Senior Salesman	23-JUL-97	31 000	02	Sales	
4218	Cohen	Engineer	25-AUG-92	21 000	04	Technical	
4936	Moore	Salesman	30-JUN-95	19 500	02	Sales	4 206
5833	Bradley	Technician	08-SEP-98	14 500	03	Technical	7 663
6223	Hamilton	Accountant	21-FEB-88	20 000	01	Accounts	3 255
7663	Newman	Engineer	15-AUG-92	28 000	03	Technical	
8253	Evans	Salesman	13-JUN-93	17 500	02	Sales	4 206
9743	Fletcher	Chief Clerk	29-OCT-91	18 000	03	Accounts	3 255
9773	Nicholson	Accountant	09-JUL-90	15 000	04	Accounts	3 255

Branch table

Name	Null?	Type
BranchCode	NOT NULL	VARCHAR2(2)
BranchName		VARCHAR2(10)
City		VARCHAR2(12)
Manager		VARCHAR2(4)
Budget		NUMBER(9,2)

BR	BRANCHNAME	CITY	MANA	BUDGET
01	South	London	1001	300
02	West	Liverpool	4206	250
03	East	York	7663	350
04	North	Aberdeen	3876	200
05	Europe	Paris		

Implementations

Like all programming languages, SQL is best learned by doing plenty of practical exercises. Most people learning SQL find that, at least to begin with, the declarative nature of SQL makes the composition of the queries much easier than writing procedural programs. However, as the complexity of the queries grows, SQL can become quite challenging. To learn SQL properly requires practical experience using a DBMS with a suitable interpreter. In this section we provide some guidance for achieving this. The tutorials have been prepared using the Oracle 10g SQL*Plus interpreter (which is a simple text-based interface) but, with a few provisos they can be used equally well with other systems. Some graphical interface systems are available which can potentially make the development and test process more convenient. Specifically, the systems considered are:

- Oracle SQL*Plus text interface and Oracle 10g Express Edition
- MySQL console text interface and MySQL Query Browser
- Microsoft Access.

Oracle

The tutorial notes have been prepared using the SQL*Plus interpreter. This comes with all versions of Oracle and is a simple text-based interface. It provides a simple editing facility using an external editor. The Express Edition of Oracle 10g contains a useful development environment that facilitates creation of tables, indexes etc. and the testing of queries. Figure HOA.1 shows an example of a query being executed in this environment.

FIGURE HOA.1 Oracle express edition interface

For academic use, Oracle 10g is available for free download from http://www.oracle.com/technology/software/products/database/oracle10g/index.html.

MySQL

MySQL is obtainable free from the website at http:www.mysql.org. There will typically be a number of versions, such as the current 'generally available' edition and other alpha and beta releases. The generally available release is normally the best choice unless you particularly want to use a new feature of a later edition.

MySQL also provides a basic 'command line' interface and a graphical environment. The latter is illustrated in Figure HOA.2.

FIGURE HOA.2 MySQL query browser

Microsoft Access

Although the main query system of Access is the QBE-style grid, Access supports the use of SQL. Indeed, queries are stored internally by Access in SQL. This indicates the equivalence of SQL and the QBE version; in fact, SQL is a superset of QBE, since it supports all QBE queries but also provides the CREATE and the UNION commands.

However, as a learning environment for SQL, Access is somewhat less convenient than the other options. While it is straightforward to enter and test a query, Access will often reformat the query so that it may appear different from the version entered. For instance, it will add full qualification of table names and additional bracketing. However, this does not prevent successful use of Access for SQL learning.

SQL implementation differences

We have provided some general notes below on the differences between Oracle and the other two implementations that are important in relation to this section. Note that we are using only a very small subset of the features of these SQL implementations, sufficient to cover the tutorials; for more details, consult the relevant website for the implementations. See the references at the end of the chapter.

Main differences in MySQL

The vast majority of the queries formulated for Oracle in this chapter will work unchanged using MySQL. The main differences in terms of identifiers, datatypes and functions are detailed below.

Identifiers

Identifiers are constructed in a similar way to Oracle (i.e. can consist of letters, digits and underscores and start with a letter) except that they are limited to 18 characters in length and embedded spaces are not allowed.

Datatypes

Numerical data

Numerical data is specified in a wide range of types, conforming to the SQL standard; most common are fixed point types DECIMAL and NUMERIC, which are synonymous. These are similar to Oracle's NUMBER. The scale and precision of the value can be specified in parentheses; e.g.:

- DECIMAL(6,2) holds values from $-9\,999.99$ to $+9\,999.99$.

- INT is commonly used for integer values; e.g. INT(4) holds a positive or negative integer value with maximum value of 9 999.

- FLOAT and DOUBLE are available for single and double precision floating-point values.

Character data

Character data generally uses the VARCHAR datatype rather than VARCHAR2.

Date/time

Dates are very difficult to manage in a database system due to the complexities of representation, the need to handle time as well as date, time zones, etc. In these notes, the use of dates is very limited in the interest of simplicity in this introductory text.

The DATE datatype is used as in Oracle. However, the 'input' date format is the SQL standard YYYY-MM-DD. Hence, entering dates in formats such as 23-Mar-07 or 23/3/07 is not allowed, although some latitude is available: YY-MM-DD or YYYY/MM/DD or YY/MM/DD are acceptable on input; note that they are stored in the standard form. Also, single digit M or D is allowed, for example 2007–5–9. Internally, date/time is stored as a numeric string of the format YYYYMMDDHHMMSS.

Functions

Numerical

ROUND, ABS, POWER, SQRT are all the same as Oracle.

Character

1 LOWER, UPPER, LPAD, RPAD, LTRIM and RTRIM works in a similar fashion to Oracle.

2 The LIKE operator uses the same wildcard codes; i.e. % indicates any number and _ (underscore) indicates one character position.

3 LENGTH(String) returns the length of a string, same as Oracle. Note that MySQL returns the number of *bytes* in a multi-byte character (e.g. Unicode) sentance case: 'Unicode', not the number of characters. CHAR_LENGTH always gives the number of characters.

4 CONCAT(S1, S2, S3, . . .). Concatenates a series of values indicated by the parameters. MySQL's CONCAT function can have one or more parameters. In Oracle it has two only.

5 The || compound symbol is also available in Oracle to specify concatenation; e.g. 'ABC' || 'DEF' returns the value ABCDEF. In MySQL, by default, || represents the logical OR operator. However, this behaviour may be changed by applying a 'server SQL mode' so that it becomes the more generally acceptable Oracle version. MySQL server modes are used to configure certain aspects of how the server executes SQL statements. In particular, the concatenation behaviour by the 'ANSI' mode; this can be set by means of configuration statements, the startup command or at run-time by the command SET sql_mode = 'ANSI';

Date/time

There is considerable variation in the facilities provided to handle dates. MySQL provides dozens of date/time functions, so that anything possible in Oracle will certainly be possible with MySQL, but there is likely to be variations in the function design.

SYSDATE, which returns the current date and time, operates in a similar way in Oracle and MySQL. Note that in Oracle SYSDATE is not a function, but a 'pseudo-column'; i.e. a value provided by the Oracle server which can be used as if it was a defined column. The main implication of this is that it does not use parameter brackets: SYSDATE but not SYSDATE(). Simple date arithmetic also works with dates in both systems; e.g. in MySQL, SYSDATE() +7.

Oracle function	MySQL function	Description
ADD_MONTHS(*date*, *num*)	DATE_ADD(*date*, INTERVAL *num* MONTH). See Note 1.	Returns a date obtained by adding *num* months to *date*
MONTHS_BETWEEN (*date2 – date1*)	There is no direct equivalent of this function. An approximate value can be obtained by using DATE_DIFF. See Note 2.	Returns a *number* equal to the months between *date1* and *date2*.
LAST_DAY(date)	Same as Oracle	Returns the date of the last day of the month of the given *date*.
TO_CHAR(date, 'format')	DATE_FORMAT(date, 'format'). See Note 3.	Returns a *text* value obtained by formatting the given date to the pattern specified by format.

TABLE HOA.1 Comparison of functions in Oracle and MySQL

NOTES

Note 1 This shows just one illustration of the DATE_ADD function. The INTERVAL can be DAY, WEEK, HOUR, MINUTE etc. – indeed just about any interval you might require.

Note 2 The DATE_DIFF(*d1*, *d2*) function takes two date values, parameters d1 and d2, and returns the difference in days between these. If this value is then divided by 30.3 (approximate average days per month) a reasonable approximation can be obtained.

The PERIOD_DIFF (*p1*, *p2*) function returns the number of months between two 'dates' specified by p1 and p2. However, the parameters are not of date type, but are numerical or string values.

Note 3 The structure of these functions is similar, but the details of the 'format' parameters are totally different. The websites of the respective suppliers should be consulted for the details – see under References at the end of the Hands-On section.

Main differences in Access

An important factor to note with respect to Access is that Access holds metadata that is not supplied to or accessible by SQL. For instance, the table design facility enables the specification of format information that might be supplied within an SQL command in Oracle and MySQL. Details that would be supplied by a CREATE TABLE command in SQL would usually be provided in the graphical table design interface in Access. Difference are described in terms of identifiers, datatypes and functions.

Identifiers

Identifiers are constructed in a similar way to Oracle (i.e. consist of letters, digits and underscores and start with a letter) except that they are limited to 64 characters in length and identifiers with embedded spaces must be enclosed in square brackets.

Datatypes

Numerical data

Numerical data is specified by the NUMBER datatype. The detailed format such as integer/real and the number of decimal places is generally entered using the table design interface. However, a full range of numeric types is provided.

Character data

Character fields are specified with the TEXT datatype. The table design facility also permits control of input and output formats and constraints.

Date/time

Date and time fields are defined by the DATE datatype. The table design facility also permits control of input and output formats and constraints.

Functions

Numerical

ROUND() and ABS() are same as Oracle.

POWER() is not available, but Access allows use of the exponentiation operator $\wedge$. For instance: Length $\wedge$ 2.

The Access function SQR() corresponds to the Oracle SQRT().

Character

The Access character functions are somewhat different from Oracle; they are described and compared below.

    1   UCASE is used to change the case to upper as in Oracle UPPER. Similarly, LCASE is used to change to lower.

2 LEN corresponds to Oracle LENGTH.

3 MID corresponds to Oracle SUBSTR. Access also provide functions LEFT and RIGHT which respectively return a sub-string starting on the first character or ending on the last character. For instance, LEFT('database', 4) would return the string 'data'.

4 LTRIM and RTRIM are the same as Oracle.

5 The concatenation operator is the ampersand &, corresponding to the Oracle ||.

Date/time

The following table summarises the main features of Access date functions and their relationship with the Oracle version.

Oracle	Access	Description
ADD_MONTHS	DATEADD	Add months to a date Oracle: Add_Months('21-Feb-07', +3) Access: DateAdd('m',2, #21-Feb-07#) both give 21-Apr-07 See also note below.
MONTHS_BETWEEN	DATEDIFF	Number of months between two dates. Months_between('1-Jan-07', '1-Aug-07') DateDiff('m', #1-Jan-07#, #1-Aug-07#) both give 7. See also note below.
SYSDATE	NOW()	Today's date
LAST_DAY	No simple method.	Date of last day of month (of param date) Last_day('14-Jan-07') is 31-Jan-07 Last_day(Sysdate) is date of last day in current month.

TABLE HOA.2 Comparison of functions in Oracle and Access

NOTES

The # symbol is used in specifying date-literal values as shown.

The Access functions DateAdd and DateDiff allow handling of other date intervals. The general formats are:

- DateAdd(interval, date, no. of intervals)
- DateDiff(interval, date1, date2)

The first parameter, the interval, can also be

yyyy	for years
m	for months
d	for days
ww	for weeks

Session 1 – Simple queries

Introduction

The most important SQL command is the SELECT command. SELECT enables you to perform queries against the database. The full SELECT command is quite elaborate, so we start with an abbreviated version that will suffice for our purposes in this session.

```
SELECT column-list FROM table-name
    [WHERE condition]
        [ORDER BY column-list]
```

To describe the format of commands within this chapter, we use a notation that helps to describe the allowable components of valid statements. Words shown in UPPER CASE are SQL reserved words that have a specific meaning in that context. Words in *italics* indicate where an entry or entries must be supplied by the user. Clauses in square brackets are optional; i.e. they provide additional functionality which may or may not be needed. Further notation conventions will be defined later.

NOTE

Although the SQL keywords such as SELECT are highlighted here in upper case, in practice SQL is insensitive to the case of keywords and user-supplied names. Literal values in single quotes, however, are *not* case insensitive and must be used consistently. See Query 1.2 below.

The SELECT command extracts rows from the table specified by *table-name*. The rows selected are defined by *condition*. The parameter *column-list* specifies the columns of the table to be shown on the output. *Column-list* can be the special value * (asterisk) that indicates that *all* columns are to be shown. *Column-list* can also contains expressions and function calls.

QUERY 1.1

Show a list of the names and positions of all employees in branch 03.

```
SQL> SELECT Name, Position FROM Employee WHERE BranchCode = '03'
```

Result:

```
NAME            POSITION
----            ----------
Stewart         Clerk
Bradley         Technician
Newman          Engineer
Fletcher        Chief Clerk
Stein           Supervisor
```

QUERY 1.2

Show all details for employees working in Admin departments.

```
SQL>  SELECT * FROM Employee WHERE Department = 'Admin'
```

Result:

EMPID	NAME	POSITION	HIREDATE	SALARY	BR	DEPARTMENT	SUPE
1534	Bell	Supervisor	28-NOV-95	2 000	01	Admin	3 876
1653	Walker	Secretary	03-AUG-87	1 550	04	Admin	3 876
3876	Hill	Administrator	27-JAN-90	2 700	04	Admin	
4102	Monaghan	Clerk	13-JUN-93	1 700	02	Admin	4 206

NOTES

Oracle uses the column names as headings but these can be truncated where the length of the column name exceeds the width of the column. For instance, in the above result, SUPERVISOR has been reduced to SUPE.

The literal value used in the condition is case sensitive so that the case of letters must match *exactly* with the table data; for instance, using . . . WHERE Department = 'ADMIN' would produce no rows in the answer. This does not apply to Access however, which ignores the case of literals.

Conditions

The WHERE clause in the SELECT command specifies a condition that each row selected must satisfy. Conditions can be expressed in a number of ways: the most common is a simple comparison of values, as used in Queries 1.1 and 1.2.

Comparative operators

The usual comparative operators are available:

=	equal to
>	greater than
<	less than
>=	greater than or equal to
<=	less than or equal to
<>	not equal to

QUERY 1.3

Show all details for employees earning more than £20 000.

```
SQL>   SELECT * FROM Employee WHERE Salary > 20000
```

Result:

EMPID	NAME	POSITION	HIREDATE	SALARY	BR	DEPARTMENT	SUPE
1001	Kennedy	Director	16-JAN-84	50 000	01		
2244	Chung	Programmer	09-APR-96	21 500	01	Technical	7 663
3255	Young	Chief accnt	19-MAR-92	30 000	01	Accounts	1 001
3691	Adams	Supervisor	01-OCT-86	23 000	04	Sales	4 206
3876	Hill	Adninistrator	27-JAN-90	27 000	04	Admin	
4206	Gomatam	Senior Salesman	23-JUL-97	31 000	02	Sales	
4218	Cohen	Engineer	25-AUG-92	21 000	04	Technical	
7663	Newman	Engineer	15-AUG-92	28 000	03	Technical	

QUERY 1.4

Show the names, hire dates and department of employees hired on or before 1st Jan 1990.

```
SQL>  SELECT Name, HireDate, Department FROM Employee
        WHERE HireDate <= '1-Jan-90'
```

Result:

```
NAME        HIREDATE     DEPARTMENT
---------   ---------    -----------
Stein       04-FEB-89    Sales
Roxburgh    21-SEP-89    Sales
Hamilton    21-FEB-88    Accounts
```

Dates can be compared, as shown by Query 1.4; earlier dates are 'less than' later dates.

Other forms of condition

BETWEEN . . . AND . . .

Range test; tests specified column for values in given range. Handy for dates.

IN (*list*)

Set membership test; tests for a value in a specified list.

IS NULL

Test for null values.

LIKE

Pattern matching test; selects values with a specified pattern, typically using wildcard characters. The wildcard character % matches zero or more characters; the wildcard character _ (underscore) matches a single character. Access uses the symbols * and? for this.

Examples of these conditions follow:

BETWEEN

QUERY 1.5

Show the names and department of employees hired between 12th March 1992 and 1st Jan 1997.

```
SQL>  SELECT Name, Department FROM Employee

        WHERE HireDate BETWEEN '12-Mar-92' AND '1-Jan-97'
```

IN

QUERY 1.6

Show all details of employees in Accounts , Sales and Technical departments.

```
SQL>  SELECT * FROM Employee

        WHERE Department IN ('Accounts' , 'Sales', 'Technical')
```

IS NULL

QUERY 1.7

Show the names and departments of employees with no assigned supervisor.

SQL> SELECT Name, Department FROM Employee WHERE Supervisor IS NULL

LIKE

QUERY 1.8

Show the names of all employees with names beginning with B.

SQL> SELECT Name FROM Employee WHERE Name LIKE 'B%'

Result:

```
NAME
------
Bell
Bradley
```

QUERY 1.9

Show the names of all employees with 5 letter names beginning with C.

SQL> SELECT Name FROM Employee WHERE Name LIKE 'C____'

The value in quotes in Query 1.9 includes four underscores.

Logical operators

Logical operators allow you to produce more elaborate conditions involving combination and negation of conditions. The available operators are:

AND   Selects rows meeting *both* specified conditions.

OR   Selects rows meeting *either* specified condition.

NOT   Negate; used with other condition tests to negate the sense of the condition. NOT can be used with any other condition format.

AND

QUERY 1.10

Show the names of all employees in the Sales department earning more than £18 000.

```
SQL>  SELECT Name, Department FROM Employee
        WHERE Department = 'Sales' AND Salary >18000
```

OR

QUERY 1.11

Show the names of all employees in Accounts and Sales departments.

```
SQL>  SELECT Name, Department FROM Employee
        WHERE Department = 'Accounts' OR Department = 'Sales'
```

Result:

NAME	DEPARTMENT
Smith	Sales
Stewart	Accounts
Young	Accounts
Adams	Sales
Gomatam	Sales
Moore	Sales
Hamilton	Accounts
Evans	Sales
Fletcher	Accounts
Stein	Sales
Roxburgh	Sales
Nicholson	Accounts

There are many traps for the unwary in the use of logical operators; particular attention should be paid to the extra notes supplied below.

NOTES

1 The above example is worthy of close study. The query above is expressed in normal English, using the 'and' connective: we want a list of all the Accounts staff and all the Sales staff. However, the correct logical definition uses the OR operator, as shown in the SQL answer.

If we expressed this as:

WHERE Department = 'Accounts' **AND** Department = 'Sales',

—SQL would be looking for rows where the Department value was equal to both 'Accounts' and 'Sales' simultaneously – clearly impossible.

2 Note that, again conflicting with English usage, we have to repeat the 'Department = . . . ' for the second comparison. That is:

WHERE Department = 'Accounts' **OR** 'Sales' is invalid.

3 Note that the IN type of query is essentially a form of OR. Use of IN instead of explicit ORs is generally neater and safer. Refer to Query 1.6 above.

NOT

QUERY 1.12

Show the names of all employees NOT in the Accounts or the Sales departments.

```
SQL>  SELECT Name, Department FROM Employee
        WHERE Department NOT IN ('Accounts', 'Sales')
```

Result:

NAME	DEPARTMENT
Bell	Admin
Walker	Admin
Chung	Technical
Hill	Admin
Monaghan	Admin
Cohen	Technical
Bradley	Technical
Newman	Technical

Multiple logical operators

You can employ two or more ANDs and/or ORs in one command.

QUERY 1.13

Show the names and salaries of all employees in the Accounts department who were hired since the beginning of 1990 and are earning less than £20 000.

```
SQL>  SELECT Name, Salary FROM Employee
        WHERE Department = 'Accounts'
        AND HireDate >= '1-Jan-90'
        AND Salary <  20000
```

NOTES

Operator precedence

1 If you use both AND and OR in one command, it is important to be aware that a rule of precedence applies, namely, that the 'ANDs' are evaluated before the 'ORs'. Failure to take this into account can produce serious errors that can be easily overlooked.

2 You can modify the effect of the default precedence by using brackets to associate conditions together. Bracketted conditions are evaluated as an independent unit (i.e. yielding either 'true' or 'false') and the result combined with the rest of the conditions.

These points are illustrated in the examples shown below.

QUERY 1.14

Show the names, department and salaries of all employees in the Accounts or Sales departments earning less than £18 000.

WRONG VERSION

```
SQL>  SELECT Name, Department, Salary FROM Employee

      WHERE Department = 'Accounts'

      OR Department = 'Sales'

      AND Salary <  18000
```

This query as it stands will select:

- all staff in Accounts (from Department = 'Accounts')
- staff in Sales earning >18 000 (from Department = 'Sales' AND Salary < 18 000)

This is not what the query asked for. The erroneous table shown below is produced. Note that it includes staff earning more than 18 000.

Result:

NAME	DEPARTMENT	SALARY
Stewart	Accounts	16 000
Stein	Sales	15 500
Young	Accounts	30 000
Hamilton	Accounts	20 000
Evans	Sales	17 500
Fletcher	Accounts	18 000
Nicholson	Accounts	15 000

QUERY 1.15

Show the names, department and salaries of all employees in the Accounts or Sales departments earning less than 18 000.

CORRECT VERSION

```
SQL>  SELECT Name, Department, Salary FROM Employee
         WHERE (Department = 'Accounts'
         OR Department = 'Sales')
         AND Salary <  18000
```

Result:

NAME	DEPARTMENT	SALARY
Stewart	Accounts	16 000
Stein	Sales	15 500
Evans	Sales	17 500
Nicholson	Accounts	15 000

ORDER BY clause

The ORDER BY clause can be used to control the sequence of output of the result. Normally the output will be produced in the physical sequence of the stored rows. If you want to see the output in some more useful sequence, the ORDER BY clause specifies a column or columns that governs the sorted output.

QUERY 1.16

Show the names and salaries of all employees in sequence of their name.

```
SQL>  SELECT Name, Salary FROM Employee ORDER BY Name
```

The ORDER BY column need not be part of the output. Also, the sequence can be reversed by use of the DESC (=descending) keyword.

QUERY 1.17

Show the names, departments and salaries of employees in the Sales department in order of salary, from greatest to smallest.

```
SQL>  SELECT Name, Department, Salary FROM Employee
         WHERE Department = 'Sales' ORDER BY Salary DESC
```

Result:

NAME	DEPARTMENT	SALARY
Gomatam	Sales	31 000
Adams	Sales	23 000
Roxburgh	Sales	20 000
Moore	Sales	19 500
Smith	Sales	18 000
Evans	Sales	17 500
Stein	Sales	15 500

It is possible to sort on multiple columns.

QUERY 1.18

Show the names, positions, BranchCode and department of all employees in sequence of name within each branch and department.

```
SQL>  SELECT Name, Position, BranchCode, Department FROM Employee
         ORDER BY BranchCode, Department, Name
```

Result:

NAME	POSITION	BR	DEPARTMENT
Hamilton	Accountant	01	Accounts
Young	Chief Accnt	01	Accounts
Bell	Supervisor	01	Admin
Roxburgh	Salesman	01	Sales
Chung	Programmer	01	Technical
Kennedy	Director	01	
Monaghan	Clerk	02	Admin
Evans	Salesman	02	Sales
Gomatam	Senior Salesman	02	Sales
Moore	Salesman	02	Sales
Fletcher	Chief Clerk	03	Accounts
Stewart	Clerk	03	Accounts

Stein	Supervisor	03	Sales
Bradley	Technician	03	Technical
Newman	Engineer	03	Technical
Nicholson	Accountant	04	Accounts
Hill	Administrator	04	Admin
Walker	Secretary	04	Admin
Adams	Supervisor	04	Sales
Smith	Salesman	04	Sales
Cohen	Engineer	04	Technical

NOTES

1 Note that the ORDER BY columns are listed in 'major' to 'minor' sequence; i.e. the BranchCodes (major sequence) are in sequence, within each branch the departments are in sequence, and finally within each Department the names are in sequence.

2 If two or more columns are used in the ORDER BY clause, it makes no sense to use a column that has unique (or almost unique) values as a major sequence key. For instance, in the clause:

   ... ORDER BY EmpId, Department

   the 'Department' component is redundant, since EmpId values on every row are all distinct.

Set operations

If the result of individual SELECT queries is viewed as a set of values it is possible to combine such sets using operators based on relational algebra. As in other parts of SQL, there is some divergence between the standard and the various implementations. The SQL/92 standard defines UNION, INTERSECT and EXCEPT; some systems only support UNION, which is the most useful. In these notes we describe the most common Oracle operator, namely the UNION.

The operators described here are subject to the restriction that the two operands (i.e. the output from the component SELECTs) must be identical in structure – i.e. they have the same number of columns and corresponding columns are of the same type. This restriction arises from the nature of the set operations, which are only defined for identically structured relations.

UNION

The UNION operator combines the results of two queries; the rows of the first query and the second query are 'ORed' together into one relation.

QUERY 1.19

Show the names, branches and departments of employees who are in branch 02 or who earn at least 20 000.

```
SQL>  SELECT Name, BranchCode, Department, Salary FROM Employee
      WHERE BranchCode = '02'
      UNION
      SELECT Name, BranchCode, Department, Salary FROM Employee
      WHERE Salary >= 20000
```

Result:

NAME	BR	DEPARTMENT	SALARY
Adams	04	Sales	23 000
Bell	01	Admin	20 000
Chung	01	Technical	21 500
Cohen	04	Technical	21 000
Evans	02	Sales	17 500
Gomatam	02	Sales	31 000
Hamilton	01	Accounts	20 000
Hill	04	Admin	27 000
Kennedy	01		50 000
Monaghan	02	Admin	17 000
Moore	02	Sales	19 500
Newman	03	Technical	28 000
Roxburgh	01	Sales	20 000
Young	01	Accounts	30 000

The trained eye will notice that the same result could be obtained more simply using the condition:

```
WHERE BranchCode = '02' OR Salary > 20000
```

Accordingly, the UNION operator would not be used in this fashion. However, if the SELECTs referred to different tables or to queries, a UNION would be necessary.

The following query is a somewhat contrived example, using the Employee and Branch tables.

QUERY 1.20

Show the BranchCode of employees who earn more than 25 000 and the branches with a budget greater than 6 000.

```
SQL>  SELECT BranchCode FROM Employee

      WHERE Salary > 25000

      UNION

      SELECT BranchCode FROM Branch

      WHERE Budget > 6000
```

Result:

```
BRANCH
------
01
02
03
04
```

The resultant relations from the two SELECTs have the same structure (a single column called BranchCode) and hence can be 'UNIONed'.

NOTE

The two component queries could potentially yield the same row; the action of SQL in this instance is to eliminate duplicate rows from the answer. If you really want to preserve duplicate rows you can change the operator to UNION ALL.

Session 2 – Calculations and functions

Calculations

In addition to columns from database tables, an SQL query can also refer to values calculated by arithmetic expressions and by the application of functions. The expressions use the basic arithmetic operators found in programming languages, namely + − / (divide) and * (multiply).

The *column-list* in the SELECT command can include arithmetic expressions:

QUERY 2.1

Show the names and monthly salaries of all employees in the Sales department. (Note: the Salary column stores annual values).

```
SQL>  SELECT Name, Salary/12 FROM Employee

        WHERE Department = 'Sales'
```

Result:

```
NAME              SALARY/12
---------         ----------
Smith                  1500
Stein             1 291.6667
Roxburgh          1 666.6667
Adams             1 916.6667
Gomatam           2 583.3333
Moore                  1625
Evans             1 458.3333
```

The display of decimal places can be controlled by the use of functions. These are described shortly.

The WHERE clause can also use expressions:

QUERY 2.2

Show the names of all employees whose monthly Salary exceeds 2 000 by more than 100.

```
SQL>  SELECT Name, Salary FROM Employee WHERE Salary/12 - 100 > 2000
```

Result:

```
NAME              SALARY
--------          ------
Kennedy           50 000
Hill              27 000
Young             30 000
Gomatam           31 000
Newman            28 000
```

NOTE

The usual precedence of arithmetic operators applies: multiplication and division are done first, then addition and subtraction. The precedence can be altered by the use of brackets.

QUERY 2.3

The annual salaries of all Technical employees are to be increased by £400 this month plus a further 5% next month. Show the names and new annual salaries.

```
SQL>  SELECT Name, (Salary+400) * 1.05 FROM Employee
         WHERE Department = 'Technical'
```

Result:

```
NAME               (SALARY+400)*1.05
--------           -------------------
Chung                     22 995
Bradley                   15 645
Newman                    29 820
Cohen                     22 470
```

NOTE

Date columns can be computed arithmetically. If you add a number *d* to a date it produces a new date *d* days after the specified date. Subtraction works similarly. If you subtract two date values, the result is the number of days between these dates.

Functions

A **function** is a program module that accepts zero or more input values and produces a *single value* answer. The input values are called the **parameters** of the function. A function is called by using the function name as a value; this value will be of some type, i.e. numeric, text, date etc. The general function call format is *function-name(parameter-list)*. All this will become clearer when we have tried a few examples.

> **NOTE**
>
> SQL standards specify a number of 'built-in' functions, but individual implementations such as Oracle, DB2 etc. appear only to conform to these rather loosely. The same functionality is often provided, but with altered syntax and with many extensions.
>
> The examples provided here are just that; they illustrate how functions are used and the general range of facilities available. The reference manuals should be consulted for the system you are using to determine the functions available for that system.

Numeric functions

These are functions that operate on numeric data items.

The ROUND function rounds a data item to the nearest value having a specified number of decimal places. For instance, to round a column *Amount* to two decimal places, we would use the expression ROUND(Amount, 2). The items in the brackets are parameters; they are the 'input' values to the function.

> **QUERY 2.4**
>
> Show the weekly salary of employee Smith, unrounded and rounded to two decimal places.
>
> ```
> SQL>  SELECT Salary / 52, ROUND(Salary / 52, 2) FROM Employee
>
>          WHERE Name = 'Smith'
> ```

Result:

```
SALARY/52          ROUND(SALARY/52,2)
----------         ------------------
346.15385          346.15
```

In query 2.4, the parameters of ROUND are Salary /52 and 2.

Other common numeric functions are

ABS(*A*)   returns the 'positive' value of *A*, regardless of whether *A* is positive or negative.

POWER(*A*, *n*)   returns the value *A* to the power *n*.

Another large group of numeric functions is available that operate on groups of rows (instead of single rows). These are described later when the SQL language elements dealing with groups are covered.

Character functions

These functions operate on text data items. The most common of these are described below:

UPPER(T)	converts the text item T to upper case.
LENGTH(T)	returns the length (in characters) of the text item T. Note that the input to this function is character but the return value is numeric.
LTRIM(T, 'c')	Removes leading 'c' characters from the text item T. This would most frequently be applied to the removal of leading spaces in text fields.
RTRIM(T, 'c')	as for LTRIM but for *trailing* characters.
SUBSTR(T, *start*, *len*)	extracts *len* characters from text T starting at Position *start*.

Examples:

QUERY 2.5

List the department names in upper case characters.

SQL> SELECT DISTINCT UPPER(Department) FROM Employee

Result:

```
UPPER(DEPARTMENT)
-----------------
ACCOUNTS
ADMIN
SALES
TECHNICAL
```

NOTE

The DISTINCT keyword causes SQL to suppress the output of duplicate values; if this was not done there would be a result row produced for every row of the table.

QUERY 2.6

List the names of employees whose names are longer than six characters.

SQL> SELECT Name FROM Employee WHERE LENGTH(Name) > 6

Result:

```
NAME
---------
Kennedy
Stewart
Gomatam
Bradley
Hamilton
Fletcher
Roxburgh
Monaghan
Nicholson
```

> **NOTE**
>
> The operation of the LENGTH function is dependent on the implementation of the column datatype. Some CHAR(n) types actually define a fixed-width column, such that the LENGTH function would return the maximum value (n) regardless of the content of the column.

QUERY 2.6a

List the names of employees whose names are longer than six characters and truncate to six characters.

SQL> SELECT SUBSTR(Name,1,6) FROM Employee WHERE LENGTH(Name) > 6

Result:

```
NAME
-------
Kenned
Stewar
Gomata
Bradle
Hamilt
Fletch
Roxbur
Monagh
Nichol
```

Date functions

Handling of dates is the most implementation-dependent area of SQL. Systems differ in the range of date formats they support and hence in the behaviour of date functions. Presented here are a small selection of the date functions provided by Oracle SQL; other systems will generally offer comparable facilities.

ADD_MONTHS(*date, num*)	Returns a date obtained by adding *num* months to *date*.
MONTHS_BETWEEN(*date2 – date1*)	Returns a *number* equal to the months between *date1* and *date2*.
LAST_DAY(*date*)	Returns the date of the last day of the current month.
TO_CHAR(*date, 'format'*)	Returns a *text* value obtained by formatting the given *date* to the pattern specified by *format*.

Some way of representing today's date is also necessary in the context of date handling; the SQL standard suggests a parameter-less function called CURRENT_DATE. The Oracle version is the global variable SYSDATE.

Examples:

QUERY 2.7

Calculate the number of months that Smith has been employed.

```
SQL>  SELECT MONTHS_BETWEEN(SYSDATE, HireDate) FROM Employee
      WHERE Name = 'Smith'
```

NOTE

The answer to Query 2.7 yields a column heading directly obtained from the SELECT item. You can output 'tidier' headings by using an **alias column name**. An alias is specified simply by providing a name after the SELECT item. If aliases are supplied, these are used as the column headings. We can restate Query 2.7 as follows, using an alias of MONTHS.

QUERY 2.7a

Calculate the number of months that Smith has been employed.

```
SQL>  SELECT MONTHS_BETWEEN(SYSDATE, HireDate) MONTHS FROM Employee
      WHERE Name = 'Smith'
```

Result:

```
MONTHS
---------
49.859547
```

QUERY 2.8

Calculate, to the nearest whole number, the number of months that Smith has been employed.

```
SQL>    SELECT ROUND(MONTHS_BETWEEN(SYSDATE, HireDate) ) MONTHS
        FROM Employee WHERE Name = 'Smith'
```

Result:

```
MONTHS
------
50
```

Date operations are very implementation-dependent. The Oracle TO_CHAR function is a case in point. The format string specifies a wide range of date representations usable in the Oracle system. Examples of format strings are shown below. The examples assume an SQL statement of the form:

SELECT TO_CHAR(HireDate, *'format-string'*) FROM Employee

Format String	Result
DD/MM/YY	27/01/97
Dy DD Month, YYYY	Mon 27 January, 1997
Day "the" ddth "of" Month	Monday the 27th of January
Day Mon YYYY	27 Jan 1997

TABLE HOA.3 Format strings and their results

NOTE

If you are experimenting with date functions (or indeed any functions) it is convenient to be able to output single item answers without reference to an real table. However, the SELECT syntax insists that a 'FROM *table*' clause be used. The way round this is to use a 'dummy' table that has only one row and one column with meaningless content. Oracle SQL provides a special table for this purpose called (rather mysteriously) DUAL, but you could define your own table if your system does not provide one. You could use DUAL like this:

SELECT TO_CHAR(SYSDATE, 'DD/MM/YY') FROM DUAL

This will produce a single value equal to today's date.

Other functions

A number of other functions are often available that work with a range of datatypes. These include:

GREATEST(*A*, *B*, . . .)   Returns the 'largest' of the parameter values; these can be of any datatype, but all values after the first are automatically converted (if possible) to the type of the first.

LEAST(*A*, *B*, . . .)   Similar to GREATEST but selecting the smallest.

NVL(*A*, *B*)   Null Value Conversion. If *A* is null, this function returns the value *B* else the value *A* is returned. This function is used to express a null value in a more meaningful manner.

Examples:

QUERY 2.9

Show the greater of Smith's salary and £17 000.

```
SQL>  SELECT GREATEST(Salary, 17000) FROM Employee
        WHERE Name = 'Smith'
```

Result:

```
GREATEST(SALARY,17 000)
-----------------------
18 000
```

QUERY 2.10

List the name of each employee in the Sales department together with their supervisor's number. If no supervisor code is present (i.e. it is null), output 'NONE'.

```
SQL>  SELECT Name, NVL(Supervisor, 'NONE') Supervisor FROM Employee
        WHERE Department = 'Sales'
```

Result:

```
NAME              Supervisor
--------          ----------
Smith             3691
Adams             4206
Gomatam           NONE
Moore             4206
Evans             4206
Stein             NONE
Roxburgh          3255
```

Session 3 – Groups and group functions

Introduction

The queries and functions we have covered to date all deal with the individual rows of a table. Another important aspect of queries is to derive information about the characteristics of *groups* of rows. For example, you might want to know the average of the salaries in the Employee table. This query, by its nature, produces a *single answer* for the whole group of rows being examined.

For the 'average Salary' query suggested above, the 'group' is the whole table. However, we may wish to subdivide the table into smaller groups, based on commonality of some attribute. For instance, we may want to know the average Salary for each of the departments. In this case, we form sub-groups of rows, each member of each group having a common department name. The salary query would now yield *n* rows in the output, where *n* is the number of departments.

These ideas will become clearer when we deal with specific examples later in this session. However, be warned that group queries can often be quite difficult to understand and formulate, so it is important that the underlying concepts be well understood before attempting complex queries.

Group functions

The list below shows the most common of the group functions. The parameter N in these functions must be the name of a numeric column.

AVG(N)   Returns the average of the values in column N of the group.

COUNT(A)   Counts the number of rows in the group. If the value in column A is null, that row is not counted. If A is *, all rows are counted.

MAX/MIN(A)   Returns the largest/smallest of the values in column A of the group.

SUM(N)   Returns the total of all values in column N of the group.

STDDEV(N)   Returns the standard deviation of all values in column N of the group.

VARIANCE(N)   Returns the variance of all values in column N of the group.

The following examples show the use of group functions applied to the 'whole table'. This does not prevent us from being selective about the rows being examined. That is, we can still use the WHERE clause. We provide only a limited number of examples at this stage; it becomes more interesting when we deal with sub-groups of the table.

Examples:

QUERY 3.1

Calculate the average salary and total salary of all employees.

```
SQL>  SELECT AVG(Salary), SUM(Salary) FROM Employee
```

Result:

```
AVG(SALARY)   SUM(SALARY)
-----------   -----------
21 809.524    58 000
```

NOTE

There is only one line in the answer because we are treating the whole table as one group. It would be incorrect to try to refer to any column names in this query; for instance:

```
SQL>  SELECT Name, AVG(Salary), SUM(Salary) FROM Employee
```

This is invalid (try it) because if we use a group function such as AVG or SUM we are committed to working with a group, not individual rows.

QUERY 3.2

Output the number of employees in the company.

SQL> SELECT COUNT(*) FROM Employee

Result:

```
COUNT(*)
--------
21
```

The * parameter in the COUNT statement causes *all* rows to be counted. Compare this with the next query:

QUERY 3.3

Output the number of employees in the company.

SQL> SELECT COUNT(Department) FROM Employee

Result:

```
COUNT(DEPARTMENT)
-----------------
20
```

One missing! When the COUNT parameter is a column name, null values in this column are not counted. In this instance, the Director has a null in the Department column.

We can apply a WHERE clause in conjunction with group functions; this simply filters the table, excluding rows from examination that do not meet the condition.

QUERY 3.4

Find out the highest salary in any Sales department.

SQL> SELECT MAX(Salary) FROM Employee WHERE Department = 'Sales'

Result:

```
MAX(SALARY)
-----------
31 000
```

GROUP BY clause

Query 3.1, we obtained the average salary for the whole company. Suppose now that we wanted to obtain the average salary for each department. We could of course simply do each department in turn:

> SELECT AVG(Salary) FROM Employee WHERE Department = 'Sales'

> SELECT AVG(Salary) FROM Employee WHERE Department = 'Accounts' . . . etc

However this is rather laborious.

A better way is to use the GROUP BY clause. This clause notionally subdivides the table into groups based on a nominated column or columns. Members of each group have the same value of the nominated column.

Examples:

QUERY 3.5

Find out the highest salary in each Department.

SQL>   SELECT Department, MAX(Salary) FROM Employee GROUP BY Department

Result:

```
DEPARTMENT    MAX(SALARY)
----------    -----------
Accounts      30 000
Admin         27 000
Sales         31 000
Technical     28 000
              50 000
```

Here our nominated GROUP BY column is 'Department' so that the rows of the table are notionally organised into groups, one group per department. Note that the result has one row per group. Note also that we can output the department name in the query because this is the 'grouping' column; i.e. the department is constant within each group. A full listing of the table divided into these groups will help in understanding all of this. For this we use the instruction:

SQL>   SELECT Name, Department, Salary FROM Employee ORDER BY Department

Result:

NAME	DEPARTMENT	SALARY	
Stewart	Accounts	16 000	
Young	Accounts	30 000	<- maximum for Accounts
Fletcher	Accounts	18 000	
Nicholson	Accounts	15 000	
Hamilton	Accounts	20 000	
Bell	Admin	20 000	
Monaghan	Admin	17 000	
Hill	Admin	27 000	<- maximum for Admin
Walker	Admin	15 500	
Smith	Sales	18 000	
Moore	Sales	19 500	
Roxburgh	Sales	20 000	
Stein	Sales	15 500	
Evans	Sales	17 500	
Adams	Sales	23 000	
Gomatam	Sales	31 000	<- maximum for Sales
Chung	Technical	21 500	
Newman	Technical	28 000	<- maximum for Technical
Bradley	Technical	14 500	
Cohen	Technical	21 000	
Kennedy		50 000	

The most important point to note when working with the GROUP BY clause is that we are dealing with the characteristics of the *groups* and not the individual *rows*. To be specific, when we use the GROUP BY clause, the data that we can select (i.e. items in the SELECT list) must be one of the following:

1 A column (or columns) value that is *constant* within the group; this must be the GROUP BY column(s). Note that if more than one GROUP BY column is used, any individual column may be output.

2 A value computed over the whole group; i.e. aggregate functions such as AVG, SUM, COUNT.

3 Expressions involving combinations of the above.

As an example of the pitfalls that you can fall into in this area, we might be tempted to extend Query 3.4 to supply the name of the person with the highest salary:

QUERY 3.6

Find the name and salary of the employee with the highest salary each department.

```
SQL>    SELECT Name, MAX(Salary) FROM Employee GROUP BY Department
```

Result:

This is wrong: Oracle produces the following error message:

```
SELECT Name, MAX(Salary) FROM Employee GROUP BY Department
       *
ERROR at line 1:
ORA-00979: not a GROUP BY expression
```

This query produces an error because Name does not conform to any of the above categories of allowable items, although the 'sense' of the query is arguably clear. This query can be answered, but not this way – it requires a **subquery**. Subqueries are described in Session 5.

If you think about it, the GROUP BY rules are quite reasonable, since they emerge purely from the nature of forming groups. However, in some situations they appear to be over-restrictive. In particular, SQL takes no account of functional dependencies within the tables. We will return to this point later after table joining has been covered, since a suitable example requires that two or more tables be involved.

HAVING clause

The WHERE clause is used to select or reject specific *rows* that participate in a normal query; in a similar fashion, the HAVING clause is used to select or reject *groups* involved in a GROUP BY query. The syntax of the HAVING clause is similar to WHERE, in terms of the use of comparative operators, etc.; however, expressions in a HAVING condition are subject to the same restrictions as discussed above for the SELECT list. That is, the HAVING clause condition can only involve the three classes of data listed in the previous section.

Examples:

QUERY 3.7

List branches with more than five employees.

```
SQL>    SELECT BranchCode, COUNT(*) FROM Employee

        GROUP BY BranchCode

        HAVING COUNT(*) > 5
```

Result:

```
BRANCH  COUNT(*)
------  -------
01      6
04      6
```

QUERY 3.8

List the branch departments whose highest salaries exceeds £22 000.

```
SQL>    SELECT BranchCode, Department, MAX(Salary) FROM Employee
        GROUP BY BranchCode, Department
        HAVING MAX(Salary) > 22000
```

Result:

BR	DEPARTMENT	MAX(SALARY)
01	Accounts	30 000
01		50 000
02	Sales	31 000
03	Technical	28 000
04	Admin	27 000
04	Sales	23 000

Session 4 – Joining tables

Introduction

In the preceding sessions we have used only one of the tables (the Employee table) defined at the start. In this section we enrich our SQL experience considerably by introducing the Branch table into our queries.

The theory and the process of joining tables was covered in Chapter 2; to recap, relational databases use tables to represent entities and relationships within the application domain. To satisfy queries against the database, tables have to be 'joined'; i.e. a new table is formed by uniting columns drawn from the component tables of the database.

Tables are joined on the basis of *primary and foreign keys*; i.e. one table contains a column (a foreign key) that holds values referring to the primary key column of the other table. When performing joins in SQL, it is essential to remember that this **join condition** must be specified; some very strange (i.e. wrong) results are obtained if you forget this.

Join definition

NOTE

There are two ways of defining join conditions: the 'traditional' way that uses a simple variation of the SELECT statement, and an alternative method defined by SQL92 that uses an explicit JOIN keyword. We will describe the traditional method first; the SQL92 method is described later, after the OUTER join has been covered.

If we want to issue a query that requires data from more than one table, the relevant tables must be declared in the SELECT command. The basic SELECT command format given at the start of this chapter is modified to the following:

```
SELECT column-list FROM table-names
    WHERE join-conditions [AND select-conditions]
        [ORDER BY column-list]
```

Notice that the FROM clause now contains two or more table names, being the tables involved in the join. Note also that the WHERE clause is now mandatory, since it must as a minimum define the join conditions for the tables. Optionally, as before, there may be additional conditions that select specific rows from the joined tables.

Example:

We can use the second table (Branch) that we defined at the start of this chapter but which, until now, has been languishing on the shelf. The Branch table holds information about the company branches. The Employee table has a foreign key column of BranchCode that refers to the Branch table primary key of the same name. Thus, the 'join condition' for these tables is:

Employee table BranchCode = Branch table BranchCode

We emphasise again: any query using both of these tables *must* include the join condition.

Example:

QUERY 4.1

List the names of each employee and the name of the branch in which they work.

```
SQL>    SELECT Name, BranchName FROM Employee, Branch

            WHERE Employee.BranchCode = Branch.BranchCode
```

Result:

```
NAME              BranchName
----------        ----------
Kennedy           South
Bell              South
Young             South
Chung             South
Hamilton          South
Roxburgh          South
Gomatam           West
Evans             West
Monaghan          West
Moore             West
Stewart           East
Stein             East
```

Bradley	East
Fletcher	East
Newman	East
Smith	North
Nicholson	North
Adams	North
Hill	North
Cohen	North
Walker	North

NOTE

Query 4.1 produces a **natural join**; i.e. the join column (BranchCode) only appears once in the output. If the * indicator is used as the select list, then an **equijoin** is produced – all columns will be shown, including two identical BranchCode columns. This does not appear to have any practical purpose.

This query requires data from both tables and hence they have been joined. Note the format of the join condition:

WHERE Employee.BranchCode = Branch.BranchCode.

Because the BranchCode column name is used in both tables, it is necessary to qualify the column names by prefixing them with the table names, as shown. This applies to any column names used anywhere in the query; if the name is not unique (across all the joined tables) it must be prefixed with the appropriate table name.

NOTE

The need to use table name prefixes as indicated above often makes the query rather long-winded. This can be relieved to some extent by the use of **table aliases** which are similar to the column aliases introduced earlier. A table alias is an alternative name defined for a table with an SQL statement. It is defined within the FROM clause and makes Query 4.1 look like this:

QUERY 4.1

List the names of each employee and the name of the branch in which they work.

```
SQL>    SELECT Name, BranchName FROM Employee E, Branch B
             WHERE E.BranchCode = B.BranchCode
```

The aliases E and B are arbitrary choices; any valid names can be used, but with regard to the purpose of these names, short ones are best.

If the query includes other conditions, the WHERE clause can be extended:

QUERY 4.2

List the name of each employee, department and the name of the branch they work in for all employees in Sales departments.

```
SQL>    SELECT Name, BranchName, Department FROM Employee E, Branch B

        WHERE E.BranchCode = B.BranchCode

        AND Department = 'Sales'
```

Result:

NAME	BRANCHNAM	DEPARTMENT
Roxburgh	South	Sales
Gomatam	West	Sales
Moore	West	Sales
Evans	West	Sales
Stein	East	Sales
Smith	North	Sales
Adams	North	Sales

We can also combine a join with a GROUP BY operation. This incidentally yields a problem alluded to in the previous session.

QUERY 4.3

List the name of each branch and the number of people employed in it.

```
SQL>    SELECT BranchName, COUNT(*) FROM Employee E, branch B

        WHERE E.BranchCode = B.BranchCode

        GROUP BY BranchName
```

Result:

BRANCHNAM	COUNT(*)
East	5
North	6
South	6
West	4

Now for the problem. Suppose we want list the BranchCode as well as the BranchName. We might be tempted to try:

QUERY 4.2

```
SQL>    SELECT E.BranchCode, BranchName, COUNT(*)

        FROM Employee E, Branch B

        WHERE E.BranchCode = B.BranchCode

        GROUP BY BranchName
```

This is wrong: Oracle produces the following error message:

```
SELECT E.BranchCode, BranchName, COUNT(*) FROM Employee E, Branch B

       *

ERROR at line 1:
ORA-00979: not a GROUP BY expression
```

What is the problem here? Well, the SELECT list item BranchCode does not qualify as a GROUP item – it is not a GROUP BY column and not a group function. However, since BranchName is functionally dependent on BranchCode, it is clear that within each BranchName group the BranchCode will also be constant. We can fix this problem simply by extending the GROUP BY parameter to include the BranchCode:

QUERY 4.3a

List the code and name of each branch and the number of people employed in it.

```
SQL>    SELECT E.BranchCode, BranchName, COUNT(*)

            FROM Employee E, Branch B

              WHERE E.BranchCode = B.BranchCode

            GROUP BY E.BranchCode, BranchName
```

Result:

BR	BRANCHNAME	COUNT(*)
01	South	6
02	West	4
03	East	5
04	North	6

In effect, the BranchCode entry here is redundant but it keeps SQL happy! Note also that the BranchCode column name has to be prefixed with a table name because it is not a unique name – it occurs in both tables. Either table name would do.

Inner and outer joins

There are actually various types of join, which so far in this chapter we have ignored. The examples above illustrate **inner natural joins**. To recap on the principle involved here, the inner join ignores rows in any of the tables being joined that do not meet any of the join conditions. For instance, in the previous query, there are no rows in the result that refer to BranchCode 05, although BranchCode 05 is appears in the Branch table. However, there are no matching rows in the Employee table; i.e. there are no rows in the Employee table for which BranchCode = 05. In real world terms, this situation could arise if a new branch were built but had not yet been occupied by staff.

If we want to see the details from the unmatched row (in this case, the information about the 05 branch), we need to use an **outer join**. An outer join enables data pertaining to unmatched rows to be output; columns of the output corresponding to unavailable data are set to null.

> **NOTE**
>
> The notation used to specify outer joins is very implementation-dependent; the technique given here is that used by Oracle. See page A46 for the more general SQL92 join formats that solve this problem.

Query 4.2 re-expressed using an outer join appears as shown in Query 4.4.

> **QUERY 4.4**
>
> List the names of each employee and the name of the branch they work in for all employees *including branches with no employees.*
>
> ```
> SQL>    SELECT Name, BranchName FROM Employee E, Branch B
>
>         WHERE E.BranchCode(+) = B.BranchCode
> ```

Result:

```
NAME           BRANCHNAME
-------        ----------
Kennedy        South
Bell           South
Young          South
```

Chung	South
Hamilton	South
Roxburgh	South
Gomatam	West
Evans	West
Monaghan	West
Moore	West
Stewart	East
Stein	East
Bradley	East
Fletcher	East
Newman	East
Smith	North
Nicholson	North
Adams	North
Hill	North
Cohen	North
Walker	North
	Europe <— this entry caused by outer join

The use of the (+) notation tells SQL to treat the associated table (Employee in this case) as though it had an extra row of null columns. Any unmatched rows from the Branch table are automatically matched with this null row. Note that, depending on the context, the (+) device can be on either side of the WHERE condition (and, theoretically, on *both* sides although this rarely has any practical value).

Question

What would be the effect of Query 4.3 if the (+) symbol were placed on the other side of the condition; i.e.

```
SELECT Name, BranchName FROM Employee E, Branch B
   WHERE E.BranchCode = B.BranchCode(+)
```

Answer

The answer would include a row for any employee BranchCode with no matching BranchCode in the Branch table. No such row exists, so the answer will be identical with that for Query 4.1.

NOTE

The presence of such a row would a imply a lack of referential integrity; i.e. a foreign key in the Employee table refers to a primary key that does not exist in the Branch table.

SQL92 join formats

The SQL92 standard introduced a new generalised method of dealing with joins by means of extensions to the SELECT command. The new syntax was introduced to resolve the variations in implementation found in different products. It enables explicit definition of the type of join at the expense of additional keywords, but does not provide any effect not achievable by the 'traditional' syntax. Availability of the new join facilities does not prevent continued use of the traditional method, since the latter depends only on the fundamental nature of WHERE conditions. Note also that there are variations in the implementation of these join facilities in different interpreters. The code examples shown below are all acceptable to Oracle; Access implements a smaller set of options, described later. My SQL supports the format shown below plus some additional features.

As there are a number of variations in the new syntax, it is helpful to see 'the full picture' in the form of syntax diagrams. The new options are effectively extensions to the FROM clause; i.e. a SELECT command is of the form:

```
SELECT column-list FROM join-expression . . .
```

where *join-expression* can be of two forms, which we will refer to the *natural form* and *on/using form*.

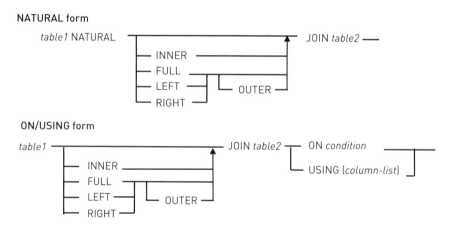

FIGURE HOA.2 SQL92 join formats

The following notes explain the principles involved in this syntax.

1 The diagrams are intended to show the valid 'paths' through the various combinations of options. For instance, the group of keywords INNER, FULL, LEFT, etc. are all optional and can be 'skipped' by traversing the line between *table1* and JOIN *table2*. This should become clearer when we cover a few examples.

2 In the natural version, the join columns are automatically assumed to be the columns of the two tables *with the same name(s)*, so no explicit join conditions are required.

3 The keyword INNER is assumed by default unless one of FULL, LEFT or RIGHT is used.

4 The keyword OUTER is also assumed if FULL, LEFT or RIGHT is used.

5 Using the ON option, the join condition is expressed as in the 'traditional' version.

6 The USING option allows you to supply a list of 'join columns' which must occur in all tables being joined.

We can now repeat some of the earlier queries using this new syntax.

Inner joins

QUERY 4.5

List the names of each employee and the name of the branch they work in.

SQL>   SELECT Name, BranchName FROM Employee NATURAL JOIN Branch

This is certainly a neater version of the original answer, exploiting the fact that the join column has the same name in both tables. The noise word INNER can be used if desired:

SQL>   SELECT Name, BranchName FROM Employee NATURAL INNER JOIN Branch

Note, however, that these joins would use *all* columns that had the same name in each table. If this is not what is wanted, another format of command would need to be used.

The same query could also be expressed using the USING or ON options:

SQL>   SELECT Name, BranchName FROM Employee INNER JOIN Branch
             ON Employee.BranchCode=Branch.BranchCode

SQL>   SELECT Name, BranchName FROM Employee INNER JOIN Branch
             USING (BranchCode)

The question could be asked: why might one choose to use the USING format rather than the NATURAL format?

The answer is that the NATURAL format will use *all* similarly named columns in the two tables; although the USING format also uses similarly named columns, it allows you to select specific columns.

Outer joins

Outer joins are intrinsically more complicated than inner joins, since they have to cope with three different ways of joining the two tables. In each example below, the keyword OUTER is used, but it should be remembered that this word is always optional.

A LEFT join means that the table on the left of the JOIN keyword is 'null-extended'; i.e. unmatched rows of this table will be shown. This is equivalent to using the (+) notation on the left of the join condition.

Similarly, a RIGHT join implies a null-extended row in the table on the right of the JOIN keyword.

For example, these two SQL queries are equivalent:

```
SQL> SELECT Name, BranchName FROM Employee E, Branch B
        WHERE E.BranchCode(+) = B.BranchCode
```

```
SQL> SELECT Name, BranchName FROM Employee NATURAL LEFT OUTER JOIN Branch
```

(The NATURAL option works as for inner joins – all matching column names are used in the join).

Alternative forms of this query are:

```
SQL> SELECT Name, BranchName FROM Employee LEFT OUTER JOIN Branch
        USING (BranchCode)
```

```
SQL> SELECT Name, BranchName FROM Employee LEFT OUTER JOIN Branch
        ON Employee.BranchCode=Branch.BranchCode
```

Similarly, the following RIGHT joins are equivalent:

```
SQL> SELECT Name, BranchName FROM Employee E, Branch B
        WHERE E.BranchCode=B.BranchCode(+)
```

```
SQL> SELECT Name, BranchName FROM Employee NATURAL RIGHT OUTER JOIN Branch
```

and similarly for the ON and USING options.

Finally, FULL joins follow the same pattern:

```
SQL> SELECT Name, BranchName FROM Employee E, Branch B
        WHERE E.BranchCode(+)=B.BranchCode(+)
```

```
SQL> SELECT Name, BranchName FROM Employee NATURAL FULL OUTER JOIN Branch
```

MySQL and Access join implementations

While MySQL and Access support the general principles of these join conventions, their implementations are slightly more limited. We have identified the differences here.

MySQL:
Implements the 'natural' join but uses *either* the NATURAL or the INNER keyword, but not both.

Does not implement the FULL outer join.

Access:
Does not implement the NATURAL join.

Does not implement the ON clause.

Does not implement the FULL outer join.

Multi-table joins

Our join examples to date have only involved two tables, but in practice joins over three or more tables are not uncommon. The general principle is simple; for n tables, $n - 1$ joins are required. For example, for three tables, two joins are necessary.

Using the basic join conventions, this means that we require an extra join condition to be specified for each extra table. As an example, assume that we have another table called Warehouse that describes company warehouses. Each warehouse is associated with a particular branch and hence contains a foreign key of BranchCode referencing the branch table. There can more than one warehouse per branch. If we assume that the format of the Warehouse table is as follows we can try a three table join example.

```
Warehouse Code      VARCHAR2(4),

Name                VARCHAR2(15),

Branchcode          VARCHAR2(2),

Address             VARCHAR2(20).
```

QUERY 4.6

List the name of each manager, the branch they manage and the names and addresses of warehouses connected to the branch.

```
SQL>    SELECT E.Name, B.BranchName, W.Name FROM Employee E, Branch B, Warehouse W
        WHERE manager = empid                (join employee – branch)
        AND B.BranchCode= W.BranchCode           (join branch – warehouse)
        AND position = 'Accountant'
```

Session 5 – Subqueries

Consider the following query and an *erroneous* attempt at an answer:

QUERY 5.1

Find the name, position and salary of the employee with the highest salary.

```
SQL>    SELECT Name, Position, Salary FROM Employee
             WHERE Salary = MAX(Salary)
```

This is wrong: Oracle produces the following error message:

```
WHERE Salary = MAX(Salary)
        *
ERROR at line 2:
ORA-00934: group function is not allowed here
```

This is invalid because we are mixing a group function (MAX) with non-group columns. Use of group functions like MAX in the absence of a GROUP BY clause tells SQL to treat the whole table as a group; this is inconsistent with our use of individual columns (Name, Position and Salary) that are not constant within the table.

In order to answer this query, we need firstly to find out what the maximum salary is and then to check each row of the table for this value. Notionally this involves two queries:

```
SELECT MAX(Salary) FROM Employee — and, using the answer from this (50 000) do -
SELECT Name, Position FROM Employee WHERE Salary = 50 000
```

Passing a value 'manually' from one query to another is clearly unsatisfactory and SQL provides an alternative – subqueries. A subquery is a query that yields an answer within the WHERE (or HAVING) clause of a main query. The above query then becomes:

QUERY 5.2

Find the name, position and salary of the employee with the highest salary.

```
SQL>    SELECT Name, Position, Salary FROM Employee
            WHERE Salary = (SELECT MAX(Salary) FROM Employee)
```

Result:

NAME	POSITION	SALARY
Kennedy	Director	50 000

We can also use a nested query within a HAVING clause:

QUERY 5.3

Find the name of the department with most employees.

```
SQL>    SELECT Department FROM Employee
            GROUP BY Department
                HAVING COUNT(*) = (SELECT MAX(COUNT(*) ) FROM Employee
                    GROUP BY Department)
```

Result:

```
DEPARTMENT
----------
Sales
```

> **NOTE**
>
> The subquery must be on the 'right hand side' of the comparison; e.g. you cannot use:
>
> ```
> WHERE (SELECT MAX(Salary) FROM Employee) = Salary
> ```
>
> This is not really a restriction, because you can always reverse the sense of the operator, although sometimes the resulting statement does not 'read' as a clear sentence.

How SQL interprets a subquery

It is important to appreciate how SQL handles a query containing a subquery. Essentially, the subquery should be executed for every row of the main query. However, in many cases the subquery is independent of the main query; i.e. it will produce the same answer regardless of the row being processed by the main query. In Queries 5.1 and 5.2, for instance, the subquery simply produces a fixed single answer. To execute the subquery for every row in the main query in these circumstances would be very wasteful in processing time. Fortunately, SQL interpreters are smart enough to recognise this situation and will take a shortcut by evaluating the subquery once and using its answer for all the main query rows.

However, in some cases, the subquery is affected by the main query; this is called a **correlated subquery**. In effect, the subquery is dependent on the current row of the main query and hence must be executed for every main query row. For example:

> **QUERY 5.4**
>
> List employees' names and salaries for employees who earn more than the average for their branch.
>
> ```
> SQL>    SELECT Name, Salary FROM Employee Emp
>         WHERE Salary > (SELECT AVG(Salary) FROM Employee
>             WHERE BranchCode = Emp.BranchCode)
> ```

Result:

NAME	SALARY
Kennedy	50 000
Young	30 000
Adams	23 000
Hill	27 000
Gomatam	31 000
Newman	28 000
Cohen	21 000

Notice use of the 'Emp' alias for the Employee table in the main query; this enables the subquery to refer to the BranchCode currently being processed in the main query.

Looking in detail at what is happening here, the main query 'scans' the Employee table row by row, so it looks first at row 1:

EMP ID	NAME	POSITION	HireDate	SALARY	BRANCH CODE	DEPARTMENT	SUPERVISOR
1001	Kennedy	Director	16-JAN-84	50 000	01		

The subquery is now executed using the BranchCode from this row; the subquery scans the *full table* but only takes in account rows meeting the condition BranchCode = Emp.BranchCode, which resolves to *BranchCode* = '01'. For such rows the average salary is calculated, yielding the value 26 917. This is then compared with the Salary value in the current main row (50 000) and, since it is greater than 26 917, the Name and Salary are displayed. The main query then moves on to the next row and the process repeats.

The previous query used only one table, but it is possible for the main and subqueries to use different tables. The same principles apply; columns named in the subquery not found in the subquery table are assumed to refer to the table in the main query. The next example uses two tables and also shows the use of grouping within the main query – This query is quite complex but worth some study!

QUERY 5.5

List those departments whose total salary is greater than 20% of the budget for the branch it is in. (Note: the budget figure in the table is in thousands.)

```
SQL>    SELECT SUM(Salary), BranchCode, Department FROM Employee E

        HAVING SUM(Salary) > (SELECT budget* 1 000 * 0.2 FROM Branch

           WHERE BranchCode = E.BranchCode)

        GROUP BY BranchCode, Department
```

Result:

```
SUM(SALARY)   BR    DEPARTMENT
-----------   ---   ------------
68 000        02    Sales
42 500        04    Admin
41 000        04    Sales
```

> **NOTE**
>
> The GROUP BY clause uses two columns, BranchCode and Department; this is necessary since the departments are effectively 'within' each branch; e.g. there is Sales department in more than one branch.

Subqueries yielding multiple rows

If the subquery yields a single-value answer (as in the above examples), you can use any of the usual operators, (=, <, >, <=, >=, <>), when comparing with the subquery answer. If the subquery can produce more than one row, these operators cannot be used on their own. Instead, you must use other additional qualifiers that are designed to work with sets of values. These qualifiers are ANY, ALL. Additionally, there are two other operators, IN and EXISTS, that can be applied to multiple row answers. These keywords are described below; first the qualifiers:

ANY: compares a value with each of a set of values; the left-hand side value is compared (using the given comparison operator) with each of the subquery result values. It returns 'true' if, and only if, the comparison is true for any row of the subquery.

ALL: compares a value with all of a set of values; the left-hand side value is compared with each of subquery result values. It returns 'true' if the comparison is true for all rows of the subquery.

The IN operator is called the **set membership** test. Note that we have already met this operator in Session 1 where it was used to test for membership of a fixed list of values. It is actually just a convenient alternative to = ANY; similarly, NOT IN is equivalent to <>ALL. In practice, the IN operator is much more intuitive than ALL/ANY and should be used in preference. However, we will look at both usages.

> **QUERY 5.6**
>
> List branches that do not employee any clerks.
> ```
> SQL>    SELECT BranchCode FROM Employee E
>             WHERE 'Clerk' <>ALL (SELECT Position FROM Employee
>                 WHERE BranchCode = E.BranchCode)
>
>         SELECT BranchCode FROM Employee E
>             WHERE 'Clerk' NOT IN (SELECT Position FROM Employee
>                 WHERE BranchCode = E.BranchCode)
> ```

Either of these queries would produce the result show below.

Result:

```
BRANCH
------
01
04
```

> **NOTE**
>
> This query uses a correlated subquery. For each row of the main query, the inner SELECT effectively produces a single column relation containing the positions within the branch indicated in the main query. The Position value of the current row of the main query is tested against this list and will *not* be reported if a match occurs.

The EXISTS operator checks to see whether a subquery yields any rows as an answer. In contrast to the other subquery operators, EXISTS is not concerned with the actual values returned – only whether there are any. Here is an example:

QUERY 5.7

List the names of branches where there are at least two salesmen.

```
SQL>    SELECT BranchName FROM branch B
            WHERE EXISTS (SELECT * FROM Employee
                WHERE Position = 'Salesman'
                AND B.BranchCode = BranchCode
                GROUP BY BranchCode HAVING COUNT(*) >= 2 )
```

Result:

```
BranchName
----------
West
```

Since the actual values derived from the subquery are irrelevant, the 'SELECT * FROM Employee' could be replaced by any other select, such as 'SELECT Name FROM Employee'. Traditionally, the asterisk is used to avoid implying some other intent in the clause.

Subqueries producing multiple columns

It is possible to compare multiple columns with a subquery result as long as the column pattern is identical on both sides of the comparison:

QUERY 5.8

List the name and position of employees who are earning the highest salary for each position.

```
SQL>    SELECT Name, Position FROM Employee
            WHERE (Position, Salary) IN
                (SELECT Position, MAX(Salary)
                    FROM Employee
                    GROUP BY Position)
```

Result:

NAME	POSITION
Hamilton	Accountant
Fletcher	Chief Clerk
Monaghan	Clerk
Kennedy	Director
Cohen	Engineer
Gomatam	Manager
Chung	Programmer
Roxburgh	Salesman
Walker	Secretary
Adams	Supervisor
Bradley	Technician

NOTE

This feature is catered for in the SQL standard, but is not implemented in every version of SQL.

Use of this technique is relatively rare but it can make certain queries, like Query 5.8, easier to follow. In the absence of this feature, some other method can generally be found. For instance, Query 5.8 could be implemented by:

```
SQL>    SELECT Name, Position FROM Employee E
            WHERE Salary IN (SELECT MAX(Salary)
                FROM Employee
                WHERE Position = E.Position
                GROUP BY Position)
```

This solution uses a correlated sub query to generate only the maximum salary belonging to the same job position as the current main query.

Note that the following query *may* yield the correct result in many circumstances, but is inherently incorrect. Can you see why?

```
SQL>    SELECT Name, Position FROM Employee
            WHERE Salary IN (SELECT MAX(Salary)
                FROM Employee
                GROUP BY Position)
```

More complex subquery constructions

Subqueries can be used in many parts of SELECT statements. For instance, they can appear within the output list in the SELECT clause. To be useful in this context, the subquery must be correlated with the main query. However, the principal use of sub-queries is in conjunction with WHERE and HAVING clauses. This section provides some examples using these clauses.

Multiple levels of nesting

Previous examples have used one subquery within a main query, but it is possible for the subquery itself to include a subquery, and so on for several levels. This yields an outline structure as shown below:

```
SELECT column-list FROM table
   WHERE value = (SELECT column-list FROM table
      WHERE value = (SELECT column-list FROM table
         WHERE value = (SELECT ...)))
```

The number of permissible levels is implementation-dependent, but will generally be more than it is realistic to need in practice. Multiple subquery levels arise in queries that effectively need a series of separate queries to evaluate.

Example:

QUERY 5.9

Find the names of employees whose salary is more than the maximum salary of anyone working at the same branch as Walker.

```
SQL>    SELECT Name FROM Employee
            WHERE Salary > (SELECT MAX(Salary)
                FROM Employee
                WHERE BranchCode = (SELECT BranchCode FROM Employee
                    WHERE Name = 'Walker'))
```

Result:

```
NAME
-------
Kennedy
Young
Gomatam
Newman
```

This query breaks down into three steps:

1 Find out Walker's BranchCode (=04).

2 Find out the maximum salary in this branch (=27 000).

3 Find out who is earning more than this salary, as shown in output result.

Logical connectives

If a WHERE or HAVING condition requires use of AND or OR connectives, subqueries can be used in each component of the condition:

QUERY 5.10

Find the names of employees whose salary is more than the average of those working in branch 02 and who are in the same position as Young.

```
SQL>    SELECT Name FROM Employee
            WHERE Salary > (SELECT AVG(Salary) FROM Employee
                WHERE BranchCode = '02')
            AND Position = (SELECT Position FROM Employee
                WHERE Name = 'Young')
```

Result:

```
NAME
-----
Young
Hill
Gomatam
Newman
```

Session 6 – Data Definition Language (DDL)

Introduction

The earlier sessions have all used a set of database tables that already exist; in this session we are concerned with DDL – the part of the SQL language that provides facilities for table creation and maintenance. There are a number of activities included in this area:

- creating a table schema and 'empty' table

- changing the structure of a table

- adding data to a table

- deleting data from a table

- amending data in a table

- deleting a whole table

- creating and deleting indexes.

It is worth noting again that there are considerable variations in the facilities offered by the various implementations (and in the standard) in this area. In particular, the range of permissible datatypes and the facilities offered by the ALTER TABLE command are subject to considerable variations. Most implementations claim to be supersets of the standard (i.e. they include all of the standard and provide additional facilities) but this is often not the case. As before, we note that these notes have been prepared using Oracle Version 9 and the syntax given reflects this version. Some additional references are made to significant elements of the SQL standard.

Table names, column names and other items created within the DDL must conform to the rules for the formation of SQL identifiers; these are summarised below. Note that there may be some variations in these rules in particular implementations.

- A name must begin with a letter, must consist of letters, numbers or the underscore character.

- A name may be up to 128 characters long; this is likely to be implementation-dependent, but all products will support names of sufficient length for practical use.

- Within one context, all names must be unique. For instance, within one table all column names must be unique, but two tables can contain columns with the same name.

- You cannot use any SQL keyword as an identifier; e.g. you cannot name a table 'SELECT' or 'WHERE'.

- The case of an identifier is insignificant; the names EMPLOYEE, Employee and employee are all considered identical.

- While it is possible to have identifiers with embedded spaces, it is necessary to enclose them (for every occurrence) in double quotes, e.g. "Date of Birth", (the quotes are part of the identifier) is valid. However, such usage is not recommended.

Creating tables

Creating a database table requires that you assign a name to the table and that you define the names and datatypes of each of the columns of the table. Additionally, each column description may include other supplementary clauses concerned with validation and integrity.

The command used to create a new database table is CREATE TABLE, which has the basic format shown below.

```
CREATE TABLE tablename

(column-definition-list)
```

where *column-definition-list* consists of a comma-separated list of column definition each with the format:

```
column-name type [additional clauses]
```

The square brackets indicate optionality. The additional clauses are concerned with validation and integrity and are mostly dealt with later. One clause however is sufficiently common that it deserves mention here. The NOT NULL option applied to a column indicates that the column must always have a value; SQL will not insert a row in the table if no value is supplied for a NOT NULL column. The NOT NULL restriction should always be applied to primary key columns and optionally to other columns where the application demands a valid value.

VARCHAR2, DATE and NUMBER are the datatypes used in this table. The first column description, for instance, defines the first column of the table to be EmpId with a datatype of VARCHAR2; this being the primary key of the table, it is also qualified with NOT NULL. Note that the NOT NULL qualifier does not *make* this column a primary key. Within the format of the basic CREATE statement used here there is no way to identify a primary key.

QUERY 6.1

Create the Employee table used in this chapter.

```
SQL>   CREATE TABLE Employee
           (
                    EmpId          VARCHAR2(4) NOT NULL,
                    Name           VARCHAR2(10),
                    Position       VARCHAR2(12),
                    HireDate       DATE,
                    Salary         NUMBER(7,2),
                    BranchCode     VARCHAR2(2) NOT NULL,
                    Department     VARCHAR2(10),
                    Supervisor     VARCHAR2(4)

           )
```

The datatype of the column governs the nature of the data to be stored in the column. In effect, it determines how the data is handled on input and output and the domain of the stored data. The SQL standard defines a range of datatypes, but again implementations differ in terms of the types offered. The table below shows the most commonly used datatypes and those used within this text.

Type	Description
CHAR(n)	Fixed length text string of n characters
CHAR	A single text character
VARCHAR(n)	Variable length text string of maximum length n characters
VARCHAR2(n)	Oracle extension; similar to VARCHAR
NUMBER	Floating point value
NUMBER(n, p)	Fixed point value with total width n digits of which p are decimal places
DATE	Date value

Creating a table from an existing table

It is possible to create a new table by copying from all or part of an existing table. In effect, the new table is derived from the result of executing a SELECT query on the current table. This sometimes called a 'make table' query.

QUERY 6.2

Create a new table containing the EmpId, Name, Position and Salary from the Employee table for all employees in the 02 branch.

```
SQL>   CREATE TABLE Employee2

           AS
```

```
SELECT EmpId, Name, Position, Salary FROM Employee

WHERE BranchCode = '02'
```

This would create a table with the following structure and content:

EmpId	NAME	POSITION	SALARY
4206	Gomatam	Manager	31 000
4936	Moore	Salesman	19 500
8253	Evans	Salesman	17 500
4102	Monaghan	Clerk	17 000

Note that, while a basic CREATE TABLE command just defines the table format, the CREATE . . . AS command also populates the new table with data from the source table.

Changing the structure of a table

If it becomes necessary to change the structure of a table, due to a error or because the design has changed, the ALTER TABLE command can help, although it is subject to certain restrictions. The basic formats of the ALTER command are defined below.

ALTER TABLE *tablename*

ADD (*column-name type* [NOT NULL])

or

ALTER TABLE *tablename*

MODIFY (*column-name type* [NOT NULL])

The first format allows you to add a new column to a table. The column will initially contain nulls.

QUERY 6.3

Add a new 'Department' to the employee2 table, defined as in the original Employee table.

SQL>   ALTER TABLE employee2

           ADD (Department VARCHAR2(10))

The new column will be filled with nulls.

The second format is used primarily to increase the width of a column; most implementations will not allow you to reduce the width of a table unless the whole column is empty (i.e. the table is empty or the column contains nulls). Also, changing the type of the column, say from CHAR to NUMBER, is generally not possible. An example of a MODIFY operation is shown below.

QUERY 6.4

Change the size of the name column in employee2 table to 20 characters.

```
SQL>    ALTER TABLE employee2
        MODIFY (Name VARCHAR2(20))
```

NOTE

The MODIFY option is not now part of the current standard, but is still supported by many implementations. The standard has an ALTER TABLE . . . ALTER COLUMN option, but its only action is to change the default value for the column.

Conversely, the standard defines a DROP COLUMN option that is not provided in Oracle.

Deleting a whole table

If it becomes necessary to completely remove a table from a database, the DROP command is used. This has a simple syntax, illustrated below.

QUERY 6.5

Delete the employee2 table.

```
SQL>    DROP TABLE employee2
```

The commands covered in next three sections describe how table data can be processed by SQL; i.e. adding, deleting and amending rows of data.

Adding rows to a table

The SQL INSERT command can be used to add one row of data to a table. The syntax of the INSERT command is shown below:

```
INSERT INTO tablename [(column-name-list)]
VALUES (data-value-list)
```

The optional *column-name-list* is used if you want to supply data only for selected columns. Columns not specified in this list would be set to null. Normally, data for all columns is supplied and the column list can be omitted. The *data-value-list* consists of a comma-separated list of values, each of which corresponds to one column of the table.

QUERY 6.6

Add a new row of data to the Employee table.

```
SQL>   INSERT INTO Employee VALUES

('6752','Ross','Programmer','12-May-95','18 000','03','Technical', '7663')
```

If we list the full table again, we can see the new row:

EMPID	NAME	POSITION	HireDate	SALARY	BR	DEPARTMENT	SUPE
1001	Kennedy	Director	16-JAN-84	50 000	01		
1045	Smith	Salesman	12-MAY-94	18 000	04	Sales	3 691
1271	Stewart	Clerk	30-APR-89	16 000	03	Accounts	3 255
1534	Bell	Supervisor	28-NOV-95	20 000	01	Admin	3 876
1653	Walker	Secretary	03-AUG-87	15 500	04	Admin	3 876
2244	Chung	Programmer	09-APR-96	21 500	01	Technical	7 663
3255	Young	Manager	19-MAR-92	30 000	01	Accounts	1 001
3691	Adams	Supervisor	01-OCT-86	23 000	04	Sales	4 206
3876	Hill	Manager	27-JAN-90	27 000	04	Admin	
4206	Gomatam	Manager	23-JUL-97	31 000	02	Sales	
4936	Moore	Salesman	30-JUN-85	19 500	02	Sales	4 206
5833	Bradley	Technician	08-SEP-88	14 500	03	Technical	7 663
6223	Hamilton	Accountant	21-FEB-88	20 000	01	Accounts	3 255
7663	Newman	Manager	15-AUG-92	28 000	03	Technical	
8253	Evans	Salesman	13-JUN-93	17 500	02	Sales	4 206
9743	Fletcher	Chief Clerk	29-OCT-87	18 000	03	Accounts	3 255
2906	Stein	Supervisor	04-FEB-89	15 500	03	Sales	
3198	Roxburgh	Salesman	21-SEP-84	20 000	01	Sales	3 255
4218	Cohen	Engineer	25-AUG-92	21 000	04	Technical	
4102	Monaghan	Clerk	13-JUN-93	17 000	02	Admin	4 206
9743	Nicholson	Chief Clerk	09-JUL-90	15 000	04	Accounts	3 255
6752	**Ross**	**Programmer**	**12-MAY-95**	**18 000**	**03**	**Technical**	**7 663**

NOTE

The items in the value list correspond to the columns of the table in sequence and type. Only one row of data can be handled by one INSERT.

Row data may be drawn from another table; a SELECT query is used to define the data. More than one row may be added by this means.

QUERY 6.7

Add to the employee2 table data from the rows of the Employee table that refer to the Sales department.

```
SQL>    INSERT INTO employee2
        SELECT EmpId, Name, Position, Salary FROM Employee
        WHERE Department = 'Sales'
```

Table employee2 is now as shown:

EMPID	NAME	POSITION	SALARY
4206	Gomatam	Manager	31 000
4936	Moore	Salesman	19 500
8253	Evans	Salesman	17 500
4102	Monaghan	Clerk	17 000
1045	Smith	Salesman	18 000
3691	Adams	Supervisor	23 000
4206	Gomatam	Manager	31 000
4936	Moore	Salesman	19 500
8253	Evans	Salesman	17 500
2906	Stein	Supervisor	15 500
3198	Roxburgh	Salesman	20 000

Updating data in tables

To update data in a current table we use the UPDATE command, which has the syntax:

UPDATE *table-name*

SET *column-name = expression or subquery*

[WHERE *condition*]

The condition is optional but if not included the change will be applied to every row. A more typical example is shown below.

QUERY 6.8

Increase the salary of everyone in the Technical department of the Employee table by 10%.

```
SQL>    UPDATE Employee
        SET Salary = Salary * 1.1
        WHERE Department = 'Technical'
```

Deleting rows from a table

The syntax of this command is quite simple:

```
DELETE FROM tablename [WHERE clause]
```

QUERY 6.9

Delete rows from the Employee table that relate to Smith or Moore.

```
SQL>    DELETE FROM Employee
        WHERE Name = 'Smith' OR Name = 'Moore'
```

If you want to delete all the rows from a table, omit the WHERE clause. Note that this is different from the DROP TABLE command; in addition to deleting the data, the DROP TABLE command also removes the table definition from the database schema, whereas the DELETE FROM simply leaves an empty table.

Indexes

Indexes were described in Chapter 4; to recap, an index is a 'look-up' dataset associated with one database table. Indexes are used to speed up direct access to specific table rows and to facilitate organisation of the table data in sequence, for example, to respond to an ORDER BY command. A table may have multiple indexes for different columns of the table.

Indexes can be specified at table creation time or at any time during the life of the table. In general, it is best to populate the table with data first as a 'one-off' index build is more efficient than a series of updates as data records are added. However, for very dynamic data this factor would have little consequence. Once created, indexes are managed and updated transparently by the DBMS. In SQL, the CREATE INDEX command is used:

```
CREATE INDEX index-name ON table-name (field-name)
```

QUERY 6.10

Create an index for the name column of the Employee table

```
SQL>    CREATE INDEX Name_Index on Employee(Name)
```

The index name Name_Index is used in cataloguing the index in the data dictionary but does not need to be referenced during its use. The SQL interpreter will use (or not use) the index as it decides during query execution.

To remove an index, the DROP INDEX command is available. As indicated in Chapter 4, it may benefit processing performance to remove an index (and therefore its concomitant update overheads) for periods when the index is not of value.

QUERY 6.11

Remove the name index for the Employee table.

```
SQL>    DROP INDEX Name_Index
```

It is also possible to build an index on multiple columns. Again, this was discussed in detail in Chapter 4.

QUERY 6.12

Create an index on department within BranchCode for the Employee table.

```
SQL>    CREATE INDEX BranchDept_Index on Employee(BranchCode, Department)
```

This might be used to speed up a query that used the clause:

```
. . . ORDER BY BranchCode, Department or
```

```
. . . GROUP BY BranchCode, Department
```

Constraints

The topic of constraints is described in Chapter 7 in the context of database integrity. This is another area of SQL that is very implementation-dependent. In this section we will highlight only a few facilities that are provided by the Oracle DBMS.

The constraints provision in Oracle is quite complex. In effect, it allows you to specify rules that restrict the allowable values for one or more columns of a table. Constraints can be applied using the CREATE command (i.e. when the table is being initially created) or using ALTER on an existing table.

Primary and foreign key constraints

Constraints can be applied at the table level or at column level. The two most important and most used constraints are those used to specify the primary and foreign keys of a table. As an example we will apply these constraints to the Employee table; the primary key of this table is EmpId and column BranchCode is a foreign key.

If the constraints are defined when the table is created, then the following column definitions would be used:

```
CREATE Employee
(  EmpId VARCHAR2(4) PRIMARY KEY,
   . . .
   BranchCode VARCHAR2(2) REFERENCES Branch(BranchCode),
   . . .
)
```

It is also possible to state all the constraints at the end of the CREATE TABLE clause. The above command would then appear as follows:

```
CREATE Employee
(  EmpId VARCHAR2(4),
   . . .
   BranchCode VARCHAR2(2) REFERENCES Branch(BranchCode),
   . . .
   CONSTRAINT PK PRIMARY KEY (EmpId),
   CONSTRAINT FK FOREIGN KEY (BranchCode) REFERENCES
                                Branch(BranchCode)
)
```

To apply table constraints to an existing table, we would issue the following commands:

```
ALTER TABLE Employee ADD PRIMARY KEY (EmpId)
ALTER TABLE Employee ADD FOREIGN KEY(BranchCode) REFERENCES
                                Branch(BranchCode)
```

CHECK constraint

CHECK constraints apply basic validity tests to new data. These can introduced in a CREATE TABLE or ALTER TABLE command. Examples:

```
CREATE Employee
   (  EmpId VARCHAR2(4) PRIMARY KEY,
      . . .
      Salary NUMBER(8,2) CHECK (salary < 90 000),
      . . .

ALTER TABLE Employee
   ADD CONSTRAINT MaxSal CHECK (salary < 90 000)
```

When constraints are added with a name such as MaxSal above, it becomes a named object in the system and can later be inspected and updated. In particular, a constraint can be dropped:

```
ALTER TABLE Employee
   DROP CONSTRAINT MaxSal
```

Session 7 – Additional SQL features

Introduction

In this session we describe a number of SQL features that have not fitted into any the categories dealt with in the earlier sessions. These features include:

- Views
- GRANT and REVOKE commands
- Transactions
- Constraints

Views

Views were described in Chapter 2. To recap, a view is a virtual relation that appears to the user to be a real table. It is derived from a query on 'real' tables. In a sense, any query produces a result which is a temporary relation; the difference a view makes is that the query definition is recorded as a named entity that can be referenced later as if it were a table.

A view is defined the CREATE VIEW command, illustrated below.

QUERY 7.1

Create a view called emp_view that shows the EmpId, name and position of all employees.

```
SQL>    CREATE VIEW emp_view

        AS

        SELECT EmpId, Name, Position, Salary FROM Employee
```

The view can now be used as if it were a table:

QUERY 7.2

List the EmpId, name and position of all salesmen.

```
SQL>    SELECT * FROM emp_view

        WHERE Position = 'Salesman'
```

Result:

```
EMPID   NAME       POSITION      SALARY
-----   --------   ----------    ------
1045    Smith      Salesman      18 000
4936    Moore      Salesman      19 500
8253    Evans      Salesman      17 500
3198    Roxburgh   Salesman      20 000
```

A view can be defined based on any valid query; in particular, the query may use group functions:

QUERY 7.3

Create a view representing the average salary of each branch and department.

SQL>

```
        CREATE VIEW emp_average

        AS

        SELECT BranchCode, Department, AVG(Salary) avg_salary FROM Employee

        GROUP BY BranchCode, Department;
```

Now test this view by the command:

```
   SELECT * FROM emp_average
```

Result:

```
BR     DEPARTMENT       AVG_SALARY
---    ----------       ----------
01     Accounts         2 500
01     Admin            2 000
01     Sales            2 000
01     Technical        2 150
01                      5 000
02     Admin            1 700
02     Sales            2 267
03     Accounts         1 700
03     Sales            1 550
03     Technical        2 125
04     Accounts         1 500
04     Admin            2 125
04     Sales            2 050
04     Technical        2 100
```

There are some caveats that must be noted when working with views. Firstly, because a view is based on a query, reference to a view will require re-evaluation of the query if the underlying real table(s) have been amended. For small tables, such as our employee table, this is not a problem; however, if the table has 100 000 rows the performance implications are more serious. This is not to say that the view mechanism *increases* the querying time; if the application requires the answer to a query over a large table, it does not matter whether a direct query or the underlying view query is used. The potential problem with a view is that the apparent simplicity of a query based on a view can obscure the processing overheads involved in rebuilding the view.

Another view difficulty is its 'updatability'; a view looks like a real table, but can it be updated like a real table? Clearly, since a view does not exist physically, a data amendment must be propagated through to the underlying source tables. However, this is not always possible because of, first, restrictions in the DBMS implementation, and second, natural limitations due to the way views are formed.

Taking the latter point first; if you look at the view emp_view above, it is clear that there is a one-to-one relationship between view rows and table rows. In this case, there is no theoretical restrictions on view updating; if you amend row *n* of the view, the corresponding row of the real table is amended.

Using the view emp_view, change the salary of employee Bell to 22 000.

```
SQL>  UPDATE emp_view

SET Salary TO 22 000
```

However, if we consider view emp_average, things are not so simple. The rows of the view correspond to a *group* of rows of the underlying employee table. The view salary figures (avg_salary), for instance, are averages of several table rows, hence an amendment to avg_salary cannot be propagated as a unique change in the employee table.

The original ANSI SQL standard specifies a list of conformance rules for view updatability; these tended to be too restrictive and many vendors' products exceeded the standard. The current standard is less prescriptive and allows for variations between products. Accordingly, the best reference for the rules in this respect lies in your DBMS documentation. As an example, you cannot update a view in Oracle SQL if the view definition query contains any of the following constructs:

- a set operator
- group function

- GROUP BY clause
- DISTINCT operator

Joins can also affect updatability but the rules in this respect are complex.

DCL commands

The Data Command Language (DCL) commands GRANT and REVOKE are used to control the granting and revoking of system and data privileges to/from database users. These commands form the basis for SQL-controlled database security. This is an area where there is substantial variation between DBMS products; also, practical systems such as Oracle provide a wealth of different options designed to cater for many operating environments. In this section we can only provide a general indication of the range of facilities one might find in a real product, with examples drawn from Oracle; for specific details, consult your own DBMS documentation. Note also that most use of these commands is by database administration staff rather than users or developers.

System privileges

System privileges refers to the right 'to do things' (such as creating tables, amending tables, etc) on the database. The command format (simplified) in this respect is:

```
GRANT system-privilege TO user [WITH ADMIN OPTION]
```

The identifier *user* is the name by which the person being granted the privilege is known to the DBMS. If the option WITH ADMIN OPTION is used, the privilege recipient (*user*) can then bestow this privilege on others. The range of available system privileges is extensive; here are a few typical examples.

ALTER ANY TABLE	Allows the grantee to alter the structure of a table.
ALTER USER	Allows the grantee to modify the system details (such as password, disk quotas) of other users.
CREATE ANY TABLE	Allows the grantee to create a table in any schema.
CREATE TABLE	Allows the grantee to create a table in their own schema.
CREATE ANY VIEW	Allows the grantee to create a view in any schema.
CREATE SESSION	Enables the grantee to log on to the database.
DROP ANY TABLE	Allows the grantee to drop any table.
INSERT ANY TABLE	Allows the grantee to insert rows into any table.
SELECT ANY TABLE	Allows the grantee to select rows from any table.
UNLIMITED TABLESPACE	Allows the grantee to use an unlimited amount of table space on disk.

Examples:

QUERY 7.5

Allow user gordon to log on to the database.

SQL>   GRANT CREATE SESSION TO gordon

QUERY 7.6

Allow user gordon to create tables within his own schema.

SQL>   GRANT CREATE TABLE TO gordon

Data privileges

The (simplified) general format for data privileges (called *object privileges* in Oracle) is:

GRANT *data-privilege* ON *data-object* TO *user* [WITH GRANT OPTION]

The *data-privilege* can be the value ALL (or ALL PRIVILEGES) or any combination of the following:

ALTER, DELETE, EXECUTE, INDEX, INSERT, REFERENCES, SELECT or UPDATE

In general, the grantee is bestowed the right to perform the given command on the specified object. The EXECUTE privilege allows the grantee to execute the procedure or function specified by *data-object*. The REFERENCES privilege allows the grantee to create a foreign key constraint in another of their tables that refers to the table named by *data-object*.

Examples:

QUERY 7.7

Allow user gordon to delete rows from the Employee table.

SQL>   GRANT DELETE ON Employee TO gordon

QUERY 7.8

Allow user karen to issue queries on, and update the Branch table.

SQL>   GRANT SELECT, UPDATE ON Branch TO karen

The REVOKE command does the reverse of the GRANT – it removes privileges from users. The formats of the command are very similar to GRANT:

REVOKE *system-privilege* FROM *user* [WITH ADMIN OPTION]

and

REVOKE *data-privilege* ON *data-object* FROM *user* [WITH GRANT OPTION]

This operates as you might expect – the privileges previously granted are revoked from the specified user.

Transactions

Transactions, including SQL facilities, are described in Chapter 6. In this section, we wish only to illustrate the concepts involved by showing transaction commands using our example tables.

The COMMIT command finalises a transaction and the amendments (since the start of the transaction) are written to disk. The ROLLBACK command aborts the current transaction and reverts the database to its state at the start of the transaction.

Before commencing the following test, it is advisable to issue a COMMIT command to commit all previous work on the current session.

First of all, we run through a sequence of commands that amends the employee table.

1 Change Adams' salary to 25 000:

```
UPDATE Employee SET Salary = 25 000 WHERE Name = 'Adams'
```

2 Change Adams' position to Manager:

```
UPDATE Employee SET Position = 'Manager'

WHERE Name = 'Adams'
```

If we now do a listing of the tables we can see these changes.

```
SELECT * FROM employee WHERE Name = 'Adams'
```

EMPID	NAME	POSITION	HIREDATE	SALARY	BR	DEPARTMENT	SUPE
3691	Adams	Manager	01-OCT-86	25 000	04	Sales	4 206

If we were to do a COMMIT command at this point, these changes would become permanent. However, if we now do a ROLLBACK command, the changes are reversed:

ROLLBACK

EMPID	NAME	POSITION	HIREDATE	SALARY	BR	DEPARTMENT	SUPE
3691	Adams	Supervisor	01-OCT-86	23 000	04	Sales	4 206

Constraints

The topic of constraints is described in Chapter 7 in the context of database integrity. This is another area of SQL that is very implementation-dependent. In this section we will highlight only a few facilities that are provided by the Oracle DBMS.

The constraints provision in Oracle is quite complex. In effect, it allows you to specify rules that restrict the allowable values for one or more columns of a table. Constraints can be applied using the CREATE command (i.e. when the table is being initially created) or using ALTER on an existing table.

Constraints can be applied at the table level or at column level. The two most important and most used constraints are those used to specify the primary and foreign keys of a table. As an example we will apply these constraints to the Employee table; the primary key of this table is EmpId and column BranchCode.

If the constraints are defined when the table is created, then the following column definitions would be used:

```
CREATE Employee
(  EmpId VARCHAR2(4) PRIMARY KEY,
   . . .
   BranchCode VARCHAR2(2) REFERENCES Branch(BranchCode),
   . . .
)
```

To apply table constraints to an existing table, we would issue the following commands:

```
ALTER TABLE Employee ADD PRIMARY KEY (EmpId)
ALTER TABLE Employee ADD FOREIGN KEY(BranchCode) REFERENCES  Branch
```

References

Textbooks

Casteel, J. (2006): *Oracle 10g SQL*, Thomson Course Technology
Mishra, S. and Beaulieu, A. (2004): *Mastering Oracle SQL*, O'Reilly
Price, J. (2004): *Oracle Database 10g SQL*, Osborne Oracle Press
Pratt, P.J. and Last, M.Z. (2006): *A Guide to MySQL*, Thomson Course Technology
Tahaghoghi, S. and Williams, H.E. (2006): *Learning MySQL*, O'Reilly
Kolfer, M. (2005): *The Definitive Guide to MySQL 5*, Apress

Websites

There are many good sites that provide tutorials for SQL, some using an active interpreter. A few suggestions are given below:

Oracle SQL reference: www.oracle.com/pls/db10g/homepage
MySQL Reference Manual: http://dev.mysql.com/doc/refman/5.0/en/index.html

Article on support for SQL standards: http://www.dbazine.com/db2/db2-disarticles/gulutzan3
Microsoft Access: http://msdn2.microsoft.com/en-us/library/aa140011(office.10).aspx

Other:

Comparison of Oracle and Access SQL: http://eis.bris.ac.uk/~ccmjs/ora_sql.htm#SQL%20 Syntax
Comparison of MySQL and Access (VBA) types: http://dev.mysql.com/tech-resources/ articles/visual-basic-datatypes.html

5

Interfacing with the database

LEARNING OBJECTIVES

In this chapter we will look at the variety of ways in which we can access databases by programming systems. After studying this chapter, you should be able to do the following:

- Describe the alternative methods that can be used to provide programmed access to a database.

- Describe the alternative ways in which SQL can be employed in programming environments.

- Explain the benefits of various standard database access interfaces: ODBC, JDBC, OLEDB, ADO.

- Explain the benefits of a fourth generation type programming system such as Oracle PL/SQL.

- Describe and explain the importance of forms and reports in database design.

- Describe the principal features of form and report management systems.

Note that the topics in this chapter overlap and impinge on the web database systems discussed in Chapter 10, since that chapter also describes techniques for interfacing to a database.

Introduction

One of the benefits of the database approach is the 'data independence' it provides. The database, in a sense, is self-sufficient; it can represent and store data pertaining to an application without immediate reference to the programming methods employed to extract and maintain the data. For instance, we can create a database in Oracle using DDL statements CREATE and INSERT without reference to how we are going to retrieve and use the data. Subsequently, we could get at this data by using a wide variety of tools: SQL DML commands, Oracle's procedural language PL/SQL, C++ programs using the ODBC interface, Java programs using the JDBC interface, among others. In this section we look at a number of database programming options.

Topics related to this area are also covered in other chapters: non-relational databases are covered in Chapter 9; web database techniques are covered in Chapter 10, including reference to ADO and ADO.NET.

Programming the database

Applications of SQL

The importance of the role that SQL plays in the database field can hardly be over-estimated. Its main virtues are that it is a widely accepted standard (well, almost) and it is a relatively simple declarative method of specifying database queries. Most students probably learn SQL by typing in SQL commands in a simple text-based interface such as the Oracle or MySQL command interpreters; however, in practice, SQL would tend to be used within the context of some other programming environment, and it is these that we will investigate in this section.

Database access interfaces

An application programming interface (API) is a software layer that provides access to a computer resource by means of functions called from application programs. In the context of SQL and databases, an API consists of a set of functions that communicate with an SQL system and deliver SQL commands. A number of such APIs exist, notably, Microsoft's ODBC and Javasoft's JDBC. These topics are covered in more detail later in this chapter.

Embedded SQL in 3GLs

In some systems where the main development is in a third-generation high-level language such as COBOL or C, it is possible to 'embed' SQL statements within the 3GL code. The HLL compiler cannot directly understand this code and hence it has to be converted into equivalent subroutine calls by means of a pre-processor. To help the pre-processor delineate the SQL commands from the normal program code, sections of SQL are introduced by the words 'EXEC SQL'. The pre-processor creates an intermediate source program which is then compiled by the language compiler in the normal way. For example, we could create a table as follows:

```
EXEC SQL
CREATE TABLE Product (
   ProdCode CHAR(4),
   ProdDesc CHAR(20),
. . . . etc.
)
EXEC SQL COMMIT
```

When a SELECT statement is executed, it notionally produces a result table. This is effectively assigned to an internal array structure which can be 'scanned' by an internal pointer called a **cursor** (not to be confused with the arrow on a Windows screen! This is a rough acronym for **cur**rent **s**et **o**f **r**ecords). The cursor can be used to reference successive elements of the result array. In this way, the program can use SQL to select some subset of the table data and then process this subset using conventional programming instructions. An example is given below:

```
EXEC SQL DECLARE K CURSOR FOR
SELECT ProdCode, ProdDesc, ProdQty  WHERE ProdQty > 100 . . . etc.
```

The above statement creates a cursor called K, then executes the given SELECT command, producing a result table. This table can then be accessed using K as a row pointer or subscript. Rows can be obtained from the cursor using:

```
EXEC SQL FETCH K INTO Pcode, Pdesc, Pqty
```

where Pcode, Pdesc and Pqty are local program variables. The FETCH command transfers data items from the cursor to local variables. The database can subsequently be updated using an embedded SQL UPDATE command.

SQL in 4GLs

Fourth generation languages (4GLs), and in particular the Oracle PL/SQL system, are discussed in more detail later in this chapter and also in Chapter 9 in relation to object-relational features. The principal difference presented by 4GLs compared with 3GLs is that in the former the integration of SQL with the procedural coding is closer. This is because the system has been designed as an integration of SQL and procedural code rather than as two separate language systems.

SQL in integrated development environments

Tools such as Microsoft Access, Visual Basic and Borland Delphi all provide for the specification of queries in SQL.

Summary of SQL applications

The general conclusion that you can glean from the above is that SQL is all-pervasive. There are very few database development tools that do not use SQL as a means of specifying query expressions. Generally, however, SQL is not sufficient in terms of the overall processing requirement, and is usually supplemented by some procedural coding, for example in Visual Basic. Oracle's PL/SQL is a useful example of how SQL and a procedural language can be combined to achieve the overall desired processing objective.

Standard database access interfaces

The principal purpose of the standard interfaces we describe here is to provide platform independence; i.e. to make it possible to access any database system using any programming environment. This objective is achieved by the use of an additional software layer between the DBMS and the application programming interface which has the task of resolving the differences between the two and suitably managing the inter-communication. The term 'middleware' is an alternative name for this software layer. While we say that the interface makes 'any' database potentially accessible from 'any' programming system, there are necessary conditions to be complied with before one can join the club, as it were. For the union to take place, both the database and the programming application must be 'compliant' with the interface and suitable interface drivers must be available. The middleware makes available an API which provides a set of functions callable from application programs.

ODBC

Microsoft's Open Database Connectivity (ODBC) specification was created with a view to making it easier for an application developer to write systems involving communication with different types of databases using SQL. The objective was to make it possible to develop an application system that would work unchanged with a variety of different databases and to facilitate the construction of systems using more than one database type. Although it was originally designed by Microsoft, it is now supported by all major database vendors and is subject to international standardisation. ODBC consists of a non-object-oriented API and a set of drivers that provide communication between the API and the database. This arrangement is illustrated in Figure 5.1.

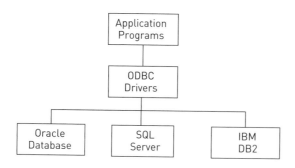

FIGURE 5.1 ODBC architecture

The application programs use the set of functions defined by the ODBC API. The API is defined as C language functions. These communicate with drivers (implemented as dynamic link libraries) that are specific to the database being accessed. The Access package itself can communicate with the ODBC drivers, either using Access Basic or by using built-in GUI procedures. Using ODBC enables communication with one or more different database types within one application system. This is particularly convenient when attempting to build upon an older application system by integrating it with newer database technology; the old and the new can operate side by side prior to a phased removal of the older system. Since ODBC is essentially based on a C language API, access to it by other systems such as Access has to be achieved via another software layer; products used in this role are DAO (Data Access Objects) and RDO (Remote Data Objects). These provide an object-based interface that is accessible by VBA coding. DAO and RDO are obsolescent and have been superseded by ADO, which is described below.

When used with Microsoft Access, ODBC provides two main facilities: attached tables and pass-through queries, which operate in quite different modes. Access allows database tables belonging to other systems to be 'attached' to an Access database. This means that Access treats these tables as if they were conventional Access tables; they can be queried, joined, updated etc. in the same way as native Access tables. Using the pass-through facility, queries (in SQL) are sent directly to a database server. No 'attachment' of tables takes place.

In order to use ODBC it is necessary to register your database with the ODBC administration software; this involves setting up a Data Source Name (DSN) that provides an association between your coding and an appropriate ODBC driver. This is achieved using the *ODBC Data Source Administrator* accessed via control panel and administrative tools.

OLE DB and ADO

Note: This section contains some programming code. The coding shown can be ignored without problem by readers who are not interested in this level of detail.

Microsoft also supports a newer system of generalised database access technologies whose most important components are OLE DB and ADO (ActiveX Data Objects). OLE DB effectively can replace ODBC, but since the latter has a large current user base it is likely that they will co-exist in the meantime. Similarly, DAO and RDO, mentioned above, currently co-exist with ADO, but are not now recommended development tools. OLE DB is an object-oriented system built using COM (Component Object Model) techniques and based on a C++ API. ADO uses SQL in the form of text strings to perform database processing. It is built on a simple object model that includes three main object types, namely Connection, Command and Recordset. The Connection object represents a connection from the VBA program to a database. The Command object is used to execute commands against a connection. When working with relational databases, this will consist of an SQL statement; it can, for instance, refer to a stored query in Access. A Recordset is used to hold records retrieved from a database as a result of a query; it is therefore similar in concept to the cursor. The diagram shown in Figure 5.2 illustrates the relationships between the various software elements.

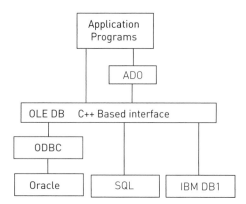

FIGURE 5.2 Interface technology

The following VBA code example illustrates the general nature of ADO coding. The code belongs to a form, within an Access database called Books.mdb, that browses through a database table called Authors. The form has two buttons that allow forward (Next) and backward (Prev) browsing through the table.

```
Private Sub MainForm_Open()
   Set cn = New ADODB.Connection              ' Note 1
   cn.Provider = "Microsoft.Jet.OLEDB.3.51"
   cn.ConnectionString = "Data Source=C:\Databases\books.mdb"
   cn.Open
   Set rs = New ADODB.Recordset               ' Note 2
   rs.Open "select * from authors", cn, adOpenDynamic,
   adLockReadOnly
   rs.MoveFirst                               ' Note 3A
   ShowData                                   ' Note 4
End Sub
Private Sub btnNext_Click()
   rs.MoveNext                                ' Note 3B
   btnPrev.Enabled = True
   If Not rs.EOF Then
   ShowData
   Else
   rs.MoveLast                                ' Note 3C
   DoCmd.GoToControl "btnPrev"
   btnNext.Enabled = False
   End If
End Sub
```

```
Private Sub btnPrev_Click()
    rs.MovePrevious                          ' Note 3D
    btnNext.Enabled = True
    If Not rs.BOF Then
    ShowData
    Else
    rs.MoveFirst
    DoCmd.GoToControl "btnNext"
    btnPrev.Enabled = False
    End If
End Sub
Private Sub ShowData()
    txtId = rs.Fields("AuthorId")            ' Note 5
    txtSurname = rs.Fields("AuthorSurname")
    txtInit = rs.Fields("AuthorInitials")
End Sub
```

5

NOTES

1 The four lines starting at Note 1 show how a Connection object cn is created and opened.

2 This line shows the creation of a recordset rs using the constructor New ADODB.Recordset.

3 Notes 3A to 3D show the use of methods of the recordset that allow repositioning of the recordset cursor.

4 The line ShowData is a call to a function, defined later, that displays the current record of the recordset.

5 In the ShowData function, the fields txtId, txtSurname and txtInit are text boxes on the form. The coding here shows how the recordset fields are accessed and copied on to the form text controls. The recordset property Fields represents the fields of the recordset records. Specific fields can be indexed using the notation shown; for instance, rs.Fields("AuthorId") references the AuthorId field of the recordset record.

JDBC

JDBC is intended to supply for Java what ODBC does for C++, but the structure and implementation are somewhat different. Like ODBC, JDBC relies on an intermediate layer, or layers, of software to connect the Java code to the database. The main difference is that JDBC is written in Java and hence the application code and the Java code effectively merge together. ODBC relies on C++ functions, so that if using another language, the intermediate software layer has to manage the communication between the languages; for instance, Visual Basic uses the ADO object system. The overall structure of an application using JDBC is shown in Figure 5.3.

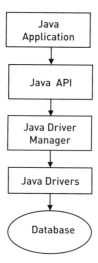

FIGURE 5.3 JDBC structure

The **Java API** takes the form of class libraries that provide a set of objects used in the connection process.

Java drivers are code modules that resolve the differences between the various databases. This is really at the heart of the JDBC concept. It means that the same Java application code (allowing for minimal set-up of specifics) can be used to reference any database without requiring special procedures for each one. The nature of Java drivers is somewhat more complex than is implied by this diagram; different types of drivers are available – see later.

The **Java Driver Manager** (JDM) is an object that manages the interaction between the Java API and the drivers. The JDM needs to be told which drivers will be used in the program; this is done by 'registering' the identity of the relevant drivers with the JDM. Note that one application can register multiple drivers and hence access more than one database type. For instance, it could read an Microsoft Access database, process the data and write to an Oracle database.

Sample JDBC program

The program shown below accesses a Microsoft Access database called Employee.mdb.

It uses the ODBC – JDBC bridge driver (type 1). This requires that the database is first registered as an ODBC data source using the ODBC utility supplied with Windows. The database has been given the data source name **employee**.

```
import java.sql.*;
public class ConnectApp
{
   public static void main(String[] arguments)
   {
      String dbURL = "jdbc:odbc:employee";
         // refers to ODBC data source for database
      try
      {
         Class.forName("sun.jdbc.odbc.JdbcOdbcDriver");
            // loads driver and registers in Driver Manager

         Connection conn = DriverManager.getConnection(dbURL,"","");
            // creates up connection object

         Statement st = conn.createStatement();
            // creates Statement object to hold SQL

         ResultSet rec = st.executeQuery("SELECT EmpId, Name,
                        Position, Salary FROM Employee");

            // executes query and creates ResultSet object

         while (rec.next()) // loop through ResultSet

         {
            System.out.print(rec.getString("EmpId")+" ");
            System.out.print(rec.getString("Name")+" ");
            System.out.print(rec.getString("Position")+" ");
            System.out.println(rec.getDouble("Salary"));
         }
         st.close();
      } catch(Exception e)
         {
            System.out.println("Error "+e.toString());
         }
   } //end main
} //end ConnectAp
```

Details of program

The line:

```
String dbURL = "jdbc:odbc:employee";
```

creates a string object containing a URL that locates the database. Remember that this works by registering the name 'employee' as an ODBC data source for the 'actual' database Employee.mdb.

The line:

```
Class.forName("sun.jdbc.odbc.JdbcOdbcDriver");
```

loads the driver and registers it with the Driver Manager. The Class class involves an interesting Java facility called 'reflection'; this system maintains 'schema' information about classes (and hence objects) defined in the program.

The line:

```
Statement st = conn.createStatement();
```

creates a Statement object that Java uses to hold SQL statements.

The line:

```
ResultSet rec = st.executeQuery("SELECT Emp_id, Name,
                Position, Salary FROM Employee");
```

creates a ResultSet object that holds the relational data.

Note that the executeQuery method is only used for SELECT statements; another method executeUpdate is used for INSERT and UPDATE commands.

The code then enters a 'while' loop that scans and outputs the ResultSet.

NOTE

Each different datatype can be read by a specialised method such as getString and getDouble. A range of these methods is available: getByte, getInt, getLong, getFloat, getDate etc. In fact, there is considerable leeway in the use of these; for instance, getString can be used for all types, although if a numerical values is read it would require conversion back to a number before being operated on numerically.

JDBC driver types

There are four types of Java drivers available, Type 1 to Type 4. The different types provide variations in performance and flexibility.

- *Type 1*: These support the ODBC bridge arrangement. While they were convenient in the early days of JDBC and continue to be a general method of accessing a range of databases, the additional ODBC layer reduces their performance.

- *Type 2*: Converts JDBC calls into calls on the client API for the database. Requires that some binary code be loaded onto each client machine.

- *Type 3*: Pure Java driver for database middleware products. Converts JDBC calls into the middleware's protocol, which then talks to the database.

- *Type 4*: Pure Java driver, converts JDBC calls into the network protocol used directly by the DBMS, allowing a direct call between the client machine and the database.

There is a large and thriving market for JDBC drivers. As well as software from the database vendors themselves, many third party companies produce 'middleware' and the various types of drivers.

Fourth generation systems

The concept of a 'fourth generation language', or 4GL, is rather ill-defined. It was a term adopted by some vendors in the 1980s for their programming products that were reputedly more productive in application development. Their promise was that systems could be written in far fewer lines of code and, because of their inherent automated features, the code would be less error-prone. The term '4GL' is based on the notion that programming languages have evolved through a series of generations; the first generation was machine code, second assembly code and third, the bulk of what we recognise as general high level languages, such as C, C++, Java etc. The term originally was supposed to describe declarative, domain-specific systems such as report and form generators and systems producing application code from CASE tools. However, it soon became associated more with systems that incorporated relatively conventional high-level language code combined with SQL and an intimate connection to a related database.

One of the earliest systems was Informix 4GL, which was developed originally in 1985. It incorporated a standard procedural language, report and forms generator, all integrated closely with embedded SQL commands. Informix is now part of IBM and the system is still in use.

As an illustration of these principles, we will look in more detail at the Oracle PL/SQL language, which displays many of the features of a 4GL and is an integral part of Oracle's repertoire of development tools.

5

Oracle PL/SQL

In its PL/SQL system, Oracle has extended the capabilities of its SQL language by adding procedural language facilities. The resulting combination of declarative SQL commands and a closely integrated procedural language is a very powerful database development tool. The procedural language provides all the facilities one would find in conventional procedural languages: block structure, procedures, functions, control instructions, range of datatypes etc. In addition there are a number of facilities to provide integration with SQL commands and the database. A PL/SQL program consists of a number of program blocks, each of which can contain nested blocks. A block has the following basic structure:

```
[ DECLARE
    data declarations ]
BEGIN
    instructions
[ EXCEPTION
    exception handlers ]
```

The items in square brackets are optional and need not appear in a particular block. The data declarations define variables used within the block; these are not database table references. A full range of datatypes are available, including character, number (various representations), Boolean etc. The instructions available are similar in effect to those provided by languages such as Java and C. In particular, module support is provided by functions and procedures.

There are one or two notable exceptions to this, however. Firstly, PL/SQL provides facilities for integrating its instructions with SQL commands. Also, it provides no input/output instructions; it is assumed that all interaction is with the database tables. Exception handlers are used to trap and process errors that occur during the execution of the program. Run-time errors can arise from a variety of sources, including programming errors and hardware failures. Normally such errors would cause termination of the program and a return of control to the operating system. The exception handling in PL/SQL enables error to be trapped; this provides an opportunity to deal with the problem within the program code and perhaps continue normally, or at least fail gracefully under control of the program.

The following sample program illustrates some of the points made above. The program is trivial and is given for purposes of illustration only. A table Employee is accessed using a cursor and new rows are added to a second table called Temp using selected columns of the Employee table. The Temp table must exist before execution of this code; assuming the existence of the Employee table with (at least) the columns shown, it could be created most easily using the SQL command:

```
create table temp as (SELECT emp_id, name, salary FROM Employee);
```

CH05.PLSQL01.sql

```
 1 DECLARE
 2 CURSOR c1 is
 3       SELECT emp_id, name, salary FROM Employee;
 4    my_id CHAR(4);
 5    my_name CHAR(10);
 6    my_salary NUMBER(7,2);
 7 BEGIN
 8    OPEN c1;
 9    LOOP
10      FETCH c1 INTO my_id, my_name, my_salary;
11      EXIT WHEN c1%NOTFOUND;
12      INSERT INTO Temp VALUES (my_id, my_name, my_salary);
13    END LOOP;
14    CLOSE c1;
15    COMMIT;
16 EXCEPTION
17    WHEN NO_DATA_FOUND THEN CLOSE c1;
18* END;
```

The following notes will help in understanding this example.

NOTES

Lines 2-3	Define a cursor (the concept of a cursor was covered in the section 'SQL in 3GLs' earlier in this chapter) called c1 that is used to accept the output from a Select query.
Lines 4-6	Define a number of local variables used in the subsequent code.

Lines 8-15	Constitutes the body of the procedure code.
Line 8	Opens, i.e., makes available, the c1 cursor. At this point it will contain the result of the Select query on line 3.
Line 9	Activates a continuous loop. The program will continue in this loop until the end of the cursor is reached. At this point the Exit command on line 11 will cause termination of the loop.
Line 10	The Fetch command extracts data from the current row of the cursor and stores the data in the local variables listed. The cursor pointer will then be moved on to the next row of the cursor.
Line 12	This is an SQL statement. It inserts a new row in the table Temp, using as values the data held in the local variables.
Line 17	Illustrates the use of an exception definition.

5

The important concepts to be learned from this example are the way in which the language system integrates SQL and procedural commands and in particular how cursors are used in this context. The close binding of the procedural language with the declarative power of SQL makes a powerful combination. It is also important to appreciate that the procedural language in PL/SQL is an advanced fully-featured language supporting procedures, function, packages, exception handling, triggers etc. It is not, however, object-oriented.

PL/SQL examples

We give three examples here:

- using a cursor to perform an update
- coding a procedure
- coding a function.

1. Using a cursor to perform an update

CH05.PLSQL02.sql

```
DECLARE
    CURSOR sal_cursor IS
    SELECT empid, salary, department from Employee
    WHERE department = 'Sales'
    FOR UPDATE OF Salary NOWAIT;
BEGIN
    FOR emp_record IN sal_cursor
    LOOP
        IF emp_record.salary < 18000 THEN
            UPDATE Employee
            SET Salary = emp_record.salary *1.1
```

```
        WHERE CURRENT OF sal_cursor;
      END IF;
  END LOOP;
  END;
```

NOTES

1 The FOR UPDATE clause causes the referenced rows to be locked while the update is performed.

2 The NOWAIT clause causes an exception if the required rows are in use by another user. If NOWAIT is not used, Oracle will wait until the rows are freed.

3 The WHERE CURRENT clause causes the most recently read row to be used in the update action. This would seem to be obvious, but in fact in the absence of this clause, explicit reference to a row id would be needed.

2. *Coding a procedure*

This procedure could be called by a program block to modify the salary of an employee specified by one parameter by a factor specified by a second parameter.

CH05.PLSQL03.sql

```
CREATE OR REPLACE PROCEDURE update_salary
   (p_empid IN Employee.empid%TYPE, p_factor IN NUMBER)
IS
BEGIN
  UPDATE Employee
  SET Salary = Salary * p_factor
  WHERE p_empid = empid;
END;
/
```

NOTES

1 This procedure could be called from another program block or by using the EXECUTE command at the SQL command interface. For example, to raise the salary of employee number 1001 by 20%:

   EXECUTE(1001, 1.2);

2 Note that the procedure is created using the CREATE command; this has the effect of permanently storing the procedure source code in the database. It then becomes available as extra functionality for subsequent queries.

3 The IN keyword specifies the direction of the parameter, which can be IN, OUT or IN OUT. The OUT parameters are subject to the usual restriction: since a value is to be returned from the procedure call, OUT actual parameters must be variables, not constant, values.

4 The element after the IN keyword is the datatype of the parameter. In the parameter employee.empid%TYPE the %TYPE suffix 'picks up' the datatype of the referenced table column. This guarantees that the types are consistent; also the type is picked up at run-time, which ensures that modification to the table design will not affect the stored procedure.

3. Coding a function

CH05.PLSQL04.sql

```
CREATE OR REPLACE FUNCTION get_maxsal(p_dept
Employee.Department%TYPE)
     RETURN NUMBER
IS
     v_maxsalary Employee.Salary%TYPE;
BEGIN

   SELECT MAX(Salary) INTO v_maxsalary FROM Employee
     WHERE Employee.Department = p_dept;
     RETURN v_maxsalary;
END;
/
```

User interfaces

Forms and report design – overview

A **form** is a screen display that is used for data entry and querying of database data. Essentially a form provides a 'window' into the database, showing the data in a convenient user-friendly format. It is an alternative to displaying the data in the simple table-based interfaces that most DBMS systems provide. Forms are primarily an end-user facility; their principal role is to facilitate the operation of the database application by clerical and administrative staff that are not familiar with the internal design of the database. To a considerable extent, the set of forms supporting a database application 'is' the database for such end-users. Typical commercial transactions such as entering sales orders, booking a theatre performance, submitting employees' overtime claims, etc. are generally managed with the use of forms. The sample Microsoft Access databases available with this text provide many examples of such forms.

Forms are available in most database systems except those using a purely SQL-based command interface. For instance, Oracle offers Oracle Forms, a component of the Oracle Developer Suite. However, a very common way of providing a forms interface is to use a web form. This topic covered in more detail in Chapter 10. For those working in Java, mention can also be made of the Java Foundation Classes and, in particular, the Swing GUI classes.

In this section, we highlight some of the main features of forms that would typically be found in a modern GUI-based database system and indicate some of the design issues of forms.

A report is a printed output of information from the database system generally derived from a query or by some processing by program. In spite of technical advances such as email, Electronic Data Transfer and on-line facilities such as the Web, there is still a very active requirement to be able to generate printed reports.

Elements of forms

A form provides a means of viewing and maintaining data held within a database. The simplest situation is that in which the form shows one row of data on screen at a time; this is illustrated in Figure 5.4.

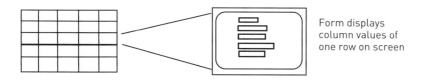

Form displays column values of one row on screen

FIGURE 5.4 Simple one-row form

However, there are several more elaborate possibilities, detailed below:

1 The form may be based, not on a physical table, but on the output from a query. A relational query by its nature produces a result that is also a relation and hence can be used as the source data of a form. When the form is used, the query may have to be executed to bring the data up to date, but this will be transparent to the user. Also, depending on the query, there may be restrictions on the updating of the data.

2 The form may display several rows of the table/query. This facility is used in mainly in browsing-type operations where the user scans manually through a range of table rows to locate some specific item.

3 The screen display may hold two (or more) forms interconnected in some fashion. The most common mode of working in this respect is the use of a form/sub-form arrangement. This is used to display two tables having a one-to-many relationship such as Order and Order Item tables in a sales order application. The main form displays the 'one' side of the relationship (the Order data) while a sub-form typically shows several lines of the 'many' table (the Order Items). An example of this is shown in Figure 5.5.

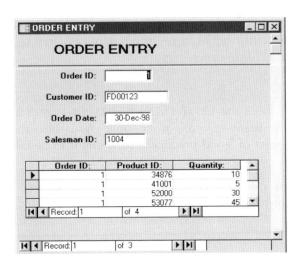

FIGURE 5.5 Form – Sub-form example

5

Form controls

In current systems using a graphical user interface (GUI), forms can be constructed using the visual objects, usually called 'controls', that the GUI supports. For the purposes of a database form, the most important of these is the text box that is used to display data from the database columns. A text box can be 'bound' or 'unbound'. Bound means that the box is linked to a column of the table underlying the form; changes made to data displayed in the text box are reflected in changes to the table. Unbound means that the text box is not linked to a table column. Unbound columns are used to hold intermediate or temporary values.

Buttons are used to initiate some specified action, such as closing the form or moving the form display to the next row of the table. They are also used to construct menu systems using unbound forms.

List boxes are used to enable selection of a data value from a list of alternatives. The list can be directly entered by the designer or be derived from a reference table.

A combo box is a combination of a text box and a list box. It presents data in a list format but also permits entry of new values.

Form applications

Forms are used for three main purposes with an application database system:

- General table maintenance, i.e. adding, amending and deleting rows from tables.

- Application transactions, i.e. performing the essential processing operations of the application, such as entering a new order, issuing an invoice, recording stock received etc. Such operations frequently use two or more tables.

- Menu construction. To navigate through the various options within the database application, a system of menus constructed from form buttons is often used. This is an alternative to conventional 'drop-down' menus.

Form design considerations

The design of a form is partly an aesthetic matter, and as such individual tastes will vary; for instance, some people will prefer many colours, others only grey, white and black. However, there are a number of factors of 'good practice' which ought to be taken into account. These, and some general design techniques, are described below.

1 **Use consistent conventions on all forms** so that the user does not have to become familiar with every form independently; e.g.

- use of header and footer

- button placements and icons

- placement and style of text and label boxes.

> **NOTE**
>
> It is possibly useful to have *some* variation in colouring or format to provide visual cues for users.

2 **Use a comfortable font size and style.**

Small font sizes can make reading difficult. If the form space permits, use larger font sizes to aid readability.

3 **Establish correct tab sequence.**

- The tab sequence is the route the focus will take through the form controls when tab (or return) is pressed. The default tab sequence is simply the order of creation of the controls on the form. This is not necessarily appropriate.

- The tab sequence is usually defined by a property of the controls. Check that the automatically generated sequence follows a natural path.

- A control can be excluded from the sequence. By default, all controls will be included (by the form generator) in the tab sequence. In many cases this serves no purpose. For instance, buttons used to navigate through the table should be excluded.

4 **Divide the form into different functional areas.**

For example, the form header could show a main title and a company logo, the form footer could hold control buttons and the central area would show the form details.

5 **Customise the system for end-users**

- Modify menu and toolbars; disable design mode, remove irrelevant options.

- Use an automatic start-up form to prevent access to database design windows.

6 **Ensure that the form has a convenient size**.

- It is generally advisable that the form covers all or most of the screen, to avoid visible 'clutter' from the rest of the screen and accidental switching to an underlying application.

- If the form is to be displayed on a number of different computers, care must be taken that the form will be clearly visible on the range of screen sizes and resolutions likely to be encountered.

7 **Apply validation to data**.

As a fundamental rule, it should be impossible for data to get into the database which is inconsistent with other data or which is not meaningful to the application. The input validation should form a barrier to such erroneous data.

8 **Use control buttons to facilitate user interaction.**

Clearly labelled buttons should be added to the form that provide the user with the necessary actions for that form, such as adding a new row, deleting a row, exiting from the form etc. In particular, it is desirable to have buttons to cancel the current transaction and to save/confirm the current transaction.

Report design

Reports produced from a database application system are normally used as a means of communication, often with people outside the company. It is important then that the report is well-designed and conveys the information correctly and clearly. Fortunately, most database systems provide extensive facilities for the automatic production of reports, so that the work involved for the database developer is dramatically reduced. In this section we look at some general aspects of report design. The Hands-On Access section later in the book provides an introduction to the report generation process in Access.

Note that reports can be generated from tables and from queries; in general, more complex reports will require data obtained from more than one table which is achieved by means of a query that joins the tables appropriately and selects the necessary data from the query output.

Report structure

In some respects, a report can be viewed as a printed form so that many of the principles of good form design (font sizes, consistent layout etc.), described above also apply to reports. There is of course, an infinite number of ways of formatting a printed report, but we can identify a number of common features:

1 We can make the broad distinction between simple listing reports and reports that subtotal and/or summarise the data. This has a bearing on the 'zoning' of the report. A listing report in effect will simply consist of a set of columns of data drawn from the input table/query. A totalling report will have subtotals and grand totals interspersed with the row data.

2 A number of zones of the print-out can be identified:

- Report heading; generally fixed heading giving a report name, date source etc.

- Page heading; usually also shows report name and date and column headings.

- Detail; shows the 'per row' detailed data from the report source.

- Page footing; possibly page numbers, page totals etc.

The typical format of a group total report is shown below. This report shows the sales of a product range, subtotalled by sales BranchCode.

Page No 1	Product Sales Report 10/09/98		
Product Code	BranchCode	Sales Quantity	Sales Value
B342	North	25	150.00
	South	31	186.00
	West	43	258.00
B342 Total			594.00
C100	North	102	1 018.98
	South	55	549.45
	West	79	789.21
C100 Total			2 357.64
E501	North	12	479.40
	South	5	199.75
	West	9	359.55
E501 Total			1 038.70
Grand Total			3 990.34

This example shows only one level of grouping, but it is possible to have many more levels. For instance, the report might be required to show the sales figures broken down into the individual salespersons at each of the branches. With increasing levels of grouping, the report becomes progressively more difficult to interpret and is it even more important to use a clear and unambiguous layout.

Summary

This chapter covered the general topic of the user interface to the database. It was divided into two main areas: access to the database by various forms of programming and user interface techniques such as forms and reports.

On the programming topic, SQL was shown to be a very significant tool in database development, appearing in a wide range of language systems. The role of standard programming interfaces such as ODBC and JDBC was also highlighted. The nature of fourth generation systems was described, using Oracle's PL/SQL as an example.

The topic of user interfaces was covered in the later part of the chapter. The nature of database forms and reports was explored.

Review questions

5

1 What is meant by 'embedding' SQL commands?

2 Outline the various programming alternatives available for accessing databases.

3 List the ways in which SQL can be used in programming environments.

4 What do the acronyms ODBC and JDBC stand for? Explain the nature of these.

5 Explain what is meant by the term '4GL'.

6 List the components of the user interface that would be provided by a DBMS.

7 Outline the main functions performed by forms.

8 What is meant by the term 'form control'?

Exercises

1 Describe the various ways in which SQL may be combined or utilised in other programming environments.

2 Draw a diagram to represent the architecture of a system employing ODBC and explain the meaning of the components of the diagram.

3 Explain what is meant by the acronym ADO and outline the purpose of its Connection, Command and Recordset objects.

4 Explain the nature of JDBC and use a diagram to show the structure of a system based on JDBC.

5 Discuss the relative merits of using a 4GL system such as Oracle's PL/SQL or Informix compared to the use of standard languages such as Java or Visual Basic.

6 Discuss the factors that must be considered in the design of forms.

References

Textbooks

Descriptions of ODBC, OLE DB and ADO tend to appear in the context of language systems such as Visual Basic or C++ or .NET etc.

Oracle PL/SQL

Allen C. (2004): *Oracle Database 10g PL/SQL 101*, Osborne Oracle Press

JDBC

Speegle G. (2002): *JDBC: Practical Guide for Java Programmers*, Morgan Kaufmann

Swing

Schildt H. (2006): *Swing: A Beginner's Guide*, Osborne/McGraw-Hill

Websites

ODBC

http://www.datadirect.com/developer/odbc/basics/index.ssp

ADO/ OLEDB

http://msdn2.microsoft.com/en-us/data/default.aspx

JDBC

http://java.sun.com/docs/books/tutorial/jdbc/

Oracle PL/SQL

http://www.oracle.com/technology/tech/pl_sql/index.html

http://infolab.stanford.edu/~ullman/fcdb/oracle/or-plsql.html

Informix

http://www-306.ibm.com/software/data/informix/tools/4gl/

Swing

http://java.sun.com/docs/books/tutorial/uiswing/index.html

6

Transactions

LEARNING OBJECTIVES

In this chapter we will look at the concept of a transaction in database processing. In particular we examine the problems that can arise in a multi-user system where multiple transactions run concurrently and potentially access the same data. The techniques that can be employed to avoid these problems are discussed. After studying this chapter, you should be able to do the following:

- Explain the concept of a transaction in database access.

- Show how the acronym ACID is used indicate the essential characteristics of a transaction.

- Describe the commit and rollback procedures associated with transaction management.

- Show by example how concurrent accesses to a database can cause erroneous results and/or database corruption.

- Describe these specific problems:

  - Lost update problem.

  - Uncommitted dependency problem.

  - Inconsistent analysis problem.

- Explain the concept of serialisation of transactions and its significance.

- Describe how locking can be used to prevent concurrency problems.

- Explain how two-phase locking improves on the basic locking method.

- Describe the different granularities of locking and compare their relative merits.

- Discuss the relative merits of optimistic and pessimistic locking techniques.

- Describe the effect of shared and exclusive locks.

- Show how locking can lead to the problem of deadlocks.

- Describe techniques for dealing with the threat of deadlock, including prevention and detection.

Introduction

Transactions are a fundamental mechanism in the management of databases. They are a major tool in the preservation of the integrity and accuracy of the database, especially when many users access the database simultaneously. In principle, a transaction is a means of grouping a series of database updates into one unit of processing in order to guarantee that the updates will all be successfully completed.

We start by examining the basic principles of transactions, then progress to the very important topic of what happens when two or more transactions are running simultaneously on the same database.

Transactions

Concept and definition

In general terminology, a **transaction** is some activity involving a transfer or exchange of goods, services or money. Used in the context of a database system, it has a related but more specific meaning: it refers to a group of changes and/or queries to the database which, for the purposes of database integrity, must be performed as a single unit. An example will quickly clarify the above statement and illustrate the need for transactions.

In a typical sales order processing application, the customer places an order for a number of items of various products. When this order is entered into the computer order processing system, the following changes need to be made to record the order:

- Add the general order information (customer details, date etc.) to the Order table.
- Add one row to the Order Item table for each item ordered.
- Update the quantity available for each ordered item in the Stock table.
- Update the Salesmen table in respect of the value of the order.

All of these changes to the database are interrelated; it does not make any sense for some of them to be carried out and not others. For instance, if all the changes except the Stock table update are carried out, the Stock table will cease to accurately represent the status of the inventory, since, when the order is executed, goods will be removed without being acknowledged in the database.

It is simple enough to ensure that all the above operations are carried out together by incorporating them into a single program procedure or procedure form, but this is not sufficient to guarantee database integrity. Problems could arise in the middle of such a compound operation:

- The computer could fail with only some of the changes completed.
- The operator may find it necessary to abandon the order entry due to lack of a crucial item of stock.
- A communication link used by the order entry system could fail.

Database transactions are designed to prevent the database being left in an inconsistent state regardless of the circumstances of the attempted update. A transaction can be defined as follows:

> A transaction is a group of database operations that is treated as an atomic unit; i.e. the operations are *all* completed or *none* of them is completed.

In effect, the DBMS must support this commitment regardless of the mode of failure of the transaction. For instance, if the sales order clerk is halfway through entering an order when a power failure occurs, they would expect to find on restarting the computer that no changes pertaining to the interrupted order had been carried out. Also, if the clerk wanted to abandon an order part way through data entry, this should not involve any complex backtracking, it should be a simple option provided by the data entry program. It is sufficient for the data entry software to signal to the DBMS that the transaction is to be aborted. This aspect of transaction management is provided by two generic system operations known as **commit** and **rollback**, described later.

ACID properties

6

The necessary characteristics of a transaction are often expressed succinctly using the ACID acronym; these properties explained below:

Atomicity

This refers to the behaviour of the DBMS in guaranteeing that either all or none of the updates of a transaction are performed. This simply reflects the essential definition of a transaction.

Consistency

The database must be left in a consistent state when the transaction terminates. This includes for instance the action of the transaction manager in maintaining referential integrity: if an update within a transaction deletes a row which is referenced from another table, the delete should not go ahead. Based on the atomicity principle, the whole transaction must then be aborted.

Isolated

Concurrent transactions are kept isolated from each, other implying that any operation such as a query cannot 'see' data, being updated within another transaction, in an intermediate state. This property is sometimes relaxed in the interests of efficiency, resulting in what is called a 'dirty read'. In effect, one may read data which is potentially being changed as it is read. Whether this is admissible or acceptable really depends on the nature of the application and the query.

Durability

This guarantees that the database will remain consistent even in the event of a serious failure of the system, such as loss of power to the computer. For example, if several parts of a transaction have been entered when the whole computer system shuts down, then the transaction management system must ensure that the effect of the partial entry is nullified.

Commit and rollback

The **commit** and **rollback** operations are supported by SQL and by any system that implements transaction management. For simplicity, their effect is described by reference to the implementation in SQL. Similar facilities are found in other non-SQL systems.

- The Commit statement signals the successful end of a series of updates within one transaction. It tells the DBMS to save all the amended data and to terminate the current transaction.

- The Rollback statement aborts the current transaction. All updates within the current transaction are cancelled and the database reverts to its state before the start of the transaction.

Note that, under this model, a transaction is considered to *start* when the first database update command is issued after the end of the previous transaction.

NOTE

Some systems (e.g. Microsoft Access and Sybase) also provide a 'Start Transaction' command, which defines a specific start point for a transaction. The implication of the presence of this command is that it is possible to perform database operations which are not governed by transaction 'bracketing'.

We can illustrate the Commit and Rollback commands by means of an example, based on the Order Input scenario given above. (For simplicity, the Salesman table update is ignored). We have used SQL commands, but a similar logic would apply if some other input mechanism were used, such as a form in Microsoft Access.

In the first case given below, the data entry proceeds without any problems and is terminated with a Commit command. This causes all the preceding commands to be applied to the database.

Enter order data

```
Insert into Orders Values ('AB1024', '12-Oct-07', S016)
```

Enter order item data

```
Insert into OrderItems Values( 'AB1024', 1, 'P234', 25)
Insert into OrderItems Values( 'AB1024', 2, 'T877', 3)
    . . .
```

Amend stock table

```
Update Stock
   Set Qty-in-Stock = Qty-in-Stock - 25
   WHERE ProductCode = 'P234'
Update Stock
   Set Qty-in-Stock = Qty-in-Stock - 3
   WHERE ProductCode = 'T877'
. . .
```

Complete the transaction

```
Commit
```

It should be clear that all these actions are part of the same 'package'; it would not be acceptable to execute some and not the others. We will suppose now that part way through this sequence a mistake in an earlier entry is noticed. The data entry operator can use the Rollback command to abort the commands entered up to that point, returning the database to its state prior to the start of the current transaction.

6

Enter order data

```
Insert into Orders Values ('AB1024', '12-Oct-07', S016)
```

Enter order item data

```
Insert into OrderItems Values( 'AB1024', 1, 'P234', 25)
Insert into OrderItems Values( 'AB1024', 2, 'T877', 33)
   ** error in previous line, 33 instead of 3 **
. . .
```

Amend stock table

```
Update Stock
   Set Qty-in-Stock = Qty-in-Stock - 25
   WHERE ProductCode = 'P234'
   ** error noticed **
```

Operator decides to abandon transaction

```
Rollback
```

Now the database is returned to its state prior to the start of the transaction, as if these commands had not been issued.

The other contingency that the system must cope with is some failure (hardware or software) occurring 'in the middle' of the transaction that prevents its proper completion, and the user is not given the opportunity of issuing either commit or rollback. In this event, failure to reach the Commit command has the same effect as the Rollback – the transaction effectively disappears. Handling of this aspect of transactions is achieved by backup and recovery techniques that are described in the next chapter.

Concurrent transactions

When a database is accessed simultaneously by two or more transactions, certain problems arise that don't exist for a single transaction. Why this should be the case is perhaps not immediately obvious; one would think that several users could read and write data to/from the database more or less independently without difficulty.

A closer inspection of what can happen during simultaneous updates reveals that serious corruption of the data can occur. These problems arise when two users attempt to update the same data simultaneously; among other problems, the possibility exists that one of the updates will be 'lost', i.e. effectively overwritten by the other. In this chapter we will look at the nature of this problem and show how it is managed by a technique known as **locking**. In addition, we discover that locking in fact produces its own problem in the form of a situation known as **deadlock**. First, we will recap on the transaction concept and introduce some important properties of transactions.

Problems of concurrency

Lost update

An example is the best way to illustrate the problems that can, arise during simultaneous updates. We assume that two clerks, Anne and Bill, are updating a customer accounts database. To appreciate the source of the difficulties, we must first examine the internal 'mechanics' of updating a row of the database.

When a database user accesses a row of data from the database with a view to amending the data (the data may be displayed on a screen form), the actual data is read from the database storage and held in a temporary buffer area in main memory. This situation is illustrated in Figure 6.1.

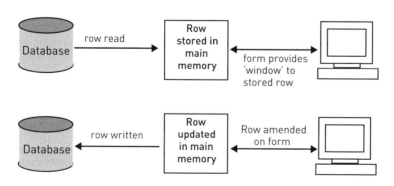

FIGURE 6.1 Data buffering

In effect, the form provides a 'window' into the memory so that the stored row can be viewed and modified. The most significant point about the above process is that a *copy* of the database row has been created and held temporarily in memory. The process of updating the database involves modifying the in-memory copy (via the form), then writing it back to the database Storage on disk.

The above narrative shows the effect of *one* user updating the database; if we extend the picture to include two users, Anne and Bill, certain complications arise.

First of all, it is probably clear that if Anne and Bill are accessing totally different parts of the database and/or working at disjoint time periods, no interference between their efforts is likely to occur. However, if they both attempt to apply an update to the *same row at the same time*, things can go badly wrong. This is illustrated in Figure 6.2.

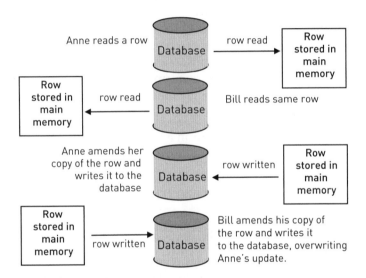

FIGURE 6.2 Concurrent updates

The result of this sequence of operations is that Anne's update of the database has been lost – this is commonly known as the **lost update** syndrome. This effect happens due to the fact that copies of parts of the database are held in main memory for the purposes of the update process. While it is perhaps fairly unlikely, the possibility exists of two users holding and amending the same row at the same time. In this situation, it is inevitable that one of these updates will be lost. In spite of the low probability of such an event, it is generally not acceptable to ignore the possibility, since it results in an undetected corruption of the database.

Additional note

The situation in practice is actually worse than that indicated above. Data transfers to and from a database actually involve at least one physical disk block possibly holding many database rows. In the example shown in Figure 6.2 Anne and Bill will each hold a copy of one such block in the in-memory buffer. Even if they are not amending the same row, Bill's rewriting of the block will cancel the effect of Anne's update. The consequence of this is that for a problem to arise the coincidence in database accessing need only apply to database blocks rather than individual rows. This is far more likely to happen. We discuss this topic in more detail later in the section 'Granularity of locking'.

Other problems can occur as a result of interleaving of transactions; two of these, known as the **uncommitted dependency problem** and the **inconsistent analysis problem**, are described below.

Uncommitted dependency problem

On completion of the transaction, the user can choose to cancel the whole sequence (rollback) or to have it finally accepted (commit). The main technique used in implementing transactions is the immediate update with transaction log: in the course of a transaction, necessary updates are written immediately to disk, while 'before images' (i.e. the previous value of the data) are written to a transaction log file. Hence, in the 'middle' of the transaction, some of the transaction updates will be actioned on the database and visible to other users, whose own updates may be affected by the uncommitted changes. If the transaction is eventually rolled back (by applying the before images), the other dependent changes are invalidated.

Consider the following example which might occur in a bank. Mr Smith's account, with an initial balance of £1 000, is being updated simultaneously by two transactions A and B and the following sequence of actions ensue:

1 Transaction A starts with a withdrawal for £600. The database is updated to show a balance of £400.

2 Transaction B reads the £400 from the database into an in-memory buffer and adds a deposit of £300, giving a balance of £700.

3 Transaction A now executes a rollback, returning the database to £1 000.

4 Transaction B now writes its in-memory balance value of £700 to the database and commits the transaction.

At this point the database has been corrupted; the balance should be £1300 but is actually £700. This effect is similar to the lost update, but differs in the timing of events. Note that the above example would not have caused a problem if the rollback had not occurred, because transaction B read the balance after update by transaction A.

Inconsistent analysis problem

This effect again arises from interleaving transaction operations and demonstrates how erroneous results can be obtained by a transaction which is only reading the database. In this instance, we assume that one transaction is reading the database to provide some analysis (say, computing a total balance value) while it is simultaneously being amended by another transaction. We assume for this example that Transaction A is reading a set of three accounts and summing the balances. Transaction B, over the same time interval, is transferring money from one of these accounts to another. We will assume that the accounts are called ACC1, ACC2 and ACC3 with starting balances of £100, £200 and £300 respectively.

1 Transaction A reads ACC1 and sets running total to £100.

2 Transaction A reads ACC2 and adds £200 to total giving £300.

3 Transaction B reads ACC2, withdraws £50 and deposits it in ACC3.

4 Transaction A reads ACC3, reads £350 and adds it to total giving final total of £650.

Note that the transfer of cash from one account to another should not have affected the overall total and hence it should still show 100+200+300 = £600. However, the summary report shows £650. In this example the database has *not* been corrupted, but a database user has obtained a query result that is quite erroneous.

Serialisation of transactions

It is clear that the potential corruption and inconsistencies described in the foregoing sections cannot be allowed to occur. In the management of concurrent transactions it is essential that the DBMS prevents such unacceptable interference. In effect, each database user should be able to access and update the database without fear of these problems occurring. The objective of the DBMS in this respect can be expressed as the concept of **serialisability of transactions**, which can be stated as follows:

> When two or more transactions are executed concurrently on a database, their effect should be the same as if they had executed serially, with one completing before the other starts.

Suppose we have three transaction TA, TB and TC that are executing at least partly at the same time. We can illustrate the relative timing of the transactions as shown in Figure 6.3(a). Note that some or all of the transactions overlap at various times. Figure 6.3(b) illustrates serial execution of the transactions, with one transaction finishing before another starts. The concept of serialisability states that the effect on the database for each of these two transaction sequences Figure 6.3 (a) and (b) should be the same.

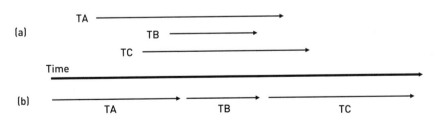

FIGURE 6.3 Serialisation

To achieve serialisability, we need some method of allowing the transactions to proceed in parallel, while at the same time avoiding the interference problems described earlier. This can be accomplished by means of a technique known as **locking**, described next.

Locking

Locking is used to implement concurrency by all commercial databases. If we examine the problems (such as lost update) that occur between concurrent transactions, we can see that they result from two or more transactions accessing the same data at the same time. The idea of locking is that interference between concurrent transactions can be controlled by enabling transactions to **lock** parts of the database data while that part is being amended, preventing other transactions from amending/reading the same data. When the amendment is complete, the lock is released, enabling other transactions to continue. If we revisit the lost update problem illustrated in Figure 6.2 we can see how locking could avoid the problem.

Note, however, that this example does not show the full picture – a further problem can occur. The nature and resolution of this additional problem is dealt with shortly.

1 Anne reads a database row into a memory buffer.

2 Anne's transaction locks the disk block holding the row.

3 Bill tries to read the same row but is prevented by the lock; his transaction enters a 'wait' state.

4 Anne writes the updated row to disk and releases the lock.

5 Bill's transaction now proceeds and reads the updated row.

6 Bill's transaction locks the block to prevent access by other users.

7 Bill updates the row and writes to disk, releasing the lock.

The two updates have been successfully made without any corruption. The process has involved a delay in completing Bill's work, but this is a small price to pay for maintaining the integrity of the database. However, the duration of the lock is obviously relevant: if Anne and Bill are online clerks dealing with, say a telephone ordering system, then lock delays could become significant.

Two-phase locking

In fact, the simple locking scheme described above does not guarantee complete protection from concurrency problems. The lost update and the other problems described above can still arise if multiple locks are applied during one transaction: although each individual update is protected, the fact that updates from two or more transactions can interleave in time can cause data corruption. As an example of how this can occur, consider the following sequence, based on the same scenario used above:

1 Anne starts a transaction and reads a row of a table after applying a lock.

2 Bill tries to access the same row but is prevented by the lock.

3 Anne updates the row, writes it to disk and releases the lock.

4 Bill now succeeds in reading the row, locks it and updates it. Note that Bill's update was based on the data *after update by Anne.*

5 Bill now write the row to disk and releases the lock.

6 Anne's transaction, for whatever reason, now fails and is rolled back, restoring the row to its state before Anne's update. Bill's update has now been lost.

The problem here is that a lock has been released too early, allowing for the possibility of interference from another transaction. A slightly more elaborate locking scheme, called **two-phase locking**, avoids this situation.

In the two-phase locking scheme, every transaction has two phases: a **growing phase** when locks are acquired and a **shrinking phase** during which locks are released. In other words, within one transaction, **all lock operations must precede the first lock release**. In the above example, at step 3, the lock would *not* be released, thereby preventing Bill from proceeding as indicated in steps 4 and 5. When the rollback of Anne's transaction eventually occurs, Bill's update is not lost, because it never took place.

The foregoing description of locking is rather simplified; there are a number of variants on this basic model that are described in the following sections.

6

Granularity of locking

A lock can be applied in a variety of 'levels' of varying severity, in terms of the relative amount of data locked; this is often referred to as the 'granularity' of the locks. The most severe would be to lock the *entire database*, preventing all other activity. This is the simplest to implement, but is very wasteful and would degrade the performance of the database dramatically. Total locking like this is only used when performing some global operation on the database such as compacting, re-indexing, etc.

A less severe lock is **table-level locking**, in which each table required by a transaction is locked, leaving other tables free for access by other transactions. This does permit some degree of simultaneity, but is still generally too restrictive. Many applications require access to several tables for one transaction; for instance, in a sales order processing system, sales order entry would use the tables Customer, Product Stock, Orders and Order Items simultaneously. Locking all these tables would bar access, for instance, to a transaction updating the Product Stock table to record the arrival of a stock delivery. Again, table-level locking would only be applied when a large-scale operation is being performed on the table such as archiving or indexing.

Probably the most logical level is **row (or record) level locking**, which locks only one row of a table at a time, providing a high degree of simultaneity. In practice, it is technically quite difficult to maintain locks at the row level and **page level locking** is used as a compromise. (Note however that some systems do implement true row-level locks). Page locking applies locks in units of whole physical blocks or pages of the database storage medium such that the row being accessed is contained within the locked zone. If the size of the row is less than or equal to the page size, then a single page lock will suffice. If the row spans several pages, all pages holding part of the row will be locked.

A drawback to page locking is that locked pages will often contain other rows not involved in the transaction. This is particularly significant for tables with a small row size, where several rows will be 'packed' into one physical page. For instance, a typical page size of 4 096 could hold 100 rows of a table with a row length of 40 bytes. The implication of this effect is that a single row lock will actually be locking another 99 rows, preventing access to these rows by other users for the duration of the lock. However, page level locking ties in with the practice in disk systems whereby the unit of transfer between disk and main memory is the physical block. Hence, the whole block will be rewritten after update of any part of it.

In principle, locks could be extended to an even finer level of granularity – to the column level. This would certainly reduce the likelihood of locks actually causing any conflict between transactions and hence would provide optimum performance. However, the technical difficulties exceed even those for row locks and no major system currently implements column locking.

Other locking variants

There are other variations on the theme of locking, in addition to the granularity of the locking. These are described in the sections below.

Optimistic and pessimistic locking

This term refers to the manner in which locks are applied relative to the reading, amending and writing activities. As the name implies, **optimistic locking** assumes that your transaction will not conflict with another and hence updating proceeds without a lock being applied. At the point of committing the transaction, a check is made to ascertain whether in fact any other transaction has accessed the same data. If so, the transactions are rolled back and must be re-started.

Pessimistic locking assumes that a conflict will occur and the data is locked at the start of the transaction. Once the data is locked, the transaction can run to completion without hindrance.

Contrasting the two approaches, optimistic locking tries to optimise system performance by minimising the duration of a lock, while pessimistic locking imposes locks for much longer periods. On the other hand, a transaction controlled by optimistic locking may not immediately succeed and may need to be re-run; this will not happen with pessimistic locking. Another advantage of pessimistic locking is that read accesses will always see the most up-to-date data; in optimistic locking, one could read a record that is currently being updated.

The choice between optimistic and pessimistic locking depends mostly on the loading of the system. If the application system is busy, with a large number of transactions being processed per hour, conflicts between transactions are therefore probable and pessimistic locking is preferable. If the loading is light, optimistic locking will generally produce a better overall performance.

Shared and exclusive locks

Another variation on the locking theme is to vary the level of 'exclusivity' of the lock. In this respect there are usually two form of lock:

Shared or S Lock : A shared lock is applied when data is only required to be read.

Exclusive or X Lock: An exclusive lock is applied when data is to be updated.

These are sometimes referred to as **locking modes**. Several transactions can apply an S lock simultaneously, enabling each user to read the database. At the same time, no transaction can apply an X lock until all the S locks terminate. If an X lock is applied to a unit of data, no other locks can be applied. In other words, at any instant, there can be no locks, one or more S locks or one X lock for one unit of data.

Deadlock

Introduction

While solving the problems inherent in concurrent access to a database, locking produces a problem of its own, known as **deadlocking**. A deadlock can occur when online users are able to apply two or more locks at the same time. This can result in a circular wait situation that brings the activity of both users to a halt. An example will clarify this concept.

Suppose we have an airline seat reservation system using concurrent access to a database. At some instant, two customers Anne and Bill are being served by the online operators. Both Anne and Bill intend to book a seat on flight AB123 and a later flight AB456. Anne's sales assistant first of all accesses the AB123 flight information, thereby placing a lock on it. At the same time, Bill's assistant accesses flight AB456 and similarly locks it. Before committing the first flight booking, each assistant now tries to access the other flight but of course finds that it is locked. Never mind, they think, it will be unlocked soon. However, the two booking operations are now deadlocked; Anne is waiting to book AB456 while holding AB123, while Bill is waiting for AB123 while holding AB456. We can summarise this sequence of events as follows:

Anne locks AB123

Bill locks AB456

Anne requests AB456 . . . waits!

Bill requests AB456 . . . waits!

A circular wait situation now exists and will persist until one user rolls back their transaction. It is important to appreciate that deadlocks occur as a *result of the locking mechanism*. Locking is used to avoid corruption of the database arising from concurrent accesses, but unfortunately it is itself marred by its potential for causing deadlocks.

Dealing with deadlocks

A number of techniques have been devised to deal with deadlocks. The most significant of these are *prevention* and *detection*.

Prevention

In the above example, each user applied two locks with a time gap between. A deadlock can be avoided if all exclusive locks are applied at the same time. Failure to lock *all* required records at the start of the transaction causes an immediate release of all locks already made, thereby preventing the circular wait situation. The difficulties with this approach are, firstly, that a number of locks may be applied for a considerable period of time, thereby limiting access by other users; secondly, in many application it is not possible to predict what records will need to be locked until later in the processing. The only way to manage this would be to release all current locks when a new lock is required, then applying all locks again; the principle applied here is that all locks are applied or none are applied.

Detection

It is possible for the DBMS to detect the presence of a deadlock by checking for circular waits within the locks and lock requests. When detected, the deadlock can be resolved by rolling back one of the member transactions. This will have the effect of removing all locks held by the transaction and hence breaking the deadlock. The online user responsible for the aborted transaction would need to be informed that the transaction did not succeed and must be re-started.

The DBMS can use a matrix technique to detect circular waits in the current resource locking situation. A 'resource' in this context refers to the unit of data that can be locked by transactions; as indicated earlier when dealing with granularity of locking, this will generally be one or more disk blocks. The current pattern of transaction requests and resource locks can be represented by a matrix as shown in Table 6.1 examples (A) and (B).

Example A

Transactions	Resource A	Resource B	Resource C
1	Locked		Wait
2		Wait	
3		Locked	Locked

Example B

Transactions	Resource A	Resource B	Resource C
1	Locked		Wait
2		Wait	
3	Wait	Locked	Locked

TABLE 6.1 Pattern of transaction requests and resource looks

In example A, each of transactions 1 and 2 are waiting on resources B and C respectively, which are both held by transaction 3. Transaction 3 is not waiting on any resource and hence will presumably eventually release B and C, so at this time no deadlock exists. However, example B shows that transaction 3 has now requested resource A which is locked by transaction 1. This now creates a circular wait.

Summary

The subject of this chapter, transactions, is at the heart of all database management systems. We have seen that transactions can help to guarantee the integrity and accuracy of database processing.

In particular, transactions are essential in the management of concurrent database accessing which of course is by far the most common practical case in enterprise computing. We saw that the process of locking is used to manage the problems that arise in concurrent transactions, and in particular it was shown that two-phase locking is necessary to ensure proper protection. Deadlock is an unfortunate by-product of the locking mechanism and must itself be managed with suitable techniques.

The topics covered in this chapter were:

1 The principles of a transaction.

2 The ACID properties of a transaction.

3 Commit and rollback transaction commands.

4 Problems of concurrency: lost update, uncommitted dependency, inconsistent analysis.

5 Serialisation of transactions.

6 Locking: general principles, two-phase locking, granularity of locking, shared/exclusive, pessimistic/optimistic locking.

7 Deadlocks: causes, dealing with deadlocks.

Review questions

1 Give a definition of a transaction.

2 In the context of transactions, what does the acronym ACID stand for?

3 What two commands are used to manage the termination of a transaction?

4 Why does concurrent access to a database give rise to potential problems?

5 What is meant by the terms: lost update, uncommitted dependency problem and inconsistent analysis problem?

6 What is meant by 'serialisation' of transactions?

7 Explain the concept of locking and why it is used.

8 What is meant by two-phase locking?

9 Explain the term 'granularity of locking'.

10 What is a deadlock and how is it caused?

11 What methods are used to manage deadlocks?

Exercises

1 Explain what is meant by transactions in the context of a database system and why they are needed. Describe the facilities that a DBMS should provide for the support of transactions.

2 Indicate what is meant by the ACID properties of a transaction and explain what is implied by each of the properties.

3 In a database system within a banking application, transaction A is transferring £1 000 from account ACC1 to account ACC2. At the same time, transaction B is processing every account record and adding interest payments by increasing each balance by 1.5%. Initially, ACC1 has a balance of £4 000 and ACC2 £5 000. The following sequence of operations shown in Table 6.2 takes place.

Transaction A	Transaction B
Read ACC1 record and lock	
Reduce balance by 1000	
Write balance	
Release lock	
	Read account ACC1 and lock
	Update balance by 1.5%
	Write ACC1 and release lock
	Read account ACC2 and lock
	Update balance by 1.5%
	Write ACC2 and release lock
Read ACC2 record and lock	
Increase balance by 1 000	
Write balance	
Release lock	

TABLE 6.2 Exercise 3 Chapter 6

What should be the final balance values if the transactions were performed serially? What is the actual final values ensuing from the above sequence? How can this error be avoided?

4 The following sequence of transactions was used earlier in the chapter to illustrate the problem of inconsistent analysis:

- Transaction A reads ACC1 and sets running total to £100.

- Transaction A reads ACC2 and adds £200 to total giving £300.

- Transaction B reads ACC2, withdraws £50 and deposits it in ACC3.

- Transaction A reads ACC3, reads £350 and adds it to total giving final total of £650.

In this scenario, transaction A reports an erroneous final total. Analyse what would happen if steps 2 and 3 above were reversed and comment on the final result.

5 Explain the purpose of locking in database processing and distinguish between shared and exclusive locks and between optimistic and pessimistic locking. By means of a suitable example, show how the use of locking in a database application can cause deadlocks.

6 The following matrix maintained by a DBMS shows the current transaction-resource situation for the database. It indicates, for instance, that transaction 1 has locked resource B and C and is waiting for D.

Transactions	Resource A	Resource B	Resource C	Resource D
1		Locked	Locked	Wait
2	Locked		Wait	
3	Wait			Locked

TABLE 6.3 Exercise 6 Chapter 6

Does a deadlock exist in this situation?

References

Websites

MySQL
Article about MySQL database engines, including handling of concurrency:
http://www.devshed. com/c/a/MySQL/Storage-Engine-Table-Types/

Oracle
Oracle article on locking: http://orafaq.com/papers/locking.pdf
Comparison of locking in Oracle and SQL Server:
http://www.devx.com/dbzone/Article/20711/0/ page/1
General article on Oracle locking:
http://www.databasejournal.com/features/oracle/article.php/ 2223371

7

Integrity and security

LEARNING OBJECTIVES

This chapter gathers together a range of topics under the general umbrella of 'integrity and security'. We are concerned here with studying techniques that ensure that the data held on a database is 'correct, consistent and secure'.

After studying this chapter, you should be able to do the following:

- Explain the concept 'application domain'.

- List and describe the threats that a database may face.

- Explain the term 'integrity' with respect to database systems and, specifically, explain 'entity integrity' and 'referential integrity'.

- Describe the techniques used in data validation, including:

  - Type checking.

  - Validation provided by DBMSs such as field-level, table-level and form-level.

  - Facilities provided by SQL.

  - Assertions and triggers.

- Describe the principles of database backup and recovery, including backup techniques, checkpoints and transaction logs.

- Explain the concept of database access privileges and permissions.

Introduction

The purpose of a database is to model some system in the real world; the system being modelled is often referred to as the **universe of discourse**, which sounds rather pompous, or by the friendlier label, **application domain**. When a database holds data that says Mr. Jones of 12 Acacia Avenue, Smalltown owes the Acme Equipment Company £200, then we would hope that this is an accurate representation of the facts. When the 'facts' change, for instance when Mr. Jones pays his debt, again we expect that the database will be changed to reflect this change in the application domain.

Regrettably, these kinds of expectations of computer databases are sometimes not realised in the real world. Some errors can be viewed as trivial; if Acacia was misspelled as Accacia, no-one would view this as a serious misrepresentation. However, it would be viewed somewhat more seriously if the amount was recorded as £2 000.

A major objective of database design must be to ensure that the database is protected from anything that might affect its accuracy. At the logical design phase, the term **constraints** is used to refer to a set of rules and restrictions that define the admissible content of the database. Some constraints are based on the domain of the data values and other natural limitations; for instance, it is readily seen that an employee's name cannot be a numeric value or their age a negative value. Some constraints, on the other hand, are determined by the application system designers as being rules and restrictions to which the application system and the database must conform. Such constraints are often called **business** or **enterprise rules**. Business rules, by their nature, can be quite arbitrary; for instance, a company may make the rule that no customer should have more than £2 000 credit, or a university cannot enrol more than 30 students on a course.

In addition to our expectations about the accuracy of the data, we would also hope that the database is safe against software and hardware failure and that it cannot be accessed by anyone not properly authorised. These aspects of database integrity and security are also described in this chapter.

Threats to the database

As this chapter discusses the subject of maintaining the integrity and security of database, it is perhaps worthwhile to reflect briefly on things that can threaten these.

User errors

The database users can accidentally (or otherwise) enter erroneous values, amend data incorrectly or delete valid data. Errors may also be generated by mistakes occurring in the data collection process prior to data entry into the computer.

Software errors

Programming errors in the database or in the application system software can introduce errors into the database.

Hardware failure

Breakdown of computer equipment, physical damage such as flooding, loss of power, etc. can result in the database being left in an inconsistent state or in the storage medium being rendered unusable.

Malicious damage

For their own motives, a database could be corrupted by authorised or unauthorised users. In particular, the Internet presents extensive threat in this regard, in the shape of viruses, worms, Trojan horses, etc. The purpose of many viruses is simply to cause damage in the victim's file system.

Breach of confidentiality

Unauthorised people may get access to the database. While this does not corrupt the data per se, it may have a serious influence on the owner of the information and indeed the future commercial or political value of the information. Again, this is very real concern in terms of hacking.

Concurrency errors

When a database is accessed by two or more users simultaneously, errors can arise due to specific kinds of interference between the actions of the users. This subject was covered in Chapter 6.

This array of threats to the database requires a corresponding array of defences to be marshalled at all stages of the database design, construction and operation. The following sections covers a range of relevant topics, which are summarised below. Not covered herein are some topics related to this area of study but which are outside the scope of this text; these include specific physical protections that might be applied in a computer installation (access controls, fire protection, etc.) and manual procedures such as batch controls.

To summarise, this chapter covers the following topics:

1 Threats to the database; a look at what can go wrong.

2 Database constraints and techniques for supporting them, including:

   ■ Data validation

   ■ Assertions and triggers

   ■ Transactions

3 Backups, checkpoints and transaction logs.

4 Database access controls.

Database integrity

The term **integrity** in the context of databases refers to the correctness and consistency of the data stored in the database. The meaning of these terms can be further detailed as follows:

Consistency implies that the data held in the various tables of the database is consistent with the concept of the relational model. Consistency is expressed in terms of two characteristics:

- **Entity integrity** is concerned with ensuring that each row of a table has a unique and non-null primary key value; this is the same as saying that each row in a table represents a single instance of the entity type modelled by the table.

- **Referential integrity** is concerned with the relationships *between* the tables of a database; i.e. that the data of one table does not contradict the data of another table. Specifically, every foreign key value in a table must have a matching primary key value in the related table. For example, if a sales order table refers to a customer code AB1212, then that code must appear in the customer table that defines such codes. This 'linking' of foreign key to primary key is fundamental to the way in which component tables are used to form an integrated database. Referential integrity was discussed in more detail in Chapter 2 in the context of the relational model.

  Referential integrity can readily be enforced within the DBMS if steps are taken to specify the necessary relationships. In Microsoft Access a relationship tool allows you to represent the table relationships graphically. This consequently prevents the insertion of a row containing a foreign key value not matched by a corresponding primary key. See Hands-On Section B for more information. In SQL, one can use the REFERENCES clause within the CREATE TABLE command to provide the same facility. See Hands-On Section B for more information.

Data integrity or *correctness* implies that data captured for entry into the computer does in fact correctly represent the 'real world' data that it is supposed to. This involves taking care with the capturing and handling of data at all stages prior to data entry to the database. Particular care has to be taken with data input; even if the 'correct' data is established prior to data input, an error can still occur in the transference of data to the computer. Common forms of error are transposition of numerical digits, misspelling of names, repetition of characters, etc.

The primary defence against invalid data is data input validation, which is described in the next section. The major contribution that can be made by the database validation is to form a barrier between the outside world and the database, ensuring that the data passing through this barrier conforms to company rules and other basic tests of reasonableness; e.g. prevents someone's age being entered as 250, or a clerk's salary as £200 000 a year.

Data validation

To provide some defence against the introduction of erroneous data into the database, a database system will typically provide a range of facilities to check data as it is initially entered. As noted earlier, data errors can occur at any time in the data collection/data entry process. Regardless of the source and cause of the errors, the philosophy applied to input data validation is that the errors should go no further than the data entry phase of processing. Data validation should provide a filter such that all data passing through the filter is sensible and meaningful to the database application system, as far as this can be accomplished. The following sections describe a typical range of validation facilities one would expect in a modern DBMS.

Type checking

The most fundamental error checking mechanism in relational databases is the 'typing' of attributes (columns); i.e. each attribute has to be declared as being of a particular 'type' such as numeric, text, date, etc. In effect, this specifies the **domain** of the data item; i.e. the 'pool' of values from which the data item is drawn. This prevents gross errors such as trying to assign text values to a date column or trying to perform arithmetic on text fields. Also, the type dictates the maximum size and 'shape' (e.g. in numeric fields, the number of decimal places; in date/time fields, the structure of the day, month, year arrangement) of a column. In effect, the type of an attribute determines its 'behaviour'; i.e.:

- the range of acceptable values on input,
- the admissible operations on the data (for instance, you can do arithmetic only on numerical or date columns),
- and how it is handled on output (e.g. left or right justified on a printed report).

Data typing is used in almost all programming languages; 'strongly-typed' languages insist on maximum adherence to the rules of type behaviour, while 'weakly-typed' languages allow the programmer to 'bend' the rules to achieve some advantage in simplicity of coding or performance.

However, the domains of common types are very large; for instance, an integer (two byte representation) has a value range of $-32\,768$ to $+32\,767$, which will generally be much wider than any integer application value such as 'quantity ordered'. Ideally, types should constitute a classification system that enables us to identify database objects (such as table attributes) as representing corresponding classes of entities in the real world. Basic types such as 'NUMBER' and 'CHAR' however are very general classifications and provide relatively little segregation of data.

Most current popular relational databases do not allow you to define your own types. However, some more recent software, referred to as 'extended-relational' or 'object-relational' databases, do provide such facilities. These systems are described in more detail in Chapter 9.

It is perhaps worth noting that the SQL standard provides for the definition of **domains**, using a CREATE DOMAIN command; an example is shown below:

```
CREATE DOMAIN VALIDPRICE NUMBER(6,2)
   CHECK (VALUE BETWEEN 10.00 AND 1 000.00)
```

This can be used in subsequent CREATE TABLE commands:

```
CREATE TABLE PRODUCT
( Product_Id      Varchar(6);
   Price          ValidPrice;
etc . . .
```

7

This ensures that values presented to the table in INSERT commands are constrained within the given value range. The expected effect of this would be simply failure of the INSERT command unless it was wrapped within some exception handling code.

While this provides some features of a new datatype, it really only provides a constraint on the data and does not provide any functionality or, in object-oriented terms, 'behaviour'. This command is not widely used at present.

In the absence of built-in facilities for defining sub-range types, database packages generally allow the user to specify explicit input validation criteria; this topic is pursued in the next section.

Validation techniques

Validation constraints should be definable within any DBMS facility that can enter or amend database data. This encompasses interactive facilities such as forms or a graphical representation of a database table, or programmed access such as SQL commands. Ideally, it should be possible to define the constraints at the table level and to have these constraints effective for any type of access, such as a form. Note, however, that forms are typically used to implement application procedures such as entering sales transactions, booking a hotel room, etc. and it may be that the validation requirements will vary from form to form; hence, validation defined at the table level may need to be modified by the specific requirements of the particular form.

As an illustration of the nature and range of validation facilities likely to be found in a practical database system, those provided by Microsoft Access are described below. (It should be noted that other techniques exist in the area of system controls applied to the general process of data entry, e.g. batch totals. These are beyond the scope of this text).

Microsoft Access

Access provides extensive facilities for validation of database data. Validation can be applied at a number of points, namely:

- Field (column) level validation. These are validations (and other constraints) specified within the definition of a field of a table. The validations applied here can only reference the field being defined. Validation defined here is carried forward to text controls of a form bound to this field. See control level validation below.

- Record (table) level validation. This are specified as a property of a table and can reference any fields of the table.

- Control level validation. This is validation applied to data entered into a text box control on a form and is applied in addition to any constraints defined for the field on which the text control is based.

- Form level validation. Validation at the form level can be applied by macros or VBA coding within an event-handling subroutine.

These validation options are described in more details in the following sections.

Field level validation

Field level validation is intended to check that the values within each field independently conform to specified criteria. These constraints are specified as an optional part of the field definition within the table design facility. There are three parts to this which are detailed below.

Input mask prescribes a basic format for the data; e.g. an order number could have a format such as AB1234. This could be defined as a mask of AAnnnn. The data entered is constrained to this format – the system simply refuses to accept data not conforming to the pattern.

Validation rule/text defines a conditional expression which is used to test the input data. If it fails, an error message appears using the supplied validation text. For instance, if a field has a maximum value of 100, the validation test would be **<=100**, and the text might be **Please enter a value up to 100**.

Required. In many applications it is not allowable to omit certain data items. The most obvious example here is the primary key field of any table; this is enforced automatically by Access. In a sales order input application, for example omitting the customer number would be unacceptable. While such errors would soon be detected by later processing, it is advantageous to prevent them occurring at the earliest possible opportunity.

An example of a validation definition for a table attribute is shown in the table design screen shown in Figure 7.1.

Record level validation

Many constraints that you may wish to apply refer to two or more fields within the one record. Since field-level validation can only deal with one field in isolation, multi-field

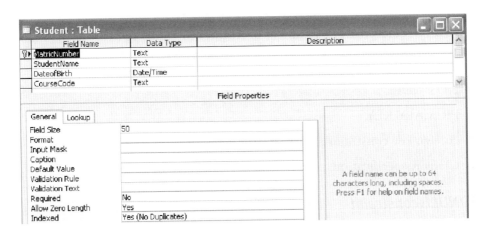

FIGURE 7.1 Attribute validation

constraints must be specified at the record (or form) level. For instance, we could check that DeliveryDate >OrderDate.

Control validation

Most form text box controls are 'bound' to fields of the underlying table (or query) which may itself have constraints defined. In general it is best to define validation at the field level, since it then applies to every form referencing the field. However, it is sometimes necessary apply more specific constraints to suit the particular form application. For instance, in a category field, a validation rule of >A and <G may be specified; in a particular form it may be necessary to apply an additional validation of <>E.

Also, control validation may be required for unbound controls and controls linked to an external database table. This can be specified as the validation rule property of the control or as an event handling subroutine in VBA (a BeforeUpdate event for the control).

Form-level validation

Constraints defined at the form level are potentially the most powerful, since they can take into account factors determined from several tables and queries that contribute to the form application. For instance, they can take account of constraints imposed by company business rules, such as:

- A hotel room is only bookable for a single night if there are more than two guests booked into the room.

- An order for more than £1 000 will only be accepted if the credit rating of the customer is A or B.

Typically, the validation would be coded as a VBA event-handler subroutine that traps an attempt to commit the current transaction (a BeforeUpdate event for the form).

SQL

The SQL standard provides a number of features intended to assist in maintaining the data integrity of the database. These are generally referred to as 'constraints'. The most important of these are:

- NOT NULL
- PRIMARY KEY
- Foreign key constraint and referential integrity
- CHECK specification

NOT NULL constraint

The NOT NULL constraint is applied to a column definition in a CREATE TABLE command. It indicates that the values inserted into that column are not allowed to be null. This would automatically be applied to the primary key of the table (see below), but can also be applied to any column that the designer decides must be available, such as the date of birth in a life assurance policy.

PRIMARY KEY constraint

The PRIMARY KEY clause indicates that the column to which it is applied has to be treated as the primary key of the table. This enforces uniqueness of values in this column of the table and also enforces the NOT NULL constraint, thereby enforcing entity integrity.

Foreign key constraint

Referential integrity can be enforced in SQL by means of the REFERENCES clause in the column definition. This clause automatically makes the column a foreign key and referential integrity is then enforced; i.e. any value in this foreign key column *must* be matched by a primary key in the referenced table. The CREATE TABLE commands shown below illustrate the above points using the Employee and Branch tables, used in the SQL notes given in Hands-On Section A.

```
CREATE TABLE branch
(BranchCode      VARCHAR2(2) PRIMARY KEY NOT NULL,
BranchName       VARCHAR2(10),
City             VARCHAR2(12),
ManagerId        VARCHAR2(4),
Budget           NUMBER(9,2) );

CREATE TABLE employee
(EmpId           VARCHAR2(4) PRIMARY KEY NOT NULL,
Name             VARCHAR2(10),
Position         VARCHAR2(15),
HireDate         DATE,
Salary           NUMBER(7,2),
BranchCode       VARCHAR2(2) NOT NULL REFERENCES
                             BRANCH1(BranchCode),
Department VARCHAR2(10),
Supervisor VARCHAR2(4) );
```

Note that NOT NULL clause applied to the foreign key clause may or may not be used. If present, it indicates a mandatory relationship in entity relationship terms; if absent, it indicates an optional relationship, i.e. it is possible for an employee to be not assigned to any branch.

CHECK constraint

In the SQL standard and in many current implementations it is possible to specify checks within the CREATE TABLE command. When a new row is added to the table, or a row is amended, the specified checks must be tested and verified or the proposed table update is rejected. For example,

```
CREATE TABLE STOCK
(
    OrderNo         VARCHAR(6),
    CustNo          VARCHAR(7),
    OrderDate       DATE,
    DeliveryDate    DATE,
    Status          VARCHAR(1),
    ...
    CHECK ( (Status in ('A', 'B', 'C', 'D') ) AND
    (OrderDate <DeliveryDate) )
)
```

The CHECK clause effectively applies constraints at the *row* level of the table, similar to validation applied as table properties in Access.

Assertions and triggers

Introduction

We consider in this section more elaborate and powerful techniques that can be applied to data validation. An **assertion** is a general term used to describe methods that impose general controls on the content of a database. A **trigger** is a term used in many systems (including Oracle) for event-handling routines.

Assertions

These can be illustrated by reference to facilities specified within the current SQL2 standard. The CREATE ASSERTION command allows arbitrary constraints to be specified. A typical expression might be:

```
CREATE ASSERTION AverageSal
    CHECK ( ( SELECT AVG(Salary) FROM Employee) <2 000 )
```

This constraint indicates that any change to the database must not make the average salary greater than 2 000. The implications of such constraints are considerable; they impose a 'business rule' type restriction on the data and any operation (data input, modification, deletion) that might break the rule must be vetted before execution. For instance, a potential breach in the above constraint could be caused by:

- increasing the salary of one or more employees,
- deleting a row or rows of the table,
- inserting new rows into the table.

In effect, if any of the above operations is requested, the query defined in the CHECK clause above must be executed to verify the transaction.

With regard to all the above SQL special clauses, it should be noted that while these are part of the SQL standard, products will vary in the degree to which these features are implemented.

Triggers

A **trigger** is a more general validation mechanism; it enables execution of units of code when certain related 'events' occur. Events in this context can be any operation that modifies a table, or they can be simply some change at the user interface, for example the cursor entering a form field, leaving a field, changing the value in a field, etc. When activated, the trigger will invoke some response that has to be programmed into the system by the system designer. (Note: In Microsoft Access, the term 'trigger' is not used, the term 'event-handler' being used in preference). The response coding will generally be defined in some procedural programming language; in Oracle, for example, it would be written in PL/SQL, which is a procedural language system that can contain SQL statements. Oracle triggers can be specified at the table level, which are activated when any operation affects the table, and at the form level, which are activated whenever a specified user interface events occurs. In Microsoft Access, event-handling code is written as a macro or as an Access Basic procedure. Figure 7.2 shows the event property list belonging to a text field on a form. It shows that a macro (Verify Date) has been specified for the After Update event and a procedure (Access Basic code) has been specified for the On Exit event.

7

FIGURE 7.2 Event handling details

Triggers provide a lower level facility that can achieve the same as the CHECK and ASSERTION techniques mentioned earlier, in that they can validate the value of table data every time it is changed. The Oracle database provides extensive trigger facilities within its forms system.

Some dialects of SQL provide commands for trigger definition. In Oracle, CREATE TRIGGER is essentially a PL/SQL command, since the trigger action is specified as a PL/SQL code block. Other SQL systems provide for the execution of SQL as the trigger action. Such commands have the basic syntax:

```
CREATE TRIGGER trigger_name
   timing
      event(s)
         ON table_name
   trigger-body
```

where `timing` is BEFORE or AFTER, `event(s)` are one or more of INSERT, UPDATE, DELETE, and `trigger-body` is a BEGIN . . . END block of PL/SQL code.

For example,

```
CREATE TRIGGER Trig1
   BEFORE
      INSERT or UPDATE
         ON Employee
   BEGIN
   . . .
END;
```

This trigger would 'fire' before any row inserts or update on the Employee table.

Backup and recovery

Backup

The most fundamental technique for protecting against loss of database data is periodically to copy the data to some other storage unit and place the copy in a secure location. This is known as **backing up** the database. Backups are generally taken when the system is inactive; this avoids the problem of dealing with transactions that are only partly completed. If some mishap later befalls the database, it is then possible to recreate it, albeit using the older data held in the backup. Transactions that were processed between the backup and the system failure have to be re-entered, either manually or with the aid of a transaction log, which is explained below. The generality of this approach means that the backup protects against a wide range of events that affect the data, from corruption by faulty software to physical damage due to fire, etc.

The frequency of taking backups is dictated by a number of factors including:

- the rate of transactions applied to the database,

- the level of availability of service demanded by the application,

- the balance of time required to perform the backup compared with the potential delay in recovery.

These factors would have to be considered by the system designers when developing a specific application.

Reverting to a backup version of the database can often imply considerable preprocessing of transactions; although this can be done automatically with the aid of a transaction log, it would be advantageous to be able to reduce the recovery time. This can be achieved by means of **checkpointing**; a checkpoint is a special record saved periodically in the transaction log that indicates the transactions that are currently executing at that time. Checkpoints are described in more detail below.

Transaction logs

A transaction log or journal is used to record the effect of all changes made to the database by transactions generated by application systems. For instance, new rows added to the database are recorded in the log; deleted rows are recorded as at the time of deletion; the values of amended rows are recorded *before* and *after* the update (called the before and after images). In the event of a system failure it is possible to recover the database by restoring the most recent backup and then re-executing the transactions recorded in the transaction log. Databases that provide transaction logging will generally provide a utility or DBMS function that will process the transactions automatically, avoiding the need for manual re-entry of the data.

Checkpoints

Checkpoints are transaction status records taken at intervals during normal processing of transactions. Typically, a checkpoint would be taken at frequent intervals during the routine processing of the database. At the checkpoint time, the following actions take place:

- Initiation of new transactions is temporarily suspended.

- All memory buffers are flushed to disk. This ensures that all committed transactions have indeed been actioned on the physical database.

- All currently active transactions are noted and recorded in the transaction log.

In the event of a failure of the database system (for instance, a power failure or program crash) where the database is not damaged but is probably inconsistent, this information enables the database to be recovered more quickly. This is achieved because it is only necessary to preprocess transactions from the checkpoint rather than returning to the previous backup. Figure 7.3 illustrates the situation; in this figure, the arrowheads indicate the start and finish (commit) points of the transaction.

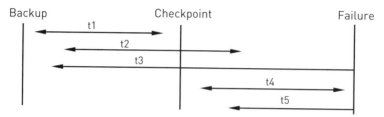

FIGURE 7.3 Checkpointing

Figure 7.3 shows the possible conditions of transactions occurring from backup time, through a checkpoint, to the point of failure. Our purpose here is to show how, in the event of failure, the checkpoint technique handles each of the transaction types illustrated.

Transaction t1 begins and ends before the checkpoint (it will not appear on the checkpoint record) and hence will be correctly implemented in the database.

Transaction t2 starts before the checkpoint and would be flagged as a current transaction by the checkpoint. Although the transaction log would show that it had committed, there would be an element of doubt as to whether the in-memory buffers were written to disk. To be certain, the after image from the transaction log would be written to disk. A similar argument applies to t4.

Transactions t3 and t5 were incomplete at the time of failure and hence may be partially written to disk. To restore the database to a known consistent condition, the before images from the transaction log would be applied. These transactions would then need to be re-executed.

Database privileges or permissions

In any enterprise running a multi-user database system, it is necessary to be able to control the data that is accessible and/or modifiable by each user and class of user. This is necessary to ensure that data can only be read or changed by users who are entitled to do so. Additionally, it is necessary to control who has system permissions such as the right to create, change or drop a table, to grant privileges to others, etc. Rather than identify the access permissions of each individual user, it is more convenient to classify users into workgroups and to assign rights to these groups. Systems will vary in the way access rights are specified and in the granularity of 'objects' that can be controlled. As an example, the security facilities in Microsoft Access are described below.

Facilities in MS Access

The security facilities of Microsoft Access effectively display a 'three dimensional' organisation, the dimensions being group or user, object (table, form, etc.) and permissions. So for instance we could assign read permission to the table Clients for the group Personnel. The database objects and the assignable permissions are described in Table 7.1.

	Database	Table	Query	Form	Report	Macro	Module
Open/Run	X			X	X	X	
Read Design		X	X	X	X	X	X
Modify Design		X	X	X	X	X	X
Administer		X	X	X	X	X	X
Read Data		X	X				
Update Data		X	X				
Insert Data		X	X				
Delete Data		X	X				

TABLE 7.1 Database objects and permissions

Note that the Administer permission allows the user or group to change anyone's permissions. It is important therefore that this permission is only bestowed where absolutely necessary.

Facilities in SQL

Access rights are specified in SQL by the GRANT and REVOKE commands. The GRANT command shown below gives the users Joe and Mary the right to view and update data in the Orders table:

```
GRANT select, update ON Orders TO joe, mary
```

The following REVOKE command removes Joe's right to update the table:

```
REVOKE update ON Orders TO joe
```

More information on these SQL commands can be found in Hands-On Section A.

Summary

The topics covered in this chapter are summarised in the following list:

Database integrity. Entity, referential and data integrity. These topics are concerned with techniques employed to preserve the 'correctness' of the database contents as it undergoes updates. Once defined by the database designer, the DBMS is able to manage subsequent preservation of these integrities.

Data validation. Techniques used to ensure that data entering the database is correct. This covered the individual topics of type checking, validation techniques, assertions and triggers.

Transactions. Transactions define groups of database operations as atomic units that must be treated as a single database update. This is a very important concept that influences many other areas of work.

Backups and recovery. Describes methods used to ensure that the database system can survive failures and other threats. This includes backups, transaction logs and checkpoints.

Database privileges or permissions. Describes methods used to control users' access to the database.

Review questions

1 What is meant by a database constraint?

2 Identify some of the problems that can threaten the integrity of the database.

3 What is meant by data validation?

4 How do datatypes contribute to the accuracy of data?

5 Distinguish between an assertion and a trigger.

6 What is a transaction log used for?

7 What are the SQL commands GRANT and REVOKE used for?

Exercises

1 Discuss the techniques that can be employed in database systems to ensure that the information stored in the database is accurate.

2 With reference to the coding shown below, explain the effect of such assertions and the specific effect of this assertion.

```
CREATE ASSERTION AverageSal
   CHECK ( ( SELECT AVG(Salary) FROM Employee) <2 000 )
```

Identify what changes to the Employee table might cause this assertion to fail, explaining why the change would potentially have this effect.

3 Describe the techniques employed by database systems to ensure that the data can be recovered in the event of failure or damage to the database.

Reference

Afyouni, S. (2005): *Database Security and Auditing: Protecting Data Integrity and Accessibility*, Thomson Course Technology.

7

8

Network and distributed systems

LEARNING OBJECTIVES

In this chapter, we look at how databases can be employed in systems consisting of a number of separate networked computers. After studying this chapter, you should be able to do the following:

- Explain the client-server concept including three-tier working.

- Discuss the advantages of the client-server approach.

- Explain the concept of peer-to-peer working.

- Explain how separate databases can be organised into a distributed database system.

- Distinguish between homogeneous and heterogeneous distributed systems.

- Identify the benefits of using database replication within a distributed system.

- Explain the concept of transparency and define location, replication and fragmentation transparency.

- Discuss the problems of schema management, query processing and concurrent transactions that arise in distributed database systems.

- List and explain Date's 12 Objectives for a distributed database.

- Discuss the advantages and disadvantages of distributed databases.

Introduction

In this chapter we cover a number of topics with the common theme of networking. Using a number of computers interconnected by a network introduces new opportunities and problems. We start by discussing the **client-server** technique that is used extensively in multi-computer environments, identifying its strengths and weaknesses. Also considered in this context is three-tier architecture in which the system work is handled in three levels of operation.

This leads us to the concept of **distributed databases** in which the data is stored in a number of physically separate computers (connected by a network) each having its own database files. The benefits and drawbacks of a range of different distribution techniques is explored.

Web database systems also use a client-server approach; these are sufficiently important that the topic is covered separately in Chapter 10.

Client-server systems

Concept

The philosophy of *server* systems arose within local area network technology. LANs enable multiple personal computers to share common resources such as file stores, printers, electronic mail, etc. To facilitate this sharing process, it was found convenient to place each resource under the control of one dedicated computer within the network. These dedicated computers are referred to as resource *servers*; hence we have printer servers, disk servers, email servers, etc. For instance, if an application program wants to produce printed output, it sends the data to the printer server, which services the request. Another common mode of working is to provide disk storage on a large server computer that can be used as general storage space for other computers on the same LAN. To the user, this space is identical in nature and functionality to 'local' storage; in Windows systems, for instance, server disk volumes can be assigned conventional drive letters such as E:, F: etc. and directories and files within this disk space can be addressed using normal pathnames. This mode of working, whereby application programs run on some computers and servers on others, became known as *client-server*, reflecting the fact that some computers (the clients) send requests to a provider of services (the server) which attempts to comply with the requests.

Client-server is a well-established architecture for data management, particularly for personal computers within a local area network. In effect the functions of the DBMS are split into two parts:

- The client or 'front-end' interfaces with the user; it is where application programs execute and it provides facilities such as interactive querying, report generation, transaction forms, etc.

- The server or 'back-end' provides the database engine that manages the physical data and responds to queries sent from the client.

In modern systems SQL plays a major role; SQL is used as the communication language that enables the client to define the queries that are sent to the server for execution. It is important to distinguish between an SQL-based client-server system and *file server* systems. In a file server, the user's computer has its own DBMS but accesses database files held on the server. Application programs request data via the local DBMS, which transmits the request to the server. The server resolves the query and returns data blocks to the application program. This is illustrated in Figure 8.1.

In an SQL server environment, the client application sends SQL queries to the server, which responds with the query 'answer', in the form of rows of data. Figure 8.2 illustrates an SQL client-server system.

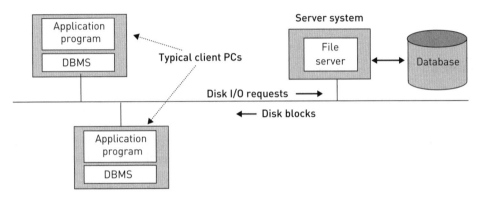

FIGURE 8.1 File server system

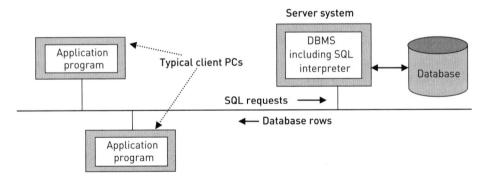

FIGURE 8.2 SQL Client-server system

Three-tier architecture

The three tier (or three layer) architecture is a client-server architecture in which the user interface, the processing logic and the data storage and access are each in a separate computing resource. This is illustrated in Figure 8.3.

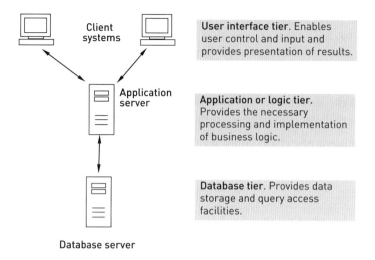

FIGURE 8.3 Three-tier architecture

This naturally benefits systems where the overall tasks to be carried out can be readily and conveniently split into three centres of processing. In principle, the concept of dividing up the processing tasks could be extended to more than three centres. The two and three tier approaches can then be seen as instances of a general multi-tier architecture.

Web systems are generally constructed using the three-tier structure:

1 A front-end browser providing the user interface, communicating over the Internet.

2 A middle Web and application server.

3 A database server that supplies dynamic content.

Advantages of client-server approach

The client-server approach provides many benefits, the most important of which are listed below. In this respect, the approach is being compared with the use of a centralised database facility or a network system using only file servers.

- Scalability; it is easier to expand the size of a system. This can be done 'horizontally', i.e. by adding more client and/or server machines, or 'vertically', by making the server machines larger, perhaps moving to a new platform such as UNIX or a mainframe.

- The computers used in the system can be optimised for the role they play. The client machines can be PC workstations that can provide very effective user interfaces at a low cost. The server machines can be configured with large memory and a fast disk system to cope with their role as data providers.

- It divides the processing burden between client and server; much of the processing is performed locally, i.e. on the client system, near to where the data is produced and required. This consequently minimises network activity needed to service the application.

- It facilitates 'open systems' by encouraging the use of a mixture of different hardware and software systems. This enables the system designer to choose the 'best' products for the task in hand without the difficulty of trying to integrate disparate systems.

- Modularity of implementation; the development of an application is naturally divided into 'client' and 'server' tasks, potentially simplifying the overall design effort.

Peer-to-peer systems

In a typical client-server system, a server may itself act as a client to use the services of another server. If this principle is adopted with full generality, the distinction between client and server *computers* would disappear; any machine could act as a server and any as a client. In effect, 'client' and 'server' would be *roles* adopted by the computers as required by application systems. Such an arrangement is called a *peer-to-peer* system and forms the basis of an ultimate distributed processing model. In this model, all networked computers can offer services to, and use the services of, the rest of the network.

At this point we are digressing into the realms of general open systems architecture. To return to the more specific topic of database architectures, we continue in the next section with a description of distributed databases.

Distributed databases

8

Overview

In a distributed database, the data comprising the database is held in a number of physically separate locations, connected by a network, which can be accessed by users independently of their location. There are a number of ways in which distribution of a database may be desirable; the principal motivation is to minimise network traffic, improve access times (for locally stored data) and hence improve overall system performance by placing data near to where it is most commonly accessed.

In the following sections we cover a number of topics:

- Types of distribution: a number of techniques used in splitting the data across a number of sites. We cover homogeneous and heterogeneous systems, partitioned, horizontal and vertical distribution and replication.

- Distributed schemas: additional problems in schema in management.

- Query processing: the problems involved in executing queries when the data is stored in several different sites.

- Concurrency.

- Date's objectives: idealised requirements for a distributed database system.

- Advantages and disadvantages of distributed database.

Homogeneous and heterogeneous

Each node within a distributed database must have a local DBMS. A homogeneous distributed database has the same (or related) DBMS at each node, while a heterogeneous one does not. For instance, a system consisting of several networked computers each running the Oracle DBMS is a homogeneous system; a system with one or more computers running Oracle and others running IBM's DB2 and/or Microsoft's Access is heterogeneous.

A heterogeneous system is technically more difficult to implement in a general way (i.e. to allow an arbitrary mixture of disparate systems) than a homogeneous one, and hence the latter are much more common and more advanced in practice. Full realisation of general heterogeneous systems will need the development of some standardised approach, possibly via distributed object technology such as CORBA. CORBA is a generalised architecture developed by the Object Management Group (OMG) that allows applications running on different computers to communicate with one another no matter where they are located or what software platforms they are based on. The OMG is a association of about 800 software vendors, developers and end-users. For more information on this topic, consult the OMG Website at http://www.omg.org.

Partitioned, horizontal and vertical

These terms refer to the way in which the database is 'divided' between the sites that host portions of the database.

Partitioned

By far the simplest and most common form of distribution is to partition the *tables* of the database into separate sites; hence, one site may have the Customer, Order, OrderItems and Product tables while another site may have the Sales and Purchase Ledger tables. This form of fragmentation is well-supported in current products. The principal justification for this arrangement is that tables can be held close to where they are mainly used, thereby minimising network traffic and increasing access times, while at the same time still providing global access to all the data. It also is a useful technique where interconnection of previously separate systems is required.

Horizontal fragmentation

Horizontal fragmentation refers to the splitting of tables such that groups of rows are held at different sites. To give a crude example, rows 1 to 1 000 could be stored at site A, rows 2 001 to 4 000 at site B, etc. It is less clear why this might be desirable; in fact, this example using numerical subdivision is pretty well useless! However, consider the following example.

A chain of estate agents, with geographically dispersed offices, use a database of properties under their management. Typically, each office would only normally cater for properties within their geographical area, but occasionally they may have to respond to a client's request for properties in some other area. In these circumstances, it might be convenient to have a 'global' property database horizontally distributed on the basis of the office. That is, database rows pertaining to properties under the jurisdiction of office A would be held in office A, properties of B at office B, and so on. Figure 8.4 illustrates this principle. Note that the subdivision would be based on a key value of the table, not on physical row numbers as the figure might suggest.

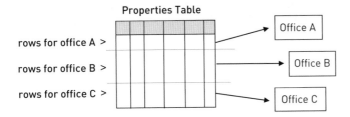

FIGURE 8.4 Horizontal fragmentation

This would provide rapid access for local enquiries while retaining the option of an enquiry over the whole (or selected parts) of the full database. Additionally, network traffic would be minimised due to the relative rarity of global enquiries.

NOTE

In this scenario, users at any one office can notionally 'see' the full database at any time. It is simply that their local enquiries will not require the system to search the local portion of the database. Horizontal fragmentation will normally be based on some such selection of rows related to the nature of the table data.

8

Vertical fragmentation

Vertical fragmentation refers to the splitting of tables such that the *columns* of the table are distributed over two or more sites. Again, it is perhaps not immediately obvious why this might be advantageous. If we return to the estate agent example, we can see that details about clients might be vertically fragmented, with local information about the client (name, address, phone, etc.) being held in the regional offices, while columns related to billing and accounting details (amount owing, invoice date, etc.) are held on a main office database. This arrangement would serve the same purpose as in the horizontal example: it optimises access times and minimises network traffic. Vertical fragmentation is illustrated in Figure 8.5.

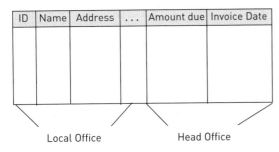

FIGURE 8.5 Vertical fragmentation

Figure 8.5 implies that each column is allocated exclusively to one fragment; a problem with this, however, is the need to preserve the primary key in each fragment so that the table data can be accessed by the key and can be re-joined for querying. As an alternative to replicating the natural primary key, a 'row number' can be assigned uniquely to each row and recorded in all fragments of the table. This can then be used as the join key when it is necessary to query over combined fragments.

NOTE

This notion of subdivision of columns based on information use is similar to the way in which the **view** mechanism is often used. Views are often used to present users with a subset of the columns of a real table, these being the columns that they require to 'see' in the execution of their job. Vertical fragmentation reflects this mode of working in a physical separation of the data.

Replication

In the examples described above, the database is fragmented for reasons of efficiency; some data is stored local to where it is produced and used and less frequently used data is held remotely. There are many situations, however, in which data produced at one location is frequently required at other locations. If the remote sites are required to access such data via a network, the network traffic will be high and the overall performance of the system in terms of access time could be poor.

An alternative approach in such circumstances is **data replication**; as the title suggests, data replication involves storing copies of data produced by one site at some or all of the other network sites, thereby avoiding cross network accesses. A database can be *fully* or *partially* replicated; i.e. the whole database is copied, or just a fragment of it. Be careful to distinguish between a fragmented database and a replicated fragment of a database. This is illustrated by Figure 8.6.

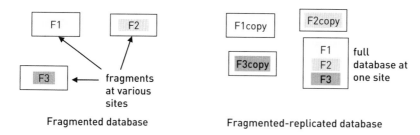

FIGURE 8.6 Replication

In the fragmented case, the 'whole' database does not exist at one site, but is dispersed between the sites. In the replicated-fragmented case, the whole database exists at one site but copies of fragments exist at other sites.

While avoiding the problems of network performance, replication creates its own problems, the principal of these being the management of the copying activity and maintenance of data consistency. These problems are discussed in a later section.

In view of the problems described above, replication is particularly suitable for databases which are essentially maintained at a central location and required principally for reference only at other sites. An example might be distribution of engineering change information from a manufacturing or software company. Note that replication is also used as a means of data security; duplicate copies of the database are maintained continuously so that, in the event of loss of one machine, the system can continue to operate using the other.

Transparency

It is a major objective of a fully-fledged distributed database that the underlying mechanisms such as fragmentation are not apparent to the user. Certainly, it is very desirable that the user need take no special action related to the location and fragmentation of the data. This objective is referred to as **data transparency**.

There are three 'flavours' of transparency that need to be considered, namely, *location*, *fragmentation* and *replication* transparencies.

Location transparency

The database user should not be concerned about the storage location of the data they are accessing. In particular, it should not be necessary to explicitly address a query to a specific location.

Replication transparency

The database user should not be concerned about whether the data being accessed is the source version or a copy of the data. Problems regarding the consistency of the data are the responsibility of the DBMS software and not the individual users.

Fragmentation transparency

The database user should not be concerned with how the data is fragmented over the network.

Schema management

Within a database system, a schema describes the information held in the database. This will include the design of tables and views, indexes, constraint definitions, etc. as well as location information indicating to the DBMS where a particular item is stored. The schema enables the DBMS to translate names (tables, attributes, etc.) used by the application programs into physical disk addresses. In conventional single site databases, the schema would naturally be stored in the database itself or at least within the same disk system. In a distributed system, the situation is somewhat more complex. The problems presented are:

- Location information is more complex; network site addresses as well as disk addresses are required.

- The schema information is required at all the sites.

- The schema requires additional information about how each table is fragmented and/or replicated.

Query processing

It is perhaps not difficult to see that processing a query in a distributed database system is more complicated than in a single database. Since the data is distributed over several physical locations, responding to a query in general will involve accessing several network sites and dealing with the implications of the query. We should note here, however, that these are problems for the DBMS to resolve; the concept of transparency implies that the database user should not be concerned with such matters.

If we use the word 'query' in a general sense to include both reading and updating of the database, then the problems inherent in query processing can be summarised as listed below.

'Fragmentation' of the query

In order to issue the query to the respective sites, it must be split into sub-queries applicable to the data fragment at that site. For example, if a query is addressed to a table that is horizontally fragmented over three sites, then the same query must be sent to each site for execution.

Distribution of updated and inserted data

If the query involves an update or insert operation, then the data must be written to the various sites as demanded by the distribution scheme. For example, if a new row is added to a table that is vertically fragmented over two sites, then it must be re-expressed as an insertion of two projections of the original row into the respective sites.

Collation of results

When individual sites respond to the sub-queries, the requesting client site must collate these into one unified answer. For instance, a select type query addressed to a table that is vertically fragmented over two sites will result in two result relations that must be joined.

Query optimisation

To resolve a query will typically involve movement of data between sites. In general, there will be several strategies available for resolving a query, involving different movements of data between the sites. The efficiency of this operation critically depends on the method chosen. For instance, suppose a table of 10 000 rows at site A is to be joined to a table of 10 rows at site B. To get the data together, it is clearly more efficient to send the 10 rows at site B to site A and to perform the join there. Typically, the optimisation process will consist of two levels: the *global optimiser* will decide how to move data across the network to best resolve the query; the *local optimiser* will then deal with the data at the target site in efficiently implementing the query.

Concurrency control

Management of concurrent transactions in a distributed environment is similar in general nature to that in a single database environment. It is still necessary to protect against loss or corruption of data arising from simultaneous access to the same data and deadlocks can still occur. However, the dispersion of the data means that a transaction may also be dispersed, i.e. it may be necessary to execute transaction code at several sites to complete the overall transaction task. In principle, if a transaction T requires separate execution of dispersed component transactions T1, T2, etc. then successful execution of the transaction requires a commit of each of the transactions T1, T2, etc. Conversely, a rollback of any of the component transactions would necessitate a rollback of *all* of the component transactions. Management of this kind of operation requires that one site acts as a coordinator for the whole system. When a site completes its part of the transaction, it will send a message to the coordinator indicating that it is ready to commit or to rollback as the case may be. If and when the coordinator receives a 'ready to commit' from *every* site, it will send a 'commit' to all the sites, which are then forced to commit. If any site fails to provide a 'ready to commit' then the whole transaction is rolled back at all sites.

8

Date's 12 objectives

The well-known authority on database matters, C.J. Date, presented a set of objectives to which a fully-fledged distributed database system should aspire. While no currently available database conforms to all these objectives, they form a useful reference standard and a target for future developments. Many of the points covered have already been discussed earlier in this chapter, so the list also forms a useful summary of the chapter.

1. Local autonomy	All sites should be independent of other sites; i.e. it should not be necessary to refer to another site before initiating a transaction.
2. No master site	There should be no site that performs special services for the rest of the sites. In particular, tasks such as transaction management should not be vested in one site.

3. Continuous operation	Making changes to one site, such as upgrading the hardware or software, should not involve closing down the whole system.
4. Location transparency 5. Fragmentation transparency 6. Replication transparency	These transparencies were described in the previous section.
7. Distributed query processing	Queries involving multiple sites should be resolved as efficiently as possible, taking into account the distribution/replication of the data and the effect of transmission delays.
8. Distributed transaction management	Management of transactions should not be vested in one site. In order to manage the commit or rollback of a transaction, it is necessary that one site acts as a coordinator, but this objective says that *any site* should be capable of undertaking this role.
9. Hardware independent 10. Operating system independent 11. Network independent	A distributed database should be capable of working on any network consisting of a mix of different computer types, e.g. PCs, minicomputers and mainframes using a variety of operating systems. Conformance to the network criterion is less of a problem; most vendors software can operate using a variety of networking architectures.
12. DBMS independent	This is possibly the hardest objective to meet. It implies that a distributed DBMS product from one vendor (say, IBM) be capable of 'talking' to a variety of local DBMS products from other vendors. This can only be achieved by the establishment of industry standards such as SQL.

Advantages and disadvantages of distributed databases

In considering the advantages and disadvantages, we are effectively comparing distributed databases with the alternative of a centralised database. In such a system, all remote sites would need to communicate over a network to a single large database.

Advantages

- Improves system efficiency due to reduced network traffic and faster access to local data. This is probably the main factor favouring distributed databases.

- Enables each site to retain control of their local data.

- Improves availability: if one site fails, the rest of the system can continue operating (at least to the extent that the services of the failed site are not required).

- By subdividing the work, the system capacity is improved.

Disadvantages

The principal arguments against distribution are concerned with the additional complexity in several areas:

- *Query processing*: data may have to be obtained from several sites, requiring additional work in resolving and optimising the query.

- *Concurrency*: there is additional complexity in managing synchronised commits and rollbacks.

- *Schema management*: it requires additional levels of schema to specify location and fragmentation of relations.

- *Update of replicated data*: it is necessary to ensure that replicated data is kept synchronised with the original.

- *Database design*: database developers have a more complex task in deciding how to distribute the data and how to administer the overall system.

Summary of distributed systems

The overall case for distributed databases could be summarised as 'worthwhile but complicated'. It provides very real practical benefits, but the design and operational complexities are daunting. Most of the design problems have been mastered by the major database vendors such as Oracle, IBM and Microsoft and practical systems can now be confidently installed. However, the management and maintenance of such systems is still a substantial undertaking for enterprises.

8

Summary

This chapter has reviewed some of the important aspects of using databases in conjunction with networks. The main topic has been distributed database systems; the main point to note in this regard is that the principal justification for the use of distributed databases is the reduction in network traffic and increased local access times. The topics that have been covered in this section include:

- **Client-server systems.**

  Advantages of client-server approach

  Two, three and multi-level client-server systems

  Peer-to-peer systems

- **Distributed databases**

  Homogeneous and Heterogeneous

  Partitioned, horizontal and vertical

  Replication

  Transparency

  Schema management

  Query processing

  Date's 12 objectives for distributed systems

  Advantages and disadvantages of distributed databases

Review questions

1 Explain what is meant by a 'client-server system'.

2 How does the three-tier architecture extend the basic client-server principle?

3 How is the three-tier architecture used in web systems?

4 In what ways is a peer-to-peer system similar to, and different, from a conventional client-server system?

5 What is meant by saying a database is 'distributed'?

6 Explain the terms 'homogeneous' and 'heterogeneous' in the context of distributed databases.

7 List the various ways in which a database can be distributed.

8 What is meant by 'database replication'?

9 In the context of distributed databases, what is meant by 'transparency'?

10 Identify the various forms of transparency.

11 Outline the problems of schema management, query processing and concurrent transactions that arise in distributed database systems.

12 List and explain Date's 12 objectives for a distributed database.

13 What are the advantages and disadvantages of distributed databases?

Exercises

1 Identify the problems inherent in performing database queries within a distributed database environment.

2 Explain what is meant by transparency in the context of distributed databases, identifying the different forms of transparency.

3 Discuss the problems faced by a database system in complying with Date's 12 objectives for distributed databases.

4 Discuss the advantages and disadvantages of distributed database systems.

References

Textbooks

For a more advanced treatment of distributed systems, see:

Elmasri R. and Navathe S.B. (2006): *Fundamentals of database systems* (third edition), Addison-Wesley Longman.
O'Neil P. and O'Neil E. (2004): *Database Principles, Programming and Performance*, San Francisco: Morgan Kaufmann.

Website

http://www.omg.org. The Object Management Group is a computer industry consortium that develops standards in many areas including database distributed systems.

8

HANDS-ON SECTION B: MICROSOFT ACCESS

Introduction

Hands-On section B is divided into three sections, which assume the student has access to a computer and Microsoft Access. The sections are:

- **Getting Started in Access.** This section guides students through the process of creating a basic database with tables, forms, queries and reports and provides a sound basis for the introduction of more advanced features. The activities are intended for the reader to follow on a computer and provides a quick introduction to the mechanics of using Access. A knowledge of database principles and design, gained from the previous theoretical chapters is assumed.

- **More about Access.** This section extends the reader's knowledge to cover many of the most commonly used features.

- **Advanced Access.** This section introduces features that enhance the power and usability of Access databases.

In addition to the notes supplied by this chapter, the text website contains a substantial amount of additional material to help you to become familiar with Access. This includes sample databases that implement the case studies described in Chapter 1 and some advice on special methods and techniques that can be employed in Access.

Getting started in Access

The database we are going to create is based on the Employee case study. This uses two tables Employee and Branch, defined below:

Employee:

```
EmpId        Text;        primary key to identify the employee
Name         Text;        name of employee
Position     Text;        employee's job within company
HireDate     Date;        date of original employment
Salary       Currency;    employee's current annual salary
BranchCode   Text;        foreign key referring to row in Branch table
Department   Text;        name of employee's department
Supervisor   Text;        the EmpId of the employee's supervisor
```

Branch:

```
BranchCode   Text;        primary key
BranchName   Text
City         Text;        location of branch office
ManagerId    Text
Budget       Number;      the annual budget for the branch, in thousands
```

NOTE

A more extensive explanation about the various datatypes is provided later; in the meantime the activities use only the types shown above.

Creating a new database

Creating a new (blank) Access database is very simple. There are a number of ways to start up Access; for instance, you can enter from the Start menu option **New Office Document** then click on **Blank Database**; or you can start Access directly via the **Start**>**Program** menu. Whatever method is used, create a new (blank) database; you have to name and save it immediately before you can work on it. The complete database is contained within one file with an MDB extension; all tables, forms, queries, etc. are held in this file. This is major simplifying feature of Access and facilitates many aspects of the management of your databases. To be consistent with the narrative below, name the database **Employee**.

When you have proceeded as above, a new window opens similar to that shown in Figure HOB.1 below. This shows the **Database** window which provides a entry point to the various objects contained within database.

FIGURE HOB.1 Main database window

For instance, the **Tables** button currently selected in Figure HOB.1 means that the names of the database tables (with other details) are listed in the main panel. Since the database has just been created, the list is currently empty. A similar list is available for the other object types such as queries, forms, etc. The buttons just below the title bar allow you to **Open** a current (selected) table to view the table data, modify the **Design** or create a **New** table.

Creating a table and entering data

From the **Database** window, select **Tables**. Create the first of the two tables required for the Employee database by clicking on the **New** button and selecting **Design** view from the New Table dialog box to start the definition of a new table. Click **OK** (Figure HOB.2).

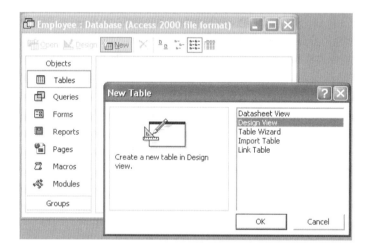

FIGURE HOB.2 Access New Table dialog box

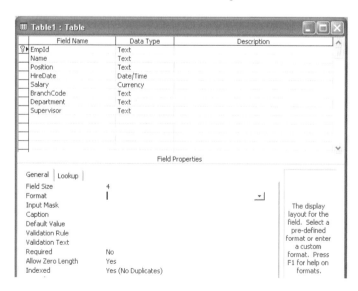

FIGURE HOB.3 Access table design view window

Figure HOB.3 shows the screen used to enter the details of the table columns (fields). The table assumes the temporary name Table 1 which can be changed later.

Enter the field names and specify the datatype by selecting from the drop-down list of available datatypes. Each field in the required table is defined on successive lines.

> **NOTE**
>
> Comments can be added, but these are purely documentary and have no effect on the table design. They do however, provide a useful reference for others who may wish to change the database in future.

Selecting each field in turn (by clicking on the box to the left of the field name), the **Field Properties** for that field are displayed in the lower pane of the window. When adding a new field, the Field Properties for that field are displayed. Some Field Property values are pre-determined by the Datatype selected, whereas others can be amended during this table design stage. For instance, the Field Size determines the format for numerical items (e.g. integer or float). A text field's Field Properties can have a range specified to limit the length of the text. The date field can have the layout of the date specified. Default values can also be set.

> **NOTE**
>
> At this early stage of design and investigation of the Access program design process, it may be easier to avoid complexity and not limit many of the Field Properties. This feature is more useful when considering the application of the database in an application, e.g. limiting telephone number entries to be e.g. fourteen digits with no spaces.

Specifying the primary key

An additional task to perform at this time is to specify the primary key column. (If you don't, Access will automatically select one itself – it inserts an additional column called ID). Figure HOB.4, shows how the primary key button used to assign the key to a field.

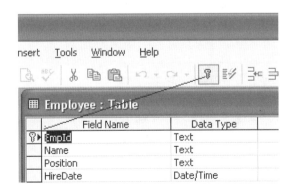

FIGURE HOB.4 Primary key

Select the primary key column (EmpId), then click the key symbol on the tool bar. The key symbol will then appear in the box as shown.

Some tables have multiple-field keys; in this case, highlight all the fields before clicking the key button.

When all the fields have been defined, close this window. At this point you are invited to give the table a name – use Employee.

Repeat this process for the Branch table.

FIGURE HOB.5 List of Table names

Close the table design dialog and return to the **Database** window, which should now list the two new tables (Figure HOB.5).

We *could* now add data to the tables. However it is best to set up the relationship between the tables first, as explained in the next section, *then* enter the Branch table information first, followed by the Employee table data. This ensures that referential integrity is preserved.

Select a table and click the **Open** button.

We get a table display into which we can insert data, as illustrated for the Branch and the Employee tables in Figure HOB.6 and HOB.7. Initially, of course these datasheets will be empty.

		BranchCode	BranchName	City	ManagerId	Budget
	+	01	South	London	1001	£300.00
	+	02	West	Liverpool	4206	£250.00
	+	03	East	York	7663	£350.00
	+	04	North	Aberdeen	3876	£200.00
	+	05	Europe	Paris		£0.00
*						£0.00

Branch : Table

FIGURE HOB.6 Datasheet view of Branch table

EmpId	Name	Position	HireDate	Salary	BranchCode	Department	Supervisor
1001	Kennedy	Director	16-Jan-94	£50,000.00	01		
1045	Smith	Salesman	12-May-05	£18,000.00	04	Sales	3691
1271	Stewart	Clerk	30-Apr-91	£16,000.00	03	Accounts	3255
1534	Bell	Supervisor	20-Nov-95	£20,000.00	01	Admin	3876

FIGURE HOB.7 Datasheet view of Employee table

The format in Figure HOB.6 and HOB.7 is called a 'datasheet'. As well as being the standard display format for the table, this format can also be used in the design of forms. This is only a sample of the data of this table.

Defining table relationships

While we are free to enter data immediately, as shown above, in practice it is desirable first to define the relationships between the tables. This is done using the main menu option **Tools>Relationships** or by using the relationships button.

FIGURE HOB.8 The relationships button

The purpose of this operation is to ensure that the two tables are correctly related. What this means in this case is that the BranchCode values used in the Employee table are all present in the Branch table. Otherwise, an employee may be assigned to a non-existent branch. Once the relationship has been set up, Access will prevent erroneous BranchCode values from being entered into the Employee table.

Initially, we get the dialog box shown in Figure HOB.9. Select each table in turn and click **Add**; then **Close**.

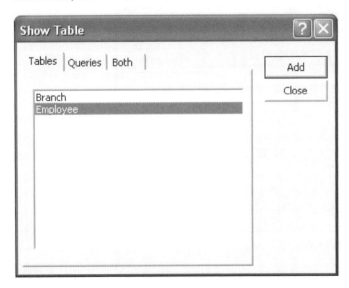

FIGURE HOB.9 Select tables

You should get the screen shown in Figure HOB.10 which shows a representation of the two database tables. The objective now is to join the tables using a line between the primary key of the Branch table and the foreign key of the Employee table, namely the two BranchCode fields.

FIGURE HOB.10 Joining tables

Now, using the mouse, click on the BranchCode in the Employee table and, holding the left mouse button down, drag it to the BranchCode field of the Branch table and release the mouse button. This opens another dialog box, shown in Figure HOB.11.

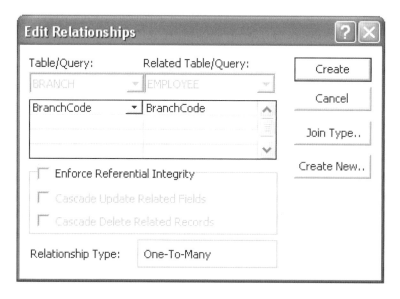

FIGURE HOB.11 Referential Integrity

Click on the **Enforce Referential Integrity** check box and then click the **Create** button. Finally, you should see the tables joined correctly, as shown in Figure HOB.12.

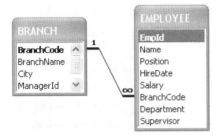

FIGURE HOB.12 Tables joined

Close and save the relationships.

Having set up the relationship between the tables, you should now enter the Branch data first, then the Employee data. This is necessary because the BranchCodes must be available in the Branch table before BranchCodes are entered into the Employee table, to comply with referential integrity.

To finish, close both tables and save then with the names Employee and Branch.

Creating forms

While data can be entered using the table interface, as illustrated above, forms are a more convenient method of interfacing with tables. In effect, forms provide a formatted 'window' through which to view the table data. To demonstrate the form creation process, we will create two basic forms to display each of our tables.

From the Database window, click the **Forms** button on the left, then the **New** button.

The **New Form** dialog should open (see Figure HOB.13). There are multiple options here, but for this example select **Autoform: Columnar** and select the Employee table in the drop-down list.

Click **OK**.

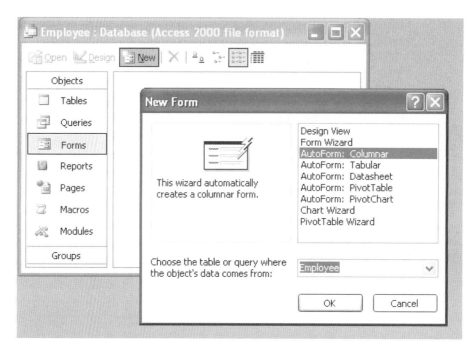

FIGURE HOB.13 New form design

An Employee form is automatically created and displayed, as shown in Figure HOB.14. Each table field is represented by a text box and a label. The text box shows values from the underlying table row. The label, by default, is simply the field name. An alternative can be defined in the caption parameter of the table design. Note the 'columnar' format: the fields of the table are arranged in a column. This layout is determined by a property called **Default View** with the value of 'Single Form'. The form objects such as text boxes are called 'controls'.

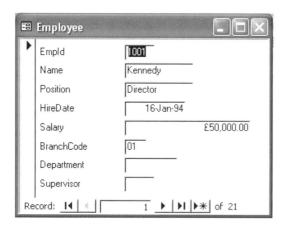

FIGURE HOB.14 Form display

At the bottom of the screen is a 'navigation bar' which allows you to move from record to record. The ▶* button creates a new empty record.

NOTE

This form has been based on a table, but it also possible to construct a form based on a query which could reference one or more tables.

Form focus

The form has a cursor that can be positioned on any control such as text boxes; the control currently holding the cursor is said to have the 'focus'. In addition, a 'tab sequence' is defined for each form which is the sequence of controls through which the focus moves as the tab key (or return key) is pressed successively. The sequence is set by the form wizard to be from top to bottom, but it can be modified by using the menu command Tools-Tab Order, including omitting controls from the sequence.

If you click **Design** icon (or select **View-Design View**), the form display changes to the Design view (Figure HOB.15). This enables you to modify the layout of the form and many other properties.

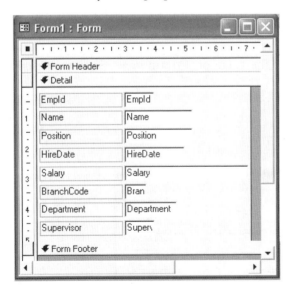

FIGURE HOB.15 Form design view

FIGURE HOB.16 The Design icon

The objects on the form can be selected in Design view by clicking, as shown in Figure HOB.17.

FIGURE HOB.17 Form object with field selected

They can then be moved and changed in size by clicking and dragging the corner or side handles around the edges of the frame boxes. Note that the text box and its label are initially locked together. They can be moved independently by pointing to the larger frame boxes on the top left of the objects. A 'finger' cursor appears.

The contents of labels such as the HireDate caption in the above form (Figure HOB.17) can be modified by clicking on the label to select it then clicking again which changes the cursor to a text cursor. While an object is selected, the properties of the object, such as colour, font size, alignment, etc. can be modified using the **Properties** box; more on this later. In addition to text boxes and labels, a form can contain a wide range of other controls; these are described in some detail later. Save the form you have created with the name 'Employee'.

Now create a form for the Branch table, but in this case use the **Autoform: Tabular** option. This will create a form as shown in Figure HO2.18. Note that the data is aligned horizontally with the labels in a header at the top. This layout is determined by a property called **Default View** with the value of 'Continuous'. See later description of object properties.

Save the form with the name 'Branch'.

BranchCode	BranchName	City	ManagerId		Budget
01	SOUTH	London	1001		£300.00
02	WEST	Liverpool	4206		£250.00
03	EAST	York	7663		£350.00
04	NORTH	Aberdeen	3876		£200.00
05	EUROPE	PARIS			£0.00
*					£0.00

Record: I◀ ◀ | 1 | ▶ ▶I ▶✱ | of 5

FIGURE HOB.18 Branch table – tabular layout

The ▶ symbol in the left column (called the 'selector bar') indicates the 'current' record to distinguish it from the other rows of data.

Tabular format is best when there are relatively few rows in the table (as for Branch) and/or you want to browse through the table quickly. Another application for tabular format is in sub-forms, covered later. The columnar format is generally best for most other situations such as entering transactions (e.g. hiring a vehicle) where you are probably dealing with single rows at a time.

Forms provide a 'window' into the tables; changes made on the form automatically cause a change to the underlying table. The form is said to be 'bound' to the table. Also, an individual text box is usually bound to a specific table field. However, it is possible to have *unbound* controls, which are simply used as work fields on the form, to show calculated values for example.

It is important to appreciate that forms can be based on queries as well as tables. Changes made to query-based forms also can update the tables on which the query is based. However, not all queries are 'updateable'. This point is pursued later.

The form consists of three main areas: Header, Detail (in centre) and Footer as shown in Figure HOB.19. The Detail section shows form data (e.g. the underlying table) and will always be used. The other sections are used to accommodate other items such as form title and control buttons. Use of these is at the form designer's discretion. Figure HOB.19 shows these sections of an empty form.

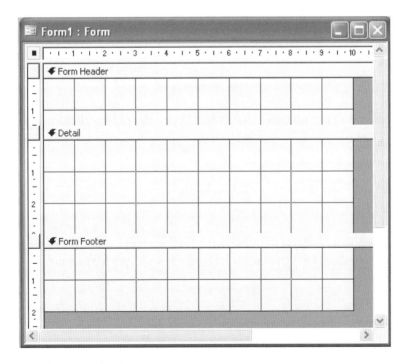

FIGURE HOB.19 Structure of a form

The Header and Footer sizes are set by the designer and these sizes are maintained at the expense of the detail section. The space left within the available window size is used for the detail. A scroll bar will appear on the Detail area if necessary.

The respective areas can be selected by clicking on the appropriate bar in order to modify its properties. The whole form is selected by clicking on the box at the top-left corner. A black square appears, as shown in Figure HOB.19.

Notice also that the usable area of the form (the grid area shown) is movable at the right-hand side.

Properties

All objects that form part of an Access design have a set of 'properties' that can be inspected (using a property box) and in many cases modified. We can illustrate how to use properties with reference to some form properties.

We will use a text box and label from the Employee form, shown earlier:

FIGURE HOB.20 Form object

The frame round the text box indicates that it has been selected by clicking on it.

NOTE

There are two controls here, close together – the text box and a label. Make sure that the correct one is selected, i.e. it has six frame handles around it as shown.

Position the cursor over the text box until a hand cursor appears, then right click the right mouse button. Select **Properties** from the menu. A text box control properties list window will appear as shown in Figure HOB.21.

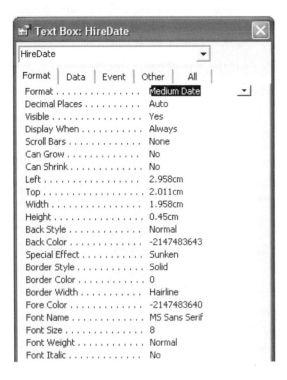

FIGURE HOB.21 Text box control properties list

NOTE

The tabs across the top enable selection of different sets of properties. The **Format** tab is currently selected, which governs aspects of the object format such as position, font attributes. The **Data** tab shows properties related to the data source for text box. The **Event** tab is used to specify the handling of 'events' that occur on the object, such as changes in value, getting the focus, etc. This topic is dealt with extensively in a later section.

Try changing some of the properties such as back color, font name etc. to see their effect. The size and position of the object can be varied using properties for exact alignment, although it is easier to drag and stretch the object frame using the mouse.

If you select a different object, the set of properties will be different. For example, selecting the whole form will give a totally different set of properties, the *form properties*.

Creating a report

Access includes a very powerful report generator that enables complex reports to be created automatically. Reports can be based on both tables and queries. The generator also incorporates a 'wizard' which can bring together one or more tables and queries to provide detail and summarised information.

We will start by generating two simple single table reports using two different layout conventions. As with forms, reports can be organised into 'tabular' and 'columnar' formats, with the report fields being arranged either vertically or horizontally respectively.

Figure HOB.22 shows the initial dialog for the report generator. Select:

Autoreport: Tabular and table **Employee** from the dropdown list box.

Do not use the **Design View** option for new reports, since it involves placing each item manually into the print layout design.

The **Report Wizard** option is useful for more complex reports, especially those using subtotalling, and starts with the screen shown in Figure HOB.22.

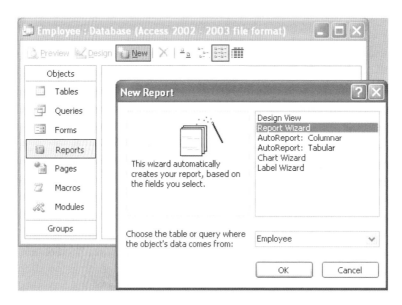

FIGURE HOB.22 Report Wizard, New Report dialog

This results in the report partially shown in Figure HOB.23 below.

Employee

EmpId	Name	Position	HireDate	Salary	BranchCode	Department	Supervisor
1001	Kennedy	Director	16-Jan-94	£50,000.00	01		
1045	Smith	Salesman	12-May-05	£18,000.00	04	Sales	3691
1271	Stewart	Clerk	30-Apr-91	£16,000.00	03	Accounts	3255
1534	Bell	Supervisor	20-Nov-95	£20,000.00	01	Admin	3876

FIGURE HOB.23 Report output

If the form is shown in design view we get the following structure layout (Figure HOB.24) which makes it possible to move the boxes around on the report, so that some arrangement between the tabular and columnar layouts can be achieved. The field values can be repositioned, reordered or deleted (not shown in this version of the report).

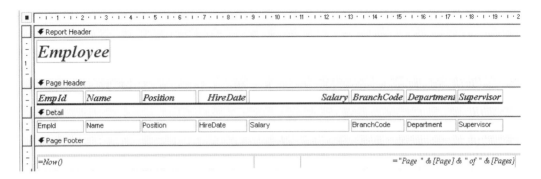

FIGURE HOB.24 Report design view

Observe the different zones of this display. The report header content will only appear once for the whole report. The page header will appear at the top of each page and similarly the footer at the bottom. As with form captions and headings, you can edit these by clicking to select them, then clicking again to get a text cursor.

Create another report (starting at Figure HOB.22) but this time select **Autoreport: Columnar**. Part of the output from this (the first row and part of the next) is shown in Figure HOB.25. As you can see, this is a less useful layout for most applications. The boxes around the values are optional.

Employee

EmpId	1001
Name	Kennedy
Position	Director
HireDate	16-Jan-94
Salary	£50,000.00
BranchCode	01
Department	
Supervisor	
EmpId	1045
Name	Smith

FIGURE HOB.25 Columnar report format

Creating a query

Access uses a special grid display for the definition of queries, although it also allows the use of SQL. The grid system and SQL are (almost) interchangeable; i.e. a query created in SQL can be shown in the grid format and vice versa. Internally, queries are saved in SQL.

Queries can be used to provide answers to specific ad hoc questions about the database tables, but are mainly used as the source of data for forms and reports. Start the query system from the Database window by selecting the **Queries** button on the left and clicking the **New** button. The dialog box shown in Figure HOB.26 appears.

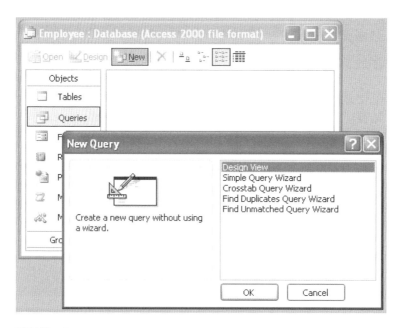

FIGURE HOB.26 Query design options

A number of options are available, but the most useful is the **Design View** shown selected. The bottom three options are more specialised queries.

The Query Wizard is useful in creating a query from two or more tables.

Click on **OK**; a **Show Table** dialog box appears. Select each of the two tables in turn and click **Add**.

This should produce the ER-style diagram shown in Figure HOB.27.

Figure HOB.27 shows the entries required to answer the question 'Show all employee ids and names from the North branch'.

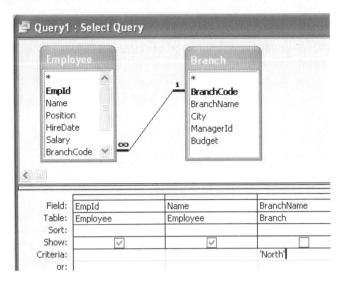

FIGURE HOB.27 Query design grid

The field names can be entered in a number of ways:

- Double-clicking on the field name.
- The **Field** row of the grid consists of drop-down boxes.
- Dragging and dropping the field name on the required column.

The action of the query grid is as follows:

- Each entry in the **Field** row (EmpId, Name, BranchName) refers to fields from the source tables; the second row indicates the table.
- If the check box in the **Show** row is ticked then that value will be displayed.
- The **Criteria** row provides conditional values to be tested against the corresponding field. In our example, the condition is BranchName = 'North'.
- Compound ANDed conditions can be expressed by using two or more entries in the **Criteria** row.
- ORed conditions use successive rows below the first criteria entry; e.g. to show employees in the North or East branches, 'East' would be entered under 'North'.

To execute the query, click the **run** button (Figure HOB.28) on the main toolbar.

FIGURE HOB.28 The run query button

You can save the query giving it a suitable name. It then becomes available for use as input to a form or report.

NOTE

The BranchName is not shown because in the design grid the check box in the **Show:** row is not set for this column.

	Empld	Name
▶	1045	Smith
	1653	Walker
	3691	Adams
	3876	Hill
	4218	Cohen
	9773	Nicholson
*		

Query1 : Select Query

FIGURE HOB.29 Query output

The query can be viewed as its SQL equivalent by selecting the **View-SQL View** menu option. This shows the SQL to be (with some reformatting):

```
SELECT Employee.EmpId, Employee.Name
    FROM Branch INNER JOIN Employee
        ON Branch.BranchCode = Employee.BranchCode
            WHERE Branch.BranchName = 'North';
```

NOTE

The original Access version uses numerous additional parenthesis which have been omitted here for clarity. The field names are fully qualified with the table names.

Queries can be saved with user-defined names and then used elsewhere as data sources for forms, reports or other queries.

Summary

After completing all the procedures in this section, you should now have a small working database consisting of:

- Two tables, Employee and Branch, with a relationship between them set up.
- Two forms, one in columnar view for the Employee table and one in tabular view for the Branch table.
- A report based on the Employee table.

Exercises

Open the Employee form in design mode and do the following:

1 Extend the size of the detail, header and footer areas and change the background colours. If there are no header and footer bars showing, click on menu **View>Form Header/Footer.** You may then have to drag the boundary lines of the header/footer to expose them.

2 Select the **EmpId** text box by clicking on it. Use the properties box to modify the font size to 12 and Arial style. This may require resizing of the box by clicking and dragging the frame handles. If the properties box is not already open, it can be opened by pointing to the selected object (hand cursor), and selecting **Properties** from the right button mouse menu.

3 Observe that you can select multiple objects on the form by clicking and dragging the cursor using the left mouse button. This generates a rectangle which selects all the objects enclosed. The properties box is now titled **Multiple Selection**. Use this to modify the font of the other text boxes.

4 Try modifying the layout of multiple items by using the features found under menu **Format>Align, Vertical and Horizontal Spacing**.

5 Write a new query that shows employee names, positions, salary, hire date, branch name and city for all employees hired after 1-Jan-95 who have a salary greater than £18 000.

6 Generate a report based on the query from question 5 above.

In Access, literal dates must be enclosed in hash symbols, so the above date would be expressed as #1-Jan-95#. The value 18 000 would not be entered with the comma included; nor would a currency symbol be used.

More about Access

The Getting Started section described the basic features of Access. In this section we expand our knowledge of Access by taking a more detailed look at tables, forms and reports.

More about tables

Tables – additional properties

In the Getting Started section we looked at the interface that enables you to design a new table or amend the design of a current table. The main properties that need to be defined here are the field names and their datatypes, but there are several other properties that can be applied to each field. The set of properties that can be set or adjusted vary depending on the datatype. Figure HOB.30 and HOB.31 show the design interface for two of the more common data types, namely text and number, side by side so you can compare their different properties. The following description also makes reference to the date datatype.

FIGURE HOB.30 Text field

FIGURE HOB.31 Number field

Figure HOB.30 and HOB.31 show that these two datatypes have a number of properties in common, such as field size, format, etc. and a few peculiar to each type, such as decimal places for number type. However, there is sufficient commonality that a common description will suffice, with variations noted. Other datatypes such as date or currency have their own properties but do not differ dramatically. Note that the properties established at this, the table design stage, are carried forward to forms design for any forms accessing this table.

Field size: For a text field, this value determines its maximum length. For instance, if it is set to 6, if you tried to enter DATABASE in the field it would be truncated to DATABA. Use of this property provides a basic validation of the data; where a field has a specific fixed length or must never be allowed to exceed a specific length the field size property can provide protection against error in this respect. However, it is important to allow sufficient space for the field application. Note that it defaults to 50. This is often larger than necessary, but there is no penalty for being generous.

Field size's use in a number field is more complex; it specifies not just the size of the field (i.e. number of digits), but also the internal format. The options are provided on a drop-down list, the main ones being:

- **Integer**   Positive or negative integer (whole number).
- **Long integer** (default)   Larger integer with more digits.

- **Byte**   8 bit number allowing only positive values from 0 to 255.
- **Single**   Single precision floating point value.
- **Double**   Double precision floating point value.
- **Decimal**   Fixed decimal representation of up to 28 digits.

More details on these formats can be obtained by selecting the **Field Length** property then clicking F1. This applies to all the other property items such as **Format**.

Format: Controls the display format of the data, i.e. they way it will appear when shown in a form or printed. For instance, for numerical amounts, you can insert commas for thousands and fix the number of decimal places shown. The notations used for text and numbers are quite complex and are ignored for the time being. For date fields the situation is simpler; dates can be shown in a number of formats such as 12 October 2007 (long), 12-Oct-07 (medium) or 12/10/07 (short). The best format is generally medium; the short format introduces the possibility of confusion between European and American conventions. The last short format date is read as the 10th of December in America.

Input mask: provides a pattern into which entered data must fit. This is also a validation mechanism; for instance we can constrain a data item to be two alphabetic letters followed by four digits by using the mask 'LL0000' (these are zeroes). So 'YZ1234' is valid but 'A999' is not. The mask can also be used to force input data to upper or lower case.

Caption: provides a value for the label attached to the field on a form. If omitted, it defaults to the field name.

Default value: determines the value inserted in the column when a new record is created. If no value is provided here, new records will contain nulls in the column being defined. This can produce erroneous results; for instance, if a numeric column contains a null, adding values to it will have no effect.

Validation rule/text: specifies a rule to which *new data* must conform. The text entry is an error message that appears when the validation fails. Note that a further opportunity for validation occurs in the design of forms. Table validations are 'carried forward' into any form created from the table, but further more specific validation can be applied within the form. Changing this entry will have no effect on currently stored records.

Required: indicates whether a null is acceptable in that field. If it is 'No', then it is not possible simply to ignore the field: something must be entered.

Indexed: allows indication that the field should be indexed. Indexing speeds up queries which reference that field. Three options are provided:

- No
- Yes (duplicates OK)
- Yes (no duplicates)

The last of these usually applies only to primary keys but can be used on other fields.

More about forms

Controls

The objects that are used on forms and reports such as text boxes, labels and buttons are referred to as 'controls' in Microsoft systems. These are essential tools in the construction of a 'point and click' style of user interface. Access provides a number of built-in controls and new controls can be implemented as ActiveX objects. A vast range of additional controls are available from Microsoft and other sources.

In this section we look at the functionality of the built-in controls.

The Toolbox

In the Getting Started section we created a form simply using the auto-form feature, which placed text boxes and labels automatically on the form. Typically, we would generate a new form in this way, then add additional controls to the form manually. We select the controls we want from a Toolbox palette, which is illustrated below. The Toolbox only appears in Design view.

The more common of the controls are described on the next page.

The top two objects in the toolbox are not 'controls' as such (selection tool and Control Wizard toggle) but assist in the form design process.

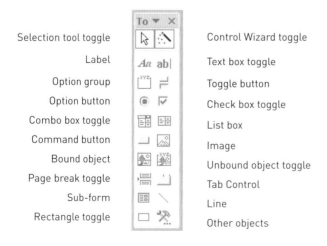

Selection tool toggle	Control Wizard toggle
Label	Text box toggle
Option group	Toggle button
Option button	Check box toggle
Combo box toggle	List box
Command button	Image
Bound object	Unbound object toggle
Page break toggle	Tab Control
Sub-form	Line
Rectangle toggle	Other objects

FIGURE HOB.32 Access toolbox

Selection tool: Used to select objects on the form.

Control Wizard toggle: When enabled, causes a wizard dialog to appear for certain controls when these are placed on the form. It is best to have this option enabled to take advantage of the wizards.

The following are control objects that can be placed on the form.

Label: A box containing a constant text string. Labels are mostly used in association with text boxes, to identify the content of the box. They can also be used for titles and other general fixed text items.

Text box: A box that can hold a variable text value. Generally shows a value obtained from the underlying table or query, called a 'bound' control. However, a box may be un-bound; in this case, it can be viewed as a storage space on the form. This might be used for temporary values held or calculated by the form.

Command button: Activates a macro or VBA procedure. Buttons are used to action some immediate command such as closing the form, saving the current record, opening another form.

Option button: Allows specification of one from a set of alternative (mutually exclusive) options. Used in conjunction with the Option frame.

Check box: Allows specification of one or more selection option. Used in conjunction with the Option frame.

List box: Displays a list of values to choose from. The values can be entered as a property of the control or can 'look up' a value from a table or query.

Combo box: A combination of a text and a list box. A value may be chosen from a given list, but alternatively a non-listed value may be entered.

Line: Draws a line to separate areas of a form.

Rectangle: Draws a rectangle to partition an area of the form.

Other objects: Provides access to other ActiveX objects that can be placed on the form. One useful example is the calendar control. Examples of using some of these controls will be covered in due course.

Event handling

Like all graphical user interfaces, Access forms use event-handling as a technique for user interaction; i.e. actions by the user in moving and clicking the mouse and in changing values cause some predetermined program action to take place.

The events that a particular object can respond to are listed in the property box for the object under the **Events** tab. e.g. On click, On change, On key down, etc. although use of many of the available events is quite rare.

Macros and procedures

The required response for a particular event for an object is defined within a macro or a procedure. These are covered in more detail later, but briefly a macro is a sequence of simple actions such as open form, goto record, close form etc. Macros provide very little in terms of programmability. A procedure is a subroutine written in Visual Basic for Applications (VBA), which is a fully-fledged programming language. With one or two minor exceptions, anything that can be expressed as a macro can be written in VBA.

Control wizard

Typical examples of using event handlers are: use of command buttons to specify actions and validation of data entered into text boxes. Fortunately, Access provides a control wizard to automate the production of VBA event-handling code for many applications. For more specialised applications it might be necessary to develop your own macro or VBA code, or to modify a wizard-generated code module.

Example

In this section we will start with the basic wizard-generated Employee form created in the first section and apply a number of enhancements to it to make the form more usable for a practical application. The specific enhancements are:

- Add a title to the header area to identify the form.

- Add buttons to the footer to close the form and to save the current record.

- Add a combo box to look up BranchCode values from the Branch table.

Add a title to the header

Create a form based on the Employee table like that shown in Figure HOB.15. Note this is in Design view. If your form does not show the **Form Header** section, use the menu option **View>Form Header/Footer** to make it appear. Then proceed as follows:

1 Using the mouse, position the cursor on the line between the **Header** and **Detail** sections – the cursor shape will change – click the left mouse button, then drag the mouse down to create some space in the detail area.

2 Click on the label icon in the Toolbox (if the Toolbox is not visible, use the menu option **View>Toolbox**.) Bring the cursor to the header area, depress the left mouse button and drag the cursor to open a rectangular area where the label will be located.

3 Release the mouse button and a text cursor will appear inside the label area. Type in a suitable title such as 'Employee Form'. Press return; the label box will be selected.

4 If it is not already opened, open the properties box. This can be done in several ways: right-mouse click, **View** menu or by a menu-bar button. Note that the label must remain selected while the properties box is opened.

5 Modify some of the label properties: change the font to Arial, the font size to 28 and the colour to red. Experiment with other properties.

Add buttons to the footer

This illustrates the process of putting a command button on the form which can be used at run time to close the form. Such buttons are usually put in the footer area.

First, give the form header and footer sections as explained in Getting Started.

1 Click on the command button icon in the Toolbox. Now move the cursor into the footer area of the form; the cursor will change to a + sign and a rectangle. The rectangle represents the button; the + sign indicates where the button will be positioned.

2 Move the cursor to a suitable location on the form, click and drag the left mouse button to open up a rectangular area as large as the button area you wish to create (including sufficient room for its label or for the user's instructions). Release the left mouse button and the button will appear on the form enclosed within a selection frame, as shown in Figure HOB.33.

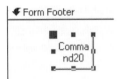

FIGURE HOB.33 Command button on a form

The control wizard should now start and produce the following dialog:

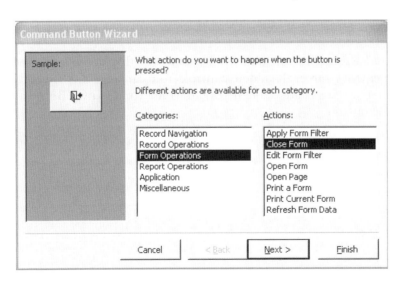

FIGURE HOB.34 Command button wizard

3 The left-hand list specifies different categories of command and the right-hand list shows the available commands within that category. We select **Form Operations** and **Close Form**. Click **Next** to give the next screen, Figure HOB.35.

NOTE

There is a wide range of operations that can be performed by the command buttons. In particular, note that from one form we can use **Open Form** to 'go' to another form. A similar **Open Report** facility exists. This can be used as the basis of a multi-level menu system to navigate through the application.

4 This dialog allows you to select an image for the button or to use a text label. Select **Picture** and accept the default **Exit** (the exit door symbol) and click **Next**.

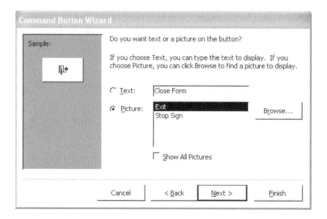

FIGURE HOB.35 Command button wizard – image selection

5 The button name created by default will be something like command20 where the number increments for each added control. You can give the button a more meaningful name. This is advisable if you are going to use any VBA or macros in relation to the button.

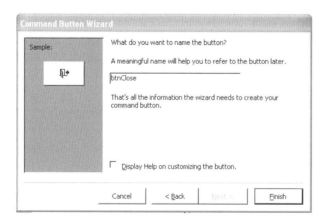

FIGURE HOB.36 Command button wizard – name

NOTE

It is conventional to use **btn** or **cmd** followed by the name commencing with a capital letter. Longer phrases, if absolutely necessary, are usually capitalised (and must not have spaces), e.g. btnTimeSubmitted. It is also advisable to link the name for the button to the text on the button in some way when designing more complex forms and user interfaces using your database.

6 Click **Finish** and the button will appear on the form. If you now save the form (using the name 'Employee'), then run it, we should see the form shown in Figure HOB.37.

FIGURE HOB.37 Completed employee form

7 Test your Employee form. If you click the newly-created button, the form will close and Access will return to the main database window.

You may be puzzled by the parallel lines that appear below the Supervisor text box. This is a 'dead zone' caused by the fact that there is 'too much' screen space available for the detail section. In the Getting Started section, we mentioned that the sizes of the header and footer are set by the designer and the detail section between them is 'squeezed'. However, if the detail section is set to a size less than that available (determined by the window size), then the dead zone appears, which will always be unused. If you use the mouse to vary the size of the window containing the form, then you will get an idea of how this works.

If you find the dead zone untidy, you can get rid of the dividing lines so that it appears as part of the detail section. At the same time we could get rid of the selector bar to the left of the screen, as this is pointless when we only have one record on the form. The selector bar is more appropriate for tabular displays such as that shown in Figure HOB.18. We can implement both these changes by using the form properties.

Open the Employee form in design view and proceed as follows:

1   Select the form, When selected, a black dot is visible in a box at the top left of the form. If it is not selected, then click in the box or use the menu option **Edit> Select Form**.

2   Open the properties box (if not open) by using **View>Properties**, the right-click menu or by pressing Alt+Enter.

3   Using the Format tab entries, set **Dividing Lines** and **Record Selector** items to **No**.

4   The properties box should now look similar to Figure HOB.38

FIGURE HOB.38 Form properties

5   Close the form properties box. Open the form. Depending on the window size, (yours may have scroll bars), the revised Employee form should look like Figure HOB.39.

FIGURE HOB.39 Revised employee form

NOTE

This form has no distinction between the header, footer and detail areas. If you want to differentiate between them, change the background colours for each section by selecting each area and modifying the Back Color property.

List and combo boxes

These controls are among the easiest to apply and at the same time are among the most useful. The functionality of the two types is similar; we will describe the list box first and then indicate the difference to the combo box. The principal purpose of these controls is to 'look-up' a value for insertion into one of the form fields. The value can be obtained from a pre-entered set of values or from a table or query.

List box

To illustrate the list box function, we will look up two values for entry onto the Employee form.

Firstly, we will use a common feature of look-up boxes to:

- **Obtain a foreign key value from another table**. In our sample system, the Employee table contains a foreign key, BranchCode, that refers to the primary key of the Branch table. It is crucial that correct values are inserted and the best way to ensure this is to pick a BranchCode value from the Branch table.

- **See a list of more meaningful values**, such as branch names, rather than anonymous numbers. With these points in mind we will put a list box on the Employee form. Fortunately, the process is automated by a wizard; on the downside, quite a few steps are involved.

List box wizard dialog

Start by opening the Employee form in design view and generate some space on the form to the right of the text boxes by 'dragging' the right-hand edge of the form work area.

1 Left click the list-box icon in the Toolbox. Move the cursor to the Employee form and use the left mouse button to place the list-box control on the form. At this point the list box wizard dialog should start, displaying the first screen, Figure HOB.40.

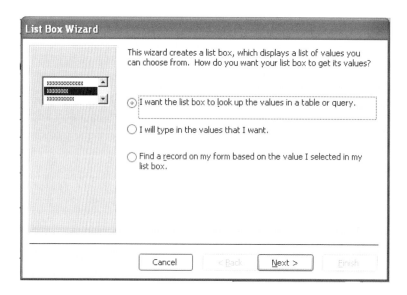

FIGURE HOB.40 List box wizard – purpose selection

2 This screen presents you with a choice of three possible actions; for our current example, choose option 1.

To recap, we intend to use the list box to select a BranchCode value from the branch table. Click **Next**.

3 The next screen (Figure HOB.41) will list all the tables available in the database (and optionally queries as well). We need to look up the Branch table, so select this table, the source for the list box. Click **Next**.

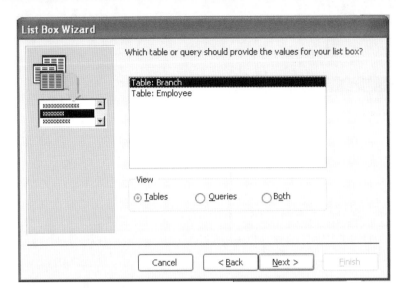

FIGURE HOB.41 Choose the source for the list box

4 A screen similar to that shown in Figure HOB.42 appears. Select the fields from the Branch table that you want to show in the list box. Select the key value, Branch-Code; any other fields you add are mainly for the purpose of identifying the correct row; in this example, the branch name should suffice, although the **City** field, might also be useful.

Note that the **>** key moves fields into the list box; the **>>** key moves all fields.

Click **Next**.

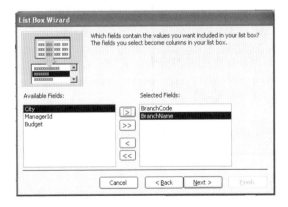

FIGURE HOB.42 Select the fields to display in the list box

5 Control the sequence of the entries in the list box using the sort in ascending or descending order using the List Wizard box shown in Figure HOB.43. This sort function is important if there are a large number of entries in the list. We have

chosen **BranchName** since we are using this identification of the branch. Click **Next**.

FIGURE HOB.43 Selecting fields to obtain a sorted results list in the list box

6 Use the list box column format dialog, Figure HOB.44, to control the appearance of the list box. The check box allows you to show the key field (BranchCode) or not as you wish.

FIGURE HOB.44 List box column format

7 Choose whether to store the value in a field, or remember the result, using the screen shown in Figure HOB.45. This box is the critical part of the process: it allows us to take the key value of the list box (BranchCode) and store it in a field of the current form. The relevant field is, of course, the BranchCode of the Employee table, thus establishing the foreign key – primary key link. Click **Next**.

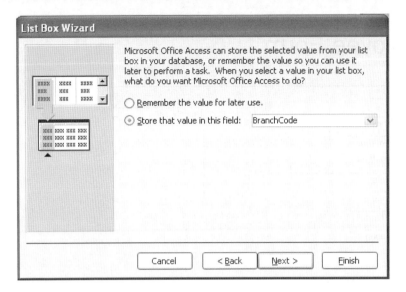

FIGURE HOB.45 Transfer value from list box to form

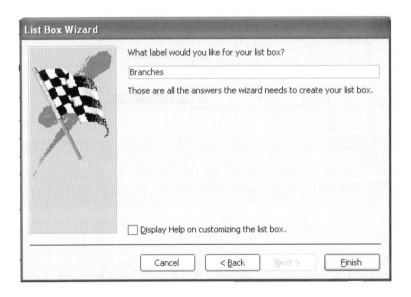

FIGURE HOB.46 Final step, define list box label

8 The final step of the wizard dialog allows us to alter the label that is associated with the list box (Figure HOB.46). Click **Finish**.

Figure HOB.47 and HOB.48 show the Design view and completed list box views of the Employee Form.

FIGURE HOB.47 Design view

FIGURE HOB.48 Form view

NOTE

Space defined by the design view frame is the fixed allocation for the list box; if it is too small in height, scroll bars will appear. The label may be moved to a more effective position or even deleted if required.

It is important to appreciate the action of the list box; when a branch name is selected in the list box, e.g. South in the example shown in Figure HOB.48, the corresponding BranchCode (01) is transferred into the **BranchCode** field on the main form. This guarantees that the BranchCode value is valid. It also avoids having to remember the codes for each of the branches; not a great problem with so few entries, but the principle applies to much larger tables.

Combo boxes

Combo and list boxes have similar purposes and functionality; the differences are as follows.

- The word 'combo' derives from the fact that it is a combination of list box and text box; i.e. it is possible to enter a value (as for a text box) which does not appear in the list.

- This, of course, negates any validation provided by the box, but this feature can be disabled by setting the property 'Restrict to list'. An example where this might be useful is in entering name information that includes titles such as Mr, Mrs, Miss, etc. While a list of the most likely cases can be assembled, the possibilities are quite diverse; e.g. Professor Sir, Lieutenant General, etc. A facility to enter an unlisted value would be essential.

NOTE

Entry of an unlisted value does *not* cause its addition to the list.

- The combo box operates as a 'drop-down' box; i.e. it initially appears as a text box but can be clicked to expose the full list. After selection the box returns to the text box shape with the chosen value displayed.

Example of combo box

We can add a combo box to the Employee form to help select the Position field of the record. Since this process is not too different from the list box dialog, we will dispense with the screenshots and indicate the action at each stage simply as numbered steps.

1 Open the Employee form in design view. Click on the combo box icon in the toolbox, then use the mouse to place the box on the form, drawing a shape roughly the size of the existing text boxes. This will activate the wizard.

2 On the first wizard dialog; select the second option available: **I will type in the values I want**. Click **Next**.

3 This dialog starts **What values do you want to see in your combo box?**. Type the Employee job positions (e.g. Salesman, Clerk, etc.) into the form provided.

   Don't press **Enter** on this form until you are finished – it takes you to the next screen; use the cursor keys to navigate down the column. Then press **Enter** or click **Next**.

4 Choose the second option **Store that value in this field** and choose **Position** from the field list. Click Next.

5 Enter a suitable label value, then click **Finish**. The combo box is now located on the form.

When using combo boxes it is normally the practice to use it entirely in place of the original text box since it appears the same when closed. Hence delete the **Position** text box and move the new combo box to replace it.

Figure HOB.49 and HOB.50 show the appearance, both 'closed' and 'open' with the drop-down combo box.

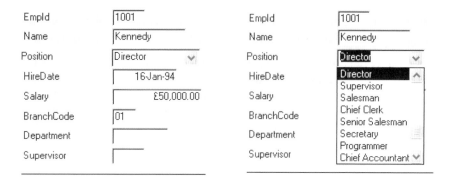

FIGURE HOB.49 Closed combo box   **FIGURE HOB.50** Open combo box

Form operating modes

By default, when a form opens it displays the first record and makes all records in the dataset available for reading and writing. It is possible modify this behaviour by suitable changes to specific form properties in Design view as described below. They appear under the properties **Data** tab:

Data entry: defaults to **No**; if set to **Yes**, the form does not show current records in the dataset. This mode is typically used to input new transactions where inspection of previous records is not relevant.

Allow edits: Normally **Yes**; if set to **No**, the form becomes 'read only' – no changes can be made to the records.

Allow deletions: Normally **Yes**; if set to **No**, deletion of records is not allowed.

Allow additions: Normally **Yes**; if set to **No**, addition of records is not allowed; note that this would be with **Data entry** = **Yes**.

More about reports

In the Getting Started section we saw how easily you can create basic reports using the Access auto-report facilities. To recap, we can generate a tabular or columnar display from rows drawn from a table or query. The generated report can then be fine tuned by suitable adjustment of the field and label positions, font sizes, shading, etc.

One of the most powerful features of the Access report generator is its ability to produce reports showing both detail and summary information such as totals and sub-totals. This is very important because such reports are used extensively in practical applications. Also, it is important to note that the generation of both detail and summary information is not convenient using SQL. For instance, we can write the following queries:

QUERY HOB.2

Show the salary and department values for each employee in the Employee table:

```
SELECT Name, BranchCode, Salary FROM Employee
```

and we can show branch total salary values:

```
SELECT BranchCode, SUM(Salary) FROM Employee
   GROUP BY BranchCode
```

With basic SQL commands we cannot show both. However, this task can be achieved by means of a wizard-generated report. We describe this process below.

Using the Report Wizard

Let's say we want to produce a report showing the details of each employee, divided into the various branches, showing the subtotalled salary bill for each branch, and an overall salary total. The first thing to realise is that this task can be implemented by means of the report generator; there is no need for any preliminary query design.

1 To begin, select the **Reports** button in the left column of the main database window and then click the **New** button at the top of the window. This will cause the first wizard dialog to open – see Figure HOB.51.

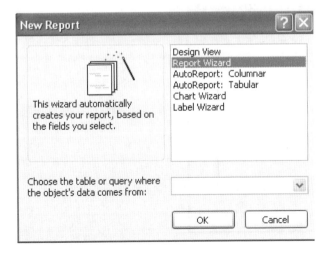

FIGURE HOB.51 Report Wizard startup

2   Select the Report Wizard option as shown in the figure; note that, for this option, no entry is required in the **Choose a table . . . box**. Click OK. The next screen, shown in Figure HOB.52, allows us to select the fields for inclusion in the report. These may come from one or more tables and queries.

3   The drop-down list labelled **Tables/Queries** allows us to select any of those that exist in the database. When one is selected, the table fields are listed as shown. We can then pick those required for the report by clicking on the **>** button. For the Branch table, select **BranchCode** and **BranchName**. Now select **Employee** on the drop down list and pick fields **EmpId**, **Name** and **Salary**. Click **Next** (Figure HOB.53).

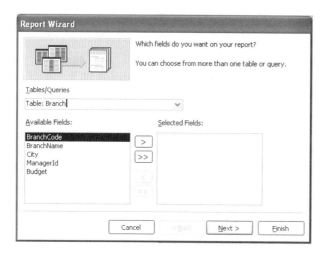

FIGURE HOB.52 Field Selection

FIGURE HOB.53 Structure of report

4 If the Report Wizard screen in Figure HOB.53 does not initially appear as shown, click on **by Branch** in the list. This screen shows a sketch of how the report will be formed. It indicates that BranchCode/BranchName will be used as a 'break-point'; i.e. subtotals will be produced for each unique value. This will become clearer once we run the report.

The next dialog screen asks **Do you want to add any grouping levels?** Since we do not want any further sub-division of the report, just respond to this by clicking **Next**.

5 The next screen, Figure HOB.54, is a little complex and services two separate design factors as described below. First, the immediate screen permits you to set the sorting sequence for the detail items in the report. In Figure HOB.54, you can see that we have selected **Name** so that the detail report lines will be ordered by the employee name.

6 This screen also contains a **Summary Options** button; this button provides entry to another screen (Figure HOB.55) that allows you to define what summary calculations are required. Note that when you finish with that screen you will be returned to the current screen. Click on the **Summary** button now.

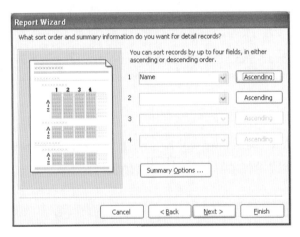

FIGURE HOB.54 Sort order

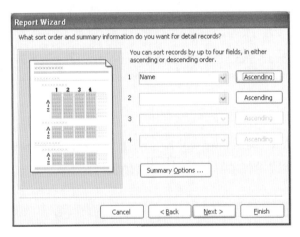

FIGURE HOB.55 Summary options

7   We can choose to calculate any of the aggregate values shown for each BranchCode/Name group. For this example, select **Sum only**. Note also that the radio button option **Detail** and **Summary** is chosen. If **Summary** is selected we get only the summary information, a bit like doing a 'GROUP BY BranchCode, BranchName' query. Clicking **OK** takes us back to the previous screen (HOB.54). From there click **Next**.

8   The next screen is headed **How would you like to lay out your report?**. This is concerned only with the general layout; just accept the default; you can experiment with the other options later. Click **Next**. Similarly, the next screen, headed **What style would you like?** is concerned only with fonts and other style considerations. Select the option **Corporate**,which is probably the most conventional of the choices.

9   The final screen allows you to set the content of the report header; set to **Branch Salaries Summary**. Now click on **Finish**; a preview of the report should appear, a part of which is shown below (Figure HOB.56).

NOTE

Salary is shown for each employee and sum of salaries values after each Branch group; a final total is also produced (not shown).

10   When you close this preview the report will be saved. You can also inspect the report in Design view as illustrated in Figure HOB.57.

Branch Salaries Summary

BranchCode	BranchName	Name	EmpId	Salary
01	South			
		Bell	1534	20,000.00
		Chung	2244	21,500.00
		Hamilton	6223	20,000.00
		Kennedy	1001	50,000.00
		Roxburgh	3198	20,000.00
		Young	3255	30,000.00
Summary for 'BranchCode' = 01 (6 detail records)				
Sum				£161,500.00
02	West			
		Evans	8253	17,500.00
		Gomatam	4206	31,000.00
		Monaghan	4102	17,000.00
		Moore	4936	19,500.00
Summary for 'BranchCode' = 02 (4 detail records)				

FIGURE HOB.56 Preview of report showing subtotals

FIGURE HOB.57 Report design showing various header/footers

Note the structure of the report that this view reveals. There are a number of nested sections bracketed by headers and footers:

Report section: this section defines the whole report. The header contains items which will be displayed once only at the start of the report. The footer is used to display the grand total.

Page section: displayed at the top/bottom of each page. The header contains column headings for the report detail. The footer is used to show page numbers.

BranchCode section: this illustrates the action taken for a **breakpoint** i.e. a change in the value of the GROUP BY value. The header holds the values of BranchCode and Branch-Name at this point. The footer contains subtotals of salaries for that Branch. If the report had more levels of breakdown then a section like this would exist for each level. For instance, the report could be further divided into the separate departments of the branches.

Detail: this section contains the detail of names, salaries, etc. and is a single area with no header and footer.

The Design view allows you to 'fine tune' the layout and make small general adjustments. For example, the size and position of text boxes can be adjusted, font sizes changed and background shading changed, etc. However, note that major changes are best implemented by redoing the report. For example, if a further break level (e.g. departments) was required, it is best to start again.

Even more Access

Overview

The topics covered in this section include:

- Menus (switchboard, button-driven)

- Sub-forms
- Querying facilities
- Events and object references.

Menus

While it is possible to select forms, queries and reports from the main database window, in a practical Access application a more convenient and user-friendly method of navigating through the various options is usually desirable. Remember that many database applications will be used by clerical staff and not by the designers of the system.

A menu system consists of a set of forms linked by command buttons arranged (in most cases) in a hierarchical structure. There are two principal methods for creating a menu:

- Using the Access supplied 'switchboard' facility.
- Building the system 'manually' using conventional forms construction.

The first method is very easy to use and provides a usable basic menu system. A table is created automatically that stores the content and structure of the menus. A form is generated based on the menu table that displays a set of buttons to be used in navigating the database forms and reports. This facility is fine for most applications; the second method does provide more flexibility in the design.

In the second method you design the menu forms yourself. From the main database window, select the **Forms** tab, then click the **New** button. From the options offered, select the top one, **Design View**. This option does not require selection of a table since you will be working on an initially blank form. Clicking the **OK** button produces a blank form on which you need to position buttons and labels. Figure HOB.58 shows an example of a top level menu for an equipment hire application.

FIGURE HOB.58 Menu screen

The top two items in Figure HOB.58 are simply labels. All but the last option provides a link to a form-based transactions. The last item is a link to another menu form that provides access to a number of reports.

The most important thing to note about this arrangement is that you must build it 'bottom up'. That is, the forms referenced by the buttons (including the lower level menu) must exist before the menu can be created.

It is possible to define an auto-executable form which the database will automatically open when the database is started. This is achieved by creating a macro called 'autoexec' which has one command of, 'OpenForm' with a parameter of 'Main Menu'.

Sub-forms

A sub-form is a form embedded in another form. Generally, there will be a relationship between the main form and the sub-form, otherwise there would be no point in the arrangement. The most common application is to represent a one-to-many relationship between two sets of data, with the main form showing the 'one' side and the sub-form showing the 'many' side. We can illustrate this principle using the Employee and Branch tables; as you recall, these tables have the relationship 'one Branch employs many Employees'. What we expect to see, therefore, is a main form based on the Branch table and containing a sub-form based on the Employee table. Let's see how this achieved. There are at least three ways of creating the form–sub-form structure:

- Create the main form first, say, based on the Branch table, then add a sub-form control to it. This will invoke a wizard which manages the design of the sub-form and its connection with the main form.

- Create a separate form for each of Branch and Employee; save the Employee form. Now drag the Employee form icon from the Database window list onto the Branch form (in Design view). The sub-form will be linked automatically to the main form. This is possible because the relationship between the tables is defined in the Relationship screen.

- Use the Form Wizard to incorporate the two tables into the one form. Again the system infers the correct relationship.

As well as being the shortest to explain, the third option is also the easiest to use and we illustrate the procedure below.

1 Starting from the main database window, select the **Forms** tab and click the **New** button; a New Form dialog appears. Here select **Form Wizard** only; there is no need to select a table in the drop down list. Now click **OK**.

2 The next dialog invites us to select the fields we want to have on the new form. Note that this dialog permits selection of fields from one or more tables. Remember that this process will build both the main form (Branch) and sub-form (Employee) so select all fields from both tables. Click **Next**.

3 The next screen (Figure HOB.59) shows the 'logical' structure of the new form.

FIGURE HOB.59 Form – sub-form structure

This illustrates that the main form will hold the Branch data and the sub-form will contain the Employee data. Note also that the radio button options have the default **Form with sub-form** selected.

The subsequent screens ask the following questions (respond as indicated):

> **What layout would you like for your sub-form?** Choose **Datasheet**.
>
> **What style would you like?** Accept the default or your own preference.
>
> **What titles do you want for your forms?** Set appropriate names, then click **Finish**.

Your new form will now be displayed and should look something like Figure HOB.60.

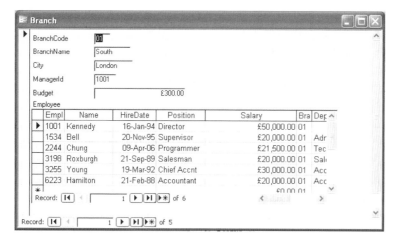

FIGURE HOB.60 Generated form – sub-form

As it stands, the layout format as shown Figure HOB.60 is a bit untidy, but a little work in the Design view can make it more presentable.

Note the following features of this process:

- The form and sub-form data are 'tied' together. Try browsing through the Branch records using the lower navigation bar; note that the content of the sub-form shows only the employees of the current branch.

- The sub-form is in Datasheet layout (as used in the table management part of Access). There is also a navigation bar for the sub-form.

The mechanism by which the two forms are tied together is worth noting. The first point to note is that the sub-form is contained within a 'sub-form control'; in Design view you can select this control; you should see a frame around the sub-form. If you now inspect the properties (right-click) of this control, it should look like Figure HOB.61.

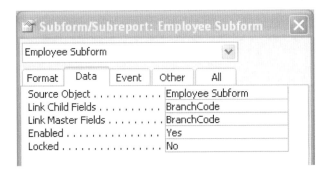

FIGURE HOB.61 Properties of sub-form control

Be sure that you are looking at the control properties and not the sub-form properties. The **Source Object** indicates the data source of the sub-form, namely the Employee table. (Note that it is possible to show the results of a query in a sub-form). In the **Link** properties, **Master** refers to the main or primary table, i.e. Branch, while **Child** refers to the Employee table.

Query facilities

In an earlier section we briefly examined how to create a simple select-type query. There are a number of other operations that we can perform with queries, namely update, delete, append, grouping and make table. These operations, except for append, correspond to the various SQL query types.

Queries are used extensively in Access. Two of the principal applications are to extract selected information required by an application and/or to join tables for subsequent processing. However, other operations are provided for.

Querying techniques

Access provides two techniques for querying, SQL and the query grid (formerly known as QBE, Query by Example). These two techniques are *almost* equivalent; i.e. a query expressed in one will convert into the other. The only exceptions are the SQL commands CREATE and UNION, which cannot be expressed in QBE.

Whether you use SQL or QBE is a matter of personal preference; simple commands are generally expressed faster by QBE, but those adept at SQL may find expression of grouping and sub-queries easier in SQL.

Types of query

Access provides facilities in the QBE grid for the expression of several types of queries. After opening the query design screen, the toolbar will have a 'query type' drop-down list (two overlapping rectangles). Exposing this list shows the selection shown in Figure HOB.62.

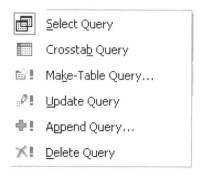

FIGURE HOB.62 Query types

The options presented by this list are described below. There is also a 'totals' button showing the Greek sigma symbol Σ, used to activate grouping in select queries.

Select: this is the default and most common query type. It simply provides a conditional extraction of data from the input table or tables. If more than one table is used, then these are joined.

Crosstab query: Used to generate a tabular output that displays the correlation between sets of values.

Select with grouping: if the totals button is pressed, the query grid format now includes a **Totals** row for the specification of groups and aggregate function (sum, average, etc.). Queries involving grouping typically present the most problems for students, whether SQL or QBE is used.

Update: this implements the SQL UPDATE command. It enables one or more rows of a table to be modified in accordance with an update specification. The latter includes:

- Selection of row(s) to be modified.

- Change(s) to be made to specific column(s).

Most commonly, update is used to make bulk changes to data, for instance raising all salaries by 5%, rather than changes to a single row.

Append: the append query adds data drawn from an input table or tables into an output table.

Delete: the delete query enables conditional deletion of row(s) from a table. For instance, delete would typically be used to remove all rows from a table that were older than, say, three years.

Make table: the make table query creates a new table with data derived from input table(s). It corresponds to the SQL SELECT . . . INTO command.

Sub-queries: These have to be specified in QBE by using an SQL clause within the criteria row of the main query. Given that you have to resort to SQL anyway, it is generally best to specify the whole query using SQL.

SQL only: Create and Union operations can only be achieved using SQL.

Field row of query grid

The **Field** row of the query grid corresponds to the SELECT list in SQL; it can contain column names (of input tables) or expressions based on column, arithmetic operators and functions. For expressions, alias names such as **Expr1** are generated by Access; these can be renamed if desired.

Use of parameters

A **parameter** is a value supplied at run-time to qualify the effect of a query. For example, you may want a query that selects rows from a student table for students who enrolled between two specified dates.

Parameter specifiers are placed in the criteria row of the QBE grid and consist of any text within square brackets. See Figure HOB.63. This causes a dialog box displaying this text to pop up when the query starts.

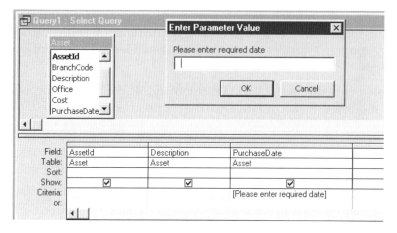

FIGURE HOB.63 Query parameters

An alternative to using parameters in this way is to use a form on which you enter the necessary parameter values in text boxes. These values can then be 'picked up' by the query. In this case, the query criteria holds (within square brackets again) a reference to the form text boxes. In fact, Access first tries to identify the contents of the brackets as an object somewhere in the system. Unidentified names are assumed to be parameters.

Invoking queries

A query may be executed in a number of different contexts:

- Directly: by opening the query from the main database window or by clicking the relevant '!' icon from the query design screen.

- Via forms and reports: if a form or report is based on a query, the query is executed 'silently' prior to activation of the form or report.

- Within VBA code: it is possible to activate a predefined query within a VBA program and to process the query output.

Updating of query result

If you base a form on a query, it is reasonable to expect that if you change the data displayed by the form that the change would be reflected in the underlying source tables. However, not all queries are 'updatable' in this sense. Since the number of permutations of table joins and query types can be very large, the exact rules with regard to updatability are complex. It hinges on whether a change to the query output can be interpreted unambiguously in terms of changes to the table data.

The main possibilities are:

- Queries involving groups are *not* updatable.

- Queries involving one-to-one and a single one-to-many relationship *are* updatable.

- Queries involving a one-to-many-to-one relationship can be updated using a form.
- more complex queries are generally not updatable.

Access query types – examples

See Figures HOB.64 and HOB.65.

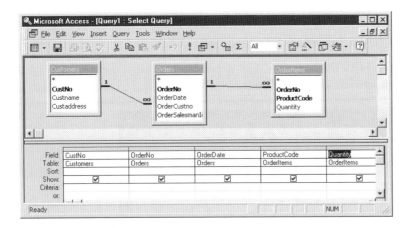

FIGURE HOB.64 Basic select query

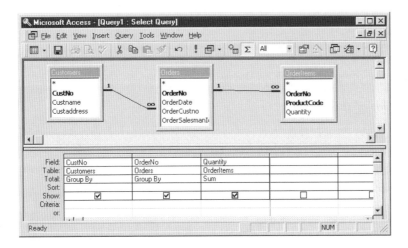

FIGURE HOB.65 Select query with grouping

Note the extra 'Total' row, produced by the sigma button. There are a number of options available in the **Total:** row of the grid; these correspond to the options available in a

GROUP BY form of SQL query:

Group by	Specifies the field(s) on which the data is to be grouped.
Where	Corresponds to the SQL WHERE clause; i.e. it selects rows to be involved in the grouping operation.
Aggregate functions	E.g. Sum, Avg, Count etc. These specify numerical operations to be callated for each group. See column three of grid in Figure HOB.65.
Expression	Indicates a calculation involving (only) the Group By fields and aggregate functions, e.g. Avg(Salary) * 2.

To specify the SQL HAVING clause, it is necessary to put a conditional value in the **Criteria** row of the grid as shown in Figure HOB.66.

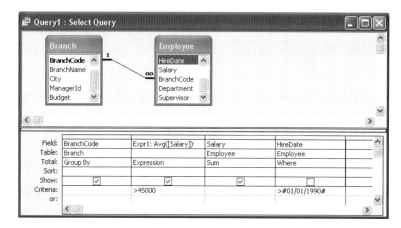

FIGURE HOB.66 More complex GROUP BY Query

The SQL equivalent of this query is:

```
SELECT Branch.BranchCode,
   Avg(SALARY)*2 AS Expr1, Sum(SALARY) AS SumOfSALARY
   FROM Branch INNER JOIN EMPLOYEE
      ON Branch.BranchCode = Employee.BranchCode
         WHERE Hire_Date > #1/1/1990#
            GROUP BY Branch.BranchCode
               HAVING Avg(SALARY)*2 > 45000;
```

Object references and events

Object references

Components used in Access databases (forms, controls etc) are handled as 'objects' by the software.

A naming convention is used to enable reference to objects.

Some objects are organised into sets called 'collections' – for instance the forms in a database are contained in the collection 'Forms'.

All objects have properties that can be viewed in the Properties dialog.

Most objects also have events that can be detected and handled. An event handler is either defined as a macro or in Visual Basic code as an event procedure.

Common events are Click (usually applied to buttons), BeforeUpdate (text boxes), OnGotFocus, etc.

Object naming conventions

Object references use a special notation illustrated by Table HOB.1.

To refer to a	Use	For example
Form	Forms!formname	Forms!Employees
Form property	Forms!formname.property	Forms!Employees.Visible
Control on a form	Forms!formname!control	Forms!Employees!Address
Property of a control on a form	Forms!formname!control.property	Forms!Employees!Address. Visible
Control on a sub-form	Forms!formname!sub-formname. form!control	Forms!Employees!Salaries. Form![Initial Salary]
Methods of an object	Objectname!method	[Results Table].MoveNext
Column of list box	Forms!formname!control.column(n) n=column no from 1 up	Forms!Employees!JobList column(2)

TABLE HOB.1 Object naming conventions

NOTE

It is often possible to abbreviate the reference name; for example, when referring to a control on the current form, the prefix Forms!formname can be omitted.

Objects, such as Forms, must be 'open' when referenced by the above notation.

Reference expressions can be constructed by using the Expression Builder; this is the 'magic wand' symbol that appears in the menu bar when in design view.

Object naming rules

The basic rules for object naming are as follows:

- Use the '!' symbol before objects that you have named yourself. For instance, Forms!Customers.

- Use a dot (the '.' symbol) before properties or methods that Microsoft Access itself names. For instance, Forms!Customers.Enabled or [Employee Table].Close.

- Use square brackets (the '[ ]' symbols) to enclose objects or control names that contain spaces. Because brackets must be used, some programmers avoid using spaces in their object names.

NOTE

Microsoft Access uses the '!' and '.' operators to distinguish between its own properties and methods and ones that you create yourself. This ensures that your code will not break in future versions.

Object references can often be generated by a wizard.

Events

Graphical user interfaces such as Access forms are described as being 'event driven'; this means that the behaviour of an interface is controlled by 'events' such as mouse clicks, changes in the content of a text box, etc. In Access, events are assigned names such as (for a form) OnOpen, OnClose, etc. and the designer can associate a macro or VBA procedure with each event (called an event-handler) that performs some action in response to the event. For instance, in response to a form OnOpen event, a macro could be activated that maximises the form.

The action to be taken for a particular event is defined in the Properties box under the 'Events' tab. An example of an Event list is shown in Figure HOB.67.

FIGURE HOB.67 Event list in properties dialog

The possible events for this object (in this case the HireDate field) are listed down the left-hand side. Against each can be entered a reference to an event handler. If this entry is [Event Procedure] then the handler is written in Visual Basic. Otherwise the name of a macro is shown. To see the Visual Basic procedure code or the content of the macro, click the ... button.

The following Visual Basic code is the procedure generated for a 'close form' button:

```
Private Sub comClose_Click()
On Error GoTo Err_comClose_Click

    DoCmd.Close

Exit_comClose_Click:

    Exit Sub

Err_comClose_Click:

    MsgBox Err.Description
    Resume Exit_comClose_Click
End Sub
```

It takes the form of a subroutine with the name generated from the object and the event; comClose_Click. Most of the code simply relates to error handling; the only 'effective' code here is the DoCmd.Close command. This simply closes the form in which the code resides, returning to the level above.

In a form of the equipment hire database, there is a button that reduces a quantity in stock figure by 1 then saves the record. The macro entry for this is shown in Figure HOB.68.

FIGURE HOB.68 Macro design

The SetValue action has two parameters, shown at the bottom. **Item** refers the object being amended and **Expression** is the new value for the object.

The next action is a procedure RunCommand; this has a parameter (not shown here) of SaveRecord – which does as it says. RunCommand actions just invoke menu operations.

Further example of form calculations

The Calculations database (available from the website) provides a simple demo of how to implement calculations within an Access form. It contains a single, simple table called Values with three fields:

Field	Datatype
Item	Text
Field1	Number
Field2	Number

This table is used to demonstrate the working of controls on a form based on the table.

Let's take a 'bare' form clear of any superfluous content on which we can demonstrate simple calculations using macros, VBA code and formulae inside the form definition. The form, which we will call Form1, is based on the Values table. We will add a number of bound and unbound text boxes to this form to illustrate what we can and can't do. A text box is said to be 'bound' when it is tied to a field in the table or query on which the form is based; it is said to be 'unbound' if it is not related to any such field. A unbound text box therefore is just a variable value that 'sits' on the form.

The form Form1 shows how you can perform an 'on-form' calculation of an unbound text box value by simply setting the **Control Source** property to the required expression. The **Control Source** property usually refers to the field in the table or query on which the form is based.

An unbound text box is *not* connected to any value in the table or query on which the form is based; so you cannot automatically update a table value by simply setting the Control Source property to an expression – since then it would not refer to any table value.

It also shows that you can perform a calculation by activating a macro using a SetValue action or by using a simple equation in a Event Procedure.

Also, the Calcfield1 macro is invoked by an AfterUpdate event of Value1 so that changing the content of this box will cause a change to Field1.

Note that Field1 and Field2 are bound values; i.e. they are 'tied' to the fields in the table on which the form is based.

References

Anderson, V. (2003): *Microsoft Office Access 2003: The Complete Reference*, Osborne.

Heathcote, P.M. (2002): *Successful ICT Projects in Access* (third edition), Payne-Gallway Publishers.

Anderson, V. (2003): *How to Do Everything with Microsoft Office Access 2003* (second edition), McGraw-Hill Publishing Co.

9

Post relational databases

LEARNING OBJECTIVES

After studying this chapter, you should be able to do the following:

- Describe the limitations of relational databases that have prompted the development of alternatives.

- Outline the main principles of object orientation.

- Describe how object features are combined with relational features in object-relational databases.

- Identify typical object-relational products.

- Assess the significance of object-relational databases in today's development environment.

- Describe the nature of the object-oriented database.

- Compare an object-oriented database with an object-relational database.

- Explain the concept of transparent persistence.

- Compare an object-oriented database with a relational database.

- Explain the concept of object-relational mapping and justify its use.

- Describe the general principles involved in object-relational mapping.

Introduction

Databases built on the relational data model command the largest part of the database market. This is in spite of the fact that the rest of the computing world is now dominated by the object orientation paradigm. This chapter examines this conundrum and describes a number of newer database technologies that offer alternatives to the relational model or provide some degree of compromise between relational and object-oriented databases. The main topic areas are:

- Assessment of the relational database

- Object-relational databases

- Object-oriented databases

- Object-relational mapping

Given the outstanding success of the relational database over three decades, it might seem a little superfluous to worry too much about its limitations. It is not as if there have been no alternatives presented to the market; object database have been the subject of research since the mid 1980s and several advanced products have been available from early 1990s. However, apart from the academic interest in constantly appraising current technology, the main factor that might lead one to assess the current position of the relational database is the potential impact of the current popularity of object-oriented programming and system design. Writing systems in object-oriented terms and storing persistent data using the very non-object-oriented relational model produces stresses that suggest that some re-appraisal of the relational versus object models is worth pursuing.

Accordingly, in this chapter we examine the advantages and disadvantages of both relational and object-based databases, and also look at possible avenues of compromise between them. We start with a critical look at relational databases, examining the reasons for their popularity and the problems that they present. Next, the concept of an object-relational (or extended relational) database is offered as a possible solution to the object versus relational conflict; here, the strict enforcement of relational principles is relaxed to allow storage of complex data. The prospects for the adoption of true object databases is then considered, in which the relational model is essentially abandoned. Finally, the idea of simply living with the two competing models is considered; using object-relational mapping, the programs are written in object-oriented code, but the data is transformed to relational form for storage. A software mapping layer transforms the data in each direction.

The chapter generally provides a description of the important concepts involved, together with some practical working and examples. More elaborate examples and references are provided on the book's website for readers wishing for more detailed practical assistance.

Since the subject matter of these topics frequently deals with programming languages and systems, this chapter contains a certain amount of program code. Readers not interested in the coding aspects of the topic can still learn much from the narrative descriptions and can safely ignore the coding.

Advantages and limitations of relational databases

Advantages

The advantages of the relational model are described below:

Simplicity of concept

The relational model is based on the essentially simple concept of a two-dimensional table. This inherent simplicity has enabled non-specialist users to become familiar with the idea and has facilitated the development of packages.

Good theoretical basis

The underlying mathematical base of the relational model has facilitated research into databases that has assisted their development. For instance, normal forms and SQL are products of such research.

Data independence

The relational database provides a much higher degree of data independence than earlier databases. This arises because the data descriptions (schema) are maintained independently of the data itself, unlike earlier systems where physical links existed within the data records. As a consequence, it is relatively easy to make changes to the schema design even after the database is live and contains data. Changes such as adding a column, extending the size of a column and modifying the column type can often be implemented. Of course, there are predictable limits to such changes: changes impinging on referential integrity are not admissible; deleting a column may or may not be acceptable depending on the application. Modifications deemed acceptable by the DBMS are implemented transparently; no 'manual' conversion is required of the user. For example, if a new attribute is required in a table after the database is live and the table is populated with thousands of records, it is generally possible to simply add a new column to the schema design and save it. The table will now have a new column filled with null values, but no modification to current programs is necessary.

Improved security and integrity

The organisation of the data into tables and the use of high level languages such as SQL facilitates the maintenance of improved security and integrity.

Suitable for high-level languages

The simple structure has facilitated the use of declarative languages such as SQL and other high-level 4GL languages and interactive non-programming environments found in current software.

Limitations of the relational database

The limitations of relational databases are described below:

Proliferation of tables

Even relatively simple applications seem to produce a disproportionate number of separate tables. Most are logically acceptable, since they correspond to 'real world' entities, but many are created to satisfy first normal form or simply to link other tables.

Processing overheads

A consequence of having to use many tables is that it is necessary to gather information from several tables to satisfy the requirements of a query. This is potentially very expensive in processor and disk access time and is only made feasible in the general case by the use of indexes and the application of query optimising techniques.

Scaleability

Access times for a relational database increase disproportionately with table size; i.e. if the table size is increased by a factor of 10, the average access time increases by much more than 10.

Lack of semantic power

The term 'lack of semantic power' means, first, that the relational database holds only limited information about the 'meaning' of its data, and also that it is limited in its ability to express certain data relationships:

- The normalisation process fragments the 'natural' expression of the data into multiple tables; at the same time, the original connections between the parts of the data are not preserved automatically. For instance, related tables have to be joined by explicit operations at run time. Note that current systems generally permit the specification of relationships in the form of foreign and primary key constraints; these can be defined using a graphical interface, as in Microsoft Access, or by using SQL clauses available for this purpose. These features, although helpful, do not avoid the need for run-time joining of the tables.

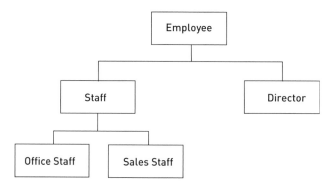

FIGURE 9.1 Sub-typing example

■ It is difficult or awkward to express sub-typing (i.e. a specialisation relationship) using relational tables. Consider the example of an Employee database; this could be viewed as a hierarchical structure as illustrated in Figure 9.1.

Considering only the first level of sub-typing:

The general Employee details are: **Employee No, Name, Address, Age**, etc.

The Staff entries would include: **Department, Salary, Responsible-to**, etc.

The Director entries would include: **Responsibility**, etc.

This can be implemented in two ways, neither very satisfactory:

Implemented as a single table with nulls used where the attribute is not applicable. For example, a Director's entry would look like:

Employee Number	Name	Address	Age	Dept	Salary	Resp-to	Responsibility
1234	Jones	London	49	NULL	NULL	NULL	Sales

Data for a staff member would look like this:

Employee Number	Name	Address	Age	Dept	Salary	Resp-to	Responsibility
2987	Smith	Bristol	31	Sales	28 000	3002	NULL
3002	Brown	London	48	Sales	46 000	1234	NULL

Implemented as three tables:

Employee

Employee Number	Name	Address	Age
1234	Jones	London	49
2987	Smith	Bristol	31
3002	Brown	London	48

Staff

Employee Number	Department	Salary	Responsible-to
2987	Sales	28 000	3002
3002	Sales	46 000	1234

Director

Employee Number	Responsibility
1234	Sales

The single table version needs to use many null columns; use of nulls can produce complications in the interpretation of query results and is generally regarded as undesirable. The three table version is probably more in the spirit of the relational model, but complicates querying. For any particular type of employee, it is necessary to join two tables; i.e. Employee–Staff or Employee–Director. Of course, in a more complex hierarchical application, these complications would intensify. For instance, the sales staff sub-category may use a sales commission percentage, which would be absent from the office staff. As we shall see later in this chapter, sub-typing can be more readily modelled using inheritance in an object-oriented database.

- It is not possible to use user-defined types. In particular, you cannot invent types using composite data items or array elements or to define sub-types. The principal restriction in this respect is the need to conform to first normal form: data items must be single-valued and based on a fixed set of datatypes. Another problem here is the fact that the built-in datatypes of a relational system have a fixed 'behaviour' known to the system. For instance, numerical values can be manipulated arithmetically and display right-justified. Date values have a prescribed format and are subject to some limited arithmetical operations. If new datatypes were to be allowed (as in object-oriented systems), some facility would be required to allow specification of type behaviour.

These points are discussed in more detail later in the chapter.

Unsuitable for long transactions

The transaction systems used in relational databases, using Commit, Rollback and locking, are only appropriate where transactions are 'short'; in some applications, notably in CAD/CAM systems, transactions could be very long, possibly hours. This arises when, for instance, a design is being developed; parts of the design will be in an incomplete state for long periods while being amended, which, using a relational database, would require extensive locking of tables and rows, effectively preventing any other users from gaining access.

Example

The first three of the above points (proliferation of tables, processing overheads and lack of semantic power) are interrelated. The following example illustrates these points.

Consider the data required for a bibliographic database system:

Reference Num

Title

Authors

Publisher

Date

Keywords, etc.

'Authors' probably consists, in the majority of cases, of a single name; however, allowance must be made for the general case where there might be two, three or possibly many names. Hence, in terms of first normal form, a separate table is required for the authors. A similar argument applies to the keyword values – another separate table is required, producing three tables, as shown below:

Reference table

Reference Num	number
Title	char(30)
Publisher	char(20)

Author table

Reference Num	number
Author	char(20)

Keyword table

Reference Num	number
Keyword	char(15)

Note that in producing tables in this form , there is no inherent linkages between the tables; such linkages have to be re-established using join operations. This seems an excessively complicated solution for a simple problem. Essentially, it would be convenient to be able to use a 'set attribute' so that the Author and Keyword data is stored as a neat parcel with the general information, but this is not possible for relational systems. In terms of programming languages and database facilities, such an arrangement would need some additional mechanism to enable processing of the set members.

The object data model

Before proceeding with an examination of object-based databases, it is perhaps worthwhile to review the underlying object data model on which these systems are based. Many readers may already be familiar with object orientation principles and may wish the skip the section; in particular, if you are familiar with Java or C++ it is unlikely that this section will present you with anything new. However, it would do no harm to revise the topic and ensure that we agree on the terminology of the area.

Basic principles

The Object Orientation (OO) philosophy views the world as a set of objects which communicate with each other. This view is applied to the design of computer systems that model and service real-world applications. An object is a representation of a real-world entity (e.g., person, component, company, etc.) which takes part in a computer application. This representation consists of data and procedures. The object data defines the state of the object at any time (hence are often called the 'state variables') and the procedures, usually called 'methods' in this context, provide a set of allowable operations on the data. It is also said that the methods define the 'behaviour' of the object. Figure 9.2 shows a graphical representation of an object.

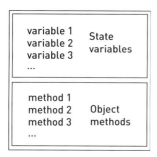

FIGURE 9.2 Structure of an object

Note that, conceptually, the only way to access and/or modify object variables is by using the object methods. This provides a high degree of encapsulation, which is considered desirable in programming terms, since it isolates the object data from the rest of the program. In this respect, OO may be considered an extension to the concept of modularity, but OO extends the notion of encapsulation beyond that found in non-object programming. This potentially provides several benefits:

- The object may be modified, with less danger to the program as a whole, as long as the external 'effect' of the object remains the same.

- Since the object performs some complete self-contained role, it could be reused in another application.

- Each object has a clearly defined interface which facilitates programming.

In addition to the basic object concept, OO philosophy encompasses a number of other important concepts that are important in programming and database development. These concepts are listed below and described in subsequent sections.

- Messages; objects are viewed as communicating by sending messages to each other.

- Classes; generic specifications of object design.

- Identity; all objects are given a system-wide unchangeable code that uniquely and permanently identifies each object.

- Inheritance; derivation of more specific object classes from existing classes.

- Polymorphism; a mechanism whereby different object classes respond differently to the same message.

Note that in practical systems, object variables and methods (particularly the latter) can be defined as 'public' or 'private'; public methods in effect represent the public interface of the object and are callable by any other object. Private methods are callable only by other methods of the object; in effect, they assist in the internal implementation of the object's functionality.

Object examples

In a simulation program we might wish to model the behaviour of a vehicle. An object specification for this could appear as shown below:

```
VEHICLE:
State variables
   X-pos, Y-pos
   Speed
   Direction
Methods
   Start
   Accelerate
   Brake
   Change direction
   Where - return current location
   What speed - return current speed
```

An OO program takes the form of a large number of objects which communicate with each other. Typically there will be some object or objects which initiate communication, often by themselves receiving 'outside' stimulus, such as data input from the program user. Communication between objects is viewed as a process of 'message passing'; this concept is dealt with in the next section.

A more mundane option might be the description of an employee in a company:

```
EMPLOYEE:
State variables
   Employee Id
   Name
   Address
   Department
   Date of birth
   Salary
Methods
   SetName     change the Name value
   GetName     return the Name value
   SetAddress  change the Address value
   GetAddress  return the Address value
   GetAge      return employee's age computed from date of birth
   etc.
```

Many methods are of the 'get' and 'set' variety; as mentioned earlier, direct reference to object variables is forbidden and these methods present a public interface that provides access to the variables in a controlled manner.

Messages

Object orientation systems use what is often called the 'object-message' convention. Objects model 'things' of interest in the application domain; these communicate by sending messages to each other. A message, send from object A, notionally has the components:

- A target object, B

- The name of a method being requested

- The arguments of the method.

The message, in a programming language, can be expressed in a number of different formats, but the most common in current languages is *B.methodname(argument-list)*. For instance, in a stock inventory application we could have an object *stock* that represents one item of stock; a method of this object is *adjustQuantity* which has one argument *change* so that the message to decrease the stock quantity by 100 would be *stock.adjustQuantity(−100)*. In some systems, such as event-driven aspects of an operating system, the concept of message processing is very real; events at the user interface such as mouse clicks or data entry are formulated as messages to the event handler to await processing. In other systems, message passing is more of a metaphor; the calling object simply invokes the method by means of a conventional procedure or function call. This is the case in Java and C++ for example, which are the principal OO languages. However, it is important to realise that program activity consists of objects invoking the methods of other objects, with suitable argument values.

Classes

Real-world objects are typically not one-offs. In the simulation suggested above, for example, we would have many vehicles, not just one. An object can be viewed as one item belonging to a set of such items. The term 'class' is used to refer to the generic specification of a set of objects; essentially, the class is a template which defines the structure and behaviour of each object of that type. It is similar in many ways to the notion of type (e.g., char, int) used in Pascal and other languages. Types, however, are built into the language and have a fixed predefined behaviour; for instance, we can use arithmetic operators and functions with int and real variables, but not char variables. Classes, on the other hand, are user-defined, with modifiable behaviour. In OO programming languages, we first define the classes we wish to use in our application. Within the application programs, we can then declare objects which are 'instances' of these classes.

The process of creating objects of a specific class with its own set of state values is called 'instantiation' and is carried out by a special method of the class called the 'constructor'. The constructor method usually has the same name as the class. In fact, there may be more than one constructor (all with the same name) but they must differ in their parameter configuration. The descriptions given above for VEHICLE and EMPLOYEE in effect constitute class outlines. An instance of class VEHICLE would represent a specific vehicle with a set of current state values for each of its variables.

In typical object-oriented languages, instances of objects are declared in a program by expressions of the form:

objectname classname for example: *Vehicle myCar*;

To reference members of the object, we use a dot notation: *myCar.speed*, *myCar.start()*, etc.

In general discussion, the terms *object* and *class* can be used somewhat interchangeably; in particular, object is often used when class would be more appropriate. No confusion should arise from this usage if you are aware of the problem and if you remember that a class is purely a template or description (it is not stored in memory) while an object is similar to a program variable; it takes up space in memory.

Collections

Some object-oriented languages support the concept of a *collection*, a special kind of object that can contain a number of other objects (of the same class). Collections come in a range of flavours such as *set*, *list* and *bag*; the usual interpretation of these terms is:

- A set is a collection of items where the items are ordered and do not repeat (i.e. no duplicate values)
- In a list, items are ordered and may repeat
- In a bag, items are not ordered and may repeat.

These mechanisms provide a straightforward way to represent one-to-many relationships in the data and hence are useful in database applications. Later in this chapter we look at the extended relational features of Oracle that offer collection facilities. In current languages such as Java and C++ collections are not part of the language as such, but are supported by library functions or classes.

9

Object identity

Real-world things that are modelled by objects in an object-oriented programming environment are considered to have a separate and unique identity so that different objects can be distinguished from each other. On creation, each object is assigned an object id, a system-generated value that is unique to the object and which is never changed or reused. This contrasts with the relational model wherein the role of identification is provided by the primary key concept. However, the primary key is usually one attribute (or combination of attributes) that is unique for the relation involved, and is generally a value used in the actual application. The possibility exists that the primary key could be changed, which could have serious repercussions for database integrity. In object-oriented systems, the object id is not used and is generally unseen in applications. The object ids are used to interconnect objects; object A can be linked to (or refer to) another object B by holding the value of B's object id in A.

Inheritance

Typically, a graphics program will require complex graphical objects, such as lines, rectangles, circles, etc. However, these objects share a number of common features, such as position and whether they are currently visible. The OO inheritance mechanism enables more complex classes to be derived from simpler, previously defined classes. For example, we could start with a primitive GRAPHIC class that has features required by all graphical objects. This might look like the following:

```
CLASS GRAPHIC:
State variables
   X-pos, Y-pos  — point coordinates
   Visible       — true/false value indicating whether the object is visible
Methods
   Move object
   Show object
   Hide object
   Where — return current X-pos, Y-pos values
```

More specific classes such as a rectangle could be derived from this; a rectangle has a position (of one corner, say) as provided for in the GRAPHIC class and can be visible or invisible. However, a rectangle also requires two lengths for the sides. We could define a rectangle class, for example, by inheriting the point class and adding to it and/or overriding certain variables and methods:

```
CLASS RECTANGLE: Inherit from GRAPHIC
State Variables
   SideX Length
   SideY Length
Methods
   Show          these are methods which are overridden from
   Hide          the GRAPHIC version.
   SetFillColor  these are methods peculiar to RECTANGLE
   ChangeSize
. . .
```

In effect, inheritance provides a system of specialisation and generalisation and enables us to define a hierarchy of classes. For example, consider the following taxonomy of workers employed in a company:

```
Employee
   Office Employee
      Office Manager
      Secretarial
         Supervisor
         Secretary
. . .
   Works Employee
      Line Supervisor
      Welder
      Fitter
. . .
```

```
Sales Employee
   Area Manager
   Salesperson
 . . .
 etc.
```

Descending through such a hierarchy produces increasing specialisation, while ascending produces increasing generalisation. Another way of looking at this is to say that it expresses an 'IS-A' relationship, e.g., an Office Manager IS-AN Office Employee, an Office Employee IS-AN Employee. A specialisation-generalisation can best be recognised by applying this IS-A test. This, of course, is the sub-typing modelling concept, which as we saw earlier presents some complications for relational databases. The benefits of being able to use inheritance are:

- it permits a more natural representation of sub-typing relationships that exist in the application

- it potentially saves coding effort because code implemented at a higher level can be reused at a lower level.

Using inheritance structures makes it possible to develop programs in terms of routines dealing with the general cases, qualified and complemented by routines for the various specialised cases. For example, a simple routine to print the employee's name and address would be common to all and would be defined at the EMPLOYEE level; however, in a payroll system, office staff and works staff would all be paid under different terms and conditions (e.g., monthly salary, weekly salary, hourly paid, etc.) and would have specialised program routines defined for each class of staff such as WORKS EMPLOYEE, OFFICE EMPLOYEE, etc. Within WORKS EMPLOYEE, the supervisor might differ from line workers, and so on.

The overall expectation is that object-oriented design should minimise the amount of specialised coding and should facilitate reuse of more general routines.

Polymorphism

The Greek derivation of this word means 'many forms'. In the field of programming, it refers to the ability of a language to use the same identifier (e.g. function or procedure name) to perform different operations depending on the class of the variables involved. For instance, we might want a method called Print whose role is to display the contents of objects presented to it as parameter values. The actual effect of Print will depend on which object is involved. In the absence of polymorphism, a separate method would be required for each different object class. Note that polymorphism is utilised in inherited classes; in the GRAPHIC/RECTANGLE example above, the Show method of the GRAPHIC class is overridden with a method of the same name. If we use the call *Show (object)* it will execute the GRAPHIC Show method; if we use the call *Show(rectangleobject)* it will execute the RECTANGLE method.

The benefit of this facility is that programs can be written to deal with objects dynamically, i.e., the precise effect of a command is determined only at run-time when the methods 'discover' the class of objects being passed to them.

Post-relational systems

The relational database has many significant merits and its domination in the area of persistent data storage for over two decades is fully deserved. As we highlighted in an earlier section, in spite of a range of perceived limitations, it has continued to be employed in the majority of computer applications.

Essentially, the main problem in working with a relational database is its conflict with object-oriented principles. The object-orientation paradigm has largely taken over the world of computing today: UML dominates the system modelling arena and Java, C++ and other object-oriented programming languages account for the vast majority of that market. In the 1990s, a number of object-oriented databases appeared on the market which abandoned the relational model altogether in favour of an architecture that stored objects persistently (on disk) while preserving their structure. In spite of showing great promise, these products failed to capture a significant share of the overall database market and tended to be employed in a number of specialised areas. In essence, the advantages of the relational model prevented any general move to the new technology. It must also be appreciated that over this period relational database products constantly improved in performance, convenience and reliability, thereby dissuading developers from investigating other products.

In spite of the general failure of the object-oriented database to capture a sizable part of the market, the general benefits of the OO paradigm have driven the development of technologies that seek to accommodate both object and relational principles. We refer to these systems as *post-relational databases*.

At first glance, these divide into two categories, object-relational and pure object-oriented, but in terms of external functionality they appear to be very similar. However, in order to highlight their underlying principles, we will preserve this category distinction in describing each of the technologies.

In the following sections we describe two examples of object-relational systems, **Oracle's extensions to SQL**, in compliance with object-relational features described in standard SQL:1999, and **Intersystems Caché**, a novel system with a sophisticated graphical interface and a wide range of storage and access functionality.

Object-relational databases

The underlying principle of object-relational databases is to enhance the relational model by some relaxation of relational principles. The alternative name of 'extended relational' perhaps reveals some of the motivation for the technology. Essentially, these systems are still based firmly in the relational domain in that they retain the use of tables, primary and foreign keys, SQL compatibility etc. The changes introduced by the new technology are:

- Relaxation of 'two dimensional' structure. Conformity to first normal form demands that datatypes are chosen from a prescribed set of scalar options, such as text, number, date etc. This fundamental change opens the door to the introduction of the following two extensions.

- Use of user-defined types. New datatypes can be defined, generally in the form of object types or classes, with arbitrary structure and complete with their own functionality (methods).

- Use of compound structured datatypes. Built-in data structures such as arrays and nested tables.

SQL:1999 standard

The SQL language has gone through a number of minor and major revisions since its initial development in about 1980. At the start of the 1990s, the standard was labelled SQL-92 or SQL2 and this version was the basis for most of the implementations during the 1990s and into the 2000s. At about the same time, an organisation called the Object Database Management Group was formed to promote and standardise the emerging object-oriented database systems. As part of this development a revision of SQL was initiated, called variously SQL3 or, when it was nearer completion, SQL:1999. The objectives of this new standard were:

- To overcome some of the perceived shortcomings of the relational model by the introducing object-oriented features.

- To permit object-based data (e.g. data used in Java or other language applications) to be stored in a relational database.

- To enable relational data to be viewed in an object-oriented fashion.

However, in order to utilise these new features, database vendors would have to implement corresponding functionality in their database products, changing them from pure relational systems to 'extended relational' or 'object-relational'. Many database vendors tackled this major change and developed object-relational features in their products. As an illustration of the scope of these developments, we will look at Oracle's offering in this area.

9

Oracle's SQL:1999

Introduction

Oracle introduced extended relational features to their databases at Version 8. These notes provide an overview of some of the features of Oracle's system.

User-defined datatypes

Oracle allows the specification of **object types**, i.e. new datatypes composed of standard types (varchar, number, date etc.) or other object types. The term 'object type' corresponds to the concept of a class as used in object-oriented systems. As in the class concept, the object type is simply a *template* for objects; it occupies no storage but is used to produce **objects**, i.e. actual instances of the type. These are often embedded within other data structures such as table rows or within other type definitions.

Methods and constructors

Methods are procedures associated with an object type that provide means of examining and modifying objects. It is possible to write methods for Oracle object types in PL/SQL or other languages.

There are three categories of methods: *Member*, *Static* and *Comparison*:

- *Member* and *Static* correspond to the Java/C++ instance and static methods; Member methods belong and refer to an instance of an object type and implicitly refer to the owing instance.

- *Static methods* belong to the object type itself and do not refer to a particular instance. There is a special case of static method called a *constructor* that generates a new instance of an object. Constructors are implicitly defined from the specified structure of an object; i.e. you do not have to supply a definition.

- *Comparison methods* are used to place objects in order. For simple built-in types such as text and number, the ordering of values (for example, as required by an SQL ORDER BY query) is implicit; if the same functionality is required for objects the programmer must provide a function that compares two objects of the same class and returns a value that indicates the relative ordering of these objects. For instance, we could prescribe an ordering of PERSON objects by comparing the surnames, so that Adams would appear before Brown. Alternative comparison methods could be defined; we may choose to sort by postcode for example.

Row and column objects

Oracle makes a distinction between *row* and *column* objects. Column objects are held within one column of a table – varrays and nested tables, which are described next, are column objects. Row objects represent rows of table data that are held in one table and referenced from another. These are described later under 'References'.

Collections

Collections are compound objects containing a number of other data objects. They are often used to represent one-to-many relationships in data and provide an alternative to the relational method of utilising separate tables linked by foreign/primary keys.

Oracle supports two main collection mechanisms: nested table and varray, which are described below. They are similar in many ways but also have differing characteristics that indicate specific areas of application. Oracle provides different ways of scanning these structures.

Nested tables

A nested table is a table within a table. A nested table is a collection of rows held as a distinct structure within a cell of a main table. Each row of the main table will have its own nested table in that column. The number of rows in a nested table is indefinite.

Consider a table that contains information about projects and engineers where each project employs many engineers. In a relational database this would be implemented as two tables connected by a primary key. Using a nested table, the Engineer table could be held within the Project table.

Varrays

A varray is a set of objects of the same datatype. The size of the array is set when it is created. It can be visualised as a fixed-size array of objects which can be held within one cell of a main table. Hence it is like a nested array, but with a fixed number of rows.

As an example of their use, varrays can be used to simplify many-to-many relationships; in a relational database, this would require three tables: e.g. Engineer-Project-Assignment, necessitating a two-way join to resolve queries such as 'list the engineers on project alpha'.

The extended relational alternative would be to have an engineer and a project table and to include a varray of engineers within the projects table and vice versa. This would certainly simply access and querying, although it would possibly complicate other update tasks.

Object tables and references

Nested tables and varrays are *embedded* objects; they are notionally stored within the owning object/table. A *referenced object* is an object that is separate from an owning object but referred to, or 'pointed' to by a reference in the owning object. Note that nested tables are physically stored separate from the owning table, but this is an implementation issue and does not affect the notional 'embedded table' concept. Nested tables and varrays are 'column objects'.

An object table is a table in which each row is treated as an object, with a unique Object Identity (OID) value. These row objects can be referenced from other tables or objects in a similar fashion to the reference mechanism in Java or C++.

A row is given an OID when it is inserted into the table. Functions REF and DEREF are provided; REF returns the value of the OID for the current row of an object table. REF can also be used as a type descriptor in another table to define a column that refers to the object table.

Object views

Object views allow you to interpret existing pure relational tables as object-based storage. For example, you can create an abstract datatype based on an existing table's definition. This would allow you to process the data in OO terms (e.g. via Java code) even though it is still in relational format.

Worked examples

Understanding of these principles is greatly assisted by trying some worked examples. The tutorial sequence below covers most of the important points; if you have access to an Oracle system (Version 9 or later) these examples may be tested.

Defining new datatypes

The PL/SQL commands contained in this example are held in the script **CH09.Client Example.sql**.

First, an ADDRESS type is defined:

```
create type ADDRESS_TY as object
   (street  varchar2(25),
    town     varchar2(20),
    postcode varchar2(12)
);
/
```

Next, a PERSON type is defined, using the ADDRESS type:

```
create type PERSON_TY as object
   ( name   varchar2(20),
     address  ADDRESS_TY,
     DOB      Date
);
/
```

Finally, a table is created utilising the person type:

```
create table client
(
   client_id    number(6),
   client_data  PERSON_TY
);
```

We can now enter data using a suitably extended INSERT syntax:

```
insert into client values ('123', PERSON_TY('Jones', address_ty('99 High St.',
'Glasgow', 'G5 6JK'), '21-Mar-88' ));
insert into client values ('456', PERSON_TY('Smith', address_ty('2 North Rd.',
'Aberdeen', 'AB7 2GG'), '1-Jun-78' ));
insert into client values ('789', PERSON_TY('Brown', address_ty('81 West St.',
'Paisley', 'PA2 3CZ'), '13-Apr-85' ));
```

Note the use of the object constructor syntax such as:

```
ADDRESS_TY('99 High St.', 'Glasgow', 'G5 6JK')
```

Let us check the content of the table:

```
select * from client;
CLIENT_ID CLIENT_DATA(NAME, ADDRESS(STREET, TOWN, POSTCODE), DOB)
--------- ----------------------------------------------------------------------------
      123 PERSON_TY('Jones', ADDRESS_TY('99 High St.', 'Glasgow', 'G5 6JK'), '21-MAR-88')
      456 PERSON_TY('Smith', ADDRESS_TY('2 North Rd.', 'Aberdeen', 'AB7 2GG'), '01-JUN-78')
      789 PERSON_TY('Brown', ADDRESS_TY('81 West St.', 'Paisley', 'PA2 3CZ'), '13-APR-85')
```

The format of this output is far from ideal and this is a relatively simple structure. Remember, however, that this kind of data would generally be accessed programmatically using, say, PL/SQL or Java, rather than being viewed in a simple interactive interpreter.

Selecting data from embedded object

The method of referencing data which is part of the embedded client_data object is somewhat unexpected: the containing table must be given an alias and this used to qualify object references:

```
select c.client_data.name from client c;
```

Strangely, use of the table name as prefix does not work:

```
select client.client_data.name from client; ** WRONG
```

Writing methods for an object type

The principles of object-orientation require that the behaviour and functionality of objects need to be defined. In Oracle, this is achieved by:

- adding a METHOD declaration to the CREATE TYPE command, and

- defining a CREATE TYPE BODY command that contains the method definition.

Here is a simple illustration of this, available in the script **CH09.RunClientExample.sql**:

First, we revise the definition of the address type to include a procedure declaration:

```
create type ADDRESS_TY as object
   (street varchar2(25),
   town varchar2(20),
   postcode varchar2(12),
   MEMBER PROCEDURE print_address
);
/
```

Now add a BODY definition:

```
CREATE TYPE BODY ADDRESS_TY
AS
MEMBER PROCEDURE print_address
BEGIN
   DBMS_OUTPUT.PUT_LINE('Street: ' || street);
      DBMS_OUTPUT.PUT_LINE('Town: ' || town);
      DBMS_OUTPUT.PUT_LINE('postcode: || postcode);
END;
```

This procedure can now be used in PL/SQL code such as:

```
declare
   cursor client_cursor is
   select * from client;
begin
   for client_rec in client_cursor
   loop
      DBMS_OUTPUT.PUT_LINE('Name: ' || client_rec.client_data.name);
      DBMS_OUTPUT.PUT_LINE('- -');
         client_rec.client_data.address.print_address;
      DBMS_OUTPUT.PUT_LINE('- - - - - - - -');
   end loop;
end;
/
```

Using a VARRAY
Scenario:

You want to keep a record of which CDs your friends borrow from you.

Step 1: Define a varray type to represent a set of borrowed CDs.

```
create type CD_VA as varray(5) of varchar2(20);
/
Type created.
```

Step 2: Create a table to hold borrowers names and the CDs they have borrowed.

```
create table borrower
( name  varchar2(25),
  CDs   CD_VA        CDs is the attribute name, CD_VA is the type
)
/
Table created.
```

Step 3: Insert data into table.

```
insert into borrower
    values ('Ann Brown', CD_VA('Classics Vol1', 'Kylie', 'Madonna'));
insert into borrower
    values ('Jim White', CD_VA('Leonard Cohen', 'Lionel Richie'));
/
1 row created.
```

Step 4: Display the contents.

```
SQL> select * from borrower;
NAME        CDS
------------------------------------------------------------
Ann  Brown  CD_VA('Classics  Vol1',  'Kylie',  'Madonna')
Jim  White  CD_VA('Leonard  Cohen',  'Lionel  Richie')
```

The above code is in script **CH09.CDExample.sql**.

Reading the table with PL/SQL (script **CH09.CD.PL.sql**)

```
 1   declare
 2     cursor borrower_cursor is
 3       select * from borrower;
 4   begin
 5     for borrower_rec in borrower_cursor
 6       loop
 7         dbms_output.put_line('Borrower name:'||borrower_rec.name);
 8           for i in 1..borrower_rec.cds.Count
 9           loop
10             dbms_output.put_line(borrower_rec.cds(i));
11           end loop;
12       end loop;
13*  end;
```

Output:

```
Borrower name: Ann Brown
Classics Vol1
Kylie
Madonna
```

> **NOTE**
>
> In line 5, borrower_rec is a for-loop cursor variable that is defined by its appearance in the for-loop.
>
> In line 8, Count is an attribute of the varray whose value is the number of items in the varray.
>
> Line 10 shows that the elements of the varray CDs can accessed using the notation 'borrower_rec.cds(i)'

Using a NESTED TABLE

Scenario:

We will construct a table containing sightings of birds by birdwatchers. The watchers' names, the bird type, and the location and date of sighting are recorded. This can be implemented as a single main table with an embedded nested table.

Step 1: Define an BIRD object type.

```
create type BIRD_TY as object
   (SPECIES   VARCHAR2(25),
    LOCATION  VARCHAR2(25),
    SIGHTED   DATE
);
/
Type created.
```

Step 2: Define a table type BIRD_NT.

```
create type BIRD_NT as table of BIRD_TY;
/
Type created.
```

Note: The 'as table of' phrase identifies BIRD_NT as a nested table.

Step 3: Create a BIRDWATCHER table embedding BIRD_NT.

```
create table BIRDWATCHER
   ( Name   VARCHAR2(25),
     BIRDS  BIRD_NT
   ) nested table BIRDS store as BIRDS_NT_TAB
/
Table created.
```

9

The nested table command specifies a separate table to physically hold the nested table, although, conceptually, it is part of the BIRDWATCHER table.

Step 4: Insert some data into the BIRDWATCHER table.

```
insert into BIRDWATCHER values
  (  'Jane James',
       BIRD_NT(
         BIRD_TY('Sea Eagle', 'Mull', '31-Mar-05'),
         BIRD_TY('Osprey', 'Aviemore', '23-Jan-04'),
         BIRD_TY('Woodpecker', 'Braemar', '19-Sep-06')
         )
  )
  1 row created.
```

NOTE

The notation BIRD_TY ('Sea Eagle', 'Mull', '31-Mar-05') is effectively a call to the constructor for BIRD_TY.

Step 5: Display the contents of the table.

```
SQL>  select * from birdwatcher;
NAME BIRDS(SPECIES, LOCATION, SIGHTED)
--------------------------------------------------------------------------------
Jane James BIRD _NT
             (BIRD_TY('Sea Eagle', ' Mull ', '31-Mar-05'),
             BIRD_TY('Osprey', 'Aviemore', '23-Jan-04'),
             BIRD_TY('Woodpecker', 'Braemar', '19-Sep-06'))
```

Note that the above Oracle output has been re-formatted to show the individual items more clearly. The script **CH09.BirdWatcher.sql** contains the above sequence of commands.

Referencing data in nested tables

The queries above only make reference to the 'whole' nested table; if we need to refer to individual items within the nested table, we require an additional syntactic element. The nested table must be listed in the select list of the query in the format:

TABLE (*nested-table-name) alias*.

Items in the table can now be referenced via the alias.

Query:

List the name of any birdwatcher who has spotted an Osprey.

```
select name, BirdTab.Sighted from birdwatcher,
   TABLE(birdwatcher.birds) BirdTab
   where BirdTab.Species = 'Osprey';
```

Note the use of the alias BirdTab.

Query:

List all birds sighted since the end of 2005, showing the location and date.

```
select BirdTab.Species, BirdTab.Location, BirdTab.Sighted
from birdwatcher, TABLE(birdwatcher.birds) BirdTab
  where BirdTab.Sighted > '31-Dec-04';
```

Varray objects are referenced in a similar way, using the TABLE notation; the word TABLE indicates to Oracle that the value is a collection and not a simple scalar value.

The queries above are available in script **CH09.BirdWatcherQueries.sql**.

Using object tables and references

The following scripts demonstrate how to use object tables in PL/SQL. The scripts are available in **CH09.ObjectTable.sql**.

Scenario: Animals and keepers

Step 1: Define an animal object type.

```
create type ANIMAL_TY as object
   (Breed   VARCHAR2(25),
   Name    VARCHAR2(25),
     Birthdate DATE
   );
/
Type created.
```

Step 2: Create an object table each row of which is an ANIMAL_TY.

```
create table ANIMAL of ANIMAL_TY;
Table created.
```

Step 3: Insert some rows.

```
insert into ANIMAL
   values ('Mule', 'Francis', '12-Jun-93');
insert into ANIMAL
   values ('Dog','Benji', '03-Sep-93');
```

Alternative form using constructor for ANIMAL_TY. This would be required if component types were user-defined.

```
insert into ANIMAL
   values (ANIMAL_TY('Tiger', 'Tigger', '14-May-97'));
```

Step 4: Table can be displayed as normal.

```
SQL> select Name from ANIMAL;
NAME
--------
Francis
Benji
Tigger
```

This works just like a normal table to this extent. Since each row is a separate object, the component attributes are treated as columns of the object table.

Step 5: Displaying the OID.

```
select REF(A) from ANIMAL A where Name = 'Francis'

REF(A)
--------------------------------------------------------------------------------
0000280209FC0E66FB15E64790A25D86231DBB49543757DD18AF4647308518F12E3622071F02C004
```

This is a generated random value. Clearly, its value is of little practical interest.

Step 6: Create another table that will reference the ANIMAL table.

```
create table KEEPER
   ( KeeperName  VARCHAR2(25),
     AnimalKept  REF ANIMAL_TY);
```

REF indicates that AnimalKept points to an object of type ANIMAL_TY.

Step 7: Insert a row into the Keeper table.

```
insert into KEEPER
   (select 'Joe Bloggs', REF(A) from ANIMAL A
      where Name = 'Francis');
```

Step 8: Display the Keeper data

```
select * from Keeper;

KEEPERNAME
--------------------
ANIMALKEPT
-------------------------------------------------------------------------
Joe Bloggs
0000220208FC0E66FB15E64790A25D86231DBB49543757DD18AF4647308518F12E3622071F
```

Basic select shows a numerical OID. To see the AnimalKept data, use DEREF.

```
select DEREF(K.AnimalKept) from Keeper K;
DEREF(K.ANIMALKEPT)(BREED, NAME, BIRTHDATE)
-------------------------------------------------------------------------
ANIMAL_TY('Mule', 'Francis', '12-JUN-93')
```

Oracle's object-relational features – summary

The foregoing section has outlined some of the main features of Oracle's implementation of the SQL:1999 standard relating to object-relational facilities. It is helpful to examine the changes required to SQL to enable it to deal with object features.

Intersystem's Caché object-relational database

Overview

Caché is a significant database-oriented development product. While it is very modern in its appearance and range of features, it is derived from much older developments in novel database and programming architectures, principally the MUMPS system and M language. Of interest in the Caché system is the way in which the object and relational (SQL) features are neatly integrated. This requires a well-defined translation scheme that converts between the object and relational views. The description of this conversion process is interesting as a workable solution to the problem of working with both object and relational models.

The database is based on an internal structure called a 'multi-dimensional array' and implemented using a sparse array technique. However, the internal structure is not of direct relevance, as it presents to the user the appearance of an extended or object-relational database. A database can be designed using classes and/or tables and access is possible using object-oriented (and other) languages as well as SQL.

Caché is a fully featured database product with multiple programming interfaces, extensive security features, distributed capability etc. and hence it takes a considerable effort learn fully. We shall concentrate on looking at specific features that are of interest to us, namely the way in which it combines object-oriented and relational capabilities.

The main features of Caché are summarised below:

- Caché's principal interface allows the definition of an object-oriented database using a tool called Caché Studio, which is a wizard-driven system. All the facilities one would expect from an object-oriented system are available: class definition (properties and methods), inheritance, collections etc.

- Class methods can be expressed in a range of languages; the default is ObjectScript, which is a powerful but cryptic scripting language based on the original M language. Alternative languages are Basic, Java and C++.

- The collections available are lists and arrays. A list is a simple set of ordered values. An array is a set of values each of which has an associated key value for look-up purposes.

- Caché has its own web interaction language (similar to ASP) called Caché Server Pages (CSP). CSP is the standard tool for generating user interfaces in both web and direct interface applications.

- Data structures defined in Caché Studio can be optionally referenced using the SQL Manager. The object-oriented class definitions are 'projected' to corresponding relational definitions using a defined mapping regime. This aspect of the system is discussed in more detail below.

Caché's object-relational features

Caché essentially defines the database in object-oriented terms, but also provides an SQL interface to the same database structures. To achieve this, Caché defines a 'projection' of object structures to corresponding (almost) equivalent relational ones. This technique is worthy of study because, as well as demonstrating how object and relational models can be united, it also details one method of implementing object to relational mapping.

It should be appreciated that due to the intrinsic differences between the object and relational models, it is not possible to project all aspects of the object design to a relational equivalent; hence there are features available in the Caché class definition that cannot be accessed from the relational version.

To a first approximation, a class projects to a relational table and an instance of the class (an object) is a row of the table. Object properties become columns (fields) of the table. More specific details follow.

Conversion rules

The table below describes how each object concept is mapped to a corresponding relational concept. It must be appreciated that this is purely a virtual realisation of the tables – no actual tables are generated. It is to be seen as the manner in which each object structure is mapped to a 'flat' SQL equivalent.

Object concept	Relational equivalent
Class	Table
OID (Object Identity)	Identity field – see note 1
Class property	Table column (field)
Reference property	Reference field – see note 2
Embedded object	Group of fields – see note 3
List property	List field – see note 4
Array property	Child table – see note 5

NOTES

1 In the object model, every object is given a system-provided unique, immutable identity value called the Object Identity or OID. In the relational model, the primary key is usually a designer-provided value that is used in the application, such as an employee number. For the purposes of this projection, Caché generates a column called ID and assigns the OID value to it. This column is not modifiable by SQL. Also, if a new row is inserted using an SQL INSERT statement, the ID value is not mentioned in the INSERT command and is automatically provided by the system.

2 In the object model, a reference property in effect 'points' to another object to express some relationship. The relational equivalent is a foreign key value referring to the primary key of another table. Caché renders this by creating a foreign key field which can contain the ID value of the referenced row. It is interesting to note that in a conventional relational database, a foreign key, in a sense, does not 'know' what table it is referencing; for example, an employee table may contain a BranchCode field that refers to some row in a branch table, but the connection between these tables has to be expressed by an SQL join. Other than the BranchCode value, the employee table contains no information about the related table. In contrast, a true reference in an object-oriented system points explicitly to a unique object.

3 The object design permits a class definition to contain another object; this mechanism has no relational equivalent. In Caché, the embedded object is projected as multiple columns in the parent table. For instance, an Employee class may contain a Home property which is represented by an object of class Address. The Address class might have properties Street, Town and Postcode. This is projected by inserting table columns Home_Street, Home_Town and Home_Postcode in the relational version.

4 A List property is a Caché collection data item used to express a multi-valued property. It consists of a simple ordered list of items of some type, for example, string. Again, there is no relational equivalent; indeed, this, and the array property considered below, are specifically disallowed by the relational model first normal form stricture. Caché renders this by concatenating the list values into a comma-separated string. This is perhaps not entirely satisfactory, as the component items in the list (except the first) are not immediately available for querying.

5 An Array is another Caché collection type; it consist of a dictionary list, i.e. a set of key and value pairs. Caché projects an array property to SQL as a separate child table. The name of the table is formed from the concatenation of the containing class and the name of the array property. The child table contains three columns: the first is a foreign key reference to the parent table, the second is a key value (user supplied) and the third is the data value.

9

Inheritance

Inheritance enables the derivation of a new class by extending the design of a previously designed class. This permits expression of sub-typing (i.e. where one class is defined as a sub-type of another) enabling expression of the IS-A or generalisation-specialisation relationship. This, of course, is not available in any direct form in the relational model.

In the discussion earlier in this chapter regarding the limitations of the relational model, we indicated that there are a couple of techniques available for managing sub-typing in relational tables. The particular method used by Caché is to flatten the classes; i.e. the sub-typed table consists of all the columns of the super-class plus the additional columns defined for the sub-class. For instance, suppose we have a Employee class that inherits from a Person class: i.e. Employee is a sub-class of the super-class Person. The relational projection will consist of an Employee table that has all the attributes of Person class and the additional attributes of the Employee class.

Object-oriented databases

The object-relational database techniques described in the foregoing sections attempt to reconcile the object and relational worlds by incorporating features of both models. In this section we examine object-oriented databases which do not attempt to preserve any semblance of relational working and opt instead for a purely object-based environment. Given the perceived problems with the relational model, this seems an eminently sensible decision, especially if our applications are written – as is most probable – in an object-oriented language. If fact, object-oriented databases have been around from the early 1990s, but have yet to capture a major share of the market. The main reasons for this appears to be the fact that 'big names' in the software world would not venture into this market while their relational products became more and more powerful and feature-rich. It seems that the limitations of the relational model have been of little consequence in this respect. However, this is not to say the object database concept has died out, and a number of systems maintain an active presence in the market. The overwhelming success of the object model in the field of programming may perhaps cause a reassessment of the merits of the object database since, by elimination of the object-relational barrier, it would appear to offer a much simplified environment for object persistence.

In this section we outline the general principles of these databases, indicating their strengths and weaknesses.

Persistence for objects

If one is programming in an object-oriented environment such as Java, C++ or C# (which is very likely nowadays), there is a need to preserve data in persistent storage. As we have seen the relational database, while being the most common form of computer-based storage, is not convenient for object-based data due to the very different data models. This is the principal motivation for the object database, which attempts to preserve the object-based, structure of data while stored on disk, so that no conversion of structure in transferring between memory and storage is necessary. If a relational database is used to store object data, a 'flattening' process is required which involves

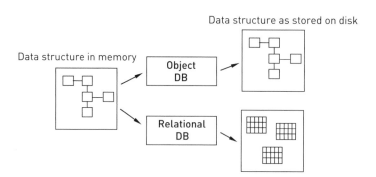

FIGURE 9.3 Comparison of relational and object storage

extra programming and incurs a run-time overhead. The term *impedance mismatch* is used to express this conflict in data models; this is illustrated in Figure 9.3 which contrasts the two modes of storage.

We should mention at this juncture the process known as *serialisation*, which is supported by some object-oriented languages such as C++ and Java. This provides the facility to transfer objects in memory to persistent storage and retrieve them at a later time. However, this mechanism is very basic and does not meet the requirements of proper database storage. What we really need is a system that provides us with both the features of object-oriented programming *and* database systems. We can list these as:

Object-oriented programming features

- Object model
- Data encapsulation
- Object identity
- Inheritance
- Polymorphism

Database features

- Persistence
- Transactions
- Concurrency
- Security, Integrity and recovery
- Standard querying facilities

These are the expected features of a true object-oriented database system and many current products meet these requirements. An additional characteristic supported by most of these systems is 'transparent persistence', which is described next.

Transparent persistence

This concept is at the heart of OODBS systems. Transparent persistence in object database products refers to the ability to manipulate data stored in a database using an object programming language. With transparent persistence, the manipulation and traversal of persistent objects is performed directly by the object programming language in the same manner as in-memory, non-persistent objects. There is no need to read or write every object from the database explicitly. Key objects are found (say, by some kind of query) and related objects are retrieved automatically by reference. Similarly, new/amended objects are saved on disk automatically, either when transactions complete or when the system cache memory becomes full. This enables the programmer to view the data as a one-level store rather than a memory-disk structure, in contrast to a database sub-language as used by embedded SQL or a call interface as used by ODBC or JDBC.

Remember that objects need not be related to some larger data feature such as a table; each object is in a sense self-sufficient, although its relationships with other objects is supported by the system. We can illustrate this point by the example in Figure 9.4.

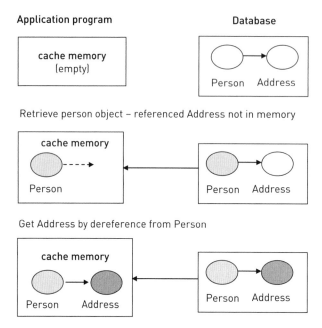

FIGURE 9.4 Transparent persistence

Object identity and references

While objects reside in memory, references between them are based on memory addresses. For example, in a Person object a reference to an Address object would consist of a memory location value. When stored on disk, these memory addresses are meaningless; if the objects are re-stored to memory they will probably be in different locations. To resolve this, some method must be employed to retain knowledge of references while the objects are stored on disk. The process of restoring objects references when objects are returned to memory is called **pointer swizzling**. The process of storing objects and recording (by some means) inherent references between objects is called **un-swizzling**. To some extent the need for this activity detracts from the ideal of transparent persistence, since the stored objects have to be mutated when moved to disk, but there is no way of avoiding this. Several methods have been used to implement un-swizzling, but the most common is to replace a pointer in an object with the object identity (OID) of the referenced object. Clearly, swizzling then replaces this OID value with an actual memory address when the referenced object is returned to memory.

OODBMS standardisation

Standardisation of object databases has been done by an organisation called the Object Data Management Group (ODMG) (http://www.odmg.org). The group was formally wound up in 2001, as it had completed its assigned task of defining this standard.

The standard refers to matters such as:

- Definition of an object model (types, type creation, collections etc.) that a conformant product should support.

- Definition of an object definition language, ODL. (Note: not all object databases use such a language).

- Definition of an object query language (OQL). This is an extension to SQL that deals with querying of more complex structures such as collections. It is expected that an implementation of OQL would support interactive ad hoc queries and embedded use, similar to current SQL usage.

- Language 'bindings'; i.e. how object database processing is integrated into various language such as C++ and Java.

The work of this group has effectively been carried on by Object Database Management Systems or ODBMS (http://www.odbms.org). This organisation was launched in 2005 and provides an up-to-date collection of free materials on object database technology via the Internet. Their website is an excellent starting point for researching the topic of object databases and sourcing software, lecture notes etc.

9

Comparison with RDBMS

Advantages

- Richer modelling capability; e.g. representation of sub-typing, definition of user-defined types.

- Removal of impedance mismatch.

- More flexible accessing mechanisms; e.g. navigational access.

- More suitable for applications that require complex data such as CAD.

- Improved performance? This is not a clear-cut matter; some applications can yield massive improvements, but this does not apply generally.

Disadvantages

- Lack of experience; compared to RDBMS, few programmers have experience of OODBMS. Requires Java or C++ experience.

- Continued competition from improving relational and extended relational products.

- Difficulty in providing graphical user interfaces.

- Lack of support for security mechanisms; e.g. ability to grant selective permissions to different users.

- Complexity – systems required for management of object databases are more complex than RDBMS.

Current practical systems

Object databases are currently actively used in many applications, but they have yet to challenge the dominance of the relational database in general enterprise computing. This section identifies a number of the active players in this market and provides a little more detail in one product, db4o ('database for objects'), which is possibly the most straightforward to illustrate. Object databases are generally accessed via programs written in Java or C++, since the data model does not lend itself to convenient graphical representation. Links to websites for these products are provided at the end of this chapter.

Versant

Versant is a major company in this area. Already successful with their own products, their capability was enhanced by taking over a German company called POET that had some success during the 1990s.

Objectivity

Once could claim to support the world's largest database (system supporting the Stanford Linear Accelerator, SLAC, at Princeton University) but this was transferred to an in-house developed system when it was about 1 petabyte (a million gigabytes). This figure indicates that object database technology cannot be accused of having limitations of scale! The company is a main player in the large object corporate database market.

Matisse

A well-developed product of French origin. Supports its own variant of OQL. Principally targets the .NET market.

Db4o

Db4o is targeted at embedded applications (e.g. in equipment or PC software) i.e. single user, non-DBA situations, although it does have a client–server mode of working. It offers an alternative to serialisation with minimal code size. It is a pure object database that can be employed directly with Java and .NET systems. By 'directly' is implied that it is not necessary to work via an additional software layer between application programs and the data store. The application code communicates directly with the database, providing a single level programming model. Database access is largely transparent – which, of course, is one of the main objectives of object database systems. Its claimed benefits are its speed, simplicity and small memory footprint (i.e. small main memory requirement). The latter features makes the system attractive for use in embedded systems where memory is often limited.

Since db4o is effectively an extension to the programming language, an explanation of it unavoidably refers to program code.

Creating the database

In a more conventional database such as Oracle, one would use some tool or utility to create the database, which would typically have a nontrivial internal structure. In contrast, the database in db4o is generated 'on-the-fly' when first referenced by application code. In Java, an openFile method is called using the chosen path name of the database file. If the file already exists, it is opened; if not, it is created. The openFile call returns a 'handle' which is a reference to an ObjectContainer object; this handle is then used in subsequent application code to refer to that database. In Java, this would look something like this:

```
ObjectContainer db = Db4o.openFile("C:/database/myDb.yap");
```

This creates a database called myDb.yap in the subdirectory/database. The 'yap' extension is the conventional extension used in db4o. The object db is the handle which serves to identify this database in later operations.

Storing objects

To store an object in the database is trivially simple. Assuming we have defined an class called Person, which has as attributes a name and a city, a typical operation might be:

```
Person p = new Person("Andrew", "London");
db.set(p);
```

9

The object containing the name Andrew is now in the database.

Updating an object

Updating an object is achieved by retrieving the object (as described in the next section), modifying it, then using the set method to re-store the object. How does db4o know this is an updated object and not a new one? It uses the object ID to maintain the connection between the in-memory object and the database stored object.

Retrieving objects

Db4o generously provides the user with three forms of query, namely, query by example (QBE), native queries and simple object database access (SODA). We will describe these briefly below.

QBE is a generic title applied by querying methods that use a prototype pattern to indicate the desired selection from the database. The term used to be applied to the graphical method used in Microsoft Access, but in the db4o context it refers to a language technique. In db4o, a prototype object of the required class is created and attribute values that you want to use as search criteria are assigned search values. All other attributes are set to null. Typical code would look something like this:

```
Person p = new Person(); // empty object
p.setname("Andrew"); // the name is set to Andrew
ObjectSet result = (ObjectSet)db.get(p);
```

ObjectSet is a db4o result set container and will be loaded with all objects having the name Andrew.

Native queries is a relatively new concept in language based database queries that allows expression of queries in the application language, such as Java or C#. The concept was introduced in a 2005 paper (Cook and Rosenberger, 2005). The authors point out that a common weakness in many systems is that a query is expressed by means of a statement within a string such as select * from student where student.age <20. This usage is common in, for instance, ADO or JDBC coding and also in object query languages such as OQL. This has many ramifications (described in the paper) but the main ones are:

- The variables in the string are not validated at compile time for correctness or type.

- Object attributes (such as student.age) are referenced directly, rather than via a method call such as student.getAge(), which in effect breaks the usual object-orientation principle of private attributes.

- A query string cannot be easily parameterised; in practice, query strings are composed piecemeal within the application code based on data input and other factors.

You may initially think that setting a query in the application code has always been an option but is too laborious and error-prone. Is that not the whole point of SQL, for example? The idea presented by native queries is that a prototype query expression is defined and wrapped within other code that serves to perform the iterative search of the object's extent. This produces a result set indicating those objects that meet the query specification. In Java this results in an expression such as that shown below:

```
new Predicate() {
   public boolean match (Student student) {
      return student.getAge() < 20
   }
}
```

This code creates an object of class Predicate with a method called 'match'. This method returns a Boolean value of true if the specified condition is met; this condition can be tested against each object in the class's extent to produce a list of matching student objects.

SODA

Db4o also provides yet another query system called 'simple object database access' (SODA). This technique in effect traverses the objects of classes involved in a query. Constraints can be specified for each object class, thereby creating a 'query graph' of all accepted objects. This query graph is used to return a list of objects that satisfy the query. The use SODA has been deprecated in favour of native queries and the QBE method.

Object-relational mapping

Probably the most common approach to the relational versus object models dichotomy is simply to live with it. Programmers are happy to work with objects in Java, C++ or Visual Basic then contrive to store them on disk by 'flattening' them into relational tables. Working in, say, ADO, object data has to be converted into some representation as an ADO recordset. There may be very specific reasons for the decision to work in this mode: e.g. an existing and indispensable relational database, or a technical or political reason for using a particular database and implementation language; or it might be that it seems simpler to avoid involvement with another bundle of software.

The idea behind object-relational mapping tools is make this process more transparent by automating the object-relational inter-conversion. In effect this is another software layer interposed between the object programs and the relational database.

This is illustrated by the diagram in Figure 9.5. The mapping process is often expressed in an XML file.

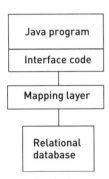

FIGURE 9.5 Object-relational mapping

There are a number of ORM standards and products available which are described below.

Current significant products

Java Data Objects (JDO)

JDO is not actually a product, but a specification defined by Sun, and hence it requires an implementation; several such implementations exist, such as CocoBase, TOPlink, Castor JDO etc. It echoes ADO in that it provides database independence – the same code will work with a range of databases – but it is more specifically targeted at implementing the object-relational mapping function. It is particularly of interest to developers working with large Java-based applications, as it is integrated with Java enterprise systems. To get a feel for the nature and benefits of JDO we can probably do no better than reading Sun's own description:

> The Java Data Objects (JDO) API is a standard interface-based Java model abstraction of persistence, developed as Java Specification Request 12 under the auspices of the Java Community Process. Application programmers use JDO to directly store their Java domain model instances into the persistent store (database).

> Alternatives to JDO include direct file I/O, serialisation, JDBC, and Enterprise Java Beans (EJB) Bean Managed Persistence (BMP) or Container Managed Persistence (CMP) Entity Beans.

> If you are an application programmer, these are the benefits for you in using JDO:

> **Portability:** Applications written with the JDO API can be run on multiple implementations without recompiling or changing source code.

> **Database independence:** Applications written with the JDO API are independent of the underlying database.

> **Ease of use:** Application programmers can focus on their domain object model and leave the details of persistence (field-by-field storage of objects) to the JDO implementation.

> **High performance:** Application programmers delegate the details of persistence to the JDO implementation, which can optimise data access patterns for optimal performance.

> **Integration with EJB:** Applications can take advantage of EJB features such as remote message processing, automatic distributed transaction coordination, and security, using the same domain object models throughout the enterprise.

Source: http://java.sun.com/products/jdo/overview.html

Hibernate

Hibernate, a popular product in this market, is a powerful, high performance object-relational persistence and query service. Hibernate lets you develop persistent classes following the object-oriented idiom – including association, inheritance, polymorphism, composition, and collections. It allows you to express queries in its own portable SQL extension (HQL), as well as in native SQL, or with an object-oriented criteria and example API. According the Hibernate website:

> Hibernate not only takes care of the mapping from Java classes to database tables and from Java datatypes to SQL datatypes, but also provides data query and retrieval facilities that significantly reduce development time. Hibernate's design goal is to relieve the developer from 95% of common data persistence related programming tasks by eliminating the need for manual, hand-crafted data processing using SQL and JDBC.

Source: http://www.jboss.com/pdf/HibernateBrochure-Jun2005.pdf

Apache ObjectRelationalBridge – OJB

Apache ObjectRelationalBridge (OJB) is an object-relational mapping tool that allows transparent persistence for Java objects within relational databases. It is developed within the Apache Software Foundation, which is a community of developers and users committed to the concept of open source collaborative software development.

Summary

In this chapter we started by identifying the perceived limitations of databases based on the relational model. One significant factor that appeared in this analysis was the fact that the relational database does not 'fit' well with the current popularity of object-oriented programming systems. Much of the rest of this chapter was concerned with how this difficulty can be resolved – or at least approached, since it is probably true to say that no ideal solution currently exists. We examined other database technologies that provide better accommodation with the object-oriented paradigm. These are referred to generically as 'post-relational' databases.

First, the object-relational model was considered; products adopting this technique preserve the basic structure of the relational database in that data is still organised in tables but the strictness of the relational model in terms of the admissible table contents is relaxed. This permits the representation of object-oriented data in the database without losing all the benefits of the established relational model. Examples of products using this technique were described.

Next, the pure object-oriented database was examined. Here, the precepts of the relational model are abandoned and the database is now seen as a managed repository of program objects. Since it is based on a specifically programming concept, it is not surprising that the object database typically is much more integrated with application programming systems such as Java, C++ and C#.

The final section described object-relational mapping, which tries to resolve the relational-object problem in another way – by providing an interface between a relational database and object-based programs that automatically provides conversions between the relational and object data versions. Another alternative was mentioned – managing the object-relational mapping 'by hand', i.e. for each application, doing ad hoc conversions between application objects and a relational database.

The subject matter of this chapter is currently in a state of flux; as yet, there has been no major shift from relational databases to pure object databases and most developers either simply work within the relational paradigm or use some form of object-relational mapping. Neither of these is entirely satisfactory and in the longer term this must increase the likelihood of a more general shift to the pure object database.

9

Review questions

1 What are the advantages of the relational database?

2 What are the disadvantages of the relational database?

3 What is meant by saying that the relational database 'lacks semantic power'?

4 Explain what is meant by sub-typing.

5 Why is it difficult to implement sub-typing in a relational database?

6 Define the basic structure of an object.

7 Why is this structure thought to be advantageous in program development?

8 Explain the concept of a class in object-orientation.

9 Explain the concept of inheritance.

10 Show how inheritance can be used to implement sub-typing.

11 What is the essential philosophy of object-relational databases?

12 Explain the nature of Oracle's varray and nested table collection features.

13 Describe the approach taken by Intersystem's Caché system in providing relational and object features.

14 Distinguish between 'object-relational database' and 'object-relational mapping'.

15 Describe the essential nature of a pure object database.

16 What is meant by 'pointer swizzling'?

Exercises

1 Explain the concept of 'sub-typing' and identify the problems involved in representing a sub-typing relationship in a relational database.

2 Compare the approaches taken respectively by object-relational and object-oriented databases in providing object-oriented capabilities within a database.

3 Describe the limitations of the relational database model in representing multi-valued attributes and explain how object-relational systems overcome this limitation.

4 The following code is written in Oracle extended SQL. Explain the meaning and effect of these items.

```
1. create type SalesItem_TY as object
   ( ProductCode  Varchar2(4),
     Quantity     Number(4)
   );
2. create type Items_NT as table of SalesItem_TY;
3. create table SalesOrder
   (
     OrderNo     Number(6),
     Customer_ID Varchar2(5),
     OrderDate   Date,
     Items       Items_NT
   );
```

```
4. insert into SalesOrder values
   (1089, '123', '19-Jul-03',
   Items_NT(
     SalesItem_TY('P020', 2),
       SalesItem_TY('P101', 3)
     )
   );
```

5 For the code in question 4, identify which elements of this code differ from conventional SQL syntax. Show how this code would need to be implemented in conventional SQL and discuss the relative merits of the two versions.

6 Systems and programming development is now predominantly object-oriented. Discuss the impact that this has had or might have on the adoption of post-relational database technology.

7 Identify the respective features of object-oriented programming and of databases that you would expect to be combined in an object-oriented database.

8 Explain the concept of 'transparent persistent' indicating its relevance in object-oriented database design.

9 Describe the motivation and principles behind the idea of 'object-relational mapping'.

9

References

Textbooks

Oracle
Rahayu W., Taniar D. and Pardede E, (2005): *Object-oriented Oracle*, Cybertech Publishing

Caché database
Kirsten, W., Ihringer, M., Kühn M., Röhrig, B. and Rudd, A.S. (Translator) (2003): *Object-Oriented Application Development Using the Caché Post-Relational Database*, Springer-Verlag: Berlin

Db4o database
Paterson, J., Edlich, S., Hörning, H., Hörning, R (2006): *The Definitive Guide to db4o*, Apress: Berkeley
Cook and Rosenberger (2005): *Native Queries for Persistent Objects*, Dr. Dobbs Journal, Dec. 2005 also available at:
http://www.cs.utexas.edu/~wcook/papers/NativeQueries/NativeQueries8-23-05.pdf

Websites

SQL

SQL background

http://en.wikipedia.org/wiki/SQL

SQL:2003

http://www.sigmod.org/sigmod/record/issues/0403/E.JimAndrew-standard.pdf
http://www.service-architecture.com/database/articles/sql1999.html

Commentary on SQL standards conformity

http://www.dbazine.com/db2/db2-disarticles/gulutzan3

Object (extended)-relational databases

Oracle object-relational

http://www.dba-oracle.com/art_oracle_obj.htm
http://www-db.stanford.edu/~ullman/fcdb/oracle/or-objects.html
http://www.lc.leidenuniv.nl/awcourse/oracle/appdev.920/a96594/adobjint.htm
http://www.oracle.com/technology/products/oracle9i/htdocs/ort_twp.html
http://osiris.sund.ac.uk/~cs0dne/teaching/CIFM01/OracleORTutorial.pdf
http://www.oracle.com/technology/products/oracle9i/pdf/simple_strat_for_complex_rel2.pdf

Caché database

www.intersystems.com

Object-oriented databases

Wikipedia

http://en.wikipedia.org/wiki/Object_database

Transparent persistence

http://www.service-architecture.com/object-relational-mapping/articles/transparent_
    persistence.html

ODBMS group

http://www.odbms.org/index.html

Versant object-oriented database

http://www.versant.com/
Versant and Poet products: http://www.versant.com/developer/downloads/index.html

Objectivity
www.objectivity.com

db4o – object database
www.db4o.com

Matisse
www.matisse.com

Object-relational mapping

Object-relational mapping principles
http://en.wikipedia.org/wiki/Object-relational_mapping
http://www.objectmatter.com/vbsf/docs/maptool/ormapping.html
http://www.howtoselectguides.com/dotnet/ormapping/

Guide to products

Apache ObjectRelationalBridge:
http://db.apache.org/ojb/ – ObjectRelationalBridge (part of Jakarta project)

Hibernate – Relational Persistence for Java and .NET:
http://www.hibernate.org/
http://www.hibernate.org/362.html – example of coding
http://www.jboss.com/pdf/Hibernate-Brochure-June 2005.pdf

JDO (Java Data Objects):
http://java.sun.com/products/jdo/
http://jcp.org/en/jsr/detail?id=012
http://www.devx.com/database/article/16406
http://www.solarmetric.com/Software/Documentation/2.3.0/jdo-overview.html

Castor JDO:
http://www.castor.org/jdo-introduction.html
http://www-128.ibm.com/developerworks/java/library/j-castor/

JDO developer's community:
http://www.jdocentral.com/index.html

9

10

Web databases

LEARNING OBJECTIVES

This chapter deals with the techniques available for utilising databases in World Wide Web applications. Although we use the above title, there is actually no such thing as a 'web database' in the sense of a database specifically designed for web use. Rather, databases used in web applications are the same databases as those in conventional applications. The novel aspects of this topic lie in the way in which database access features are integrated into normal web page design and this is the subject of this chapter.

This chapter is primarily addressed to readers who have some knowledge of programming and unavoidably contains a fair amount of coding. However, much of the general principles can still be appreciated even if the coding elements are ignored.

After studying this chapter, you should be able to do the following:

- Outline the general principles of the Internet, the World Wide Web and associated technology, including HTML.

- Understand the need to provide database access for websites.

- Explain the client–server principle as applied to web database systems.

- Describe the principles and problems involved in utilising a database from a website.

- Explain in outline the techniques and technologies used in the web databases including cgi-bin, ASP (Active Server Pages) and ASP.NET, JSP (Java Server Pages) and servlets and PHP.

- Appreciate the problems inherent in developing web database systems.

Introduction

Historical background

Everyone nowadays is familiar with the general nature of the World Wide Web, often simply called 'the web' or WWW. The web is based on a set of applications that run on the Internet. The Internet is made up of a set of interconnected networks, all of which utilise common communication protocols such as **TCP/IP**. In principle, this enables any connected computer, equipped with suitable software, to communicate with any other. For web applications, this communication is generally conducted in client-server mode; i.e. some computers act as 'servers' and provide information to other computers, 'the clients'. Client-server working is described in more detail in the next section.

The Internet was conceived and originally developed during the Cold War days of the 1960s and 1970s. The US Air Force wanted a decentralised communications system that would be resilient in the event of a nuclear attack. The system adopted is called 'packet switching'. In this system, messages are sent in a series of relatively small 'packets' of data, with each packet being viewed as an independent unit of transmission. This avoids having to dedicate an 'end-to-end' link of circuits for the duration of the transmission; such a connection would be vulnerable to failure of some intermediate point in the link. The packets are dispatched into the system and may take different routes in reaching their destination, where they are re-assembled into the original message. The original network designed on this basis was called ARPANET (Advanced Research Projects Agency Network).

Another crucial development was the adoption in 1976 of TCP/IP (Transmission Control Protocol/Internet Protocol) as the working protocol for ARPANET. This protocol provides a numerical addressing scheme which enables any computer connected to the network to be referenced. In 1983, the Domain Name System (DNS) was created. This allowed packets to be directed to a domain name, the web addresses with which we are now familiar, which are translated by domain name servers into the corresponding IP number. Domain name servers reside transparently on the Internet and perform this valuable translation service. This makes it much easier for users since it avoids the need to remember specific numerical addresses. Web addresses are expressed in a format called a Uniform Resource Locator (URL); this is a broadly defined format that is utilised by a number of protocols including HTTP, FTP (File Transfer Protocol) and mailto (email address) and has the basic structure: **protocol://host:port/path?query**.

For HTTP, the URL has the following components:

protocol	Identifies the protocol to be used, such as HTTP, FTP, mailto, file etc.
host	The domain name of a network host, such as a web server.
port	Optional numerical port address; defaults to 80.
path	A relative path reference from the home directory of the server.
query	A string of name-value pairs, supplied by the sender or by a GET request.

The World Wide Web was originally conceived by Tim Berners-Lee working in CERN, the European high-energy physics research centre in Geneva. The original motivation was to provide a hypertext system to facilitate efficient information transfer between members of the international physics community. Two technologies are important in this development: the hypertext protocol HTTP and the hypertext mark-up language HTML. HTTP is a protocol that is used on the web to manage communications between the client and the server. HTML is a language used to express the design of web pages. HTTP is a low-level protocol and Internet users and application developers do not need an extensive knowledge of it. A knowledge of HTML, on the other hand, is important for web application development and a brief description of it is given below.

Client-server architecture

In a client-server architecture, there exist 'clients' who request a service and 'servers' who provide the service. Typically, the client and the server are on separate computers and frequently widely separated geographically. This mode of working is covered in more detail earlier, in Chapter 8 but since the client-server concept features strongly in web database environments, it is worthwhile to review the main characteristics of such a system.

In a simple web dialogue, the client employs a browser such as Internet Explorer or Firefox to access remote web servers. If a database is to be accessed, then the web server takes on the role of a client and requests a service from the database server. Such requests are typically expressed in SQL. Hence we have a three-tier system as illustrated in Figure 10.1.

10

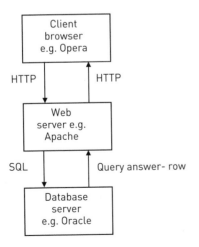

FIGURE 10.1 Three-tier server

A significant aspect of this arrangement is that the processing activities of the system are distributed over three locations: the browser, the web server and the database server. This has the advantage of distributing the processing effort and specific processing tasks can be located where they can best be performed. For instance, script languages such as JavaScript or VBScript can be employed in the browser to perform preliminary tasks such as data validation within forms.

On the other hand, the separateness of the system elements introduces its own problems. For the website designer, a major consideration is that the clients will use a range of different browsers whose design is not within their control. Hence, the designer must work within constraints of the known characteristics of commonly available browsers.

HTML

Hypertext Markup Language, HTML, is used to define the content and, to some extent, the format of a web page. An HTML web page design consists of a simple text file (usually with an .htm or .html extension) containing HTML language elements that specify the text and image content of the page. Such pages are stored on a web server and are requested by users by using a browser program such as Internet Explorer, Firefox or Opera. The browser downloads the HTML definition and renders the text and graphical content on the user's display.

While HTML forms the backbone of web page handling, current web page design frequently uses a number of additional technologies to improve the functionality of web pages. For instance, cascading style sheets (CSS) are used extensively to control the presentation of web pages. Also, Java and JavaScript are used to introduce programmability to the page. Java programs in the form of 'applets' are downloaded from the server (in the same way as text, images etc.) and is executed by the browser. JavaScript code is included simply within the text of the page and, again, interpreted by the browser. CSS and JavaScript in particular are very widely employed in modern page design.

In the following section we provide a brief introduction to HTML, covering the basic concepts and enough of the language elements to enable you to follow the explanation of the more advanced web technologies such as ASP. It does not constitute a full course on the subject; for more information and assistance, consult the references provided at the end of the chapter.

Introduction to HTML coding

The purpose of an HTML document is to specify the content and layout of the elements (text and images) of a web page for display using a browser. It uses a system of *tags* to define each page element. HTML tags consist of a left angle bracket ($<$), a tag name and a right angle bracket ($>$). There are a range of tag types that constitute the HTML language, each tag type having a predefined effect in the rendering of the page. Tags are often paired with a 'start' tag and an 'end' tag enclosing between them an element value. For example, the HTML command to define a title for a web page:

```
<TITLE>This is the title </TITLE>
```

Note that the end tag is the same as the start tag but preceded by a slash. There are also unary tags that do not have an end version; for example, <BR>, the 'break', command, causes a new line to inserted in the text. There is no </BR> tag.

A simple example is shown below (HTML.Example01.html):

```
<html>
<head>
<title>Simple HTML Example </title>
</head>
<body>
   <h1>Main Heading </h1>
   <h2>Second Heading</h1>
   <p>Hello! This is a text paragraph.
   It is written over several
   lines but it is rendered as one paragraph.
   </p>
   <br>
   <table border = "1">
      <tr><td>Table 1,1 </td><td>Table 1,2 </td><td>Table 1,3 </td>
      <tr><td>Table 2,1 </td><td>Table 2,2 </td><td>Table 2,3 </td>
   </table>
   <br><br>
   <a href = "http://www.cengage.co.uk">Hyperlink to Cengage Learning website:
   </a>
</body>
</html>
```

10

This produces the output shown in Figure 10.2.

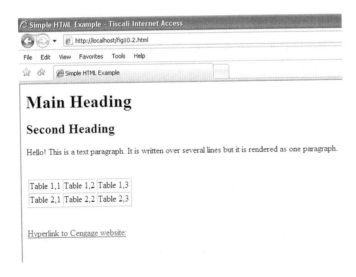

FIGURE 10.2 Simple HTML example

Some general points can be made here:

1 A number of tags are used, such as `<html>`, `<title>`, `<head>`, etc. and each tag has an associated end tag. Tags can be nested; for instance, the `<html>` tag pair encloses the whole of the document and the `<title>` tag pair is contained within the `<head>` tags. The meaning of the tags is explained in the next section.

2 Spaces in the HTML document are insignificant except in separating words within the text. Even there, extra spaces are simply ignored. Note that several spaces after the word 'Hello!' have been removed. This process is often rather mystifying to novice users of HTML who expect the control provided by a word processor or publishing software; the document is intended primarily to specify content rather than the final layout, which is left to the browser. Similarly, line breaks in HTML are insignificant. In fact, HTML does have some control over the format and it is possible to influence the appearance using a STYLE tag or by a separate style file.

3 HTML is insensitive to case; hence, `<TITLE>`, `<Title>` and `<title>` are all treated identically. However, as discussed in the next chapter, with the introduction of an XML language for website design, which enforces a more strict syntax, the advice now is to use lowercase tags throughout. The language, XHTML, is a version of HTML designed using XML; it provides the same features and characteristics as HTML but, as in XML, requires use of a stricter syntax, including lowercase letters for all tags.

Parameters

In the HTML example above, the element `<h1>Main Heading </h1>` specifies an h1 header with a value of 'Main Heading'. In addition to their value, some tags can also have *parameters*. These define other properties of the element that affect its appearance or functionality. For example, header tags such as h1, h2 etc. can use an *align* parameter:

```
<h1 align = left>Main Header </h1>
```

which, as you may guess, affects the alignment of the header text. Other examples of parameters will be encountered in the rest of this chapter.

Common HTML tags

HTML	The `<HTML>` tags bracket the complete web page document and are mandatory.
HEAD and BODY	The HTML document is divided into two sections, the head and the body, bracketed by `<head>` and `<body>` tags. The head section containing identifying information, such as the title, while the body contains the main page content definition.

TITLE	This tag is contained within the head area of the document and supplies a title for the page. The title does not actually appear on the rendered web page but browsers generally place it on the title bar at the top of the window.
P	Denotes a paragraph. All text within the <p> and </p> tags is treated as a single paragraph.
H1, H2, etc.	The H1, H2, . . . H6 tags, denote a hierarchy of headings. Browsers will typically render these in different character formats, usually larger than normal text.
TABLE, TR, TD	These tags are used to define a table. <table> and </table> bracket the overall table definition. A table consists of a number of rows, each defined by <tr> . . . </tr>; each row in turn contains a number of data cells defined by <td> . . . </td> entries. These tags all have various parameters that affect the table format. For instance, the table tag has a parameter border = "1" which sets a relative size for the borders around the table cells.
A	The anchor tag is used to specify both the source and target for a hypertext link (hyperlink). The example above shows the definition of a hyperlink to a web URL. The text between the <a> and </a> tags is typically presented in a different format (underlined in the example – see Figure 10.2) to emphasise its 'clickable' nature. Hyperlinks can also target another point in the same HTML page or some point in another page of the same website.

10

Forms

An important component of HTML coding is the definition of 'forms'. The form is the main vehicle in establishing interaction with the web server and much of the technology in this area involves forms. A form is an 'input' mechanism that consists of a set of text boxes, buttons and other objects displayed by the browser. Data entered into the form by the browser user can be transmitted to the server for processing. HTML itself has no capability in this respect and the processing has to be achieved by means of one of the technologies described in this chapter, such as CGI, ASP etc. A knowledge of HTML forms is therefore an essential prerequisite for studying these subjects. Also, note in passing at this point that ASP.NET, a derivative of ASP, provides for the definition of non-HTML forms; instead, the forms are defined and processed by ASP.NET coding.

A form is defined within a <form> ... </form> pair which contain a set of input elements; these are either <input>, <textarea> or <select> (dropdown list) elements. Each <input> can specify one of a range of form objects; common objects are: text box, button, radio button and check box.

A simple example using these is shown below – **HTML.Example02.html**:

```
<html>
<head>
<title>HTML Form Example </title>
</head>
<body>
<br>
<form method=post action="Page2.asp">- - - - - - - (1)
Make: <input type=text name=make size=20>- - - - -(2)
<p>
Colour:
   <input type=radio name=colour value="R">Red - - (3)
   <input type=radio name=colour value="W">White
   <input type=radio name=colour value="B">Blue
<p>
Price range:
<select name=price size=1>- - - - - - - - - - - -(4)
   <option>Less than £10000
   <option>Less than £15000
   <option>More than £15000
</select>
<p>
<input type=submit>- - - - - - - - - - - - - - - (5)
</form>
</body>
</html>
```

The output from this code is shown in Figure 10.3 and the lines indicated by numbers in the code are explained on the next page.

FIGURE 10.3 HTML form example

1 The 'action' parameter specifies the URL to be followed when the Submit button is pressed (see note 5). This is significant in ASP and other programming technologies, as the action parameter will specify a web page or program that processes the form data. The 'method' parameter specifies one of two modes of data transference from the form to the action agent. The POST value in the example sends the data, in name-value pairs, within an HTTP protocol message to the server when the 'submit' button is pressed. The alternative method, GET, specifies that the form data is to be appended, in name-value pairs, to the end of the URL that is sent to the server.

The main difference between these techniques is that the GET method exposes the content of the form on the URL, which may be a security risk in some applications. See the explanation of the ASP Request object later in this chapter for more details on how the form data is handled.

2 Input type = text defines a text box used to enter data. The text is treated as character data; the code processing the data can interpret it as required.

3 Input type = radio defines a set of radio boxes. These provide a number of selectable options, only one of which can be chosen.

4 The select element defines items in a dropdown list.

5 Input type = submit defines a button that is used to terminate the entry of data and to send the form data to the 'action' destination. Note that, in order to try this example, the file Page2.asp must exist in the same directory as the HTML file and should 'handle' the data received. We will return to this point when working with ASP.

We will elaborate further on these principles when we have progressed further into our description of the web technologies such as ASP.

10

Overview of interactive web technologies

In this section we describe a number of technologies that are commonly used in web database communication. Essentially these technologies are designed to provide websites with user interaction capability. HTML on its own cannot provide any interaction; it simply delivers web pages as requested by the client browser. For example, a basic HTML site cannot accept values and return a computed result. A particular requirement here is to handle data supplied by the client on an HTML form. Forms are extensively used in other processing contexts (such as a database user interface) to collect various related items of data from the user for transmission to some server for processing. Without some kind of interactive capability, the web server could do nothing with the transmitted form data.

In the context of web–database interaction, what we require is that the browser can, say, issue a query which is presented to the database for execution. The query result can be dynamically formatted as a web page and returned to the browser. Many examples of this process are shown in the following sections.

Note: Dynamic HTML (DHTML) does provide some interaction features, but these only handle graphical aspects of the web page such as font sizes, text positioning, animation etc. It cannot perform general computational tasks as required for database interaction.

Within the confines of a single chapter in a more general textbook, it is not possible to provide a study in depth on the range of topics described. We try only to provide a general explanation of the techniques used in the area and to provide a useful comparison of the relative merits of the various products. The technologies described are listed below:

CGI   The earliest of the methods used, CGI is a general technique that enables a web page to execute a program that can perform some processing (such as database access) then generate appropriate HTML code.

ASP   A Microsoft product, ASP was the earliest of tag-based systems, where program code is interspersed with HTML code.

ASP.NET   A derivative of ASP that introduces many significant advancements including event-handling and server-side controls.

PHP   A popular language with a modest beginning that is now possibly the most popular language in this area.

JSP   Java Server Pages is a technology that is part of the Java environment and hence is popular for web development in Java systems.

We will now describe these in more detail in the following sections.

CGI

The Common Gateway Interface or CGI was the earliest technique introduced to provide website interaction and in nature differs somewhat from the other techniques described here. Put simply, CGI enables us to initiate execution of a program on the server by a URL reference to the address of the program (in a CGI directory of the server system) in HTML code. The program can be written in any language supported by the server system, such as C++ or Visual Basic, but the most popular language for this purpose is the script language Perl. Scripting languages are preferred in this application since they avoid the need for a compilation system. Typically, the Perl program will output HTML code which is sent to the browser for display. Of course, in generating the HTML code, the CGI code can perform any necessary computations and, in particular, access a database.

The main distinction between CGI and the other techniques described below is that in CGI a program (e.g. a Perl script), held separately on the server, is invoked and executed. In the other methods, the executable code is embedded in the HTML code, but also executes on the server. In both cases, the ultimate result is an HTML page that is delivered to the browser, although it could be substantially enhanced by the inclusion of generated JavaScript code. CGI is principally employed on UNIX systems using the Apache web server. It is possible to use it on Microsoft platforms using IIS but it can be somewhat complex to implement. In any case, ASP or ASP.NET is generally the preferred vehicle for website interaction on Microsoft systems.

ASP and ASP.NET

Introduction

ASP or **Active Server Pages** is a technique used to produce interactive web pages; i.e. web pages that can respond to user input and obtain data from other sources (notably databases) to generate web output dynamically. It is not the only such technique, but it is probably the most widely used in practice today.

ASP works by combining conventional HTML with code written in a scripting language and embedded in the HTML code using ASP-specific bracketing notations. The in-built code typically has the effect of generating additional content within the HTML document and the updated document is then delivered to the client browser for display. The most common scripting language used in this respect is VBScript, which is a derivative of (but not the same as) Visual Basic. However, other languages such as JavaScript can also be used. For our purposes, we will use the most common option of VB Script. An additional element that is required if we wish to use ASP to communicate with a database is ADO (ActiveX Data Objects). An introduction to ADO is also provided in this chapter.

ASP pages have to be interpreted by a web server that is equipped to process it; this includes Microsoft's IIS and PWS. With suitable add-ins, ASP can also be used with the Apache web server.

ASP.NET is a derivative of ASP and effectively renders ASP obsolescent; i.e. ASP will not be developed further and ASP.NET is now the standard Microsoft offering for website interaction. However, many sites exist running ASP and it is still used by many developers, so a study of it continues to be relevant. There are many points of similarity between ASP and ASP.NET. The features of ASP.NET will be described later.

A sample ASP file is shown below. Note the use of the .asp extension. This alerts the server to the fact that the file contains ASP code. However, even if the file were pure HTML, IIS would not complain.

ASPExample1.asp

```
<%@ Language = VBScript %>
<HTML>
<BODY>
Output:<BR>
<%
```

10

```
hours = 24*7
%>
There are
<%
Response.Write hours
%>
hours in a week.
</BODY>
</HTML>
```

ASP files contain a mix of HTML and ASP/VBScript code. The shaded areas bounded by <% and %> brackets are ASP and the rest is HTML. The server executes the ASP and any output generated by the code is inserted at that point in the text, thereby updating the HTML content.

The line hours = 24*7 is actually a VBScript instruction performing a simple multiplication. The line Response.Write hours is using the built-in Response object of ASP. ASP provides a set of built-in objects that are used to simplify interaction between the browser and the server; these are explained in more detail shortly.

This will generate the output (as a web page):

```
Calculate hours in a week:
There are 168 hours in a week.
```

Sample ASP scripts

The following scripts provide other illustrations of how ASP can be used and also serve as an overview of the more common VBScript instructions. The dotted lines are *not* part of the code but refer to the explanatory notes given on the next page.

ASPExample02.asp

```
<%@Language = VBScript%>
<%Option Explicit %>
<! - ASPExample02.asp Displays date and time from server - >
<html>
<head>
<title>ASPExample02.asp - Server Date and Time
</title>
</head>
<body>
<%
Dim dt, tm - - - - - - - - - - - - - - - - - - -(1)
dt = Date - - - - - - - - - - - - - - - - - - -(2)
tm = Time

Response.Write "The date is " & dt & "<br>" - - - (3)
Response.Write "The time is " & tm
%>
<br>
</body>
</html>
```

Output:

> The date is 27/01/2006
>
> The time is 11:53:43

Notes:

1 The Dim statement (short for Dimension) is used to declare variables used in the script. This is strictly speaking not necessary, as VBScript will assume a type based on the context and usage. However, it is good practice, and the command Option Explicit at the top of the script forces explicit declaration. In case you are wondering where the term 'Dim' comes from, we can offer the following explanation: in very early versions of Microsoft Basic, Dim was originally used to declare the dimensions of an array – no other type declarations were used. It seems to have been later adopted for all type declaration even for scalar variables.

2 These statements use functions Date and Time, which return the current date and time values. These are assigned to the variables dt and tm.

3 These lines output the values of the dt and dm variables, which in effect embeds these values in the generated HTML script. The ampersand (&) is the text concatenation operator; i.e. it chains together the component text values in the line. Note how the text value <br> is also output to generate a line break at this point.

10

ASPExample03.asp

```
<%@Language = VBScript%>
<%Option Explicit %>

<!-- ASPExample03.asp
   Illustrates the use of the FOR loop -->

<html>
<head>
<title>ASPExample03.asp - FOR loop
</title>
</head>
<body>
<%
Dim i
For i = 1 to 5
   Response.Write "number is " & i & "<br>"
Next
%>
<br>
</body>
</html>
```

Output:

```
Number is 1
Number is 2
Number is 3
Number is 4
Number is 5
```

ASPExample04.asp

```
<%@Language = VBScript%>
<%Option Explicit %>

<!- - ASPExample04.asp
   Illustrates the use of the Select Case statement - ->

<html>
<head>
<title>ASPExample04.asp - Select Case statement
</title>
</head>

<body>
<%

Select Case WeekDayName(WeekDay(Now) ) - - - -(1)
   Case "Monday"
     Response.Write "Start of the Week"
   Case "Tuesday","Wednesday", "Thursday"- - -(2)
     Response.Write "Mid-week"
   Case "Friday"
     Response.Write "End of the week"
   Case Else
     Response.Write "Weekend"
   End Select
%>
<br>
</body>
</html>
```

1 The Select Case statement uses a test value and selects one of a number of possible actions dependent on this value. The test value in this example is WeekDayName(WeekDay(Now)) which is a nested function call expression. The Now function returns today's date. Applying the WeekDay function to this produces a number from 1 and 7, representing the days of the week from Sunday to Saturday. The WeekDayName function converts this numerical value to the name of the day.

2 Note how multiple case values can be used.

3 The output from this code would vary depending on the day of the week that it is run. For instance, running it on a Friday would produce the answer 'End of the week'.

To provide user interaction, ASP includes a number of built-in objects; these are considered in the next section.

Overview of ASP objects

Introduction

ASP objects are data structures maintained by the IIS web server that are automatically available when an ASP script is invoked on the server. They provide the programmer with facilities essential to managing effective interaction with the web server.

ASP includes five standard objects for global use:

- **Request** – to get information from the user

- **Response** – to send information to the user

- **Server** – to control the Internet Information Server (IIS)

- **Session** – to store information about and change settings for the user's current Web server session

- **Application** – to share application-level information and control settings for the lifetime of the application

10

Here we will look, in overview, at the objects mentioned above.

The Request object

The Request object is used to get information from the user that is passed along in an HTTP request. The Request and Response objects support collections:

- **ClientCertificate** – holds the certification fields from the request issued by the Web browser.

- **QueryString** – holds items held in the parameter list appended to a URL, possibly by a GET method in a form.

- **Form** – holds data from an HTML form, sent using the POST method.

- **Cookies** – holds the values of application-defined cookies.

- **ServerVariables** – holds HTTP information such as the server name.

The Response object

The Response object is used to send information to the user. The Response object supports only cookies as a *collection* (to set cookie values). The Response object also supports a number of properties and methods. The properties currently supported are:

- **Buffer** – set to buffer page output at the server. When this is set to true, the server will not send a response until all of the server scripts on the current page have been processed, or until the Flush or End method has been called.

- **ContentType** – to set the type of content (i.e: text/HTML, Excel, etc.).

- **Expires** – sets the expiration (when the data in the user's cache for this web page is considered invalid) based on minutes.

- **ExpiresAbsolute** – allows you to set the expiration date to an absolute date and time.

- **Status** – returns the status line (defined in the HTTP specification for the server).

The following methods are supported by the Response object:

- **AddHeader** – Adds an HTTP header with a specified value

- **AppendToLog** – Appends a string to the end of the web server log file

- **BinaryWrite** – writes binary data (e.g. Excel spreadsheet data)

- **Clear** – clears any buffered HTML output

- **End** – stops processing of the script

- **Flush** – sends all the information in the buffer

- **Redirect** – to redirect the user to a different URL

- **Write** – to write into the HTML stream. This can be done by using the construct

`Response.write("hello")` or the shortcut command `<% = "hello"%>`

The Server object

The Server object supports one property, ScriptTimeout, which allows you to set the value for when the script processing will time out, and the following methods:

- **CreateObject** – to create an instance of a server component. This component can be any component that you have installed on your server (such as an ActiveX or COM component.).

- **HTMLEncode** – used during output of text to encode the specified string in HTML. Converts characters with special meaning within HTML, such as <and >, into special character encoding &lt and &gt.

- **MapPath** – to map the current virtual path to a physical directory structure. You can then pass that path to a component that creates the specified directory or file on the server.

- **URLEncode** – applies URL encoding to a specified string.

The Session object

A Session object is used to maintain user information while the user is online, i.e. accessing the website. Each user's visit is represented by a Session object, the object being created when the first page is accessed. Because WWW connection is 'stateless' there is no intrinsic record of successive accesses by a user to the website. In order to maintain the notion of an online session, ASP generates a unique SessionId for a user when the site is first accessed. This is maintained as a **cookie** as explained in a section below.

Session properties

SessionId	Value generated for each user session. Only guaranteed to be unique as long as the web server is not restarted.
TimeOut	Specifies the maximum time in minutes of user inactivity until the session is considered abandoned.

Session method

Abandon	Immediately terminates the session and releases all resources. Can be used when an explicit logout is provided in an application.

10

Session events

Session_OnStart	Called by ASP when the client requests the first ASP file from the web application.
Session_OnEnd	Called when the session is closed. Happens when the session times out or the *Abandon* method is called.

Event handlers for these events must be placed in the **global.asa** file which should be in the root directory of the website. The nature of this file is explained below, under the Application Object section.

Session cookies

A cookie is a small item of information that the server sends to the client browser which stores them on the client computer. In particular, ASP will record the user's SessionId as a cookie on the user's first access to the ASP pages. Thereafter, on each user access the cookie is retrieved and used to preserve continuity of the user's session. The topic of cookies in general is covered in a later section.

Session variables and objects

Variables and objects can be stored in a Session object. The variable notation is:

```
Session("Name") = Username
```
assuming 'Username' is a VBScript variable.

For an object, the format is:

```
Set Session("Connection") = Conn
```

The Application object

The Application object represents a single website application running within a dedicated subdirectory of a web server. The object is created the first time a user accesses a page within the application and persists until the server is shut down.

It is convenient to use it to store information that must persist indefinitely and be available to all users, such as a page counter.

Application variables

To define an Application variable, use the notation illustrated below:

```
<%
    Application("myVariable") = "Hello world"
    Application("Counter") = 12
%>
```

Since Application variables are accessible to all users, variables that can be modified must be protected against conflicting accesses by means of locking:

```
Application.Lock
Application("Count") = Application("Count")+1
Application.Unlock
```

Application events

The Application objects detect two events:

Application_OnStart	Called by ASP when the first client requests an ASP file from the web application
Application_OnEnd	Called when the server is shut down. This event can be used to store all application values to disk so that they can be restored on start-up.

Events handlers for these events must be placed in the **global.asa** file which must reside in the web application root directory.

global.asa file

The **global.asa** file is used to house the event-handling code for the application and session objects. The general structure of the file is shown below:

```
<SCRIPT LANGUAGE=VBSCRIPT RUNAT=Server>
Sub Session_OnStart
    Session startup commands
End Sub

Sub Session_OnEnd
    Session shut down commands
End Sub

Sub Application_OnStart
    Application startup commands
End Sub

Sub Application_OnEnd
    Application shut down commands
End Sub
```

Note that the <% and %> tags are not admissible; the <SCRIPT> tag must be used.

Example of global.asa use – counting site hits

Since the scope of the count is the application, it must be held in the Application object. The counter can be initialised using the **global.asa** file shown below:

```
<SCRIPT LANGUAGE=VBSCRIPT RUNAT=Server>
    Sub Application_OnStart
    Application.Lock
    Application.("Hits") = 0
    Application.Unlock
    End Sub
</SCRIPT>
```

The following ASP code must be included in every page in which you wish to register a hit. Note that it may be sufficient to include it on the home page if most visits initially go there.

```
<% @ LANGUAGE VBSCRIPT %>
<%
Application.Lock
Application("Hits") = Application("Hits") +1
Application.UnLock
%>
<HTML><BODY>
Number of hits in the application:
<% = Application("Hits") %>
</BODY></HTML>
```

More sample scripts

The following scripts provide additional examples of ASP coding and its built-in objects.

ASPExample06.asp

This script uses only HTML code. It uses a form to input two values which are submitted to the script **ASPExample06A.asp** for processing

```
<!-- ASPExample06.asp -->

<html>
<body>
Please enter text values in the boxes: <br>
<Form Action = "ASPExample06A.asp" Method = "Post">
Value 1: <input type = "text" name = "value1" size = "20"><br>
Value 2: <input type = "text" name = "value2" size = "20"><br><br>
<input type = "submit" name = "submit" value = "Submit Form">
</form>
</body>
</html>
```

ASPExample06A.asp

This script receives two values as form data from **ASPExample06.asp** and displays them concatenated.

```
<!-- ASPExample06a.asp -->
<html>
<head>
<title>ASPExample06A.asp - Receives two text values and concatenates them
</title>
</head>

<body>
<%
X = Request.Form("value1")
Y = Request.Form("value2")
Ans = X & " " & Y
%>

X: <% = X%><br>
Y: <% = Y%><br>
Ans: <% = Ans%><br>

</body>
</html>
```

The form displayed by ASPExample06 is shown in Figure 10.4.

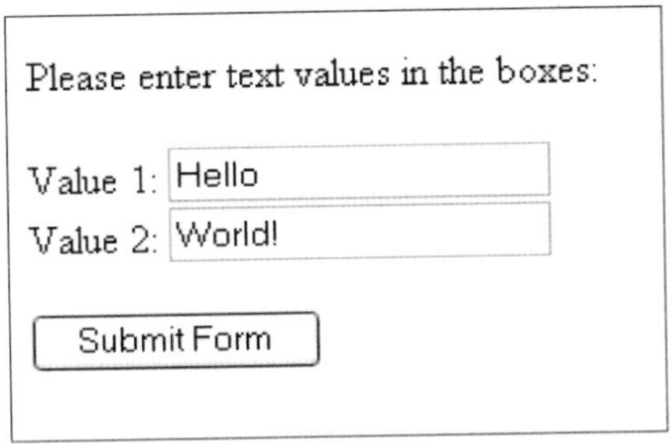

Please enter text values in the boxes:

Value 1: Hello

Value 2: World!

Submit Form

FIGURE 10.4 ASPExample06 form display

The following display is produced by this form.

X: Hello
Y: World!
Ans: Hello World!

ASPExample07.asp

This ASP example combines **ASPExample06.asp** and **ASPExample06A.asp** into one script. It consists of two section subject to an If . . . else test. The If test checks to see whether the request object has received any data yet by checking a Request object server variable identified by CONTENT_LENGTH. This property indicates the length of the data received in a POST operation and will be zero if no form has been executed yet. If this is the case, 'else' code is executed which contains an HTML form. The form ACTION parameter uses the Request server variable SCRIPT_NAME, which is the name of the current script. Hence the script re-executes itself when the form is submitted but this time the form values will be received. The code within the 'if' part of the script will then be executed.

```
<!-- ASPExample07.asp -->
<%
Response.Expires = 0

Dim X, Y, Ans

If Request.ServerVariables("CONTENT_LENGTH") <>0 then
X = Request.Form("value1")
Y = Request.Form("value2")
Ans = X & " " & Y
%>
```

10

```
<html>
<head>
<title>ASPExample07.asp - Receives two text values and concatenates them
</title>
</head>

<body>

X: <%=X%><br>
Y: <%=Y%><br>
Ans: <%=Ans%><br>

</body>
</html>

<%
Else
%>
<html>
<body>
Please enter text values in the boxes: <br>
<Form Action="<%=Request.ServerVariables("SCRIPT_NAME") %>" Method="Post">
Value 1: <input type="text" name="value1" size="20"><br>
Value 2: <input type="text" name="value2" size="20"><br><br>
<input type="submit" name="submit" value="Submit Form">
</form>
</body>
</html>
<% End If %>
```

NOTE

The script ASPExample08 is similar to ASPExample07 except that two numerical values are added. This simply changes the line Ans = X & " " & Y to Ans = X + Y

ADO – ActiveX Data Objects

Introduction

ActiveX Data Objects (ADO) provide access to information stored in a database (or in another tabular data structure) that complies with the Open Database Connectivity (ODBC) standard.

ADO embodies Microsoft's Universal Data Access Model, the goal of which is to provide language-independent access to data, regardless of its location. Microsoft's aim is that all data in an enterprise, from a humble email message in a mailbox to monthly sales and stock inventories in relational DBMSs, can be accessible in a uniform way. ADO represents one aspect of this strategy.

Underlying ADO is a fairly complex object hierarchy that includes the object types described below.

ADO object types

Connection

The Connection object represents a single connection to an underlying data provider. In the context of Web applications the connection object represents one connection from the web server to the database management system.

Command

The Command object allows you to define and manipulate database commands and execute a command string on a Connection object.

Recordset

The Recordset object represents the records returned from a query. The Recordset embodies a concept called a **cursor** which notionally allows traversal of the recordset in various modes. The etymology of 'cursor' is uncertain but Oracle resolves it as 'CURrent Set Of Records' which seems plausible.

ADO supports the following cursor types:

- **Dynamic cursor** – Allows you to see additions, changes, and deletions by other users and all types of movement through the recordset are allowed.

- **Keyset cursor** – Like a dynamic cursor, except that you cannot see additions by other users, and it prevents access to records that other users have deleted. Data changes by other users will still be visible.

- **Static cursor** – Provides a static copy of a recordset for you to use to find data or generate reports. Additions, changes, or deletions by other users will not be visible. This is the only type of cursor allowed when you open a client-side Recordset object.

- **Forward-only cursor** – Similar to Static but only allows forward scrolling through the Recordset. Additions, changes, or deletions by other users will not be visible. This mode improves performance in situations where you only need to make a single pass through a recordset and is the default.

10

Field

A recordset has a Fields collection consisting of a set of Field objects; each of these represents one column of one row of data.

Streams

The Stream object allows you persistently to store a set of records or data in memory. By setting the Destination property of a recordset to a valid stream object, all the data in the recordset can be stored and subsequently manipulated, copied, and saved to file.

With ADO we can, for example, connect to a Microsoft Access or Oracle database to query or update its contents using SQL.

Sample scripts using ADO

These scripts use an Access database called **Asset.mdb** which is available from the text website. The database has two tables, Asset and Branch, that constitute a company's fixed assets application. The tables have the following format:

Asset: **AssetId**, *BranchCode*, Description, Office, Cost, PurchaseDate

Branch: **BranchCode**, BranchName, BranchArea

where the bold indicates a primary key and the italic a foreign key.

ASPDatabase01.asp

Displays all the rows in the Asset table using an HTML table

```
<%@Language = VBScript%>
<HTML>
<HEAD>

<TITLE>ASPDatabase01 – Asset Table Full Listing </TITLE>

</HEAD>
<BODY>

<%
Set Conn = Server.CreateObject("ADODB.Connection")
Conn.Open "DRIVER={Microsoft Access Driver (*.mdb)}; DBQ=" &_
    Server.MapPath("Assets2003.mdb")
%>
<TABLE BORDER=1><CAPTION><B>ASSETS</B></CAPTION>
<%

    sql="select * from asset"
    Set RS=Conn.Execute(sql)

    RS.MoveFirst
    Do while not RS.eof
%>

<TR VALIGN=TOP>
    <TD><% Response.Write RS("Description")%></TD>
    <TD><% Response.Write RS("Office")%></TD>
    <TD><% Response.Write RS("Cost")%></TD>
</TR>
<%
    RS.Movenext
    loop
%>

<BR>
</BODY>
</HTML>
```

The script is fairly basic and does the following:

1 Creates an instance of an ADODB connection and assigns it to the variable Conn. This is again done by using the CreateObject method of the Server object, as follows:

```
Set Conn = Server.CreateObject("ADODB.Connection")
```

2 Specifies the ODBC data source (the database from which you want data) by opening a connection to the database. For example:

```
Set MyConn = Server.CreateObject("ADODB.Connection")
MyConn.Open "DRIVER={Microsoft Access Driver (*.mdb)}; DBQ=" & _
    Server.MapPath("Asset.mdb")
```

Note that this is using OLEDB and is called a 'DSN-less' connection, used when using a remote web server (such as an Internet service provider) where one has no administration access to the server. Another approach is to set up a DSN (Data Source Name) on the web server; this is an ODBC-based connection that requires admin access to the web server. Then we can refer to the DSN to establish connection to our database.

```
MyConn.Open "SomeDataSource"
e.g. MyConn.Open "DSN=MyDatabase"
```

Setting up a DSN is done using **Settings > Control Panel > Administrative Tools > Data Sources.**

3 Uses the Database Access component's Execute method to issue a SQL command on the database and store the returned records in a result set (RSCustomerList):

```
sql = "select * from asset"
Set RS = Conn.Execute(sql)
```

4 Displays the rows returned by the query by performing a loop through the rows of the result set. The first line positions the cursor at the start of the result set:

```
RS.MoveFirst
Do while not RS.eof
%>
    <TR VALIGN = TOP>
    <TD><% Response.Write RS("Description")%></TD>
    <TD><% Response.Write RS("Office")%></TD>
    <TD><% Response.Write RS("Cost")%></TD>
    </TR>
<%
    RS.Movenext
    Loop
%>
```

The Do . . . Loop statement in the above code extract repeats a block of statements while a condition is true. The repeated statements can be script commands or HTML text and

10

tags. Thus, each time through the loop, you construct a table row (using HTML) and insert returned data (using script commands). To complete the loop, use the MoveNext method is used to move the row pointer (cursor) for the result set down one row:

```
<%
    RS.Movenext
    Loop
%>
```

Because this statement still falls within the Do . . . Loop statement, it is repeated until the end of the file is reached.

The output from this code is shown below:

ASSETS		
Desk & Chair	Accounts	410
Computer	Accounts	1 350
Filing Cabinet	Sales	450
Fax	Accounts	160
Printer	Sales	310
Scanner	Accounts	255
Computer	Technical	1 230
Desk	Sales	450
Table	Sales	35
Desk & Chair	Technical	370
Computer	Technical	1 800
Printer	Accounts	210
Table	Sales	45
Filing Cabinet	Accounts	75
Fax	Sales	60
Shelving	Sales	70
Desk & Chair	Technical	525
Printer	Sales	300
Computer	Sales	999
Table	Technical	45
Scanner	Sales	245
Desk & Chair	Sales	599
Computer	Technical	1 345
Printer	Technical	180

ASPDatabase02 and 02A.asp

Selective listing of Assets table

ASPDatabase02.asp accepts an asset id value and invokes **ASPdatabase02A**, which displays the corresponding Asset table row.

```
<HTML>
<HEAD>
<TITLE>ASPDatabase02.asp – Enter asset id and display details in ASPDatabase02A</TITLE>
<HEAD>
<BODY>

<FORM METHOD=POST ACTION = "ASPDatabase02A.asp">

Asset Id :<INPUT TYPE = "text" SIZE = "10" NAME = "Assetid"><BR>

<INPUT TYPE = "submit" VALUE = "Run"><BR>

</FORM>
</BODY>
</HTML>
```

Selective listing

```
<HTML>
<HEAD>
<TITLE>ASPDatabase02A.asp – show one record from Asset table </TITLE>
<HEAD>
<BODY>
<%
Set Conn = Server.CreateObject("ADODB.Connection")
Conn.Open "DRIVER={Microsoft Access Driver (*.mdb)}; DBQ=" & _
   Server.MapPath("Assets.mdb")

Dim RS, SqlStr, AssId
AssId = Request.Form("AssetId")

SqlStr = "Select * from Asset where assetid = " & Assid
Set RS = Conn.Execute(SqlStr)

RS.Movefirst

%>
<TABLE BORDER=1><CAPTION><B>ASSETS</B></CAPTION>
<TR VALIGN=TOP>
   <TD><% Response.Write RS("AssetId")%></TD>
   <TD><% Response.Write RS("Description")%></TD>
   <TD><% Response.Write RS("Office")%></TD>
   <TD><% Response.Write RS("BranchCode")%></TD>
   <TD><% Response.Write RS("Cost")%></TD>
   <TD><% Response.Write RS("PurchaseDate")%></TD>
   </TR>
</BODY>
</HTML>
```

10

ASPDatabase03 and 03A.asp

Update selected asset description

```
HTML>
<HEAD>
<TITLE>ASPDatabase03 - supply AssetId and New description for db update </TITLE>
</HEAD>

<BODY>
<FORM METHOD="POST" ACTION="ASPDatabase03A.asp">
Enter amendment to description<P>
<P>
AssetId <INPUT TYPE="Text" NAME="ASSETID"><P>
Description <INPUT TYPE="Text" NAME="Description"><P>
<INPUT TYPE="SUBMIT" VALUE="Run Query">
</FORM>

</BODY>
</HTML>
```

Update selected asset description

```
<HTML>
<HEAD>
<TITLE>ASPDatabase03A.asp - update description of selected asset</TITLE>

</HEAD>

<BODY>
<%
Set MyConn = Server.CreateObject("ADODB.Connection")
MyConn.Open "DRIVER={Microsoft Access Driver (*.mdb)};DBQ="& _
Server.MapPath("Assets.mdb")

Dim Assid, SqlStr, RS

Assid = CINT(Request.Form("AssetId") ) - - - - - - - - - - - -(1)
SQL = "Update Asset SET Description = "
SQL = SQL & "' " & Request.Form("description") & "' " - - - - (2)
SQL = SQL & " where AssetId = " & Assid & ";" - - - - - - - -(3)

MyConn.Execute SQL

SqlStr = "Select * from Asset where assetid = " & Assid
Set RS = MyConn.Execute(SqlStr)

if RS.EOF and RS.BOF then
   Response.Write("Record not found")
else
   RS.Movefirst

%>
```

```
<TABLE BORDER = 1><CAPTION><B>Revised value of Asset Record</B></CAPTION>
<TR VALIGN = TOP>

  <TD><% Response.Write RS("AssetId")%></TD>
  <TD><% Response.Write RS("Description")%></TD>
  <TD><% Response.Write RS("Office")%></TD>
  <TD><% Response.Write RS("BranchCode")%></TD>
  <TD><% Response.Write RS("Cost")%></TD>
  <TD><% Response.Write RS("PurchaseDate")%></TD>
<%end if%>

</TR>
</BODY>
</HTML>
```

1 The CINT function converts the form item AssetId to an integer value. All data delivered from a form is of type character. Since the AssetId in the Assets table is defined as a number it is advisable to convert the form value.

2 Note the use of the two different 'quote' values. The SQL interpreter expects to see apostrophes around constant text values as, for instance, in the expression:

```
... SET Description = 'Computer'.
```

Therefore apostrophes have to be placed round the Request.Form("description") item by enclosing them in double quotes.

3 In this line, the AssetId value is numerical and hence is not enclosed in apostrophes.

10

ASPDatabase04 and 04A.asp

Insert a new row into Assets table

```
<HTML>
<HEAD>
<TITLE>ASPDatabase04.asp - Input asset data to be added</TITLE>
</HEAD>

<BODY>
<FORM METHOD = "POST" ACTION = "ASPDatabase04A.asp">Input a new Asset:<P>
<P>
AssetId <INPUT TYPE = "Text" NAME = "ASSETID"><P>
Description <INPUT TYPE = "Text" NAME = "Description"><P>
Branch<INPUT TYPE = "Text" NAME = "BranchCode"><P>
<INPUT TYPE = "SUBMIT" VALUE = "Run Query">
</FORM>
</BODY>
</HTML>
```

Insert a new row into Assets table

```
<html>
<head>
<title>ASPDatabase04A – Add row to Asset table </title>
</head>

<body>
<%
   Set MyConn = Server.CreateObject("ADODB.Connection")
      MyConn.Open "DRIVER = {Microsoft Access Driver (*.mdb)}; DBQ = " & _
         Server.MapPath("Assets.mdb")

SQL = "INSERT INTO Asset (AssetId, Description, BranchCode) Values "
SQL = SQL & "(' "
SQL = SQL & Request.Form("AssetId") & "','' "
SQL = SQL & Request.Form("description") & "','' "
SQL = SQL & Request.Form("BranchCode") & "'); "

MyConn.Execute SQL

%>
<H1>Row added </H1>
</body>
</html>
```

ASPDatabase05.asp

Joining tables and generating grouped report

```
<HTML>
<HEAD>
<TITLE>ASPDatabase05.asp – Compute cost totals grouped by Branch </TITLE>
</HEAD>
<BODY>
<%
   Set Conn = Server.CreateObject("ADODB.Connection")
   Conn.Open "DRIVER = {Microsoft Access Driver (*.mdb)}; DBQ = " &_
      Server.MapPath("Assets.mdb")
%>
<TABLE BORDER = 1><CAPTION><B>ASSETS</B></CAPTION>
<%
   sql = "SELECT branchname, sum(cost) as sumcost "
   sql = sql +"FROM Branch INNER JOIN Asset ON Branch.BranchCode = Asset.BranchCode"
   sql = sql +" GROUP BY branchname"

   Set RS = Conn.Execute(sql)
%>
```

```
<TR VALIGN = TOP>
  <TD><% Response.Write "BRANCH"%></TD>
  <TD><% Response.Write "Total Cost"%></TD>
</TR>
<%
  RS.MoveFirst
  Do while not RS.eof
%>
<TR VALIGN = TOP>
  <TD><% Response.Write RS(0)%></TD>
  <TD><% Response.Write RS(1)%></TD>

</TR>
<%
  RS.Movenext
  loop
%>

<HR>
</BODY>
</HTML>
```

The development of ASP.Net

10

Background

ASP.NET is Microsoft's current technology for web interaction. The name indicates two of its main aspects: first, that it is derived from ASP and secondly that it operates within Microsoft's .NET framework. Although it has ASP in its ancestry, ASP.NET is radically different in many respects. The main innovations are described below:

- **Simpler programming model.** ASP and other web scripting systems involve interspersing program script code (e.g. VBScript lines) within HTML coding. This makes reading and interpretation of the coding difficult and error-prone. ASP.NET separates these by using functions based on 'server controls'. The code is class based and event-driven, making web page design more like conventional programming.

- **.NET hosted and compiled execution.** ASP.NET is part of the .NET framework and hence utilises the Common Language Runtime system. This means that any CLR-compatible language can be used in the script coding. The CLR version of Visual Basic, VB.NET, is the most commonly used language. Also, the page script coding will be compiled, leading to faster execution.

- **Automatic session state handling.** Form data is automatically maintained between successive pages, greatly simplifying management of session state.

- **Rich class library.** A wide range of useful application features can be invoked from a class based library framework, covering XML, login, email, etc.

- **Easy migration.** While ASP.NET is not upwardly compatible with ASP (i.e. ASP coding is not generally acceptable ASP.NET coding) they are compatible in that both can be used on the same website. Pages with an .asp extension are treated as traditional ASP while pages with .aspx extensions are processed with the ASP.NET engine. Hence, a website could be progressively converted to ASP.NET while retaining some of the old coding.

Main features in page design

In this section we review the main features of ASP.NET coding innovations, including the various forms of server controls and session maintenance.

Server controls

In MS-speak, the word 'controls' refers to graphical objects with some underlying functionality that are used in forms for user interaction. Common controls are text boxes, buttons, lists, check boxes and radio buttons, but the term also covers more elaborate objects such as calendars, clocks, various slider controls and, most notably, facilities for database connection and data display.

The main problem with conventional ASP coding is the close integration of HTML and ASP code, which makes it difficult to read and maintain. Distinguishing the ASP code from the HTML requires close attention to the position of the ASP <% .. %> brackets. ASP.NET overcomes this problem with 'server controls', as we describe in the following section.

ASP.NET server controls

There are three main types of server controls:

- **HTML server controls:** effectively a substitute for traditional HTML controls.

- **Web server controls:** a new set of controls, some of which also substitute for HTML.

- **Validation server controls:** controls that are used to validate form content.

HTML server controls

These look like traditional HTML controls but use a special attribute of `runat = "server"`. This causes the control to be processes at the server by the ASP.NET engine rather than simply being passed to the browser for execution. The syntax also differs from traditional HTML, avoiding the need to mix HTML and ASP coding. Required executable code is provided by an event-driven subroutine. This example requests a name from the user, then displays 'Hello name'.

AspNetExample01.aspx

```
<script runat="server">

Sub submit(Source as Object, e as EventArgs)
    Para.InnerHTML="Hello " & name.value
End Sub
</script>


<html>
<head>
<title>Simple ASP.NET test </title>
</head>


<body>

<form runat="server">
Please enter your name:<input type="text" id="name" runat="server">
<br><br>

<input type="submit" value="Press to submit" OnServerClick="submit"
runat="server">
<p id="Para" runat="server"/>
</form>


</body>
</html>
```

10

The behaviour of this script is quite complex. Notice that although HTML-like tags are used, there is no <% .. %> to delineate ASP code. In fact, the HTML tags such as <form> and <input>, having the runat="server" attribute, are processed by the server and not by the browser. The server sends a much modified script to the browser for initial display. When the form is filled in and submitted (HTML-style) the server again generates more HTML coding to effect the expected output. Note in particular the use of the paragraph tag line:

```
<p id="Para" runat="server">
```

While this looks like a simple HTML tag, the browser will never see it in this form. When the submit button is pressed, the submit subroutine is executed. The InnerHTML function intersperses its parameter value into a (conventional) <p> element for display in the browser. The resultant HTML code (as revealed by the menu **View>Source** facility) is shown below:

```
<html>
<head>
<title>Simple ASP.NET test </title>
</head>
```

```
<body>

<form name="_ctl0" method="post" action="AspNetExample01.aspx" id="_ctl0">
<input type="hidden" name="__VIEWSTATE"
value="dDwtMTAOMDMOODg4NztOPDtsPGk8MT47PjtsPHQ8O2w8aTw1Pjs+O2w8dDxwPGw8aW5u
ZXVodG1sOz47bDxIZWxsbyBSaWNoYXJkOz4+Ozs+Oz4+Oz4+Oz4BQQ4EtOHbcU6zmkg4Q1ZurmzFS
Q==" />

Please enter your name:<input name="name" id="name" type="text"
value="Richard" />
<br><br>

<input name="_ctl1" type="submit" value="Press to submit" />
<p id="Para">Hello Richard</p>
</form>

</body>
</html>
```

1 The <input type = "hidden"> control is used in automatic state maintenance; this is explained later. The value parameter is a very long string and is shown folded over several lines above.

2 These controls each map to a standard HTML control although, as we can see from the above description, the browser never sees these controls before server manipulation.

Web server controls

Some web server controls also effectively replace certain of the HTML tags, but others provide completely new functionality. The controls are identified by tags of the form:

```
<asp:control_name id = "thisid" runat = "server" />
```

An example is shown below – **ASPNetExample02.aspx**:

```
<html>
<script language = "VB" runat = "server">
Sub EnterBtn_Click(Sender As Object, E As EventArgs)
   Message.Text = "<br><br><br>Hello " & Name.Text & ", welcome to our website"
End Sub

</script>
<body>

   <h3>Example of button Onclick Event Handling (aspNetExample02.aspx)</h3>

      <form action="AspNetExaample02.aspx" runat=server>

      Please enter your name:

         <asp:text box id="Name" runat=server/>
         <asp:button text="Enter" Onclick="EnterBtn_Click" runat=server/>
         <asp:label id="Message" runat=server/>

      </form></body></html>
```

Validation controls

These controls are a useful innovation in the area of web database techniques. They permit declarative validation of the content of form textboxes. An example is shown below:

```
<html>
<body>

<form runat="server">
Enter a date between 2005–01–01 and 2005–12–31:
<br />
<asp:Text Box id="tbox1" runat="server" />
<br /><br />
<asp:Button Text="Submit" runat="server" />
<br /><br />
<asp:RangeValidator
ControlToValidate="tbox1"
MinimumValue="2005–01–01"
MaximumValue="2005–12–31"
Type="Date"
EnableClientScript="false"
    Text="The date must be between 2005–01–01 and 2005–12–31!"
    runat="server" />
</form>

</body>
</html>
```

This is an example of a RangeValidator; the various validators are shown in the table below.

Validation server control	Description
CompareValidator	Compares the value of one input control to the value of another control or to a fixed value
CustomValidator	General technique that allows you to write a method that implements the validation of the value entered
RangeValidator	The value entered is checked to ensure that it lies between two specified values.
RegularExpressionValidator	The value entered is checked against a pattern defined by a regular expression
RequiredFieldValidator	Specifies that the input control is a required field

Using this system, the validation is performed on the server. It is, of course, an option to perform such validation using JavaScript on the client-system although this would involve procedural coding, which is arguably more time consuming and error-prone.

10

Database access in ASP.NET

To complete the .NET conversion, there is a new version of ADO called, as you might guess, ADO.NET. In introducing ADO.NET as part of its overall strategy of bringing its component technologies into the .NET fold, Microsoft took the opportunity to effect a major redesign of ADO. ADO.NET performs similar tasks to ADO in enabling communication between ASP and data stores such as databases. However, the two systems differ in terms of the underlying data model, the facilities provided and the efficiency of execution. Some of the distinguishing features of ADO.NET are highlighted below:

1 The recordset concept is replaced by the DataSet; the main difference is that the latter can represent multiple tables (each represented by a DataTable object) from a database.

2 It provides a DataRelation object to model relationships between DataTables, avoiding the need for explicit join queries.

3 It provides a navigation facility which can use a relationship to navigate from one table to related records in another.

4 It uses a disconnected communication paradigm; the source tables accessed by the DataSet are only locked during record transfer, thereby reducing the loading on the database.

5 DataSets are represented internally as XML. This eases problems related to data typing as the data is self-describing. It also means that native XML data can be managed with the same techniques as relational data.

6 A Data Provider is a collection of classes designed to facilitate communication with a particular type of data store; ADO.NET comes with Data Providers to directly access Microsoft SQL Server, OLEDB compliant sources such as Microsoft Access, ODBC sources and Oracle databases.

We will consider some of the features of ADO.NET using the following categories:

1 Connections: how a connection is made to the data store and how the data is referenced.

2 Data representation: how the data is represented internally.

3 Data access: how the data can be read and updated.

Connections

ADO.NET contains a set of classes to enable interaction with specific DBMSs.

Each set of classes is identified by a *namespace* which organises the classes into a hierarchy to prevent name conflicts. Available namespaces are shown below:

Namespaces	
System.Data.SqlClient	SQL Server v. 7.0
System.Data.OleDb	OLEDB connections, e.g. MS Access
System.Data.ODBC	ODBC connections
System.Data.OracleClient	Oracle

To use a connection class, the namespace must be imported into the program by including an Import command at the start of the script:

```
<%@ Import NameSpace = "System.Data.SqlClient" %>
```

Data representation

The DataSet object is central to supporting disconnected, distributed data scenarios using ADO.NET and replaces the ADO recordset. It is not necessary to use a dataset if you are only using forward-only read-only access. This object is actually a memory resident representation of data that provides a consistent relational programming model regardless of the data source. The DataSet object represents a complete set of data including the related tables, constraints and relationships. Figure 10.5 shows the DataSet object model.

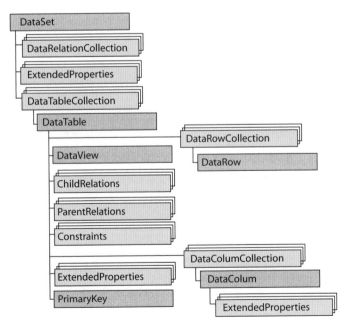

FIGURE 10.5 DataSet object

The DataSet object is a container for a number of DataTable objects which are stored in the DataSet's tables collection. The main advantage of this arrangement is that the whole system of interrelated tables can be retrieved in one access to the database. The data stored in the DataSet object is disconnected from the database. Any changes that are made are cached in a DataRow object. When it is necessary to save the changes, the DataSet provides a GetChanges method that can be used to extract only the modified rows from a DataSet. This reduces network traffic, as only the changed data is transferred to the database.

Data access

The ASP concept of the recordset cursor is replaced by DataReaders, specifically, SQLDataReader, OLEDBDataReader etc. These are forward-only, read-only readers. For more elaborate access, a DataSet must be defined. The objects of the DataSet can be scanned programmatically. The following sample program reads an Asset table in a Microsoft Access database and displays each AssetId on successive lines.

Sample program – ASPNetExample03.aspx

```
<%@ Import NameSpace = "System.Data.OleDb" %>
<html>
   <head>
   <title>ASPDatabase03.aspx </title>
   </head>
<script language="VB" runat="server">

Sub Page_Load(s as Object, E as EventArgs)

   Dim AssetDb as OledbConnection
   Assetdb = New
OledbConnection("Provider = Microsoft.Jet.OLEDB.4.0;DataSource=assets2003.mdb")

   AssetDb.Open()

   Dim cmdSelectAssets as OLEDBCommand
   cmdSelectAssets = New OLEDBCommand("Select AssetId from Asset",Assetdb)
   Dim dtrAssets as OLEDBDataReader
   dtrAssets = cmdSelectAssets.executeReader()

   While dtrAssets.Read()
      Response.Write(CStr(dtrAssets.Item("AssetId") ))
      Response.Write ("<br>")

   End While
End Sub


</script>
<body>

</body>
</html>
```

Maintaining state in web applications

Introduction

Web applications use the HTTP protocol to implement the communication between the browser and the web server. HTTP is inherently 'stateless'; i.e. each request from the browser to the server is treated as independent. This is really unavoidable given the environment in which the web operates. The alternative would be fixed sessions in which a semi-permanent connection is established between the two ends during the user's interaction with the website. This would place an enormous burden on the server in terms of keeping track of online users, most of whom in any case are only viewing pages. Also, the server would have the task of uniquely identifying connected users using for example their IP address, which could be quite complex.

For applications that require maintenance of state, such as those accessing databases and/or maintaining some activity such as a shopping basket, other techniques must be used. These notes discuss some of these methods.

ASP sessions

Microsoft's ASP technology provides the concept of a session object. This is intended as a means of creating the illusion of a continuous session of communication between the client and the server. When the client first makes contact with the web page, a session object is created containing a unique identifying session ID and any other values the application wishes to store about the client. This can be used to preserve continuity between successive accesses to the site if the session ID of the client can be established. Unfortunately, due to the way HTTP works, variables such as a session ID are lost after completion of page processing. ASP's way of retrieving the ID is the use of cookies, explained below. The session object can be used to store any data that is required by the application and preserve it between successive page accesses, provided the session ID can be retrieved (by a cookie or other method). However, it requires an amount of memory-based data to be held for each active session, and this has serious scalability problems.

10

Cookies

The most common method used for state maintenance and probably the best is 'cookies'. A cookie (the origin of the name is unknown) is a small data item that is stored on the client's disk. When a web page is visited by the client browser, the server may return an HTTP message containing the cookie, which identifies the sending website address and other data. If the browser is 'cookie-enabled' it will store the cookie in a disk directory reserved for this purpose. On later visits to that web address the browser checks its cookies and will return any cookies originating from that address. The server can read the cookies and recover data that was abandoned after the previous contact.

One main task that is implemented using a cookie is to maintain a 'session'; the ASP session object depends on the preservation of a session ID and ASP attempts to implement this by sending a session cookie.

The main problem with the cookie method is that some users do not enable cookies on their machine, thereby preventing the system from functioning altogether. Cookies have in the past received a fair amount of ill-informed criticism, with the result that many people believed that cookies somehow compromised the security or privacy of their computer. The reality is that the storage and retrieval of cookies on a computer is under the control of the browser and the remote website has no influence other than to send cookies and to read cookies that are returned.

Cookies can be managed in ASP (at the server) using the Response (sending to client) and Request (reading from client) objects, which hold cookie collections. For example,

```
Response("MyCookie") = "Chocolate"
myvar = Request("MyCookie")
```

You can also interpolate Request calls within HTML code:

```
<font = "<%=Request("MyFont")%>"
```

URL-encoded variables

Web pages often contain HREF entries that link to other pages the user might want to visit. Within the server code of such pages it is possible to append name-value pairs to the target URL. These can carry identification and other data to the next page, which can be used to continue the session. The URL would look something like:

```
http://www.mysite.co.uk?id=1234&name=smith&company=acme
```

Unfortunately, the data in the URL will be visible to the user and hence there is a security issue with this technique. However, it is quite usable in situations where the security aspects are not important. Another disadvantage is that the URL can become long and cumbersome and requires interpretation by the server. Web page script languages generally have some method of reading the appended data; ASP, for instance, manages this quite well by means of the QueryString collection of the Response object.

Hidden form variables

In a web session that uses forms, it is possible for the server to send a form page to the client that contains form elements (such as a text box or label) that are not visible to the client and which contain identification information such as a session ID. When the user completes and returns the form, the hidden data (unchanged) is returned to the server, enabling continuation of the session. It is best to use this with the POST method of form transmission; using GET the 'hidden' data will appear appended to the URL, similar to the URL-encoded method described above. The hidden data is incorporated into the form as an <INPUT> item such as:

```
<input type=hidden name=userID value="12345">
```

It is possible, at the client computer, to modify the hidden data before it is returned. This is achieved by saving the web page, editing the HTML and sending it back. There are, therefore, potential security risks in this technique. However, it is quite usable in many applications where security is not of the essence.

One limitation of the two preceding methods is that they only retrieve data from the previous page; if data has to be preserved over multiple pages it all has to be passed from page to page.

Database storage

To get round the scalability problem related to the use of the session object, it is possible instead to use a database to save user session data. Again, this will depend on the retrieval of the session ID to use as an access key for the database. This would avoid the potentially excessive use of server memory, but has performance and maintenance implications; in order to continue a session, a database access is required. The data held on disk will need to be purged consistently to remove 'dead' session information.

Using cookies

Cookies are small items of information sent from the server and stored by the browser on the client machine. If the same web address is later accessed by the browser, the cookie is sent along with the HTTP request from the browser to the server. Only the server that sent the cookie will ever receive it.

Cookies come in two flavours: **session** and **permanent**. Session cookies persist only as long as the session. Permanent cookies persist until a specified expiry date.

A cookie is created by the server and sent to the client. Since this involves server to client data transfer, the natural medium is the Response object; the code below illustrates how a cookie is assigned a value and sent to the client:

```
<%
Response.Cookies("myCookie") = "Chocolate"
%>
```

The brackets are to remind you that this code is issued within an ASP block. They are omitted in the following notes.

'Cookies' is a collection referenced by the Response (and the Request) object. This syntax will either create a new cookie with the value shown or will re-assign a value to an existing cookie.

In this form the cookie is a session cookie since, no expiry date is given. To make it permanent, issue a command as illustrated below:

```
Response.Cookies("myCookie").Expires = #31-Dec-07#
```

or use a relative date (example gives the expiry date as one month from today):

```
Response.Cookies("myCookie").Expires = DateAdd("m",1,Now() )
```

10

It is possible to assign multiple values within one cookie in the form of key-value pairs – sometimes referred to as a 'dictionary'.

```
Response.Cookies("User1")("Joined") = #25-Feb-07#
Response.Cookies("User1")("NumVisits") = 0
```

To retrieve and show a cookie value within a script, use the notation:

```
<% = Request.Cookies("User1")("Joined") %>
```

The <% = notation is equivalent to <% Response.Write.

To determine whether a cookie has keys, use the Haskeys method:

```
Request.Cookie("User1").Haskeys returns True or False
```

PHP

Introduction

The first version of PHP was developed from 1994 onwards by Danish software developer Rasmus Lerdorf and 'PHP' originally stood for 'Personal Home Page'; the accepted interpretation is now the recursive 'PHP Hypertext Processor'. To a first approximation, PHP is similar to other web techniques such as ASP and JSP, in that it uses special embedded scripting within an HTML template. However, PHP has its own characteristics and peculiarities, which are described in this section.

Availability

Since PHP arose within the world of public domain and open source programming, it is no surprise that Apache is the most common choice for hosting of PHP-based pages. Also, in the spirit of the open source movement, MySQL is a popular database used in conjunction with PHP. Nevertheless, it is possible to use PHP with IIS, PWS and other servers. Note however that while it can be compiled as a module within Apache, for the other servers PHP runs as a free-standing interpreter. This will unavoidably be slower than the compiled Apache version. This is further exacerbated by the fact that the interpreter is invoked as a CGI process and hence will incur overheads related to process creation and management within the server.

General principles

PHP pages are written in a similar fashion to ASP; i.e. an HTML template is used into which PHP coding is embedded, enclosed between pairs of opening and closing tags. There are a number of tag conventions, which are described later. In contrast to ASP and JSP, which respectively use the general purpose languages VBScript (usually) and

Java as the coding language, PHP has its own language, specifically designed for this purpose. The PHP language syntax borrows strongly from C and Perl but it also supports classes. As with ASP, displayed output from the PHP code becomes incorporated into the HTML framework and the resultant combined text is sent to the client. The following sections provide an overview of the main features of PHP coding.

PHP coding

This section covers:

- Tag conventions
- Definition of variables
- Getting information from the user
- Outputting information
- General processing
- Database connectivity

Tags

PHP supports four tags, illustrated below. (Note: the echo command displays values following)

- `<?php echo("the conventional style"); ?>`

- `<? echo ("shortened version"); ?>`
  `<?= expression ?>`This is a shortcut for `"<? echo expression ?>"`

- `<script language = "php">`
  `    echo ("Least likely to offend web page editors");`
  `</script>`

- `<% echo ("Optional ASP-style tags"); %>`
  `<%= $variable; # This is a shortcut for "<% echo ..." %>`

Of the four tags described above, only two,

- `(<?php ... ?>` and
- `<script language = "php"> ... </script>)`

are always available; the others can be turned on or off from the `php.ini` configuration file.

While the short-form tags and ASP-style tags may be convenient, they are not as portable as the longer versions. Also, if you intend to embed PHP code in XML or XHTML, you will need to use the `<?php ... ?>` form to conform to XML conventions.

PHP language

PHP embodies its own language. In this section we briefly review some features of the language to indicate its nature. Many aspects of the language are borrowed from C/C++and hence will appear familiar.

Datatypes

PHP has integer, double and string datatypes and composites arrays and objects. The language is weakly typed, i.e. you do not need to declare variables – they are automatically declared when a value is assigned to them, their type is determined from the context and can change at run-time. It is also possible to find out and modify the type of a variable at run-time.

Variables

All variable must be preceded by a '$' symbol; otherwise they are composed much the same as in other languages.

Operations

The language contains the usual procedural coding facilities, essentially following C syntax. The available statements are:

```
if
switch . . . case
while
do . . . while
for
```

Arrays

PHP provides a range of interesting features for creating and accessing arrays. As well as the conventional style of arrays based on an integer index, PHP also provides a mechanism called an associative array.

Conventional arrays are created dynamically and have dynamic bounds, e.g.:

```
$country[0] = 'UK';
$country[1] = 'France';
$country[2] = 'Spain';
$country[3] = 'Portugal';
$country[4] = 'Italy';
```

Another way to create an array is to use the array() function:

```
$country = array('UK','France','Spain','Portugal','Italy');
```

is equivalent to the previous lines.

Array elements can be accessed by an index value, e.g.

```
$home = $country[1];
```

An array can also be scanned using a for loop:

```
for (i = 0; i< = count($country) ; i++)
    echo $country[i] . "<br>";
```

Associative arrays

In an associative array, keys are associated with the values. Values are retrieved using the key rather than a numerical index. This is sometimes also known as 'content addressing'. For instance, we could store capital cities associated with the country name:

```
$capital['UK'] = 'London';
$capital['France'] = 'Paris';
$capital['Spain'] = 'Madrid';
```

or by using the array() function:

```
$capital = array('UK' =>'London', 'France' =>'Paris', 'Spain' =>'Madrid');
```

However, it is now not possible to iterate through the array using an indexed for loop. PHP provides a foreach loop for this purpose:

```
foreach($capital as $country =>$city)

{
echo "Capital of $country is $city" ;
echo "<br>";
}
```

which would produce:

```
Capital of UK is London
Capital of France is Paris
Capital of Spain is Madrid
```

10

Functions

Functions are defined using the basic structure indicated in the following example.

```
function cube($val)
{ return $val * $val * $val; }
```

A call to this function might be cube(5);

By default, parameters are passed by value but it is possible to pass by reference, as in C++ and Java. A reference parameter is specified by prefixing it with '&' as in C++.

Classes

Classes can be defined and objects instantiated in PHP. Again, the format is similar to C++ or Java. Normally in PHP variables do not need to be declared, but within a class definition the nature of the class attributes has to be specified explicitly. For this purpose, the var keyword is used, although no type information is required.

```
    class Student
    {
      // define the attributes
      var $name;
      var $matricno;
      var $courseno;
// define the methods
    function getname()
    {
      return this ->$name;
    }
    function setname($n)
    {
        this->$name = $n;
    }
        etc.
} // end of class
```

User communication

GET and POST support

Information received via HTTP requests can be 'picked up' very easily using PHP. Variables supplied either by a POST (HTTP header values) or GET (query string values) are available within built-in PHP arrays $_POST and $_GET. These are associative arrays that are indexed simply by using the form control names. This is illustrated in the following scripts; the first presents a form to the user and invokes the second. The second script displays the value posted from the form.

PHPExample01.php

```
<html>
<form action="PHPExample01A.php" method=post>
   Please enter your name: <br>
   <input type=text name="username"><br>
   <input type=submit value="submit">
</form>
</html>
```

PHPExample01A.php

```
<html>
<?php
   echo "Welcome, " . $_POST['username'];
?>
</html>
```

NOTE

'Echo' is used to display values. The dot is the string concatenation operator.

Sessions and cookies

Since Version 4.0 PHP has supported cookies in a similar fashion to ASP. A session identifier is used to reference a client transactions over multiple page accesses. A function `session_start()` is executed at the start of a script which generates a unique session identifier and an associative array $_SESSION which can be used to store session variables. This provides similar facilities to the ASP session object. The session identifier is restored on each page access (by calling `session_start`), either by using a cookie or some other state maintenance technique such as URL encoding. The following scripts illustrate session variable handling.

PHPExample02.php

```php
<?php
session_start();

$_SESSION['user'] = 'Colin';
$_SESSION['password'] = 'sesame';
?>
```

PHPExample03.php

```php
<?php
session_start();

echo $_SESSION['user'];
echo $_SESSION['password'];
?>
```

10

NOTE

It is important to note that the `session_start()` call must be issued before any HTML coding.

Using cookies

PHP provides the function `setcookie()` to write a cookie to the client machine. The function has six parameters: cookie name, value, its expiry date, its path and domain and a Boolean flag used to indicate security status. Only the first argument is mandatory.

Example:

```php
<?php
// write a cookie called 'username' with value 'fred'
// with an expiry time of 1 hour
setcoookie('username', 'fred', mktime()+3600);
?>
```

The `mktime` function returns the current date and time.

To retrieve a cookie value that is already stored, the associative array $_COOKIE is used. Based on the preceding code, that cookie could be referenced by $_COOKIE['username'] which would equal the value 'fred'.

Database connectivity

PHP differs from other similar systems in that it does not (generally) use a system of drivers or intermediate interface to separate the application code from the database interface. For instance, ASP uses ADO and OLEDB and JSP uses JDBC. Instead, PHP has a separate set of interface functions for each database. For instance, to communicate with MySQL, the functions mysql_connect, mysql_select_db, mysql_query etc. are available. To 'talk' to an Oracle database, another set of similar functions exist. The only exception to this is that a set of interface functions exist for ODBC and hence can be used to access any ODBC compliant database. This does incur an overhead however.

This system appears to fly in the face of the principle of program independence adopted by other systems, since different coding is required for each database. However, it does have these advantages:

- No intermediate software layer exists and hence performance should be better.

- Since the functions are prepared specially for each database, they can exploit the specific features of the database. For a proprietary system, having many different function sets would be a major inconvenience, but PHP is developed and maintained by many independent users so the various versions are not so problematic.

- For situations in which only one database type is in use, the lack of flexibility is not an issue. For instance, many PHP installations use MySQL. The other systems might be more convenient in situations where multiple databases were in use within a single enterprise or where conversion to another database might be required.

- Conversion of coding from one database to another is not too onerous; the program structure is likely to be unchanged and many functions will simply require a one-to-one conversion.

Other features

PHP has benefited greatly from its open source, public domain status and has been extended considerably in a number of areas. Of particular note are its XML capabilities. PHP has built-in support for various processing tasks based on XML-constructed websites. For instance:

- It can perform smart searches through XML code, searching for specific tags and returning required associated information.

- It can convert an XML document into equivalent HTML for use where the browser is not XML-enabled.

■ It can present different views of the same XML data at varying levels of detail by enabling or disabling nodes within the structure.

Example of simple form handling

PHPExample04.php

```
<html>
<head>
<title>
PHPExample04.php – Inputs two text values and concatenates them
</title>
</head>
<body>

<?php
if (!isset($_POST['submit'])) .... .... Note 1.
{

?>
Please enter text values in the boxes: <br>
<Form Action="<?=$_SERVER['PHP_SELF']?>" Method="Post">
VAL1: <input type="text" name="value1" size="20"><br>
VAL2: <input type="text" name="value2" size="20"><br><br>
<input type="submit" name="submit" value="Submit Form">

</form>
<?php
}
else
{
    $X = $_POST['value1']; ... ..... Note 2.
    $Y = $_POST['value2'];
    $Ans = $X . " " . $Y;
    echo "X: " . $X ."<br>";
    echo "Y: " . $Y ."<br>";
    echo "Ans: " . $Ans ."<br>";
}
?>
</body>
</html>
```

1 This form uses the 'self re-entrant' method also used in .ASP. The $_POST array contains the values posted from the form. The isset function checks to see whether an item in the array has any value; a false result means that the form has not been actioned yet.

2 Note use of $_POST array to obtain form values.

10

Example of database access in PHP

PHPReadTab1.php

```
<html xmlns = "http://www.w3.org/1999/xhtml" xml:lang = "en">
<head>

<title>Test PHP</title>

<body>

<?php
   $host = "localhost";
   $username = "root";
   $password = "leonard";
   $database = "assets";

$connection = mysql_connect($host, $username, $password) or
die(mysql_error());
mysql_select_db('assets') or die('Unable to select database db1');

$query = 'SELECT * FROM asset';

$result = mysql_query($query);

$noofrecs = mysql_num_rows($result);

echo 'No of records = ';

echo $noofrecs;

echo '<table width=90% cellpadding=5 cellspacing=0 border=3 >';
echo
'<tr><td><b>Assetid</b></td><td><b>Branchcode</b></td><<td><b>Description
</b></td>';

while ($row = mysql_fetch_row($result))
{
   echo '<tr>';
   echo '<td>' . $row[0] . '</td>';
   echo '<td>' . $row[1] . '</td>';
   echo '<td>' . $row[2] . '</td>';
   echo '</tr>';
}

echo '</table>';

mysql_free_result($result);
mysql_close($connection);

?>

</body>
</html>
```

Java servlets and JSP

Java servlets is a Java technique introduced by Sun to effect an improvement over CGI technology in generating dynamic web pages. It uses Java code that executes on the server; the code generates HTML code dynamically that is sent to the client browser.

Java Server Pages (JSP) is a development from servlets; it uses an HTML framework into which Java code is interspersed, in a similar way to ASP and PHP. Both of these are now an integral part of the J2EE technology that Sun promotes for the design and construction of enterprise-scale software projects. Servlets and JSP are not mutually exclusive; sites can be built using a mixture of both and combined with conventional (server-based) Java code.

We will look at the two technologies in turn, starting with servlets.

Java servlets

Effectively, a servlet is to the server as an applet is to the browser – it extends the capability of the server by supplying functionality in the form of Java code. A servlet is accessed from a browser simply by referencing it using a URL. For instance, an HTML page could include a hyperlink to a servlet file on the server. In order to make use of servlet functionality a web server must be servlet-enabled, i.e. support the execution of servlets. Many servers now support servlets, certainly most of the non-Microsoft offerings. The Microsoft IIS server does not explicitly support servlets, since they compete with ASP, but it can be enhanced using a third party plug-in called Tomcat.

10

Since Java runs in a Java Virtual Machine (JVM), the server incorporates a JVM. In this context, the JVM is called a *servlet engine* or, a more recent term, a *web container*.

When a servlet is invoked by a client HTTP call (from a browser), it begins execution and receives two objects from the server that manage the interface between the server and the client:

- ServletRequest, which encapsulates the communication from the client to the server.

- ServletResponse, which encapsulates the communication from the servlet back to the client.

These are analogous to the Request and Response objects as used in ASP.

ServletRequest interface

The ServerRequest interface allows the servlet access to information sent in the HTTP request from the client and to a stream of data sent by the client from GET and POST methods.

ServletResponse interface

The ServletResponse interface gives the servlet methods for replying to the client. In particular, it is possible to set up HTTP parameters such as MIME type and content length and to send data back to the client.

In contrast to ASP, where response text is interspersed with HTML-generated text, data sent by a servlet must be entirely generated by the ServletResponse writer output. Except for trivial unformatted text this necessitates generation of HTML tags around the text being formed. This is illustrated in the example shown below. When the text is returned to the client, the browser of course interprets the HTML tags and displays the data accordingly.

Java servlets simple example

```java
import java.io.*;
import java.text.*;
import java.util.*;
import javax.servlet.*;
import javax.servlet.http.*;

public class HelloWorldExample extends HttpServlet {

public void doGet(HttpServletRequest request,
                              HttpServletResponse response)
   throws IOException, ServletException
{
   response.setContentType("text/html");

   // Create a servlet output stream
   PrintWriter out = response.getWriter();

   // generate some HTML
   out.println("<html>");
   out.println("<body bgcolor = \"white\">");
   out.println("<head>");
   out.println("<title>" +"Simple HTML " + "</title>");
   out.println("</head>");
   out.println("<body>");

   out.println("<H2>Hello World! </H2>");

   out.println("<H3>");
   out.println("This is some text that is sent back");
   out.println("to the browser and formatted using simple tags");
   out.println("</H3>");

   out.println("</body>");

   out.println("</html>");
   }
   }
```

The servlet code, at minimum, must implement the doGet method (actually it overrides the doGet method from the inherited class HttpServlet) which services a HTTP GET command from the client.

Java server pages

Overview

Java server pages or JSP was introduced to simplify the use of servlets and to provide a Java-based alternative to ASP.

Servlets are very much an advanced programmers tool and are not usable except by programmers with extensive knowledge of Java. JSP actually use servlets but provides a more user-friendly interface that can be used by less specialised developers.

JSP uses the same general idea as ASP, namely incorporation of special coding entries interspersed within a template provided by HTML (or XML). However, JSP uses a more elaborate tag system with different types of tag, described later. Also, the two techniques differ considerably in the actual execution of the pages. In ASP, the special ASP coding is executed and any textual output then incorporated into the HTML framework for transfer to the browser. In JSP a more complex procedure unfolds which is described below.

JSP architecture

JSPs are built on top of Sun's servlet technology. JSPs are essentially HTML pages with special JSP tags embedded. These JSP tags can contain Java code. The JSP file extension is .jsp rather than .htm or .html. The JSP engine parses the .jsp and creates a Java servlet source file. It then compiles the source file into a class (bytecode) file; this is done the first time the page is called and this why the JSP is slower the first time it is accessed. Any time after this the special compiled servlet is executed and therefore returns faster. The overall scheme is illustrated in Figure 10.6.

10

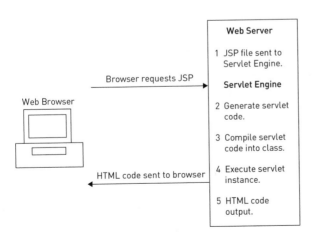

FIGURE 10.6 JSP model

The following steps are required for a JSP request, and correspond to the numbers in Figure 10.6:

1 The user goes to a website made using JSP. The user goes to a JSP page (i.e. has a .jsp extension). The web browser makes the request via the Internet.

2 The JSP request is sent to the web server.

3 The web server recognises that the file required is special (.jsp), therefore passes the JSP file to the JSP servlet engine.

4 If the JSP file has been called the first time, the JSP file is parsed. Otherwise the process continues from step 7.

5 The next step is to generate a special servlet from the JSP file. All the HTML required (including the HTML present in the original page) is converted to `println` statements.

6 The servlet source code is compiled into a class.

7 The servlet is instantiated, calling the `init` and `service` methods.

8 HTML from the servlet output is sent via the Internet.

9 HTML results are displayed on the user's web browser.

JSP tags

The tags employed in JSP are more elaborate than in ASP. There are five main tag types:

1 Declaration tag

2 Expression tag

3 Directive tag

4 Scriptlet tag

5 Action tag

Declaration tag (<%! %>)

This tag allows the developer to declare variables or methods. The declaration is placed between these tags. Code placed in this tag must end in a semicolon (;). For example,

```
<%!
    private int counter = 0 ;
    private String get Account ( int accountNo) ;
%>
```

Expression tag (<% = %>)

This tag allows the developer to embed any Java expression and is short for `out.println()`.

A semicolon (;) does not appear at the end of the code inside the tag.

For example, to show the current date and time.

```
Date : <% = new java.util.Date() %>
```

Directive tag (<%@ directive . . . %>)

A JSP directive gives special information about the page to the JSP engine.

There are three main types of directives:

- Page-processing information for this page.

- Include – files to be included.

- Tag library – tag library to be used in this page.

Directives do not produce any visible output when the page is requested but change the way the JSP engine processes the page.

For example, you can make session data unavailable to a page by setting a page directive (session) to false.

Page directive

This directive has 11 optional attributes that provide the JSP engine with special processing information. Examples of some of these attributes are shown below:

```
<%@ page language = "java" %>
```

Specifies the page language as 'java'. Actually, this is the only option at present, but it allows for future developments.

10

```
<%@ page import = "java.util.*" %>
```

Causes other pre-complied Java code modules to be loaded so that the code available can be called by the JSP page.

```
<%@ page errorPage = "/error/error.jsp" %>
```

Defines another page that deals with errors occurring on the current page.

Include directive

Allows a JSP developer to include the contents of a file inside another file. Typically include files are used for navigation, tables, headers and footers that are common to multiple pages.

Here are two examples of using include the files. To include the HTML from privacy.html found in the include directory into the current JSP page.

```
<%@ include file = "include/privacy.html" %>
```

To include a navigation menu (jsp file) found in the current directory:

```
<%@ include file = "navigation.jsp" %>
```

Taglib directive

A tag library is a collection of custom tags that can be created by the developer and used in subsequent page design. These tags initiate some defined action when included in a web page and are used to enhance the built-in JSP tags and to hide complex coding from less-skilled page designers. Assuming a tab library called 'mylib' has been created, a tag such as 'hello' could be defined as:

```
<mylib:hello>
   <%= yourName %>
</mylib:hello>
```

The tag library must be declared within the JSP page:

```
<%@ taglib uri="http://www.oursite.com/tags" prefix="mylib" %>
```

Scriptlet tag (<% ... %>)

General Java coding in the JSP page is enclosed between <% and %> tags. The term *scriptlet* is used in Java parlance. This code can access any declared variable or bean.

For example, to print a variable.

```
<%
   String username = "John Smith" ;
   out.println ( username ) ;
%>
```

Action tag

There are three main roles of action tags:

- To enable the use of server-side Javabeans.
- To transfer control between pages.
- To provide browser independent support for applets.

Javabeans

A Javabean is a special type of class that has a number of methods. It is analogous to ActiveX components in Microsoft systems. The JSP page can call these methods so that most of the code for the page is in the Javabeans. For example, suppose you wanted to make a feedback form that automatically sent out an email. By having a JSP page with a form, when the visitor presses the submit button this sends the details to a Javabean that sends out the email. This way there would be no code in the JSP page dealing with sending emails (JavaMail API) and your Javabean could be used in another page (promoting reuse).

To use a Javabean in a JSP page, use the following syntax:

```
<jsp:usebean id = "..." scope = "application" class = "com..." />
```

To get or modify a property of a Javabean, the following actions are available:

```
<jsp:getProperty ...>
<jsp:setProperty ...>
```

Transfer

The tag `<jsp:forward ....>` redirects the execution to another specified page and hence is similar to the ASP redirect command.

Browser support

The `<jsp:plugin ....>` generates HTML that contains browser-specific elements (OBJECT or EMBED) needed to execute an applet with the Java plug-in software.

JSP example script

```
<%! private static final String DEFAULT_NAME = "World"; %>

<html>
<head>
<title>Hello Java Server Page </title>
</head>
<%-- get a name from somewhere, possibly a posted form value --%>

<%
String name = request.getParameter("name");
if ( (name = = null) || (name.length() = = 0 ) )
{
    name = DEFAULT_NAME;
}
%>
<body>bgcolor = 'white'>

<b>Hello, <% = name %></b>

</html>
```

Summary

In this chapter we have described the general principles one needs to have a understanding of web database systems. There is no such thing as specifically web oriented database systems; database utilised in a web context are simply conventional database systems such as Oracle and MySQL accessed via the Internet. There are, however, a vast range of technologies and products that are employed to facilitate the interaction of web users with databases. Within the limited scope of this chapter we have provided a overview of some of the main technologies currently available in this area.

Review questions

Client-server architecture

1 Describe the structure and mode of operation of a three-tier web/database server system.

HTML forms

1 Outline the main elements used in the construction of HTML forms.

2 Explain the significance and importance of HTML forms in the design of web interfaces.

3 In an HTML form, describe the effect of a submit button.

CGI

1 Explain how CGI is used in a web – database connection.

2 What is the main difference between CGI and other web interaction technologies such as ASP and PHP?

ASP, ADO

1 Explain how ASP coding is embedded in HTML documents.

2 Outline the role of the Request and Response objects in ASP programming.

3 Explain the purpose of the Application object and identify the two events handled by the object.

4 What is the global.asa file used for?

5 Explain the general nature of ActiveX Data Objects (ADO).

6 Outline the main object types supported by ADO.

7 Explain what is meant by a 'recordset' and how a cursor is used in conjunction with a recordset.

ASP.NET

1 How are ASP and ASP.NET related?

2 What are the principal innovations of ASP.NET?

3 List the categories of server controls provided by ASP.NET.

4 Identify the main features of the Dataset object that ADO.NET maintains.

Cookies

1 Explain what is meant by a 'cookie' and describe the mechanism used in communicating cookies between the web server and client computers.

State maintenance

1 Explain the concept of, and the need for, 'state maintenance' in web sessions.

2 Outline the principles underlying the following state maintenance methods: sessions, URL-encoded variables, hidden form variables.

PHP

1 Describe the general principles of the PHP language for web interaction.

2 How does PHP differ from ASP with regard to the languages used?

3 How does PHP differ from other web interaction systems with regard to database access?

JSP/Servlets

1 Outline the essential nature of Java servlets.

2 Describe the role played by the servlet objects ServletResponse and ServletRequest.

3 Explain why JSP was introduced to the Java web system.

4 Describe the processes involved in handling JSP requests.

5 Outline the JSP tag system.

10

Exercises

In this topic area, exercises that the student can undertake will depend on the facilities available to them. However, many of the software systems referred to in this chapter are available online and can be downloaded free. For Microsoft operating systems, ASP and ASP.NET are available free. For Microsoft and UNIX/Linux systems, PHP and JSP are available free. The following exercises have been expressed with reference to ASP but could be implemented in any of these systems. The website for this text contains coding examples in ASP, etc. Also, the case studies covered in the text are all available as Microsoft Access databases on the website. Some of the following exercises make reference to the Employee database. In coding these exercises, use the sample scripts and the Assets database given in the body of the chapter as guide to the coding.

General ASP

1 Write ASP code to display the word 'Hello' five times on successive lines, each time increasing the font size by 1.

2 Use a form to enter three numerical values which are then displayed in sorted sequence.

Database

Use the Access database, Employee.mdb in writing the following scripts.

1 Write a script that uses a form to input a BranchCode, then display in a table layout all employees' names, positions and salaries.

2 Repeat the form input as in (1) but now display each position (e.g. Salesman) together with the average salary for that position.

3 Use a form to input an employee id value and a percentage value (e.g. '10' for 10%). The salary of the referenced employee should be increased by that percentage amount. Display the new salary value for that employee.

Cookies

1 Design an ASP page WriteCookie.asp that uses a form to gather user information: Username, name, a date of birth and an address consisting of two lines and a postcode.

2 Save this form as a set of cookies: the first two items are individual cookies while the rest is a cookie with keys (e.g. 'line1', 'line2').

3 The username cookie should be given an expiry date one month ahead using the function DateAdd("m",1,Now()).

4 Write a second script ReadCookies.asp that uses the following code to report all the stored cookies:

```
<% @LANGUAGE = VBScript %>
<% Option Explicit %>
<html>
<body>
<%
Dim cookie, key
For Each cookie In Request.Cookies
  If Not Request.Cookies(cookie).HasKeys Then
    Response.Write cookie & " = " & Request.Cookies(cookie) & "<br>"
```

```
      Else
      For Each key In Request.Cookies(cookie)
        Response.Write cookie
        Response.Write " Key: " & key
        Response.Write " = "
        Response.Write Request.Cookies(cookie)(key)
        Response.Write "<br>" & vbCrLf
      Next
    End If
Next
%>
</body>
</html>
```

Execute this immediately after running WriteCookies. Study this code to ensure that you understand the functionality involved.

References

If one includes all the language technologies such as ASP, JSP, PHP etc. the volume of published work in this area is massive. A few books are suggested below which are worth examination.

Textbooks

Oracle
Ostrowski C. and Brown B. (2005): *Oracle Application Server 10g Web Development*, Osborne Oracle Press
Gogala M. (2006): *Easy Oracle PHP: Create Dynamic Web Pages with Oracle Data*, Rampant Techpress

MySQL
Williams H.E. and Lane D. (2004): *Web Database Applications with PHP and MySQL*, O'Reilly (second edition)

ASP
Kauffman J., Spencer K. and Willis T. (2003): *Beginning Asp Databases*, Apress

ASP.NET
Kauffman J. and Millington B. (2006): *Beginning ASP.NET 2.0 and Databases*, Hungry Minds

10

11

XML and databases

LEARNING OBJECTIVES

After studying this chapter you should be able to do the following:

- Understand in outline the nature and purpose of XML and associated tools such as XSL, XPath and XQuery.

- Justify the need to be able to support XML data within a database system.

- Distinguish between XML-enabled databases and native XML database (NXD).

- Summarise the available XML support tools.

- Understand the features available in current XML-enabled databases.

- Understand the features available in current Native XML databases.

Introduction

The purpose of markup languages is to hold, within the one document, textual data together with information about the structure of the data and about how the data should be presented. Originally, markup in the form of manual additions to printed documents was used in the publishing industry in the communication of printed work between authors, editors and printers. The best known computer-based markup language at present is HTML which is used to specify the design of web pages. This chapter is concerned with another markup system, XML or Extensible Markup Language, which has a much broader range of applications.

XML is derived from the older but more complex markup language SGML, on which HTML is also based. It was formally ratified by the World Wide Web Consortium (W3C) in 1998. The objective of the language was to provide a data definition system that would enable the design of other languages that would provide specialised markup for a range of different applications including, in particular, web page definition.

XML's inherent power and essential simplicity appears to have caught the interest and imagination of the industry, resulting in its application far beyond these initial objectives. It is now a general method of representing and communicating data between applications such as transfer of data between databases and the specification of configuration files. It is also widely used in applications such as product catalogues, media archiving, commerce interchange etc. Developing the potential of XML has necessitated the development of a host of other associated software tools such as XSLT, XQuery, XPath etc.

The purpose of this chapter is to examine how the worlds of databases and XML intersect and interact. Given the potential size of this topic and the constraints of this text this is necessarily an overview. We will concern ourselves primarily with outlining the major types of systems without delving too deeply into the practicalities. We will include XML-enabled databases, Native XML databases and other tools for managing the XML–database interface.

We start in the next section with a brief description of XML, sufficient to enable understanding of the rest of the chapter. Readers who are already conversant with the principles of XML can safely skip this section. The following section describes the more important software tools that are used in conjunction with XML. Again, readers familiar with this area can skip this section.

XML overview

As indicated, XML bears some resemblance to HTML in terms of its hierarchical structure, construction of tags and elements, etc. (The nature of HTML was covered in Chapter 10; knowledge of that chapter would assist in understanding the following notes.) The main difference is that, while HTML is based on a fixed set of predefined tags, in XML a set of tags is designed to suit the needs of the application. XML, like SGML, is a meta-language – it is a language used to define other languages. It is not a language for a specific application in the way that HTML is used to specify web pages. A couple of simple examples will help to explain this point. The first example below is HTML:

```
<html>

<head>
<title>        Simple HTML example    </title>
<h1>           Main Heading  </h1>
</head>
<body>
<p>     Some data <em>here </em>  </p>
</body>
</html>
```

The main point to note here is that the element tags used such as <html> and <title> are all predefined and are meaningful to a web browser. The expected effect of the HTML code is specified in standards issued by the W3C, although this leaves browsers with a certain amount of latitude in forming the output. In HTML it is not possible to introduce new tags for a special purpose. Note also that as well as data, HTML supplies an indication of how the data should be displayed. The <em> element requests 'emphasis', which in most browsers is rendered as italics. HTML can be enhanced in this respect by the use of **cascading style sheets** (CSS).

This is an example of XML:

```
<?xml version="1.0"?>
<!-- Music Collection -->
<musicCollection>
   <musicItem>
      <musicItemID>1</musicItemID>
      <title>Tubular Bells</title>
      <artist>Mike Oldfield</artist>
      <yearReleased>1973</yearReleased>
   </musicItem>
   <musicItem>
      <musicItemID>2</musicItemID>
      <title>Ten New Songs</title>
      <artist>Leonard Cohen</artist>
      <yearReleased>2001</yearReleased>
   </musicItem>
</musicCollection>
```

11

The structure of this is superficially similar to HTML, but there are a number of significant differences. None of these tags is immediately recognised by a browser and the tags are not intended to show what the data should look like. The XML is concerned only in expressing the content and the hierarchical structure of the data. However, within the context of an application (such as the music recordings in the example), the tags are meaningful: it is obvious what the interpretations of 'title' and 'artist' are. Hence, XML provides a general means of storing data with a degree of self-documentation.

There are explicit relationships defined in an XML document between the root, parent and child nodes. In the above example: musicCollection is the root element which has child elements: musicItem. MusicCollection is said to be a parent element. A valid XML document must always have a root element that encloses the rest of the coding. MusicItem is also a parent element of musicItemID, title, artist, yearReleased and media – these are called 'siblings' or sister elements. An element encompasses a start tag, contents and end tag.

While the XML example above is meaningful to a human reader, it cannot immediately be interpreted by computer. If this is presented to a web browser the best that it can achieve is to display the hierarchical structure. To enable processing and utilisation of the data, the XML has to been complemented by two other definitions:

- A logical structure definition – this specifies what tags are allowable and how these can be organised within an XML document. This role is performed by a Document Type Definition (DTD) or by some form of XML schema definition; the most common of these is called simply XML Schema. These are described briefly below.

- A style sheet specification that indicates how the data is to displayed. This is provided by the Extensible Stylesheet Language (XSL). The standard web style system CSS can also be used with XML.

These topics are described in the XML Technologies section below.

XML tags are case sensitive and each tag must have a matching end tag. HTML is less strict about such matters; an HTML browser will typically tolerate missing end tags and simply ignore tags it does not recognise, but an XML processor will not and will reject the document.

XML documents should begin with a declaration of the XML version being used (e.g. `<?xml version="1.0"?>`). This allows the XML processor to check the version of a document and reject versions it does not support.

Attributes

In addition to the data held in each XML element, an element can also contain attributes. An attribute is a value associated with that element. The distinction between 'data' and 'attribute' is not clearly defined and the designer of the XML document has a measure of choice in making a data value a data element or an attribute of a parent element. For example, the music collection example above could be modified to:

```
<musicCollection>
  <musicItem musicItemID = 1>
    <title>Tubular Bells</title>
    <artist>Mike Oldfield</artist>
    <yearReleased>1973</yearReleased>
  </musicItem>
```

In the example, the musicItemID value has been changed from an element value to an attribute of musicItem. Typically, elements are used to hold 'pure' data and attributes are used to hold information about the data. For instance, the musicItemID is not an intrinsic part of the music data but simply an identifying code.

Associated XML technologies

The technologies related to XML described in this section are:

- DTD
- XML Schemas
- XSL, XSLT, XPath
- XQuery
- Xlink and Xpointer

DTD

An XML document must be supported by a logical definition of its tags, and a DTD (Document Type Definition) is one of the methods that fulfil this role. A DTD is (usually) contained within a separate file with extension .dtd and referenced through a DOCTYPE declaration, although internal declarations, are also possible. For example:

```
<!DOCTYPE musicCollection SYSTEM "MusicCollection.dtd">
```

The DTD can be used to indicate the relationships between the user-defined tags as well as some basic datatype/values information.

Let's look at DTDs for our music collection XML. Basically, the DTD code is:

```
<!ELEMENT musicCollection  (musicItem+)>
<!ELEMENT musicItem  (title, artist, yearReleased, media)>
<!ATTLIST musicItem musicItemID CDATA #REQUIRED>
<!ELEMENT title  (#PCDATA)>
<!ELEMENT artist  (#PCDATA>
<!ELEMENT yearReleased  (#PCDATA)>
<!ELEMENT media  (#PCDATA)>
```

As you can see, each element such as musicItem is individually defined. Where the element is compound, it can be expressed as a set of one or more other elements or as a set of specific other elements. An example of the former is musicCollection (musicItem+) which indicates that a musicCollection consists of one or more musicItem elements. The expression musicItem (title, artist, yearReleased, media) indicates that a musicItem consists of title, artist etc. For 'leaf' elements (i.e. non-composite) the data

11

is specified as #CDATA, which indicates simple character data, or #PCDATA which indicates 'parsed character' data. The latter implies that the text may contain XML tags that can be parsed.

The DTD code can be incorporated into the XML file:

```
<?xml version="1.0"?>
<!DOCTYPE musicCollection [
   <!ELEMENT musicCollection (musicItem+)>
   <!ELEMENT musicItem (title, artist, yearReleased, media)>
   <!ATTLIST musicItem musicItemID CDATA #REQUIRED>
   <!ELEMENT title (#PCDATA)>
   <!ELEMENT artist (#PCDATA)>
   <!ELEMENT yearReleased (#PCDATA)>
   <!ELEMENT media (#PCDATA)>
]>
<musicCollection>
   <musicItem>
      <musicItemID>1</musicItemID>
      <title>Tubular Bells</title>
. . . etc.
```

or it can be held in a separate file and referenced from the XML:

```
<?xml version="1.0"?>
<!DOCTYPE musicCollection SYSTEM "MusicCollection.dtd">
<musicCollection>
   <musicItem>
      <musicItemID>1</musicItemID>
      <title>Tubular Bells</title>
. . . etc.
```

XML Schema

An alternative to DTDs for defining the rules of an XML document is to use an XML Schema. XML Schemas are actually XML documents in themselves and have a number of advantages over DTDs, including their extensibility, reusability, programmability and support for datatypes. The schema for the music collection example is shown below:

```
<?xml version="1.0"?>
<xsd:schema
   xmlns:xsd="http://www.w3.org/2001/XMLSchema"
        targetNamespace="http://www.colinr.net/music">
   <xsd:element name="musicCollection">
   <xsd:complexType>
   <xsd:sequence>
      <xsd:element name="musicItem" minOccurs="1"
           maxOccurs="unbounded">
         <xsd:complexType>
            <xsd:sequence>
```

```
<xsd:element name="title" type="xsd:string"/>
<xsd:element name="artist" type="xsd:string"/>
<xsd:element name="yearReleased">
  <xsd:simpleType>
    <xsd:restriction base="xsd:positiveInteger">
      <xsd:pattern value="[1–2][0–9][0–9][0–9]"/>
    </xsd:restriction>
  </xsd:simpleType>
</xsd:element>
<xsd:element name="media">
  <xsd:simpleType>
    <xsd:restriction base="xsd:string">
      <xsd:enumeration value="CD"/>
      <xsd:enumeration value="MD"/>
      <xsd:enumeration value="LP"/>
      <xsd:enumeration value="Cassette"/>
    </xsd:restriction>
  </xsd:simpleType>
</xsd:element>
</xsd:sequence>
  <xsd:attribute name="musicItemID"
        type="xsd:positiveInteger" use="required"/>
  </xsd:complexType>
</xsd:element>
  </xsd:sequence>
  </xsd:complexType>
</xsd:element>
</xsd:schema>
```

As you can see, this is an elaborate definition that provides more information about the application, including more precise datatype definitions. Note also that the schema is itself an XML document, which makes it amenable to processing by XML tools.

XSL

XSL, eXtensible Stylesheet Language, was developed as a stylesheet language for XML documents. It consists of three components:

- XSL-FO (extensible stylesheet formatting), often just called XSL.

- XSLT (extensible stylesheet language transformations).

- XPath; this is described below.

The role of XSL is to tell a browser how to display user-defined XML tags. XSL is a set of languages that can:

- Transform XML into XHTML

- Filter and sort XML data

- Define parts of an XML document

- Format XML data based on the data value – e.g. displaying negative numbers in red

- Output XML data to different media, like screens, paper, or voice

XSLT (XSL Transformations) is a language that allows us to transform an XML document into another XML document or another type of browser-friendly document. We can also use XSLT to add and remove elements from the collection and, in addition, using XPath, to select parts of the original document to include in the resultant document.

Browser support

XSLT in Internet Explorer 5 is not compatible with the official W3C XSL recommendation, however, Internet Explorer 6 fully supports it. The XML Parser 3.0, which is shipped with Internet Explorer 6.0 and Windows XP, is based on both the W3C XSLT 1.0 and the W3C XPath 1.0 recommendations. Netscape 6 is in a similar position to Internet Explorer 5 while Netscape 7 supports the official W3C XSLT recommendation.

Stylesheet rules

To define a stylesheet we must refer to the stylesheet rules as follows:

```
<xsl:stylesheet version="1.0"
   xmlns:xsl="http://www.w3.org/1999/XSL/Transform">
```

As a simple example, let's look at a stylesheet which transforms our XML document above into an XHTML table display as shown in Figure 11.1.

Music collection

Title	Artist	Year Released	Media
Tubular Bells	Mike Oldfield	1973	CD
Ten New Songs	Leonard Cohen	2001	CD

FIGURE 11.1 Output from stylesheet transform

The stylesheet looks like this.

```
<?xml version="1.0"?>
<xsl:stylesheet version="1.0"
   xmlns:xsl="http://www.w3.org/1999/XSL/Transform">
<xsl:template match="/">
<html>
<body>
   <h2>Music Collection</h2>
   <table border="1">
   <tr>
      <th>Title</th>
      <th>Artist</th>
      <th>Year Released</th>
```

```
    <th>Media</th>
  </tr>
  <xsl:for-each select="musicCollection/musicItem">
  <tr>
    <td><xsl:value-of select="title"/></td>
    <td><xsl:value-of select="artist"/></td>
    <td><xsl:value-of select="yearReleased"/></td>
    <td><xsl:value-of select="media"/></td>
  </tr>
  </xsl:for-each>
  </table>
</body>
</html>
</xsl:template>
</xsl:stylesheet>
```

The template element is used to indicate the rules which have to be applied. For example, match="/", tells the processor to deal with the whole document. Each row of the table is formed using the for-each command with the path for musicItems while the value-of command constructs each cell by selecting each of the child elements of musicItem.

XPath

XPath is a language for addressing and extracting parts of an XML document based on some criteria. A basic path mechanism is used to identify the elements you are interested in and paths can be qualified to only select those elements whose values match a specified criterion. XPath itself goes no further than defining some portion (or all) of an XML tree structure; other tools are utilised to display or otherwise process the XPath selection. For instance, XPath is used in XSLT, XPointer and XQuery.

There is a library of standard functions which can be used in various contexts (e.g. using JavaScript in an HTML document) to handle the data. XPath uses a range of notations to specify locations in the XML document tree and elements at that point. The following notations are used to indicate parts of the tree as shown; some similarity with UNIX style path conventions may be noticed:

nodename	Selects all 'child' nodes; i.e. all nodes below the named node.
/	Selects starting from the root node.
//	Selects nodes in the document from the current node that match the selection no matter where they appear in the document.
.	Selects starting from the current node.
. .	Selects the parent of the current node.
@	Select attributes.

Here is a range of examples that illustrate the main features of this notation.

The following paths identify parts of the XML document described earlier:

`/musicCollection`	Selects the whole music collection document.
`/musicCollection/musicItem`	Selects all music items from the collection.
`/musicCollection/musicItem/title`	Selects only the title of each item.
`//musicItem`	Selects all musicItem elements below the current node.

It is also possible to use conditional expressions (predicates) to limit the selected set of elements:

`/musicCollection/musicItem/[yearReleased=2001]`	The square brackets denote the predicate
`/musicCollection/musicItem[@musicItemID<5]`	The @ symbol indicates an attribute.

Example

Based on the music collection XML example, a possible query might be:

'Select all titles from the music items released after 1980'.

A solution might be developed as follows:

1 `doc("Music.XML")` the doc function opens the named XML file.

2 `doc("Music.XML")/musicCollection/musicItem/title` selects all titles in the document. This would yield the output:

   `<title>Tubular Bells</title>`

   `<title>Ten New Songs</title>`

3 To apply conditions to the query, a predicate expression is added at the end:

   `doc("Music.XML")/musicCollection/musicItem/title[yearReleased>1980]`

   This would reduce the output to:

   `<title>Ten New Songs</title>`

4 The query can be asked to yield any part of the tree structure:

   `doc("Music.XML")/musicCollection/musicItem[yearReleased>1980]` would yield:

```
<musicItem>
   <musicItemID>2</musicItemID>
   <title>Ten New Songs</title>
   <artist>Leonard Cohen</artist>
   <yearReleased>2001</yearReleased>
</musicItem>
```

XQuery

The XQuery language is intended to provide for XML what SQL provides for databases – the ability to extract required information from an XML document by means of a compact query specification. XQuery 1.0 became a W3C recommendation in January, 2007 and is supported by the main database vendors such as Oracle, IBM and Microsoft. Also, it is often the main query facility for the new wave of Native XML Databases (NXD) that is currently appearing. It is, therefore, a very significant technology in the current XML market.

XQuery in effect, incorporates XPath; i.e. any valid XPath expression is also an XQuery query. However, it also has an additional query syntax, referred to as FLWOR – which is an acronym derived from the processing elements For – Let – Where – Order – Return. This topic is covered briefly here since it is of some interest in terms of the relationship between XML and SQL.

Use of XQuery

Query can be used for the following

- Generate ad hoc summary reports from XML data.

- Transform XML data to XHTML. The XQuery output can be embedded in an outer framework of XHTML.

- Search web documents for relevant information. This might be used in many contexts such as within an SQL query to an XML-enabled database.

FLWOR

The processing terms For, Let etc. convey an impression that we are dealing with a procedural command system, and an initial inspection of some FLWOR code tends to confirm this impression. However, closer inspection shows it to be declarative like SQL. The 'for' and 'let' clauses are simply used to express the scope of the command and the 'where' clause is a predicate specification similar to the SQL WHERE. The 'order' clause is analogous to the SQL ORDER BY and the 'return' clause is similar to the SQL Select since it defines the items to be returned. The following section describes a range of examples which hopefully will clarify the working of this innovative language. The $x code that appears in the examples operates in a fashion similar to a control variable in a conventional language, but technically in XPath, 'variables' cannot be updated; in fact, on each iteration $x is a new value.

11

Examples

1 Selective listing of titles. The XPath expression (introduced earlier):

```
doc("Music.XML")/musicCollection/musicItem[yearReleased>1980]/title
```

may be expressed alternatively in FLWOR as:

```
for $x in doc("Music.xml")/musicCollection/musicItem
where $x/yearReleased>1980
return $x/title
```

2 Embedding XML output in an HTML framework. In this example the XML output is bracketed within a unordered list <UL> HTML tags. Each title value is enclosed in <LI>, list items, tags.

```
<ul>
{
for $x in doc("Music.xml")/bookstore/book/title
order by $x
return <li>{$x}</li>
}
</ul>
```

The result of this would be the HTML fragment:

```
<ul>
<li><title>Tubular Bells</title></li>
<li><title>Ten New Songs</title></li>
</ul>
```

3 Using an if..else construct.

```
for $x in doc("Music.xml")/MusicCollection/musicItems
return if ($x/yearReleased<1980)
then <old>{data($x/title)}</old>
else <recent>{data($x/title)}</recent>
```

This would produce:

```
<old>Tubular Bells</old>
<recent>Ten New Songs</recent>
```

XPointer and Xlink

These conventions provide the means for creating hyperlinks in XML documents. They provide a similar feature as the <A> tag and HREF attribute in HTML, but are somewhat more elaborate. While of importance to general XML usage their use does not impact greatly on XML databases and they will not be considered further here.

XML databases

Introduction

The first question that must be addressed is; 'What is the rationale for XML databases?' It is not difficult to appreciate that XML documents need to be stored in some form of persistent storage, but given that they are simply text files, what is the problem?

It is of course perfectly possible for an XML document to be stored as text and at a later date retrieved into a suitable programming context. This was effectively done in the earlier implementations of XML-enabled databases using, for example, a CLOB (character large object) datatype. This is an improvement on a simple text file, as the database can provide lookup facilities and other basic DBMS features such as security, concurrency etc. However, such a system views the XML text as a 'black box' with no directly accessible internal structure. No opportunity is provided for applying queries to the XML data other than by dispatching the document data to another environment where querying is available.

The intention of recent more highly developed XML database features is to improve the facilities we have to query, extract and manipulate XML data from the stored documents. There are two main classifications of database in this respect, called 'XML enabled' and 'Native XML' databases. These are summarised below.

XML-enabled database

This is a conventional relational, object-oriented or object-relational database that provides facilities to manage XML documents within its normal storage system. There is clearly a requirement here to accommodate the XML data into the natural storage features of the database; for instance, an XML document would have to be accommodated into the tabular structure of a relational database. We will look at how this might be done shortly.

11

Native XML database (NXD)

This is a database that has been specifically designed to store and access XML data. Although this definition does not dictate the underlying storage mechanism, it can be assumed that this is not a feature of the system that is of concern to the developer or user. Being specifically designed for the purpose, we would expect that NXDs would be more convenient to use and to execute faster, but there could be issues regarding the higher-level functions expected of a database, such as scalability, security, concurrency etc., all of which are well-developed in current conventional databases. Note also that NXDs provide a very specialised service and do not in any way compete with the general capabilities of relational databases.

Another distinction which is often used is between 'data-centric' and 'document-centric' applications, terms which try to characterise the main usage of the information to be held in XML. These terms are clarified below.

Data-centric documents

XML is used as data transport and designed for machine consumption. Here, it is not important to the application or the database that the data is, for some length of time, stored in an XML document. Examples include sales orders, flight schedules, and scientific data.

These collections have a fairly regular structure with fine-grained data and relatively little mixed content. As is the case in relational data, the order of elements is generally not significant. Data can originate either in a database to be transmitted as XML, or from outside the database, and be stored in a database in XML.

Document-centric documents

These types of documents contain data for human consumption and have a more textual basis. Examples include books, email, advertisements, archives and XHTML documents. They have a less regular or irregular structure with larger-grained data and lots of mixed content. The order of elements is often significant. The content of documents is usually prepared manually in some format which is then converted to XML using suitable tools. They usually do not originate in the database.

These terms only provide a coarse categorisation and do not form rigid boundaries, since many applications may display characteristics of both categories.

Other terms used in categorising data are *structured*, *semi-structured* and *unstructured*. Structured data is typical of conventional relational database applications where the data must conform to strict schema-defined patterns; potential structural variations must be accommodated within the defined structure, often requiring a proliferation of separate tables. The classic example of unstructured data is a web page; here, the data can be arranged and modified without the constraints of any predefined format. Semi-structured data is somewhere in between, with some semblance of order but with substantial variations and irregularities; such data is more amenable to representation by XML.

XML-enabled databases

Overview

Given the importance of XML, database vendors have lost no time in providing some measure of support in their products. Generally, the minimum to be expected would be the ability to store and retrieve whole XML documents and to be able to convert from relational tables to a corresponding XML version, but ideally of course it would be 'nice' to go beyond this basic provision. In this section, we indicate the current support provided by our exemplar systems in this area. We start by reviewing the SQL/XML standard, which is an attempt to provide a standard approach to storing and accessing XML data in relational databases.

SQL/XML standard

A significant contribution to this area are the international standards SQL/XML:2003 and SQL/XML:2006; these latest SQL revisions (more formally: INCITS/ISO/IEC

9075-14:2003 and 'INCI TS/ISO/IEC 9075-14':2006), provide support for using XML in the context of an SQL (i.e. relational or extended relational) database system. The development of the new standard has been driven by the desire to:

- Be able to present information from the vast body of data held on relational systems in XML form.

- Be able to hold XML data within a relational system making it amenable to XML-oriented querying and integration with standard relational data.

- Facilitate the exchange of data between relational and XML repositories.

The main features of the SQL/XML standard are:

- Provision of an XML datatype which is intended to hold data in the form of an XML structure within conventional relational tables.

- Methods associated with the XML datatype.

- A range of built-in operators which facilitate creating, amending and retrieving data stored in relational tables. These include extract and extractValue, XMLElement, XMLForest, XMLGen, XMLConcat and XMLAgg, etc.

Oracle has supported many features of SQL:2003 and SQL:2006 since Version 9i with further enhancement in Oracle 10g. As an illustration of the new SQL/XML features, some of the facilities provided by Oracle are illustrated below. Also indicated in later sections is the support provided by Microsoft Access and MySQL for the management of XML data.

Oracle XML features

- Oracle XML support is its XML DB feature, which is a component of the 10g database designed to facilitate storing and retrieving of XML data.

- SQL/XML support; e.g. XMType, XMLGen etc.

- XSU – refers to the XML SQL Utility. This is a set of programming tools accessible from Java, PL/SQL and from a Java command interface. See references for more details.

- A host of packages such as DBMS_XMLSCHEMA, DBMS_XMLSTORE, DBMS_XMLSTORE to provide procedural support for XML processing in PL/SQL.

Some of the XML DB and SQL/XML features are outlined below.

XMLType

Oracle provides the XMLType datatype to enable storage of XML. XMLType may be specified as the type of a column of a table or as the whole row.

Oracle sample commands

Script CH11.OracleXML1.SQL on the book's companion website contains this code

11

Create table with XML field

```
create table XMLTab
(
   BookRef Varchar2(4),
   BookData XMLType
)
```

Insert three rows

```
declare           -- declare three CLOB variables and assign XML code
XML_Text1 CLOB :=
'<Book>
   <title>Bleak House</title>
   <author>
      <fname>Charles</fname>
      <surname>Dickens</surname>
   </author>
</Book>';
XMLText2 CLOB :=
'<Book>
   <title>Made in America</title>
   <author>
      <fname>Bill</fname>
      <surname>Bryson</surname>
   </author>
</Book>';
XMLText_3 CLOB :=
'<Book>
   <title>The Selfish Gene</title>
   <author>
      <fname>Richard</fname>
      <surname>Dawkins</surname>
   </author>
</Book>';

begin
insert into XMLTab values ('AB01', XMLType(XML_Text1));
insert into XMLTab values ('AB02', XMLType(XML_Text2));
insert into XMLTab values ('AB03', XMLType(XML_Text3));
end;
```

An expression such as XMLType (XML_Text1) is using an XMLType constructor. It is also possible to put the XML text directly into the constructor instead of using the intermediate XML_Text1 variable. For example:

```
XMLType('<Book>
   <title>Bleak House</title>
   <author>
```

```
        <fname>Charles</fname>
        <surname>Dickens</surname>
    </author>
</Book>')
```

Extract, ExtractValue

These SQL/XML functions allow extraction of parts of an XML document within the context of an SQL command. Extract will return a properly formed XML expression, while extractValue obtains the data portion of the referenced XML location. In both cases, the required data is defined by an XPath expression. An example based on the above book scenario is shown below:

CH11OracleXML2.sql

```
select bookref, extract(Bookdata, '/Book/title') from xmltab
where extractValue (Bookdata, '/Book/author/surname') <>'Dickens'
```

Output

BOOK	EXTRACT(BOOKDATA,'/BOOK/TITLE')
AB02	<title>Made in America</title>
AB03	<title>The Selfish Gene</title>

This example extracts the <title> elements from the table where the book author's surname (obtained using extractValue) is not Dickens.

SQL/XML functions – examples

A range of SQL/XML-based functions are described below, using the Oracle implementations. These are all used to generate XML documents or fragments from a relational source.

SYS_XMLGEN generates XML elements derived from the specified selection from a relational table:

CH11OracleXML3.sql

```
select SYS_XMLGEN(name) FROM Employee where empid < '1 500'
```

SYS_XMLGEN(NAME)
<NAME>Kennedy</NAME>
<NAME>Smith</NAME>
<NAME>Stewart</NAME>

11

SYS_XMLAGG aggregates all the documents or fragments generated by the first parameter and produces a single XML document. An enclosing element with a default name of ROWSET is added.

CH11OracleXML4.sql

```
select sys_xmlagg(SYS_XMLGEN(name)) FROM Employee where empid < '1 500'
```

SYS_XMLAGG(SYS_XMLGEN(NAME))
\<ROWSET\> \<NAME\>Kennedy\</NAME\> \<NAME\>Smith\</NAME\>
\<NAME\>Stewart\</NAME\> \</ROWSET\>

XMLElement facilitates the formation of XML elements by extraction from a relational source:

CH11OracleXML5.sql

```
select xmlelement(name "Employee",
    xmlelement(name "Id", e.empid),
    xmlelement(name "Surname", e.name)) as "EMPLOYEES" from employee e
where Empid < 1 500
Result:
```

EMPLOYEES
\<Employee\> \<Id\>1001\</Id\> \<Surname\>Kennedy\</Surname\> \</Employee\>
\<Employee\> \<Id\>1045\</Id\> \<Surname\>Smith\</Surname\> \</Employee\>
\<Employee\> \<Id\>1271\</Id\> \<Surname\>Stewart\</Surname\> \</Employee\>

This same result can be achieved more compactly by using the **XMLForest** function. This creates a 'forest' of sibling nodes derived from a variable number of parameters:

CH11OracleXML6.sql

```
select xmlelement(name "Employee",
    xmlforest(e.empid as "Id", e.name as "Surname")) as "EMPLOYEES"
from employee e
where Empid < 1 500
```

Finally, this example shows how the **XMLAttributes** function can be used to generate XML code that includes attributes:

CH11OracleXML7.sql

```
select xmlelement(name "branch", xmlattributes(b.branchcode),
    xmlforest(e.name as name)) as "Selected Names"
from employee e, branch b
where e.branchcode = b.branchcode
    and name <= 'Cohen'
```

Microsoft Access XML features

Microsoft Access is not targeted at the larger applications found in enterprise computing and the support for XML at the time of writing is not so extensive as that in other systems. Note however, that Microsoft's Server system provides features comparable with that of Oracle. The features provided by Access may be summarised as:

- Importing XML data into an Access database.
- Exporting Access tables and queries in XML form.
- Generating XSLT data from Access sources.

We will review these facilities below.

Importing XML to Access

Access can accept an XML document and convert it to one or more relational tables. The general principles of this conversion process are:

- The XML declaration and the document element are ignored. However, a document element must exist which encloses the rest of the XML data.
- A top-level data element is converted to a table. Elements contained within the toplevel are converted to fields of this table. The same principle is applied to successive levels of nesting of the XML text.
- The data values of the field elements are accepted as the field data.
- Attributes are ignored.

Note that in the process of generating the tables, no linking fields are generated; i.e. foreign key values are not inserted where they should exist. Ignoring the attribute values is also a limiting factor in the use that can be made of this facility.

To import XML data into Access, select **Get External Data** then **Import** . . . A dialog box allows you to select the XML document to be imported. A further window shows the hierarchical structure of the selected document, but provides no further control over the process.

Exporting XML from Access

Access database tables may be exported in the form of XML documents, including the XML text itself, together with related XSLT and XML Schema files.

To apply the XML export facility in Access:

1 From the database window, select the table or query that you wish to export.

2 From the **File** menu, click on **Export**.

3 In the **Save as type** box, click **XML(*.XML)**.

4 Enter, or select the required folder and filename in the **Save in** and **File name** boxes.

11

5 Click on **Export**.

6 This produces an **Export XML** dialog box. Here you can select to output any combination of XML, XSL and XML Schema derived from the Access source.

This is potentially a useful feature if it is necessary to transfer the contents of an Access database, in a 'one-off' operation or regularly, to another database environment or other application that uses XML.

Access program-level facilities

In addition to the 'higher level' features of Access that support XML, it is also possible to use VBA programming to provide a greater degree of control. This topic is beyond the scope of this text. The best source of information in this area is the Microsoft Developer Network (MSDN) website. See the reference section at the end of this chapter for specific links into the MSDN site which, incidentally, also provides some good general introductions to XML and associated technologies.

MySQL XML features

At the time of writing, MySQL versions 5.1.5 and 5.1.8 provided some support for XML text handling. This consists of two functions extractValue and UpdateXML; the first of these is the same as that described for Oracle earlier. These are essentially designed to handle XML code stored in a database as a large text field. Both use XPath expressions to locate the processing within an XML text body. The following sections illustrate the working of the functions.

ExtractValue

Assume we create a table consisting of a single text column, which we use to hold an XML document.

```
CREATE TABLE XTab (XMLDoc VARCHAR(200))
```

Assume that the musicCollection XML document (described earlier) is inserted into this table; e.g.

```
INSERT INTO XTab VALUES
( ' <?xml version="1.0"?>
<! -- Music Collection -- >
<musicCollection>
  <musicItem>
    <musicItemID>1</musicItemID>
    <title>Tubular Bells</title>

  . . . etc.
```

We can now use the extract function to obtain a selected portion of the XML data:

```
SELECT extractValue (XMLDoc, '/musicCollection/musicItem/title') FROM XData
```

This will produce a list of all titles:

```
Tubular Bells
Ten New Songs
```

Note that the function uses XPath to identify the referenced location but extracts only the tag data; i.e. it does not return the tag notation surrounding the data, as expected in XPath itself. Various XPath expressions can be used, although at the time of writing MySQL does not support all XPath constructs.

Example 1

```
SELECT extractValue (XMLDoc, '//artist') FROM XData
Mike Oldfield
Leonard Cohen
```

Example 2

```
SELECT extractValue (XMLDoc, '//title[yearReleased>1980]') FROM XData
Tubular Bells
```

UpdateXML

The *UpdateXML* function has three parameters. The first two are the same as for the extract function, i.e. reference to the XML document and an XPath expression to identify a portion of the XML. The third parameter specifies an XML fragment that is to replace the selected one. The function returns the whole of the updated document.

Note carefully that, although the extract function simply extracts the data portion of the XML selected, this update function refers to the whole of the XML fragment including tags. Hence the replace parameter must similarly indicate a properly-formed XML expression. An example may clarify this:

```
SELECT UpdateXML( XMLDoc, '//yearReleased', <yearReleased>9999</yearReleased>)
```

This code will change all year released dates to 9999

Native XML databases (NXD)

Overview

Given the enormous interest in and potential of XML technology and the need for storage of large XML documents, it is not surprising that developers have addressed the idea of a database specifically for this purpose. Clearly, the motivation would be to produce a system that, by virtue of being specifically designed for the purpose, would be more efficient and convenient that one accommodated within a relational framework. We shall not attempt to address the relative performance of NXD and XML-enabled systems; some benchmarking activities are already under way which should be researched if this is of interest.

Although the data stored by an NXD is ostensibly in standard XML format, the storage system itself does not conform to a specific model, in the sense that relational data is held in two-dimensional tables. The internal organisation would be determined by the particular product. This could be purely textual or could involve some compacted or pre-parsed format designed to optimise performance. This is not a serious problem, because the nature of the data (i.e. XML) means that communication of the data between different proprietary systems is not going to be difficult. It is best simply to see an NXD data repository as holding textual XML documents.

There is of course the need to be able to extract required parts of the data and for that purpose some querying system is required. While XML-enabled databases would typically employ extended SQL commands, an NXD would use XPath and XQuery commands.

Advantages and disadvantages of NXD

The main advantages of NXDs are:

- You can insert the data as XML and retrieve it as XML.

- The storage system used can be optimised for the purpose.

- Potentially better performance is achieved due to specialised design.

- Good integration with web server systems is offered.

The main disadvantages are

- At present, all products are relatively new and therefore lacking in practical assessment.

- Conventional products such as Oracle, DB2 and Microsoft Server are very highly developed and provide extensive enterprise-level features for the developer.

- NXDs may be limited in their ability to mix in conventional relational features such as extensive amounts of numerical data.

Current XML software implementations

In the burgeoning world of XML it is not surprising many products have appeared to compete in this potentially exciting market. We have identified a few of these below that may be of interest in finding a suitable vehicle for trying out XML exercises. Most are available on a trial basis and a few are free or reasonably priced.

XML Tools

Saxon

An open source product that is primarily an XSLT and XQuery processor although an XML parser is also available. This is probably a good choice for starting work on these tools.

StylusStudio

This offers a wide range of XML-related tools. A trial edition is available, as well as a low-priced 'home' version.

Altova XMLSpy

This offers a wide range of tools for XML, DTD, Schema, XPath, XQuery etc. A trial edition is available.

Native XML databases

Tamino

A large scale enterprise level database system.

TigerLogic XDMS – XML Data Management Server

Claims to provide high performance management and querying of XML data.

EXist

A Java-based open source database with indexed XQuery facilities. EXist provides a powerful environment for the development of web applications based on XQuery and related standards. Entire web applications can be written using XQuery, XSLT, XHTML, CSS and JavaScript. Probably a good choice for an economical way to learn about this topic.

11

Summary

This chapter has attempted to provide an insight into a relatively new development area of databases. In spite of its infancy, considerable progress has been made in establishing standards and developing practical implementations.

The most significant developments are:

- **SQL/XML standard.** This assists current relational systems to maintain a level of standardisation while establishing their position in this new market.

- **XQuery.** Provides for XML-based systems what SQL has provided for relational systems.

- **Native XML databases.** The conventional relational system vendors are faced with more competition from a host of newcomers and will be working hard to retain their domination of the database market.

This is perhaps reminiscent of the introduction, some years ago, of new products based on the object-oriented database model. In that area, the market penetration of the newcomers was relatively limited; while the intention of object-oriented databases is addressing the 'impedance mismatch' between the de facto default programming paradigm and the non-object nature of relational databases, in the event, most developers seemed to be reluctant to abandon the relational model. However, it is perhaps arguable that the XML databases are addressing a more specific need, namely the marshalling of the rapidly growing volume of data being generated in XML. Time will tell if the new NXD systems will display benefits that will be sought out by the market.

Review questions

1 Distinguish between the nature of tags as used in HTML and XML.

2 Explain why XML requires the use of a supporting DTD or Schema document.

3 What are the two main categories of database in terms of XML support?

4 Describe the nature of XPath and XQuery.

5 Outline the main features of SQL/XML, including the XMLType data type.

6 Describe the operation of the extract and extractValue functions.

7 Outline the purpose of the functions XMLElement, XMLGen, XMLForest and XMLAttributes.

Exercises

It is, of course, more beneficial to be able to perform exercises in a working environment, so the reader is encouraged to obtain the means of building XML documents and databases. Many systems as available free or on short-term test or reasonably priced. For instance, Saxon provides an open source tool for trying out XML, XPath and XQuery. Other XML tools such as Oxygen, StylusStudio and AltovaSpy have trial offers. MySQL and certain versions of Oracle are free for personal and academic use. In particular, Oracle 10g can be downloaded, which has one of the most advanced implementations for supporting XML.

Note that at the time of writing, the Oracle 10g Express Edition did **not** support XQuery. For NXDs, eXist provides an open source database for use with Java.

1 Design an XML document called movie.xml that holds data on films. Include about four–five films as a test sample. It should include title, year, director, main stars, etc.

2 The film element should include a 'filmid' attribute, a numerical value.

3 Create a DTD for movie.xml, called movie.dtd.

4 Create an XML Schema for movie.xml, called movie.xsd.

5 Write an XPath statement that would list the titles of every film.

6 Repeat Exercise 5 using an XQuery FLWOR expression.

7 Create an Oracle database to hold the film data. Use a two-column table where the first column holds the film id value and a second column holds the XML data as described above.

8 Write select queries incorporating ExtractValue and XPath expressions to make selective queries of the data.

9 Create a conventional relational table to hold the film data described in Exercises 1 and 2; i.e. a set of columns holding film id, title etc. Use the XMLElement, XMLForest and XMLAttributes functions to generate the XML as defined in Exercises 1 and 2.

References

There is currently an explosion of articles and sources on XML and XML databases and it is impossible to reference anything but a small selection here. However, the newness of the topic means that there are very few textbooks on XML databases at present. We reference two useful texts below.

Textbooks

For a general source of current research and practical systems, see:

Chaudhri, A., Rashid, A., and Zicari, R. (eds) (2003): *XML Data Management: Native XML and XML-Enabled Database Systems*, Addison Wesley

The following text provides a good guide to the practical implementation of databases:

Powell G. (2006): *Beginning XML Databases*, Wrox

Websites

A selection of useful websites is referenced below, under various categories. The Cengage Learning website for this book also contains a more convenient method of browsing the references.

General and introductory

General XML database articles – starting point: http://www.service-architecture.com/xml-databases/index.html

Survey of many XML database products: http://www.rpbourret.com/xml/XMLDatabaseProds.htm

A survey of XML standards:

- Part 1: http://www-128.ibm.com/developerworks/xml/library/x-stand1.html

- Part 2, including SQL/XML:

    http://www-128.ibm.com/developerworks/xml/library/x-stand2.html

    This site relates to an XML database benchmarking initiative:

    http://monetdb.cwi.nl/xml/

11

XML

W3C Specification of XML: http://www.w3.org/TR/xml/

FAQ on XML: http://xml.silmaril.ie/

Benefits of XML: http://www.softwareag.com/xml/about/xml_ben.htm

Extensive guide to very wide range of standards and other information:

     http://xml.coverpages.org/xml.html

Introduction to XML: http://www.xml.org/xml/resources_focus_beginnerguide.shtml

Good XML tutorials:

     http://www.zvon.org/index.php?nav_id=tutorials&mime=html

     http://www.softwareag.com/xml/about/starters.htm

XML applications:

     http://www.softwareag.com/xml/applications/xml_app_at_work.htm

XML tools

XPath description: http://www.w3.org/TR/xpath

XPath tutorials:

     http://www.w3schools.com/xpath/default.asp

     http://www.expertrating.com/courseware/XMLCourse/XML-XML-Styles-7-2.asp

     http://www.zvon.org/xxl/XPathTutorial/General/examples.html

XQuery:

     http://www.w3schools.com/xquery/xquery_intro.asp

     http://www.stylusstudio.com/xquery_flwor.html#

XML-enabled databases

General sources: http://www.xml.org/xml/resources_focus_rdbms.shtml

SQL/XML

Introduction to SQL/XML: http://sqlx.org/

     http://www.sigmod.org/record/issues/0109/standards.pdf

Oracle

Oracle Database 10g Release 2 XML DB – Introduction and link page for a range of articles:

     http://www.oracle.com/technology/tech/xml/xmldb/index.html.

Technical white paper that include a significant overview of Oracle system:

     http://download-west.oracle.com/otndocs/tech/xml/xmldb/TWP_XML_DB_10gR2_long.pdf

Selection of general articles:

http://www.oracle.com/technology/oramag/oracle/05-mar/o25xmlex.html

http://www.oracle.com/technology/oramag/oracle/05-sep/o55xquery.html

http://www.orafaq.com/faq/xml

Detailed description of SQL/XML functions:

www.psoug.org/reference/xml_functions.html

Succinct and easy to follow Oracle examples: http://www.oradev.com/xml.jsp

Futher Oracle examples:

http://www.oracle.com/technology/sample_code/tech/java/sqlj_jdbc/files/9i_jdbc/
XMLTypeSample/Readme.html

Very good general site for Oracle information:

http://www.oracle-base.com/index.php

See especially http://www.oracle-base.com/articles/9i/Articles9i.php#XML for XML

XSU (XML SQL Utility):

http://download-east.oracle.com/docs/cd/B10501_01/appdev.920/a96621/
adx08xsu.htm#1013816

http://www.devx.com/xml/Article/32046

Microsoft Access

Access XML info:

http://msdn.microsoft.com/XML/BuildingXML/XMLinOffice/default.aspx

MySQL

MySQL XML support:

http://dev.mysql.com/doc/refman/5.1/en/xml-functions.html

http://dev.mysql.com/tech-resources/articles/mysql-5.1-xml.html

XML databases

General XML database articles – starting point:

http://www.service-architecture.com/xml-databases/index.html

Native XML databases

Introduction to NXDs:

http://www.xml.com/pub/a/2001/10/31/nativexmldb.html

Description of the XML:DB interface and the dbXML NXD:

http://www.xml.com/pub/a/2001/11/28/dbxml.html

List of NXD vendors: http://www.service-architecture.com/products/xml_databases.html

Some current products

XML tools

Saxon XML, XSLT etc. tools: http://saxon.sourceforge.net/

StylusStudio; range of XML-related tools: http://www.stylusstudio.com/

Altova XMLSpy; range of XML tools: http://www.altova.com/simpledownload1.html

Oxygen XML editor; range of XML tools: http://www.oxygenxml.com/

NXD vendor's websites

eXist open source native XML database: http://exist.sourceforge.net/

TEXML server:

   http://www.ixiasoft.com/default.asp?xml=/xmldocs/webpages/textml-server.xml

TigerLogic XDMS: http://www.rainingdata.com/products/tl/

Ipedo: http://www.ipedo.com/html/ipedo_xml_database.html

Tamino: http://www.softwareag.com/corporate/products/tamino/

Appendix
Answers to review questions

Chapter 1

1 **How do older file systems and the database approach differ in terms of the relationship between the data and the application programs?**

File systems were generally 'application-oriented'; i.e. a system was constructed for particular applications. Database systems tend to be 'data-oriented' – the required data is organised as a self-consistent repository and applications are constructed around this.

2 **What are the two most significant properties of a database?**

- It holds data as an integrated system of records.

- It contains self-describing information.

3 **List the data models that provide the bases for database organisation.**

The main data models are:

- Hierarchical model

- Network model

- Relational model

- Object model

4 **What are the principal disadvantages of hierarchical and network databases?**

- They use pointers embedded in the data to represent the data structure, making it difficult to modify the structure.

- Access is primarily by navigation.

- General-purpose query systems are not easily written.

- Design and maintenance require skilled staff.

5 **List the stages of the waterfall development model.**

The stages are analysis, logical design, physical design, implementation, maintenance.

6 **List the possible methods of introducing a new system.**

Pilot running, parallel running, phased introduction, direct introduction.

7 Outline the basic structure of a relational database table.

A table consists of a *fixed* number of columns (each of which holds one attribute of the table) and a *variable* number of rows.

8 Explain the meaning of the rows and columns of a relational database table.

The rows of the table each describe one instance of the entity class that the table models.

Each column describes one attribute of the entity instance and must be a simple single-valued data item.

9 Explain how separate tables in a relational database are linked together.

A column value (called the foreign key) in one table has the same value as a primary key in the other table.

10 What is meant by the term 'schema'?

A schema is a description of the structure of the tables within a database.

Chapter 2

1 Distinguish between the application domain and the domain of an attribute.

'Application domain' is a real-world environment within which an information system and/or a database is being employed. The domain of an attribute is the range of possible values for that attribute.

2 List the properties of a relation.

Columns in the relation are all single values; i.e. arrays of values or other compound structures are not allowable.

Entries in any column are all of the same datatype; e.g. integer, real number, character, data, etc.

No two rows of the relation are identical.

The order of the rows in the table is immaterial.

The order of the columns in the table is immaterial.

Each table contains an identifying column or columns (the ruling part or primary key).

3 The above properties of a relation indicate that the sequence of the rows and of the columns are immaterial. How can a particular row and column be located?

Rows are identified by a primary key value which can be used in a search query. Columns are located only by name; the names are recorded in the database schema.

4 Distinguish between the terms primary key, candidate key and foreign key.

A candidate key is one or more attributes that can serve as a primary key (because each has a unique value in each row). The primary key is one of the candidate keys that is chosen to act as the unique identifier for the table. A foreign key is an attribute in one table that refers to the primary key of another table. This is the basic linking mechanism used to associate tables together.

5 **What does it mean to say that one attribute of a table is 'functionally dependent' on another?**

If attribute B is functionally dependent on attribute A, then every instance of a specific value of A automatically determines a specific value of B. If A has value x in one row and B has value y in that row, then every row containing A = x will also have B = y.

6 **Explain the purpose of nulls in database tables and indicate why it is not quite correct to talk of a 'null value'.**

Nulls are used to 'fill' attribute values where an actual attribute value is unavailable for some reason e.g. the value is not known or is not applicable for that row instance. A null is not a value, but the 'state of having no value' and should not be confused with a space character in a text attribute or a zero in a numeric attribute.

7 **How are separate tables in a relational database notionally connected together?**

One table has a column, called a foreign key, that holds a value equal to the primary key column value in a row of the other table.

8 **Explain the concept of referential integrity and its importance in relational database practice.**

Referential integrity is concerned with the correctness of foreign key to primary key links between the database tables. Every non-null foreign key value must have a matching value which is a primary key in one of the database tables. It is a method of enforcing consistency in the database.

9 **Define the term 'view'.**

A view is a virtual table whose content is defined by a query specification. Since it has the characteristics of a relation, it can be treated in many respects like a real table. However, the data values of the view are not stored in the database, only the query definition; the query is re-executed when the view data is required.

10 **What is the essential nature of relational algebra?**

A relation is a mathematical concept concerned with the mapping from one set to another. Relational algebra defines a set of operations that can be performed on relations to generate new relations based on selecting certain components from the relations or by combining relations.

Chapter 3 – Part 1

1 **Distinguish between an *entity* and an *entity set*. Which one is represented in an ER diagram?**

'Entity' is a term used to refer to any 'thing' – object, person, concept – which you wish to model in an ER diagram. An entity set is the set of all instances of the kind of entity being modelled. An ER diagram represents the entity set.

2 **List the possible variants of cardinality.**

One-to-one, one-to-many and many-to-many.

3 **How is the 'many' end of a relationship denoted in ER diagrams?**

By a 'crowsfoot', i.e. a splayed group of three lines.

4 **Explain what is meant by saying that a relationship is 'optional'.**

It means that for one (or both) entity sets involved in the relationship there may be some instances of the entity that do not have a related entity in the other entity set. For instance, in the relationship WORKS ON between entity sets Engineer and Project, the relationship is optional if one or more engineers are not necessarily working on any project and/or one or more projects do not necessarily have any engineers working on it.

5 **Explain what is meant by saying that an entity set may have 'partial participation' in a relationship.**

This conveys the same notion as optionality described in the previous answer, but expressed differently. Using the example given in Answer 4, the Engineer entity set is said to have partial participation if there are some engineers not working on a project. The optionality or participation depends on the 'rules' of the application, not on the chance values in specific entity sets.

6 **What is meant by the term 'weak entity'?**

A weak entity is one that cannot exist without another, related, entity. A hospital appointment cannot exist without a patient since it has no logical interpretation.

7 **Explain what is meant by a unary and a ternary relationship.**

A unary relationship is one in which members of an entity set are related to other members of the same set. For example, in a Employee entity set, a Supervises relationship relates one employee (a supervisor) to one or more other employees.

8 **Why is it not possible to represent a many-to-many relationship with two tables?**

It would require multiple valued foreign key values, which is not possible in relational tables.

9 **Describe the multiplicity notation used in UML style diagrams.**

The notation consists of an item of the form m..n where 'm' represents the participation and 'n' the cardinality. The m value can be any number from 1 upwards. The n value can be the number zero upward or an asterisk. Hence, examples of valid formats are 0..1, 1..*, 3..6.

Chapter 3 – Part 2

1 **List the stages of the conversion process from ER diagrams to relational tables.**

i   Convert each relation to a table.

ii Create tables for certain relationships that need to be represented by a separate table.

iii Establish links between tables using suitable foreign key to primary key pairings.

2 How do you represent a many-to-many relationship with relational tables?

A many-to-many relationship always requires a separate table containing foreign keys linking to the two original tables.

3 When is it permissible for a foreign key value to be null?

When the entity has partial participation in the relationship.

4 How do you represent multi-valued attributes in relational tables?

It requires the generation of a separate table each row of which holds one of the attribute values.

5 How do you represent time-varying attributes in relational tables?

It requires the generation of a separate table each row of which holds one instance of the value(s) per specific time.

Chapter 3 – Part 3

1 Define the term 'normalisation'.

Normalisation is the process of converting the design of database tables so that they conform to a set of defined criteria that lead to an optimal design.

2 What are the benefits of normalisation?

A normalised set of tables exhibits minimal redundancy and freedom from update anomalies.

3 Outline the process of converting from un-normalised through the first, second and third normal forms.

First NF: remove repeating values of attributes. Create a new table to hold the repeating values linked to the original.

Second NF: Remove attributes with partial dependencies (i.e. dependent only on part of the primary key) to a separate relation.

Third NF: Remove attributes dependent on non-key attributes to a separate relation.

4 List the types of anomaly that can arise if database tables do not conform to 2NF and/or 3NF.

Update anomaly – arising when certain columns are changed.

Insertion anomaly – arising when new rows are added.

Deletion anomaly – arising when rows are deleted.

5 **Define the Boyce-Codd normal form.**

A relation is in BCNF if every determinant in the relation is a candidate key.

6 **List the conditions that give rise to anomalies in non-BCNF relations.**

The conditions are:

- There is more than one candidate key.

- The candidate keys are composite.

- The attributes of the candidate keys overlap; i.e. they have an attribute in common.

7 **What is the significance of the Domain-Key Normal Form?**

It is the 'ultimate' normal form: no further normal forms are possible or necessary. However, its practical significance is limited.

Chapter 4

Outline the role of the database engine.

1 Physical data management and accessing including:

- Index management.

- View management.

- Accessing of data dictionary.

- Concurrency control.

- Security: access rights.

- Integrity: validation, referential integrity, transactions, recovery.

2 **Distinguish between an active and a passive data dictionary.**

A passive data dictionary is used purely for system documentation. An active data dictionary is accessed by the database engine and is used in working with the database.

3 **Identify the benefits of using indexes.**

There are three benefits:

- They increase access speed to individual records.

- They allow the data to be displayed in different sequences (e.g. when using the SQL ORDER BY clause) without massive sorting of the data records.

- They facilitate maintenance of unique key values.

4 **Identify the main factors to be considered when choosing a database product for a proposed new application.**

The main factors are:

- Scale

- Performance

- Support for datatypes

- Connectivity

- Processing complexity

5 **What datatype would be the best choice for:**

a) **An amount of money?**

b) **Quantity of televisions in stock?**

c) **The dimensions of molecules?**

a) If a currency type is available then this is best. Otherwise a fixed-point representation, say, DECIMAL(12,4) or a FLOAT type.

b) An integer type is ideal, such as DECIMAL(5) or NUMBER(5), making sure that the scale is adequate; e.g. the foregoing types provide for up to 99 999 televisions.

c) A double-precision real type such as DOUBLE would be best.

6 **Can you suggest conditions within which a limited de-normalisation might be acceptable?**

De-normalisation is acceptable only on the basis of performance issues or in the interests of simplicity (as in the postcode example). Examples are:

- Using a limited number of repeated columns instead of a separate table-where the number of repeats in small and fixed.

- Maintaining a calculated total cost in an order table instead of using a query to calculate the value when required.

7 **It was stated earlier that to end-users the set of forms supporting a database application 'is' the database. Explain what is meant by this statement.**

The forms of an application serve as a window into the system. Often, it is all that the user is aware of in using the system, since the internal details such as tables and indexes are not directly visible.

8 **Why is it advantageous that each form within an application system has a consistent appearance and uses similar functionality?**

This enables the user to become more competent, comfortable and accurate in their use of the forms.

9 What is meant by saying that indexes are an 'implementation feature' and not a theoretical feature of relational databases?

The principles of the relational model do not include reference to the use of indexes and hence it is possible to operate a relational database system without indexes. However, the improvement in performance obtained by the use of indexes makes them all but essential.

Chapter 5

1 What is meant by 'embedding' of SQL commands?

SQL commands can be incorporated into the program code of other languages. SQL is used to query the database and extract required data. The other language code is then used to process the data.

2 Outline the various programming alternatives available for accessing databases.

Options are:

- Query language (e.g. SQL).

- SQL embedded in conventional languages.

- Conventional languages using standard interfaces such as ODBC and JDBC.

- 4GL style languages such as Oracle PL/SQL.

3 List the ways in which SQL can be used in programming environments.

- Free-standing command interpreter.

- Embedded in a conventional language such as C.

- Within a 4GL system such as Oracle PL/SQL or Informix 4GL.

- Within an integrated development environment such as Visual Basic.

4 What do the acronyms ODBC and JDBC stand for? Explain the nature of these.

- ODBC – Open Database Connectivity.

- JDBC – usually taken to mean Java Database Connectivity, though actually a trademark of Sun.

These are standard interfaces that provide a software layer between a programming system and various databases to enable the program code to be relatively independent of the database accessed.

5 Explain what is meant by the term '4GL'.

4GL stands for Fourth Generation Language, which refers to a high-level language offering more advanced facilities than conventional languages such as Java and C. Generally, 4GLs are associated with a database and have intimate communication with the database engine.

6 **List the components of the user interface that would be provided by a DBMS.**

- Schema manager

- Forms generator

- Query processor

- Report generator

- Programming interface

7 **Outline the main functions performed by forms.**

Forms provide a user-friendly means of viewing database tables and the output from queries.

They are used to manage application transactions; e.g. in an order processing system, entry of new orders, accepting payments for orders, etc.

Also used for general interface tasks such as menus, information screens etc.

8 **What is meant by the term 'form control'?**

Form controls are visual objects used on forms, such as text boxes, buttons, list boxes, etc. which are used in the form interaction process.

Chapter 6

1 **Give a definition of a transaction.**

A transaction is a group of database operations that is treated as an atomic unit; i.e. they are *all* completed or *none* of them is completed.

2 **In the context of transactions, what does the acronym ACID stand for?**

Atomicity, Consistency, Isolation and Durability.

3 **What two commands are used to manage the termination of a transaction?**

Rollback and commit. Rollback aborts the transaction and commit terminates it normally.

4 **Why does concurrent access to a database give rise to potential problems?**

The possibility arises of two users working on the same data (or data held in the same disk block). This can cause interference between the work of the two users, resulting in possible loss of updates and other problems.

5 **What is meant by the terms: lost update, uncommitted dependency problem and inconsistent analysis problem?**

- Lost update: effect caused by interference of concurrent transactions whereby a user submits a database update that appears to be actioned but is in fact over-written by another update.

- Uncommitted dependency: concurrency error caused by one transaction updating uncommitted data that is later rolled back, causing database corruption.

- Inconsistent analysis: occurs when a database query produces an erroneous result due to another user changing the data while it is being read by the query transaction.

6 What is meant by 'serialisation' of transactions?

If transactions were all executed in sequence, without concurrency, then no concurrency errors would arise. Serialisation refers to techniques that allow concurrent transactions but produce the same result as if the transactions were serially executed.

7 Explain the concept of locking and why it is used.

Locking of a part of a database (row, block etc.) by one transaction prevents read and/or write access to the data by other transactions. Locking is used to achieve serialisation.

8 What is meant by two-phase locking?

Two-phase locking is a locking technique that uses two phases – the growing phase (during which locks can be acquired) and the shrinking phase (when locks are released). This avoids the problems inherent in basic locking schemes.

9 Explain the term 'granularity of locking'.

Granularity of locking refers to the unit of storage locked in one lock operation. It can be a database, table, block or row, with block being the most common.

10 What is a deadlock and how is it caused?

A deadlock occurs when two (or more) transactions are waiting for the release of locks when the release will not occur due to a circular wait situation. It is caused by each transaction holding one lock while requesting a data item that is locked by another.

11 What methods are used to manage deadlocks?

The methods are prevention (acquiring all locks at the same time) and detection (allowing deadlock to occur but then clearing it by rolling back a transaction).

Chapter 7

1 What is meant by a database constraint?

A constraint is a definition of a limitation or restriction on the admissible values of data items in the database.

2 Identify some of the problems that can threaten the integrity of the database.

Possible threats are: hardware failure, software errors, operator errors, physical damage, concurrency errors, breach of confidentiality.

3 What is meant by data validation?

Data validation refers to the checking of data as it is entered into a database to ensure that it conforms to specified limits.

4 **How do datatypes contribute to the accuracy of data?**

Datatypes define the domain of data items; i.e. the bounds of acceptable values for the items. An attribute of a given type cannot hold values not in the domain of that type.

5 **Distinguish between an assertion and a trigger.**

An assertion is a general declarative statement of a database constraint that must be applied wherever and whenever the data concerned is altered. A trigger is a trap for a specific condition or event.

6 **What is a transaction log used for?**

A transaction log is used to record all updates applied to a database over a period of time so that the updates can be re-applied in the event of a database failure.

7 **What are the SQL commands GRANT and REVOKE used for?**

GRANT is used to bestow access, update and other rights on specified users of the database. REVOKE is used to remove these rights.

Chapter 8

1 **Explain what is meant by a 'client-server system'.**

A technique used in networked system in which some computers (the servers) provide a service to other computers (the clients).

2 **How does the three-tier architecture extend the basic client-server principle?**

In a three-tier architecture, the 'client' communicates with an intermediate software layer which in turn communicates with the server. This is an application of the 'division of labour' principle; the tasks involved in the client-server activity are shared between different software elements that are designed for the purpose.

3 **How is the three-tier architecture used in web systems?**

The client is the web browser-which communicates with a web server. This in turns communicates with a database server.

4 **In what ways is a peer-to-peer system similar to, and different from, a conventional client-server system?**

A peer-to-peer system operates in a client-server fashion but a particular site can act as both client or server at various times. These terms now refer to 'roles' of the site rather than fixed functions.

5 **What is meant by saying a database is 'distributed'?**

A distributed database is physically stored at two or more separate locations connected by a network, rather than at a single location.

6 **Explain the terms 'homogeneous' and 'heterogeneous' in the context of distributed databases.**

Homogeneous distribution involves a set of databases of the same kind (e.g. Oracle) while a heterogeneous system involves databases of two or more kinds (e.g. Oracle, SQL Server, DB2).

7 **List the various ways in which a database can be distributed.**

The possibilities are:

- Tables stored separately.
- Tables split into groups of rows (horizontal distribution).
- Tables split into groups of columns (vertical distribution).
- Combinations of these.

8 **What is meant by 'database replication'?**

Database replication refers to the storing of one or more copies of a database at other network locations.

9 **In the context of distributed databases, what is meant by 'transparency'?**

Transparency refers to an objective of distributed systems whereby the user of the system need not be aware of the distribution and/or replication of the database they are using.

10 **Identify the various forms of transparency.**

Transparencies are locations, replication and fragmentation.

11 **Outline the problems of schema management, query processing and concurrent transactions that arise in distributed database systems.**

Schema management:

Each site requires global schema information which is updated locally and requires to be synchronised. Access to data requires location information in addition to disk addresses.

The schema requires information about how the data is fragmented and/or replicated.

Query processing: queries must be resolved into sub-queries and distributed to the relevant site. The resultant recordset must then be collated. Updating and insertion can involve several operations at multiple sites. Query optimisation is required to minimise data movement between sites.

12 **List and explain Date's 12 Objectives for a distributed database.**

These are described in some detail on page 225 of the text.

13 **What are the advantages and disadvantages of distributed databases?**

Advantages are:

- Reduced network traffic and faster access to local data.

- Local control of data.

- Improved availability.

- System capacity is improved.

Disadvantages:

Additional complexities in the areas of query processing, concurrency, schema management and database design. In replication system, there is additional work in keeping replicated data synchronised.

Chapter 9

1 **What are the advantages of the relational database?**

A summary list includes:

- Simplicity of concept

- Good theoretical basis

- Data independence

- Improved security and integrity

- Suitable for high-level languages such as SQL

2 **What are the disadvantages of the relational database?**

- Proliferation of tables

- Processing overheads

- Do not scale well

- Lack of semantic power

3 **What is meant by saying that the relational database 'lacks semantic power'?**

It is not possible to express deeper semantic properties such as the relationship between tables or sub-typing.

4 **Explain what is meant by sub-typing.**

This refers to some data item being defined as a more specialised version of another. This is achieved in object-oriented systems by inheritance.

5 **Why is it difficult to implement sub-typing in a relational database?**

There is no natural mechanism included in the relational model, so be it has to be implemented in some ad hoc fashion.

6 **Define the basic structure of an object.**

An object consists of a set of attributes (also called properties or state variables) and a set of methods which are procedures and/or functions which can be applied to objects of a class.

7 **Why is this structure thought to be advantageous in program development?**

It provides 'information-hiding' whereby the attributes are hidden from the rest of the program and modification of the object has to be done using the available methods. This provides many useful benefits such as re-use, debugging, program maintenance etc.

8 **Explain the concept of a class in object-orientation.**

'Class' refers to the generic specification of a set of objects; essentially, the class is a template which defines the structure and behaviour of each object of that type.

9 **Explain the concept of inheritance.**

Inheritance is an object-oriented mechanism whereby sub-classes can be created as more specialised versions of a base class. In this way, a generalisation/specialisation hierarchy can be set up.

10 **Show how inheritance can be used to implement sub-typing.**

Inheritance allows the design of one object (child) to be based on the design of a previously defined object (parent). The child object can modify and add to the properties of the parent thereby providing a hierarchy of specialisation/generalisation which is the nature of sub-typing.

11 **What is the essential philosophy of object-relational databases?**

An object-relational system is generally based on a conventional relational database but uses extensions to and relaxations of the relational model to permit object features.

12 **Explain the nature of Oracle's varray and nested table collection features.**

These are built-in compound datatypes provided by Oracle so that multi-valued attributes can be employed in a table. A varray is an array of objects or types; a nested table is a table embedded within another table.

13 **Describe the approach taken by Intersystem's Caché system in providing relational and object features.**

Objects are created using an object database system. Data can accessed by means of a 'relational mapping' that enables the data to be viewed as a relational tables.

14 **Distinguish between 'object-relational database' and 'object-relational mapping'.**

An object-relational database is database that combines features of a relational and an object database. Object-relational mapping refers to the process of storing object-based data in a conventional relational database using an intermediate software layer to resolve the differences between the external (programming) representation and the stored version.

15 **Describe the essential nature of a pure object database.**

A pure object database manages the storage and retrieval of data in the form of objects as defined within a programming environment without extensive re-structuring of the data between memory and persistent storage.

16 **What is meant by 'swizzling'?**

In program memory, an object will be referenced by a memory address pointer and on disk by a disk address. When a previously saved object is returned to memory, it will most probably be in a different memory location. Swizzling refers to the process of updating references to the object to allow for its new location in memory.

Chapter 10

Client-server architecture

1 **Describe the structure and mode of operation of a three-tier web/database server system.**

Refer to Figure 10.1 in the text.

HTML forms

1 **Outline the main elements used in the construction of HTML forms.**
The main elements are text boxes, buttons, drop-down lists, radio boxes and check boxes.

2 **Explain the significance and importance of HTML forms in the design of web interfaces.**

Forms are the means by which the browser can communicate data to the web server. It is therefore an important element in the interaction between the user and the server.

3 **In an HTML form, describe the effect of a submit button.**

The submit button causes the contents of the form to be sent to the server.

CGI

1 **Explain how CGI is used in a web – database connection.**

An HTML command is used to activate a program that resides on the server. This program can perform any programming tasks, such as accessing a database and preparing data for return to the browser. This is done by generating HTML code into which the data is formatted and which is returned for display by the browser.

2 **What is the main difference between CGI and other web interaction technologies such as ASP and PHP?**

CGI uses an external program (often in the Perl language) that generates an output which becomes the HTML code that is returned to the browser. In other techniques, the web page contains embedded code such as VBScript, JavaScript or PHP that interacts directly with the server system to generate the resultant HTML.

ASP, ADO

1 **Explain how ASP coding is embedded in HTML documents.**

Coding is bracketed between special ASP tags. When the web page is interpreted by the ASP-aware server, this code is interpreted first and is used to modify the content of the page before transmission to the browser.

2 **Outline the role of the Request and Response objects in ASP programming.**

These objects contain certain data items and support methods that facilitate communication between the client browser and the web server.

3 **Explain the purpose of the Application object and identify the two events handled by the object.**

An Application object in effect 'represents' a website application running on the web server. It is created the first time a user accesses a page of the site and persists until the server is shut down. Two events are On_Start and On_End.

4 **What is the global.asa file used for?**

This file is used to house the event-handling code for the Session and Application objects.

5 **Explain the general nature of ActiveX Data Objects (ADO).**

ADO is software layer that facilitates communication between other program code such as ASP coding and a database to make the coding 'database independent'.

6 **Outline the main object types supported by ADO.**

The principal ADO objects are: Connection, Command, Recordset, Field and Streams.

7 **Explain what is meant by a 'recordset' and how a cursor is used in conjunction with a recordset.**

A recordset is a virtual array structure that contains the results of a query. A cursor is a notional pointer associated with the recordset that can be used to 'scan' the rows of the recordset.

ASP.NET

1 **How are ASP and ASP.NET related?**

ASP.NET is derived from ASP and both can be used on the same website but not on the same page. However, ASP.NET is a more elaborate and extensive system and uses a number of more effective mechanisms.

2 **What are the principal innovations of ASP.NET?**

- Simpler programming model
- Separation of HTML and script coding
- Automatic session state maintenance
- NET hosting provides extensive facilities from class libraries

3 **List the categories of server controls provided by ASP.NET.**

- HTML server controls
- Web server controls
- Validation server controls

4 **Identify the main features of the Dataset object that ADO.NET maintains.**

The Dataset object is provides an in-memory representation of a relational database. It contains objects that represent all aspects of the database organisation including table schema, constraints, relationship etc.

Cookies

1 **Explain what is meant by a 'cookie' and describe the mechanism used in communicating cookies between the web server and client computers.**

A cookie is a (small) item of data that is held in the client computer's file system and supplied by the website being accessed. On later accesses to the same site, the browser reads the cookies for that site and sends them to the site server. These are used to maintain session state.

State maintenance

1 **Explain the concept of, and the need for, 'state maintenance' in web sessions.**

State maintenance refers to the preservation of client-based information during successive accesses to a website. Inherently, each access to a website, even though the series of accesses are related (e.g. in conducting an online purchase), is an independent event from the point of view of the server.

2 **Outline the principles underlying the following state maintenance methods: sessions, URL-encoded variables, hidden form variables.**

- ASP maintains information between related website accesses to provide the notional existence of a continuous communication session between client and browser. A session object in conjunction with cookies is used for this purpose.

- URL-encode variables are data appending to the end of a URL string after a '?' symbol. By sending this data in successive accesses continuity can be maintained between client and server.

- A hidden form variable is used in the same way as URL variables, but the continuity data is held in a form variable which does not appear on the browser screen.

PHP

1 Describe the general principles of the PHP language for web interaction.

PHP uses special bracketing tags contained within HTML pages. Within the tags program code in the PHP language is used for web server interaction.

2 How does PHP differ from ASP with regard to the languages used?

'ASP' strictly refer to the bracketing system and the various supporting objects. The script language can be one of several options, such as VBScript or JavaScript. PHP only employs PHP language coding.

3 How does PHP differ from other web interaction systems with regard to database access?

It does not use an intermediate software layer such as ADO to resolve the differences between the various databases. Hence, different database access functions are required for each type of database.

JSP/servlets

1 Outline the essential nature of Java servlets.

A servlet is a code module written in Java which is activated on the server by referencing it by a URL in a web page. The servlet provides interaction facilities between browser and the web server.

2 Describe the role played by the servlet objects ServletResponse and ServletRequest.

- ServletResponse is a program object that provides facilities for servlets to send data from the server to the browser.

- ServletRequest is a program object that processes data sent from the browser in GET or POST messages.

These objects are analogous to the Response and Request objects of ASP.

3 Explain why JSP was introduced to the Java web system.

The development and maintenance of servlets is non-trivial and labour intensive. JSP is a means of providing the same features but in a more user-friendly environment.

4 Describe the processes involved in handling JSP requests.

This is a complex process; check the body of the chapter for full details. Briefly, the first time a reference is made to a web page containing JSP code, the code is converted to an equivalent Java program that regenerates the HTML of the web page combined with output from the JSP coding. On subsequent accesses to the page, the compiled Java code is simply executed again.

5 **Outline the JSP tag system.**

Declaration tag: Used to declare variables or program code.

Expression tag: Allows the developer to embed any Java expression and is short for out.printn(.)

Directive tag: Gives special information about the page to the JSP engine.

Scriptlet tag: Allows definition and embedding of Java coding into the page.

Action tag: Provides additional programming within the page.

Chapter 11

1 **Distinguish between the nature of tags as used in HTML and XML.**

HTML tags are predefined and fixed. XML tags have no inherent meaning and must be defined by the user.

2 **Explain why XML requires the use of a supporting DTD or Schema document.**

Since the user can invent their own tags, they initially have no meaning. The DTD or Schema enables the structure and content of tags to be validated.

3 **What are the two main categories of database in terms of XML support?**

XML-enabled databases, i.e. conventional databases extended to accommodate XML, and Native XML databases, which are specifically designed to manage XML.

4 **Describe the nature of XPath and XQuery.**

These are XML-related language systems that support applications in XML. XPath is a language for addressing and extracting parts of an XML document based on some criteria. The XQuery language is intended to provide for XML what SQL provides for databases – the ability to extract required information from an XML document by means of a compact query specification.

5 **Outline the nature of SQL/XML, including the XMLType datatype.**

SQL/XML is an extension of SQL based on the SQL:2003 and SQL:2006 standards that enables SQL queries to contain XML-related terms. It also provides for the XMLType datatype, which is designed to enable storage of XML in a relational table.

6 **Describe the operation of the extract and extractValue functions.**

These are functions are callable within an SQL/XML query to extract parts of an XMLType data value from a table.

7 **Outline the purpose of the functions XMLElement, XMLGen, XMLForest and XMLAttributes.**

These are functions (supported by Oracle) used to generate XML documents or fragments from a relational source.

Index